UNDERSTANDING
CONTEMPORARY
LATIN AMERICA

UNDERSTANDING

Introductions to the States and Regions of the Contemporary World
Donald L. Gordon, series editor

Understanding Contemporary Africa, 3rd edition
edited by April A. Gordon and Donald L. Gordon

Understanding the Contemporary Caribbean
edited by Richard S. Hillman and Thomas J. D'Agostino

Understanding Contemporary China, 2nd edition
edited by Robert E. Gamer

Understanding Contemporary India
edited by Sumit Ganguly and Neil DeVotta

Understanding Contemporary Latin America, 3rd edition
edited by Richard S. Hillman

Understanding the Contemporary Middle East, 2nd edition
edited by Deborah J. Gerner and Jillian Schwedler

THIRD EDITION

UNDERSTANDING CONTEMPORARY
LATIN
AMERICA

edited by
Richard S. Hillman

LYNNE
RIENNER
PUBLISHERS

BOULDER
LONDON

Published in the United States of America in 2005 by
Lynne Rienner Publishers, Inc.
1800 30th Street, Boulder, Colorado 80301
www.rienner.com

and in the United Kingdom by
Lynne Rienner Publishers, Inc.
3 Henrietta Street, Covent Garden, London WC2E 8LU

Library of Congress Cataloging-in-Publication Data
Understanding contemporary Latin America / edited by Richard S.
Hillman.—3rd ed.
    p. cm. — (Understanding)
    Includes bibliographical references and index.
    ISBN 1-58826-341-X (pbk. : alk. paper)
    1. Latin America. I. Hillman, Richard S., 1943– II. Series:
Understanding (Boulder, Colo.)
    F1408.U43   2005
    980—dc22
                                                    2004029858

British Cataloguing in Publication Data
A Cataloguing in Publication record for this book
is available from the British Library.

Printed and bound in the United States of America

       The paper used in this publication meets the requirements
              of the American National Standard for Permanence of
              Paper for Printed Library Materials Z39.48-1992.

5   4   3   2   1

Contents

Illustrations

Preface

In this new edition of *Understanding Contemporary Latin America*, each chapter has been updated with analyses of current political, social, and economic developments in the region, as well as citations of up-to-date research. Several chapters have undergone extensive revision, and one is entirely new. Comprehensive appendixes of basic political data and non-independent territories also have been added. These enhancements have been designed to make *Understanding Contemporary Latin America* an even more useful resource for those interested in an informed introduction to the region.

The volume was written by Latin America specialists who believe that expanding academic, economic, and policy interests requires a basic introduction to this complex and significant part of the world. Increased numbers of scholarly studies attest to the importance of contemporary Latin America. While comprehending those studies presupposes some degree of expertise and experience in the field, *Understanding Contemporary Latin America* is intended for the many "beginners" who wish to learn about the region.

The strategic geopolitical relevance of Latin America has been recognized throughout history, and increased trade has affected hemispheric development. Nevertheless, Latin American attitudes, values, and beliefs regarding the conduct of politics, business, and life in general remain misunderstood by many. The media have sensationalized issues such as political corruption and instability, narcotics trafficking, and immigration problems, overshadowing attempts to promote democracy, trade, development, tourism, and regional cooperation. The long-term health of inter-American relations, however, is contingent on accurate awareness and mutual understanding. In this context, *Understanding Contemporary Latin America* introduces fundamental background, issues, themes, and directions in countries throughout the region. The book is designed as a basic interdisciplinary resource for use in college and university classrooms, foreign service seminars, and corporate training programs. Its wealth of graphic and textual information, presented in a straightforward style, is intended to enhance clarity, comprehension, and appreciation of the traditions, influences, and commonalities underlying the varying cultural orientations in this vital area.

The facts alone are insufficient for a complete understanding of contemporary Latin America. Insight and empathy are required for overcoming stereotypical characterizations and cultural biases. It is precisely this mix of knowledge and appreciation that is inherent in each chapter's treatment of Latin America's complex settings and challenges. After the first chapter's brief introduction, outlining the scope and themes of the book, the second chapter describes the rich diversity of Latin America's human and physical geography. Legacies of the colonial era that continue to influence current realities are analyzed in the third chapter. Chapter 4 discusses how these legacies affect ongoing political institutions, including the military, which is treated separately in the fifth chapter due to its singular importance in the region. The sixth chapter investigates the area's economic performance over time, culminating in a discussion of current problems. Some of these problems are covered further in Chapter 8, specifically those dealing with environmental degradation, population expansion, and rapid urbanization. Chapter 7 examines international relations among countries within Latin America as well as with the rest of the world. Patterns of ethnicity and class are explored in Chapter 9, the role of women in Chapter 10, and the relationship between education and development in Chapter 11. These chapters offer a human face to the problems and challenges detailed in other parts of the book, as do Chapter 12 on religious beliefs and Chapter 13 on literary expression. Finally, Chapter 14 examines where the region has been and in what direction it appears to be going. Far from a definitive closure to these matters, the book is designed to be an open-ended resource for provoking greater interest and raising more questions about a vital, complex, and increasingly important region of the modern world.

*   *   *

I am grateful to each of the chapter authors for finding time during busy academic schedules to participate in this collaborative effort and for making my tasks as editor intellectually fulfilling. Working with this talented group of scholars has been a pleasure. Also, I appreciate the support of several organizations and programs that either directly or indirectly made the project possible.

The Fulbright Scholars Program provided multiple opportunities for me to teach and conduct research in Latin America. The Institute for the

Study of Democracy and Human Rights at St. John Fisher College, supported by the U.S. State Department College and University Affiliation Program, allowed me to maintain professional linkages, particularly in Venezuela, and sponsor academic exchanges and conferences. Field research in Brazil and Cuba was facilitated by the University of Pittsburgh Semester at Sea Program, as well as the People to People Ambassadors Program. The United Nations Photographic Library and the World Bank Photographic Department gave me the opportunity to select most of the photographs that appear throughout the text. The Venezuelan Embassy supplied several photographs as well.

John Bogdal created the excellent maps that appear in the book. My graduate assistant, Amin Alexander Choukairi, prepared Appendix 1: Basic Political Data and Appendix 2: List of Nonindependent Territories; he also helped with various aspects of the editing process. Lynne Rienner Publishers provided helpful advice, and anonymous reviewers made sensible suggestions that enhanced the readability of the manuscript. I am indebted to my colleagues, and especially to my family, for encouraging, supporting, and assisting in my work. Finally, I wish to dedicate this book in loving memory of my mother, Edith Natalie Hillman (1918–2004)—may she rest in peace.

—*Richard S. Hillman*

UNDERSTANDING
CONTEMPORARY
LATIN AMERICA

Introduction

Richard S. Hillman

Two basic questions constitute a point of departure for our study: first, What constitutes Latin America, and second, Who are the Latin Americans? Responses to these questions are far more complicated than they may appear at first. Latin America can be defined as a region in a variety of ways. Some definitions are based on geopolitical and strategic concerns, others on common languages and cultures. Some include only Hispanic countries, excluding the Anglo-Caribbean, the Francophone countries, and Brazil; whereas others include these areas, as well as French Canada, part of Louisiana, southern Florida, and the southwestern United States because of their "Latin" influence and cultural connections.

Similarly, many theories have been advanced regarding the inhabitants of the Americas. The most widely accepted view holds that, initially, groups of Asians crossed the Bering Straits, migrated south, and settled in North and South America. Another suggests that these groups crossed the Pacific Ocean on rafts. Yet others maintain that human life originated in South America. José Vasconcelos, a Mexican intellectual, posited in 1948 that Latin Americans had become a "cosmic race," combining the strengths of different ethnic groups that have inhabited the region. Each theory is based on a plausible interpretation of certain aspects of the available evidence, and each definition has its own logic. Thus, a comprehensive approach is required to respond adequately to what are actually complex, rather than simple, questions about the nature of the area and the people we seek to understand.

Let us begin to formulate responses by considering one of the first encounters between a Native American and a European in the early sixteenth century. Montezuma, leader of the Aztec civilization, is reported to have told Spanish explorer Hernán Cortés, "We have known for a long time, from the chronicles of our forefathers, that neither I, nor those who inhabit this country, are descendants from the aborigines of it, but from strangers who came to it from very distant parts" (Keen 1966:47). According to Cortés's account in his letters to the king of Spain, Montezuma then related an ancient story that legitimized Spanish sovereignty in the Americas. But Montezuma added a comment that would have portentous significance in subsequent history: "Look at me," he said, "and see that I am flesh and bones, the same as you, and everybody, and that I am mortal, and tangible" (Keen 1966:48). Since the first contact between Europeans and Native Americans, Latin Americans have been trying to define themselves and their region. Who would govern this New World inhabited by the progeny of "strangers"? What kind of world would it become?

The story of Latin America's Indian origins, conquest by European powers, struggles for independence, and twentieth-century search for political and economic stability is an action-filled drama, revealing protagonists whose cultural differences have brought about conflicts as well as coalitions. Contemporary Latin America's increasingly important role in world politics makes essential a comprehensive understanding of how its history is rooted in a complex and turbulent past. Popular discussions of Latin America and inter-American affairs, however, are generally charged with high levels of passion and scanty knowledge, resulting all too often in mutual misunderstanding, due to unfortunate stereotypes on both sides. For example, some North Americans argue vehemently about their need to protect themselves against violent Latin American revolutionaries who threaten political stability in their backyard, illegal immigrants who steal jobs from U.S. workers, and narcotraffickers who poison U.S. youth. And some Latin Americans fear the malevolent intentions of the "colossus of the North" that has seemed to intervene continuously in their domestic affairs.[1] They exhibit a strong tendency to resent U.S. hegemony in the Western Hemisphere and blame the violence occasioned by drug cartels on the demands of the U.S. market. Yet, many Latin Americans seek upward mobility by emigrating to the United States, thereby causing their "love-hate" relationship to confound many observers.

During the Cold War, many U.S. citizens excitedly propounded the merits of military incursions or covert operations in places like Grenada, the Dominican Republic, Panama, Chile, Nicaragua, and El Salvador. When asked to locate these countries on a map, name their major cities, account for their economic status, or place them in historical context, however, they were clueless. Far too many North Americans are apt to locate Cuba in Central America or Argentina in the Caribbean and to assume Brazilians speak Spanish. Moreover, public opinion on many issues in both the United States and Latin America has become profoundly divided in the post–Cold War era. The plight of Cuba is a case in point. To many observers, the U.S. economic embargo and diplomatic isolation of Cuba have constituted a misuse of power to the extreme detriment of masses of Cubans, who, as a result, must endure suffering and hardship.[2] Many others believe Cuba's development problems should be attributed solely to Fidel Castro's adoption of the socialist model. In either case, ideological dogmatism has been reinforced by insufficient understanding and vilification of U.S. foreign policy on the one hand or of Castroism on the other. Could it be that this is not a mutually exclusive proposition, that, in fact, both sides have contributed to the dilemma?

Unfortunately, stereotypes and myths that have fostered public impressions, as well as political actions, are deeply embedded in popular culture. Frederick Pike (1992) has amply documented the pervasiveness of this type of thinking, from the speeches of early statesmen, like Thomas Jefferson and Simón Bolívar, to virtually continuous references in literature, art, cinema, and the media. According to Jefferson, for example, the superior U.S. culture would supplant the inferior Latin American culture. He held that "it is impossible not to look forward to distant times when our rapid multiplication will expand itself . . . and cover the whole northern, if not the whole southern continent, with a people speaking the same language, governed in similar forms, and by similar laws" (Pike 1992:19). Such thinking has fueled historical U.S. imperialism, as well as contemporary reactions to waves of Hispanic immigrants, such as the "English only" movement. Ironically, Bolívar predicted the United States would "afflict Latin America in the name of liberty" (Pike 1992:18), leading Pike to conclude that "the degree to which American stereotypes of Latin Americans are reinforced by—and perhaps sometimes even originate in—Latin Americans' stereotypes of themselves [is impressive]" (Pike 1992:116).

Impressions reflected in advertising and the popular media perpetuate myths. In a free association of ideas, what are the first images that come to mind when identifying Latin Americans? If you think of the silly Frito Bandito or *el exigente*, whose favorable judgment of a coffee bean results in an instant fiesta for a whole village, you are not alone. Nor would you be unique in conjuring up the idea of the "Latin lover" or the romantic revolutionary. Regarding politics, a U.S. traveler in Latin America reported that "the value of stability in government is something they [Latin Americans] cannot be made to understand. It is not in their power to see it, and the desire for change and revolution is in the blood" (Pike 1992:68). Similarly, *machismo* is equated with the oppression of women, the *siesta* with laziness, music and dancing with today, work and planning with *mañana* (Hillman 2003).

Many Latin Americans also hold distorted perceptions of the United

States and its citizens. These views vary from the vulgar notion that all *gringos* carry guns and walk on gold-paved streets to the more sophisticated analysis of the United States as a materialistic, mercenary culture of acquisition, devoid of the higher virtues of family loyalty, honor, and personalism. In this regard, José Enrique Rodó of Uruguay wrote *Ariel* in 1900 as a glorification of Latin America's superior cultural sensitivity. His ideas influenced other Latin American critics of the United States, such as José Martí of Cuba and Rubén Darío of Nicaragua, thus contributing to an antiyanqui sentiment. Hence, mutual misperceptions, stereotypes, and myths abound, making a more penetrating and realistic portrayal of the region particularly important in an era of global change. The basic problem, according to Pike (1992:364), is that "Americans remain reluctant to accept the fact that their country has become a frontier for Latin Americans. For generations, after all, Americans had assumed that Latin America was their frontier. Old myths, like hoary stereotypes, die hard."

Recognition of the highly misleading and counterproductive nature of portrayals of Latin America as somehow more "natural" and less civilized than the developed North is essential for understanding the region. This book is an attempt to promote such recognition through exploration of basic ideas and information that will contribute to debunking various myths about contemporary Latin America. The fundamental theme of "unity in diversity" provides a comprehensive organizing concept. Using this approach, the authors emphasize the significance of the area as a whole, along with ample references to the individual countries within the region and their history, geography, and political culture. Our examination encompasses all territory in the Western Hemisphere south of the United States. (Latin American enclaves within North America can be understood in the context of their ties to the region.) Hence, areas within Latin America include Mexico, Central America, the Caribbean, and South America. Countries within these areas form part of Ibero-, Luso-, Indo-, Afro-, and Hispano-America. Subareas such as the Anglo, French, and Dutch Caribbean are also included because of underlying similarities that transcend apparent differences.[3]

Great diversities of peoples, institutions, and geography in Latin America coalesce in common historical, social, political, and developmental patterns. Various combinations of these patterns, similar socioeconomic problems, and analogous cultural expressions permit a unified vision of Latin America. Therefore, each chapter in this volume draws examples from several countries within the various areas of Latin America, thus allowing the text as a whole to offer a balanced representation of the entire region. The authors use a variety of specific cases to illustrate their general overviews of the geographic setting, historical context, political evolution, and political issues; the role of the military; the ways in which economic systems function; the impacts of urbanization, demographic trends, and the environment; the influences of ethnicity, class, and nationalism; the role of women; the relationship between education and development; the impact of religion and of cultural and literary expressions; and the ways international relations have contributed to new trends and prospects for the future. In sum, the book is designed as a core text that introduces students to Latin America as a diverse yet inclusive region facing crucial issues at the advent of the twenty-first century.

Among the major issues discussed in the text, the most prominent are those related to socioeconomic and political development, debt, immigration, narcotics trade, and inter-American affairs. These are understood in the context of a background strongly influenced by European, Native American, African American, and the "fused" cultures of the New World, as well as by the legacies of colonialism and the predominant impact of the United States. We introduce the reader to the area by providing basic definitions, outlining major issues, discussing relevant background, and illustrating these considerations in countries within the region. Thus, the text employs both thematic and case study approaches. Each chapter contains general discussions, key concepts, ongoing questions, and bibliographic resources.

Rather than attempting to bring these issues and considerations to closure, this text is designed to advance knowledge and stimulate interest and discussion. Therefore, the contents are neither all-inclusive nor deterministic. They are selective and exemplary, based on the premises that (1) common themes tie diverse countries together in a vital region, (2) misunderstanding can be overcome through awareness of other cultures, and (3) a need exists for innovation in domestic and international policymaking, as well as in education. As stereotypes are based on partial truths distorted by ignorance and bias, a more adequate comprehension of contemporary Latin America requires that distortions be overcome and that the region be appreciated as a distinctive set of cultures, encompassing great diversity, unique amalgamations, and increasing global importance.

Latin America's more than 540 million people accounted for approximately 10 percent of the world's population and outnumbered North Americans by two to one at the beginning of the twenty-first century. Latin Americans live in a geographic region that encompasses 15 percent of the world's land surface with vast differences in terrain and climate—ranging from tropical rain forests, swampy lowlands, grassland plains, and deserts to mountainous highlands, island chains, and cays. Increasingly, demographic concentration in urban areas, especially in very large cities, has reaffirmed some cultural traditions and torn down others. European-style central cities have become surrounded by shantytowns occupied mostly by migrants displaced from rural agrarian society. These and other demographic trends have presented a variety of difficult socioeconomic challenges.

Issues relating to the environment, economic growth and distribution, and political and developmental concerns also must be understood in historical perspective. The area has an extremely interesting past in which three major ethnic groups have simultaneously clashed with each other while forming unique fusions. Much of the Latin American story is one of confrontation and accommodation among Native Americans—the Aztecs, Maya, Inca, Taino or Arawak, Carib, Aymará, and Quechua; Europeans— the Spanish, Portuguese, English, French, and Dutch; and Africans— Yoruba, Mandingo, Fulani, Hausa, and other groups. The interaction among the European conquerors, Indian civilizations, and imported African slaves during the colonization period left a legacy that has profoundly influenced subsequent development. Later, immigrants from many nations contributed to the multiplicity of groups interacting in the region.

The conquerors, who sought adventure and wealth in the New World, transferred a peculiar system of agrarian feudalism that was derived primarily from the reconquest of the Iberian Peninsula after eight centuries of Moorish domination. The land and the Indians were divided among the colonizers, who created a hierarchical social order in which the landed aristocracy was supported by the church and protected by the military. Significantly, after initial settlement, the second generation of colonizers were no longer native Europeans but creoles (*criollos*), Europeans born in the Americas. Although they were thoroughly "Spanish," "English," or "French," for example, the creoles had often never even been to Europe. Similarly caught between two cultures were the *mestizos*, offspring of Europeans and Indians. Later, the offspring of Africans and Europeans identified themselves more with the *haciendas*, large socially self-contained ranches, than with the homelands of their forebears.

The plantation economy and *hacienda* life produced interactions and traditions that have continued to influence Latin American society. Moreover, the region is rich in many natural resources that have contributed to the global economy. Latin America has produced large percentages of the world's supply of crops, such as coffee, bananas, linseed, meat, cocoa, sugar, cotton, and others. Significant percentages of the world's oil, nitrates, bauxite, tin, copper, gold, and silver, among other sources of wealth, have also been found in the region. Nevertheless, even after the colonial period ended with independence for the countries within Latin America, foreign capital predominantly exploited and foreign interests largely profited from these resources—until they were partially displaced by attempts to promote national development and social equity through state planning and governmental enterprises.

The forging of new national identities and liberation from oppressive colonial structures did not result in the rapid redefinition of political and social institutions leading to stable self-governance; nor did the region's economies develop self-sufficiency. On the contrary, confusion and disorder were manifested in *caudillo* rule, control of the people by military strongmen. Initially, authoritarian solutions to this anarchic and unstable situation prevailed, despite the democratic tradition of *cabildo abierto* (town meeting) and Bolívarian ideals of independence and order. To this day, the appeal of authoritarian populism in the face of destabilizing political, economic, and social problems can be traced to the way the Catholic kings consolidated Spain under unified control. These traditions are reflected in ongoing Latin American culture—in literary themes; in gender roles; in relations among ethnic groups, belief systems, and educational systems; and in political institutions and practices.

Latin American culture has been in transition. The combinations of strong legacies of the past, many of which are worthy of preservation, and modern challenges to the traditional order have been explosive at times. Although the multiple forces operating in Latin American societies are complicated and the overarching political cultural context is far from constant, ignoring these legacies and influences is just as naive and misleading as accepting the myriad myths surrounding the area. Evolving fusions of religious beliefs, political and social forms, and even ethnic groups have yielded a whole that is truly greater than the sum of its parts.

After the end of the Cold War, the new world order that began to emerge in the last ten years of the twentieth century set into motion a process of realignment among the developed and developing nations. Latin America has not been immune to the emergence of competitive regional economics and the apparent collapse of authoritarian regimes that came to characterize the new international dynamics. Termination of General Augusto Pinochet's dictatorship in Chile, the end of military rule in Brazil and Argentina, the negotiated truces that ended the wars in Central America, the restoration of an elected leader who had been ousted by a coup in Haiti, and fairly free elections in the Caribbean, Venezuela, and elsewhere seemed to indicate a trend toward democratization and the eventual amelioration of debilitating problems, such as political corruption, massive poverty, monetary inflation, foreign debt, illiteracy, crime, and disease.

The complex dynamics on which these hopeful interpretations are based, however, raise a series of difficult questions: How are the legacies of colonialism and nationalism being transformed in contemporary Latin America? What are the prognoses for further democratization, economic and social development, stability, and amelioration of serious crises of governance? Is a hemispheric free-trade zone inevitable? Will regional integration help to resolve or exacerbate the problems facing Latin America? In short, where has this vital region been, and where is it going? The story is far from complete. Each chapter of this book focuses on a different, yet interrelated, aspect of these open-ended questions. If we are to understand Latin America, we will continue to seek answers to these questions; develop new insights, empathy, and appreciation; and raise new questions. While to many observers the region and people are perplexing and unfathomable and their differences profound, we, as scholars, need to keep clearly in mind Montezuma's observation that, ultimately, we are all "flesh and bones, the same as you, and everybody . . . mortal, and tangible" (Keen 1966:48). This book is designed to clarify that proposition as it applies to Latin America and Latin Americans.

*   *   *

Much has occurred since publication of the second edition of *Understanding Contemporary Latin America*. The process of democratization has faced complicated challenges, globalization has accelerated, and the threat of global terrorism since the attacks on September 11, 2001, has impacted international relations. Yet, now the questions formulated in this introduction to previous editions emerge as even more significant.

While there have been transitions, there has also been durability. The elevated expectations for deeper democratization and hopes for amelioration of socioeconomic and political problems that were identified in the first and second editions have been tempered by new developments in the twenty-first century and constrained by legacies of the past. Therefore, this third edition presents a vision of the region that is the product of the new events as well as continuing patterns, building on the themes presented in earlier volumes.

Previous editions of *Understanding Contemporary Latin America* contained chapter analyses that were consistent in addressing strengths and weaknesses in confronting daunting challenges. Their general tones and conclusions reflected the great potential inherent in a region embarking on difficult transitions toward peaceful conflict resolution, social and economic equity, political democracy, environmental and cultural health, and the protection of human rights. Each chapter of this volume was updated, two contain extensive revisions, and one ("The Environment, Population, and Urbanization") was completely rewritten in order to take into account new developments and challenges. While some chapters, such as those on geography, literature, and history, are necessarily more constant in their themes and approaches, others, such as those on politics; international relations; economics; the changing roles of women; the environment, population and urbanization; and education must assess contemporary changes. Conclusions drawn from the chronicles of the past are thereby modified as contemporary history unfolds.

A common theme emerges in this third edition that is consonant with the hopefulness of previous editions, yet less sanguine about the time frame projected previously. The complex processes of democratization and economic development have faced challenges that will continue to inhibit the full realization of free and open societies in many countries in the near future. Elections in several countries have challenged existing political solutions while raising further questions about historical tendencies and the ability to consolidate democracy in Latin America. Divisive partisan struggles have characterized politics in Argentina, Chile, Peru, and Ecuador. Although the Brazilian economy has attracted large amounts of foreign investment, poverty, malnutrition, and health issues have continued to challenge President Luiz Inácio Lula da Silva's populist appeal. Haiti's President Jean-Bertrand Aristide was forced into exile by gangs of dissidents. While Venezuela's President Hugo Chávez survived both an attempted coup d'etat and a recall referendum, his regime, nevertheless, continues to be fraught with controversy and the country with extreme class-based political polarization (Cardozo and Hillman 2003; Hillman 2002, 2004).

Instability still prevails in many areas of Latin America. The conflict in Chiapas, Mexico, continues, as does the near civil war in Colombia. Peace negotiations between the Zapatista National Liberation Army (EZLN) and the Mexican government faltered. Talks between the Revolutionary Armed Forces of Colombia (FARC)—also known as *la guerrilla*—and the Colombian government suffered a similar fate. Despite several major arrests of cartel kingpins, illicit trafficking of narcotics from northern South America through the Caribbean and Mexico into the United States continues practically unabated. Mutinies in the overcrowded jails of the Dominican Republic, Brazil, and Venezuela draw attention to human rights problems in the region.

The love-hate relationship between Latin America and the "Colossus of the North" persists. The United States has been a leader in providing disaster relief to Caribbean countries devastated by hurricanes and providing upward mobility for multitudes of immigrants from the region. Yet, resentment and defiance continue to affect hemispheric relations. The U.S. embargo against Cuba persists despite failure to achieve its stated goals. Free trade in the hemisphere is welcomed by some as a vehicle for development and attacked by others in both the United States and Latin America as an expression of neocolonialism.

All of these considerations require renewed focus on the basic themes of this book and the new questions that they stimulate. Will countries struggling with socioeconomic development find a novel paradigm for political organization? Will the masses be integrated through populist leaders whose regimes devolve into authoritarianism? Or will the new paradigm deepen democracy?

Hence, the story of Latin American trends and developments remains far from being completed. This new edition of *Understanding Contemporary Latin America* continues to seek answers and raise new questions about where the region has been and where it is going and treats these and many other questions by focusing on their particular significance in the context of specific subjects organized by separate chapters.

The editor and the authors are hopeful that our efforts contribute to increased understanding among people of different cultures who may find that they have much in common. Hence, we offer this volume in the spirit of constructive analysis that characterizes the highest aspirations of our respective academic disciplines.

▨ Notes

1. An exception to this tendency is Mendoza, Montaner, and Vargas Llosa's (1996) vehement critique of theories that blame the United States, multinational corporations, and international institutions for development problems in Latin America.

2. Increased recognition of the mutually beneficial aspects of revising U.S. policy toward Cuba, as manifested in growing bipartisan efforts to normalize trade, was stultified in 2004 by the George W. Bush administration's stringent adherence to the embargo.

3. For a detailed examination of the Caribbean, see Richard S. Hillman and Thomas J. D'Agostino, *Understanding the Contemporary Caribbean*, Boulder, Colo.: Lynne Rienner Publishers, 2003.

▨ Bibliography

Alba, Victor. *The Latin Americans*. New York: Praeger, 1969.

Cardozo, Elsa, and Richard S. Hillman. "Venezuelan Foreign Policy: Petroleum, Democratization, and International Affairs." In *The Foreign Policies of Latin American States*, edited by Frank O. Mora and Jeanne A. Hey. Lanham, Md.: Rowman & Littlefield, 2003, pp. 145–165.

Harrison, Lawrence E., and Samuel P. Huntington (eds.). *Culture Matters: How Values Shape Human Progress*. New York: Basic Books, 2000.

Hillman, Richard S. "Venezuela." In *The South America Handbook*, edited by Patrick Heenan and Monique Lamontagne. Chicago and London: Fitzroy and Dearborn Publishers, 2002, pp. 45–57.

———. "Venezuela: The Tropical Beat." In *The Spanish-Speaking South Americans: Insights into Our Hemispheric Neighbors*, edited by Skye Stephenson. Falmouth, Maine, and London: Intercultural Press, 2003, pp. 343–365.

———. "Intellectuals: An Elite Divided." In *The Unraveling of Representative Democracy in Venezuela*, edited by Jennifer McCoy and David Myers. Baltimore: Johns Hopkins University Press, 2004, pp. 115–129.

Keen, Benjamin (ed.). *Americans All: The Story of Our Latin American Neighbors*. New York: Dell, 1966.

Mendoza, Plinio Apuleyo, Carlos Alberto Montaner, and Álvaro Vargas Llosa. *Manual del Perfecto Idiota Latinoamericano*. Barcelona, Spain: Plaza y Janés Editores, S.A., 1996.

Pike, Frederick B. *The United States and Latin America: Myths and Stereotypes of Civilization and Nature*. Austin: University of Texas Press, 1992.

Vasconcelos, José. *La raza cósmica* (3d ed.). México: Espasa-calpe Mexicana, 1966.

2

Latin America: A Geographic Preface

Marie Price

The popular image of Latin America as a major world region has existed for well over a century. The limits of the region are relatively unproblematic, beginning at the Rio Grande (called the Río Bravo in Mexico), usually including the Caribbean, and ending at the southern tip of South America. The region's shared history of Iberian colonization, more than the current economic status of individual states, provides its social glue. The marks of over three hundred years of Iberian rule are still evident. Roughly two-thirds of the 540 million who live in the region speak Spanish; most of the rest speak Portuguese. Catholicism is the dominant religion, although Protestant faiths have made inroads and African religious practices have long been present. Likewise, since much of Latin America lies within the tropics, its verdant forests, exotic wildlife, and balmy weather distinguish Latin America from the temperate and subarctic climates of North America. (See Map 2.1.)

Historically, the Spanish and Portuguese who settled much of the region never referred to the area as Latin America. The term was used first by French politicians in the 1860s in an effort to suggest their own "Latin" links with the Western Hemisphere. Other labels, such as Ibero-America, the Indies, and the Americas, have all been applied. Yet the term Latin America seems to be the most popular, perhaps because it is vague enough to be inclusive of different colonial histories but specific enough to distinguish it from Anglo-America. The idea of Latin America gained support during the latter half of the nineteenth century among intellectuals in the former Spanish colonies who were grappling with a way to build political and ideological unity among the new republics. They, too, stressed a distinct "Latin" identity separate from the "Anglo" North (Ardao 1980).

Map 2.1
Latin America: Countries and Capitals

Like all world regions, Latin America is diverse, and generalizations are inherently problematic. Considering the disparate levels of economic development among Latin America countries—for example, gross national products (GNPs) per capita range from $400 in Haiti to nearly $9,000 in

Barbados—as well as their diverse ethnic compositions, it would be easy to emphasize division over commonality. Consonant with the theme propounded by Richard S. Hillman in Chapter 1, however, the geographic perspective clearly illustrates unity in diversity. There is little dispute, for example, that the region's human geography was completely reworked with the arrival of Europeans. The number of Amerindian peoples declined by as much as 90 percent during the course of conquest, but the Amerindian presence remains strong in many parts of Latin America. Large numbers of African slaves were also added to the cultural mix of Europeans and Amerindians through the slave trade. Today, the African presence throughout the Caribbean, Brazil, and coastal Venezuela and Colombia is quite notable. Other immigrant groups arrived—from Italy, Japan, Germany, and India—from the late nineteenth century on, adding to the cultural complexity of the region.

In terms of physical geography, much of the area is tropical, with a mixture of grasslands and forest, as well as mountains and shields (large upland areas of exposed crystalline rock). An impressive array of natural resources includes the planet's largest rain forest, the greatest river by volume, and substantial reserves of natural gas and oil, tin, and copper. Since Christopher Columbus's journey of exploration more than five centuries ago, Latin America has provided the world with many valuable commodities. The early Spanish Empire concentrated on extracting precious metals, namely silver and gold, from Mexico and the Andes. The Portuguese became prominent producers of sugar products, gold, and (later) coffee. By the late nineteenth and early twentieth centuries, natural resource exports to Europe and North America fueled the region's growing economies. Countries tended to specialize in one or two commodities: wool and wheat from Argentina, coffee and sugar from Brazil, coffee and bananas from Costa Rica, tin and silver from Bolivia, and oil from Mexico and Venezuela. Although the national economies of Latin America have diversified since the 1950s, they continue to be major producers of primary goods for North America, Europe, and East Asia.

In the first part of this chapter, I provide a sketch of the physical environment of Latin America, drawing attention to its topographical features, climates, natural resources, and environmental issues. In the second part, I discuss the basic demographic and cultural patterning of the region, developing the concept of the Columbian exchange as a way to understand the ecological and cultural impact of the Americas' encounter with Europe. Iberian colonization, the African slave trade, and later waves of immigrants from Europe and Asia in the nineteenth and twentieth centuries produced a multiethnic and multiracial society. Current patterns of Latin American and Caribbean emigration to North America, Europe, and Japan are creating complex transnational networks that are conduits for the diffusion of Latino culture into other world regions. Each modern state of Latin America, therefore, has a diverse indigenous and migrant profile that contributes to its distinct national culture. Yet, this chapter reveals the common experiences shared by the nations in the region.

▪ Physical Setting

The movement of tectonic plates explains much of Latin America's basic topography. As the South and North American plates slowly drifted westward, the Nazca, Cocos, and Pacific plates were subducted below them. In this contact zone, deep oceanic trenches exist along the Pacific coasts, such as the Humboldt trench along the coast of Chile and Peru, producing surprisingly cool ocean temperatures for a tropical zone. The submerged plates have folded and uplifted the mainland's surface, creating the geologically young western mountains, such as the Sierra Madre Occidental in Mexico, the highlands of Central America, and the Andes. The Andes, the most dramatic of these highland areas, run the length of the South American continent for 5,000 miles, with some thirty peaks reaching over 20,000 feet. Created by the collision of oceanic and continental plates, the Andes are a series of folded and faulted sedimentary rocks with intrusions of volcanic and crystalline rock. Consequently, many rich veins of precious metals and minerals are found there. From Colombia to Chile, the initial economic wealth of these Andean territories came from mining. (See Map 2.2.)

The Andes are typically divided into the northern, central, and southern components. In Colombia, the northern Andes actually split into three distinct mountain ranges before merging near the border of Ecuador. High-altitude plateaus and snow-covered peaks distinguish the central Andes of Ecuador, Peru, and Bolivia. The Andes reach their greatest width here. Between Peru and Bolivia is a treeless high plateau called the *altiplano*. Averaging 12,000 feet in elevation, it has limited grazing potential but important mineral resources. The southern Andes are shared by Chile and Argentina. Much of this highland region was an important zone of settlement for Amerindian people, who exploited the diverse ecological niches of the mountains and domesticated a tremendous variety of native crops, such as potatoes, hot and sweet peppers, and quinoa (Gade 1999). In Peru, the magnificent mountaintop city of Machu Picchu is an example of the remains of a pre-Columbian settlement. Today, most of the people of the Andean states still live in or at the base of the mountains. Major cities, such as Bogotá, Quito, and La Paz, are in the mountains. The Andean states of Ecuador, Peru, and Bolivia are home to the majority of Amerindian peoples in South America.

The Mexican plateau is a massive upland area ringed by the Sierra

Map 2.2
Climates and Vegetation

Madre Mountains and tilted so that the highest elevations are in the South—about 8,000 feet near Mexico City and just 4,000 feet at Ciudad Juárez. The southern end of the plateau, known as the Mesa Central, supports Mexico's highest population density, including the cities of Mexico City, Puebla, and Guadalajara. The Mesa Central was historically Mexico's

High in the Peruvian Andes, Machu Picchu
is the site of a city in pre-Columbian culture.

breadbasket, but water shortages due to urbanization and rapid population growth threaten the region's productivity (Ezcurra et al. 1999). Throughout the Mexican plateau are also rich seams of silver, the focus of economic activity during the country's colonial era. Today, the Mexican economy is driven more by petroleum and gas production along the Gulf Coast and less by the metals of the plateau.

The Caribbean plate contains most of Central America, the islands of the West Indies, and part of Colombia. As the Caribbean plate moves slowly to the east, it triggers volcanic activity in both the Central American highlands and the islands of the Caribbean. The Central American highlands are composed of a volcanic chain that stretches from Guatemala to Costa Rica, producing a handsome landscape of rolling green hills, elevated basins with lakes, and conical peaks. Hugging the Pacific Coast, the legacy of some forty volcanoes is fertile soil that yields a variety of domestic and export crops. Most of Central America's 39 million people are concentrated in this zone, either in the capital cities or the surrounding rural villages. In the eastern Caribbean, the arc of smaller islands, known as the Lesser Antilles, exist within a subduction zone that also produces volcanic activity. In this area, the heavier North and South American plates go underneath the Caribbean plate, creating a chain of mountainous islands from St. Kitts to Grenada that are volcanic in origin. The latest round of volcanic activity began in 1995 on the island of Montserrat. Since then, a series of volcanic eruptions of ash and rock have forced most people off the island and the relocation of the capital, Plymouth (an interim capital was constructed at Brades Estate).

The shields are another important landform of the region. These large rocky outcroppings vary in elevation from 600 to 5,000 feet and are remnants of the ancient landmass of Gondwanaland, which began breaking apart 250 million years ago. Consequently, most shields are not noted for their agricultural potential because they lack volcanic and sedimentary soils. The Guiana and Patagonia shields are very lightly settled and have limited agricultural potential. In terms of natural resources and settlement, the Brazilian shield is the largest and most important shield. It covers much of Brazil, but in the southeastern portion of the state, a series of mountains protrude from the shield. In between these mountains are elevated basins with fertile soils, excellent for agriculture. This is where many Brazilians live and Brazil's largest cities, São Paulo and Rio de Janeiro, are located.

Historically, the most important areas of settlement in tropical Latin America were not along the region's major rivers but across its upland plateaus and intermontane basins. In these areas, the combination of soils, benign climates, and sufficient rainfall produced Latin America's most productive agricultural areas and its densest settlements. Examples of four such areas are the Brazilian shield, the Mexican plateau, the Central American highlands, and the Andes.

Major River Basins

In contrast to the western highlands, humid lowlands characterize the Atlantic side of Latin America. Across these lowlands meander some of the great rivers of the world, including the Amazon, Plata, and Orinoco rivers. The Amazon, draining some 2.4 million square miles, is the largest river in the world by volume and area and the second longest in length. The scale of this watershed is underscored by the fact that 20 percent of all freshwater discharged into the oceans comes from the Amazon. Everywhere throughout the basin, more than 60 inches of rain falls each year and in many places more than 80 inches. This is home to the largest tropical rain forest in the world and, thus, a treasure for genetic diversity. The Plata Basin begins in the tropics and discharges its water in the midlatitudes near the city of Buenos Aires. This basin has three major rivers—the Paraná, Paraguay, and Uruguay—that drain an area from central Bolivia and southern Brazil to northern Argentina. On the Paraná River is Latin America's largest hydroelectric project, the Itaipú, which produces all of Paraguay's electricity and much of the energy used by industrial southern Brazil. The other great river of the region is the Orinoco of Venezuela and Colombia.

Although just one-sixth the size of the Amazon watershed, the Orinoco's discharge roughly equals that of the Mississippi River.

Within these watersheds are vast lowlands of less than 600 feet elevation. From north to south, they are the Llanos, the Amazon lowlands, the Pantanal, the Chaco, and the Pampas. With the exception of the Pampas, which is a major center of grain and livestock production, most of these lowlands are sparsely settled and offer limited agricultural potential except as grazing lands for livestock. Long thought of as static frontiers (open lands unsuitable for permanent settlement), areas such as the Chaco and the Amazon have experienced marked increase in resource extraction in the last thirty years, especially the booming soybean market. The pressure to open new lands for agribusiness and export production is transforming much of lowland South America. Likewise, since the 1970s, the Amazon has witnessed a dramatic increase in population, with over 12 million people settling in the Brazilian Amazon alone, bringing about accelerated levels of timber and mineral extraction.

The Mexican and Central American river basins cannot match the scale of the South American ones, but they are important nonetheless. Mexico's Río Bravo (called the Rio Grande in the United States) delimits the boundary between Mexico and Texas. With headwaters in the Sierra Madre Occidental, the Río Bravo and its tributaries carry the snowmelt from the mountains through arid northern Mexico. Dams have been built on some of the watershed's major tributaries to produce electricity and to supply water to cities, towns, and farms. The rise of border cities and industrialization have combined to degrade the watershed. Surface water in the lower Río Bravo is scarce, and what does exist is badly polluted. The largest watershed by volume in Central America is the Grijalva-Usumicinta Basin, which flows through a sparsely populated tropical forest zone in southern Mexico and northern Guatemala. In the Mexican state of Tabasco, the Usumicinta joins the Grijalva and flows into the Bay of Campeche, accounting for nearly half of Mexico's freshwater river flow. Political interest in the basin has intensified over the years because the watershed may be critical for satisfying the water and energy demands of Mexico.

Climate and Vegetation

In tropical Latin America, the daily high temperatures (Fahrenheit) are in the 70s to 80s and the daily lows in the 70s to 60s (see Map 2.2). Moreover, the average monthly temperatures in localities such as Managua, Port-au-Prince, and Manaus change very little. Precipitation patterns, however, do vary and create distinct wet and dry seasons. In Managua, January and February are dry months, and June through October are the wettest months. The city of Manaus on the Amazon, however, is the reverse. June through

August are relatively dry, and the long rainy season extends from October to April. The tropical lowlands of Latin America are usually classified as tropical humid climates that are covered in either forest or savanna (grassland with few trees), depending on the amount of rainfall. The largest remaining tropical forest is in the Amazon Basin, but much of the perimeter of this forest zone has been converted into pasture or farms. In contrast, much of the tropical forest in the Caribbean and in Central America was removed long ago for agriculture and human settlement.

Important areas of Latin America are desert. The region's desert climates are found along the Pacific Coast of Peru and northern Chile, Patagonia, northern Mexico, and northeastern Brazil in an area called the Bahia (or the *sertão*). Desert areas are generally those that get less than 10 inches of precipitation a year. Thus, a city such as Lima, Peru, which is clearly in the tropics, averages only 1.5 inches of rainfall per year due to the hyperaridity of the Peruvian coast. In fact, there are parts of the Atacama Desert in northern Chile that have never recorded rainfall, giving this desert the distinction of being the world's driest. Such an inhospitable climate, however, hosts a rich assortment of phosphates and copper, so that resources from the Atacama buttressed the Chilean economy for much of the twentieth century.

Not all of Latin America is tropical. In the Southern Cone states, midlatitude climates with hot summers and cold winters prevail. Of course, the midlatitude temperature shifts in the Southern Hemisphere are the inverse of those in the Northern Hemisphere (cold Julys and warm Januarys). In the mountain ranges, complex climate patterns result, so that elevation becomes more critical than latitude. The temperate lands (*tierra templada*), at 3,000–6,000 feet in the tropics, have been described as having an eternal springtime climate with warm days and pleasant nights. The colder lands (*tierra fría*) of the tropics are found at 6,000–12,000 feet. These tropical highlands support agriculture such as wheat, tubers, and even maize, but the daytime highs are cool, and the lows can reach freezing. These normal climate patterns and the human ecological systems they support are periodically disrupted by weather events that can dramatically impact Latin America. Two of these that deserve attention are hurricanes and El Niño.

Several hurricanes form each season, and the worst ones can devastate communities and agriculture in the Caribbean, Central America, Mexico, and North America. (South America is out of the hurricane belt.) Beginning in July, westward-moving low-pressure disturbances form off the coast of West Africa, picking up moisture and speed as they move across the Atlantic. The air masses are usually no more than 100 miles across, but to achieve hurricane status, their winds must reach velocities of more than 75 miles per hour. Typically, half a dozen to a dozen hurricanes form each season and move through the region, causing limited damage. There are, of course, exceptions, and most longtime residents of northern Latin America have experienced the full force of at least one major storm in their lifetimes.

In 1998, the torrential rains of Hurricane Mitch, one of the most deadly tropical storms in a century, resulted in the death of at least 8,000 people in Honduras, Nicaragua, and El Salvador. Mudslides and flooding ravaged structures and roads, leaving upward of one-quarter of Honduras's population without shelter. Whereas Hurricane Mitch largely bypassed the Caribbean, Hurricane Gilbert took 260 lives in 1988 and pounded Jamaica and Mexico's Yucatán Peninsula before slamming into Texas. Eighty percent of the houses in Jamaica lost their roofs. Plantations of coconut palms on the Yucatán were leveled like matchsticks. Hurricane Hugo came the following year, leaving nearly everyone in Montserrat homeless, wiping out the infrastructure and tourist economy of St. Croix, and damaging Puerto Rico to such an extent that army troops were sent in to help restore order. Modern tracking equipment has improved hurricane forecasting and reduced the number of fatalities. Forecasting, nevertheless, cannot reduce the economic damage done to crops, forests, and infrastructure when a powerful storm hits.

In recent years, abnormally heavy rains have been responsible for tragic natural disasters, made worse by poverty that forces thousands of people to live in vulnerable areas. The massive mudslides on the northern side of the El Ávila mountain range that separates Caracas from the sea was caused by weeks of torrential rains in December 1999. Thousands of hillside squatter settlements vanished in the mud. The official death toll was 10,000 (2,000 more fatalities than Hurricane Mitch caused), and 400,000 were left homeless. Yet, unofficial estimates of the death toll were closer to 40,000. Similarly, in Haiti, torrential rains brought nearly five feet of water during one week in May 2004. Rain ran down the denuded hillsides, the silty rivers rose, and towns like Mapou were washed away in the floods that followed. Nearly 3,000 people perished in Haiti and the bordering villages of the Dominican Republic as a result of flooding.

The most debated weather phenomenon in Latin America, and perhaps the world, is El Niño. El Niño (a reference to the Christ child) is a warm Pacific current that usually arrives off the coast of Ecuador and Peru in December. Every decade or so, an abnormally large current arrives that produces torrential rains, signaling the arrival of an El Niño year. The 1997–1998 El Niño was especially bad for Latin America; at least nine hundred people were killed by floods or storms attributed to El Niño–related disturbances. Devastating floods occurred in Peru and Ecuador. In Peru, flooding drove some 350,000 people temporarily from their homes. Heavy May rains in Argentina and Paraguay caused the Paraná River to rise 26 feet above normal, forcing thousands of people to flee.

The other, less talked about aspect of El Niño is drought. While the

Pacific Coast of South and North America experienced record rainfall in the 1997–1998 El Niño, Colombia, Venezuela, northern Brazil, and Central America battled drought. Hundreds of brush and forest fires left their mark; the amount of smoke produced by forest fires in northern Mexico in the spring of 1998 was so great that it caused haze in the southeastern United States. Drought also brought losses, estimated in billions of dollars, to farmers and ranchers in the region. And for areas that depend on hydroelectricity, such as Colombia and Central America, drought can cause disruptions in electrical power. The indirect costs of drought, such as fire-charred hillsides vulnerable to landslides, are impossible to measure.

Environmental Issues

Given Latin America's immense size and relatively low population density, it has not experienced the same levels of environmental degradation witnessed in other parts of the world, such as in East Asia. The worst environmental problems are found in cities, their surrounding rivers and coasts, and intensely farmed zones (Roberts and Thanos 2003). Vast areas of Latin America remain relatively untouched, supporting an incredible diversity of plant and animal life. Throughout the region, national parks offer some protection to unique communities of plants and animals. And a growing environmental movement in countries such as Costa Rica, Brazil, and Guyana has yielded popular support for environmentally friendly initiatives. It can be argued that Latin America entered the twenty-first century with a real opportunity to avoid many of the environmental missteps seen in other regions of the world.

At the same time, economic pressures brought about by global market forces are driving governments to exploit their natural resources (minerals, fossil fuels, forests, and soils) aggressively. The challenge lies in managing the region's immense natural resources and balancing the economic benefits of extraction with the ecological soundness of conservation. Of the many environmental challenges facing the region, three of the most pernicious are deforestation, degradation of arable lands, and urban environmental pollution.

Due to international interest in tropical forests, deforestation is probably the environmental issue most often associated with the region. The Amazon Basin and portions of the eastern lowlands of Central America and Mexico still maintain important stands of tropical forest. Other areas, such as the Atlantic coastal forest of Brazil and the Pacific forests of Central America, have nearly disappeared because of agricultural use, settlement, and ranching. Likewise, extensive forest clearing for sugar plantations in the Lesser Antilles nearly eliminated all the tropical forest there more than two centuries ago. In the midlatitudes, the ecologically unique evergreen rain forest of southern Chile (the Valdivian forest) is being cleared to export wood chips to markets in Japan (Clapp 1998). The coniferous forests of northern Mexico are also being cut down, in part because of the boom in commercial logging stimulated by the North American Free Trade Agreement (NAFTA).

In terms of biological diversity, however, the loss of tropical rain forest is the most critical. Tropical rain forests account for only 6 percent of the earth's landmass, but at least 50 percent of the world's species are found there. Moreover, only the Amazon contains the largest undisturbed stretches of rain forest in the world. In the last forty years, the region's tropical forests were seen as agricultural frontiers that governments opened up in an attempt to appease landless peasants and reward political cronies. The forests fell as colonists created farms and large cattle ranches (Hecht and Cockburn 1989). Forest clearing also occurred due to the search for gold in Brazil, Venezuela, Costa Rica, and Guyana and the production of coca leaf for cocaine in Peru, Bolivia, and Colombia (Young 1996), as well as from logging concessions to Southeast and East Asian companies in Guyana, Suriname, and Brazil.

Soil erosion and fertility decline occur in all agricultural areas. Certain soil types in Latin America are particularly vulnerable to erosion, most notably the volcanic soils and the reddish oxisols found in the humid lowlands. The productivity of the volcanic highlands of Central America, for example, has declined over the decades, due to the ease with which these soils erode and the failure to apply soil conservation measures in many localities. The oxisols of the tropical lowlands, by contrast, can quickly erode into a baked claypan surface when the natural vegetative cover is removed, making permanent agriculture nearly impossible. Ironically, the consolidation of large modern farms in the valleys tends to push subsistence farmers into marginal areas on steep slopes. On these hillside farms, gullies and landslides are a constant threat to rural livelihoods.

The reality of poverty forcing people to degrade their environment is evident in many rural places in Latin America. Nowhere is this connection clearer than in Haiti. The inhabitants of this densely settled country are largely dependent on commercial and subsistence agriculture, which has resulted in serious problems with soil erosion and declining yields. In addition, the majority of Haitians rely on charcoal (made from trees) for their cooking fuel, which places additional strain on the island's vegetation. The deterioration of the resource base is evident from the air: aerial photos reveal a sharp boundary between a denuded Haiti and a forested Dominican Republic. The difference between the two countries is explained, in part, by the lack of affordable fuel alternatives. Whereas many Dominicans can afford to buy liquid or gas cooking fuel, many Haitians cannot.

Because the vast majority of Latin Americans live in cities, it has become increasingly clear that the environmental quality of urban settings has been a focus for local activism. While Susan Place and Jacqueline Chase discuss urban environmental issues at some length in Chapter 8, it is important to recognize here that many of Latin America's environmentalists worry about ways to make urban environments cleaner rather than about the future of distant tropical forests. In Rio de Janeiro and São Paulo alone, hundreds of local environmental organizations push for cleaner air, better water, and more green space (Christen et al. 1998).

Factories, coal- and gas-burning power plants, and vehicles all contribute to urban air pollution. The environmental regulations that exist are seldom enforced. The consequences are, in the worst cases, a serious threat to people and the environment. In the 1980s, the Brazilian industrial center of Cubatão, near São Paulo, became synonymous with environmental catastrophe. For years, people complained of headaches and nausea from the belching factory smokestacks, but their complaints were not taken seriously. In 1984, a leak occurred in a gasoline pipeline that ran through one of the poorest squatter settlements. The smell of leaking gas went unnoticed because of the stench of industrial pollutants throughout the valley. When the gas was finally ignited, as many as two hundred people were incinerated in the resulting explosion and fire. While industry leaders downplayed the disaster, traumatized residents mobilized to address the worst abuses (Dean 1995). The events in Cubatão, more than the destruction of the Amazon rain forest, are credited with invigorating the environmental movement in Brazil.

Despite serious urban environmental issues, people in Latin American cities tend to have better access to water, sewers, and electricity than their counterparts in Asia and Africa. Moreover, the density of urban settlement encourages the widespread use of mass transportation—both public and private bus and van routes make getting around most cities fairly easy. The largest cities, such as Mexico City, Buenos Aires, and Caracas, have subway systems. Increasingly cost-effective high-speed bus systems, as found in Curitiba and Bogotá, are gaining popularity. Yet, the inevitable environmental problems that come with primate (dominant or major) cities that grew rapidly and have widespread poverty cannot be overstated. Improving sewer systems, waste disposal, and water treatment plants is expensive. Chronic air pollution has caused debilitating health effects, most notably in Santiago and Mexico City. The money to clean up cities is always in short supply, especially with problems of foreign debt, currency devaluation, and inflation. And, as many urban dwellers tend to reside in unplanned squatter settlements, retroactively servicing these communities with utilities is difficult and costly.

A Bounty of Natural Resources

Historically, Latin America's abundant natural resources were its wealth. In the colonial period, silver, gold, and sugar generated fortunes for a privileged few. In the latter half of the nineteenth century, a series of export booms introduced commodities such as bananas, coffee, cacao, grains, tin, rubber, copper, wool, and petroleum to an expanding world market. One of the legacies of this export-led development was the tendency to specialize in one or two major commodities, a pattern that continued well into the 1950s. During that decade, Costa Rica earned 90 percent of its export earnings from bananas and coffee, El Salvador earned over 90 percent from coffee and cotton, 85 percent of Chilean exports came from copper, and half of Uruguay's export earnings came from wood (Wilkie 1997). Even Brazil, the region's largest country, generated 60 percent of its export earnings from coffee in 1955. By the 1990s, that figure was less than 5 percent (although Brazil remains the world's leader in coffee exports, followed by Colombia), and soy products earned Brazil more foreign exchange than coffee.

The trend throughout Latin America since the 1960s has been to diversify and mechanize resource extraction, especially in agriculture and mining. Nowhere is this more evident than in the Plata Basin, which includes southern Brazil, Uruguay, northern Argentina, Paraguay, and eastern Bolivia. Soybeans, used for oil and animal feed, transformed these lowlands in the 1980s and 1990s. Added to this crop are acres of rice, cotton, and orange groves; the more traditional plantings of wheat and sugar; and livestock. Other large-scale agricultural frontiers exist along the piedmont of the Venezuelan Andes (mostly grains) and the Pacific slope of Central America (mostly cotton and tropical fruits). In northern Mexico, water supplied from dams along the Sierra Madre Occidental has turned the valleys in Sinaloa into an intensive production zone for fruits and vegetables bound for the United States. An explosion of so-called nontraditional agricultural exports is reshaping activities in rural areas—from melons and shrimp in Honduras, to flowers and ferns in Costa Rica and Colombia. One major exception to this trend toward agricultural diversity was Cuba from the 1950s until 1990. During that period, Cuba earned nearly 80 percent of its foreign exchange from sugar. With the fall of the Soviet Union and the loss of guaranteed prices and markets for Cuban sugar, the value of Cuba's sugar exports declined by two-thirds from 1990 to 1998 (Wilkie 2002: 686).

In each of these cases, the agricultural sector is capital intensive and dynamic. By using machinery, high-yielding hybrids, chemical fertilizers, and pesticides, many corporate farms have become extremely productive and profitable. What these operations fail to do is employ many rural people, which is especially problematic in countries where one-third or more of the population depend on agriculture for their livelihood. As industrialized agriculture becomes the norm in Latin America, subsistence producers are further marginalized. The overall trend is that agricultural production is increasing, while proportionally fewer people are employed in it, and agriculture contributes less to the overall economy than it once did. In absolute terms, however, the number of people living in rural areas is about the same today as it was in 1960 (roughly 100 million). The major difference over the last forty-five years is that many of these people are worse off, because traditional rural support networks have broken down and small farmers have been forced onto marginal lands that are vulnerable to drought and erosion. Peasant farmers who are able to produce a surplus of corn or wheat earn very little from these crops, as their value is undercut by cheaper imported grains.

Mining and fossil fuels continue to shape the economies of several countries in the region. The oil-rich nations of Venezuela, Mexico, and Colombia are able to meet their own fuel needs and to earn vital state revenues from oil exports. Venezuela is most dependent on revenues from oil, earning up to 90 percent of its foreign exchange from crude petroleum and petroleum products. Venezuela and Mexico have become major suppliers of oil to the United States. In 2002, oil exports from these two countries to the United States were equal to the volume of oil exports from the Middle East to the United States. Vast oil reserves also exist in the eastern lowlands of Colombia, yet a costly and vulnerable pipeline that connects the oil fields to the coast is a regular target of guerrilla groups. By 2000, Colombian oil production had improved, making it the third largest Latin American exporter of oil to the United States (Wilkie 2002).

Besides oil, Latin America's other important exports are silver, zinc, copper, iron ore, bauxite, and gold. Like agriculture, mining has become more mechanized. Even Bolivia, a country dependent on tin production, cut 70 percent of its miners from state payrolls in the 1990s without appreciable falls in production. The measure was part of a nationwide austerity program, but it also illustrates that the majority of miners were not needed. Similarly, the vast copper mines of northern Chile are producing record amounts of copper with fewer miners. Gold mining, in contrast, continues to use artisanal methods and larger numbers of miners. Gold rushes are occurring in remote tropical regions of Venezuela, Brazil, Colombia, Guyana, and Costa Rica. Many gold strikes are made illegally on indigenous lands or within the borders of national parks (as in Costa Rica and Guyana). However, because gold is such a valuable export commodity, the borders of protected areas are seldom enforced.

■ Human Geography of Latin America

Today, more than half a billion people live in Latin America. This is a striking figure when one considers that in 1950, Latin America comprised 150
million people, which equaled the population of the United States at that
time. Now, Latin America's population is almost double that of the United
States. Like the rest of the developing world, Latin America experienced
dramatic population growth in the 1960s and 1970s. It outpaced the United
States because infant mortality rates declined and life expectancy soared. In
1950, Brazilian life expectancy was only 43 years; by the 1980s, it was 63;
and by 2000, it was 68. In fact, most countries in the region experienced a
twenty- to thirty-year improvement in life expectancy between 1950 and
2000, which pushed up growth rates. Today, the average life expectancy for
the entire region is 71 years, compared to 78 for the United States. Four
countries account for two-thirds of the region's population: Brazil, with
almost 177 million; Mexico, 105 million; Colombia, 44 million; and
Argentina, 37 million (Population Reference Bureau 2003).

During the 1980s, population growth rates suddenly began to slow, and
during the 1990s, most countries reported growth rates of less than 2 percent. The region is still growing, but the sudden slowdown in growth surprised many demographers. For example, in the 1960s, a typical Latin
American woman had six or seven children. By the 1980s, the average
woman was having three children. A number of factors explain this, including more urban families, which tend to be smaller than rural ones;
increased participation of women in the workforce; higher education levels
of women; and state support of family planning and better access to birth
control. Today, the average number of children per woman is 2.7. Only a
few poorer and more rural countries (Guatemala, Honduras, Haiti, Bolivia,
and Paraguay) have averages higher than four children per woman
(Population Reference Bureau 2003).

The distribution of population away from rural areas and into cities is
the other major demographic change for the region. A staggering 75 percent
of Latin Americans live in cities, which is a rate comparable to Europe and
North America. This makes Latin America the most urbanized region within the developing world. The cities in the region are noted for high levels of
urban primacy, a condition in which a country has a primate city that is
three to four times larger than any other city in the country. Examples of
primate cities are Lima, Caracas, Guatemala City, Havana, Santo Domingo,
Buenos Aires, Mexico City, and Santiago. In Brazil and Ecuador, two cities
dominate all others in the country in terms of size and economic importance: Guayaquil and Quito in Ecuador and São Paulo and Rio de Janeiro in
Brazil are examples of dual primacy. Primacy is often viewed as a liability,
because too many national resources are concentrated into one urban cen-

ter. In an effort to decentralize, governments have intentionally built cities far from primate cities, such as Ciudad Guyana in Venezuela and Brasília in Brazil. Despite these efforts, the tendency toward primacy remains strong. In order to appreciate the magnitude of population growth and the dominance of cities, it is important to address the demographic consequences of Iberian conquest in the Americas.

Conquest and Settlement

The Iberian colonial experience imposed a political and cultural coherence on Latin America that makes it a distinguishable region today. Yet, this was not an uncontested transplanting of Iberia across the Atlantic. As a result of the papal-decreed Treaty of Tordesillas in 1493, Spain received the majority of the Americas, and Portugal received a small portion of eastern South America that eventually became Brazil. Through the course of colonization, Spain shifted its attention to the mainland colonies centered on Mexico and Peru. This left the Caribbean and the Guianas vulnerable to other European powers, most notably England, France, and the Netherlands, and each of these countries established territorial claims.

Nevertheless, Spain was able to conquer and administer an enormous territory in less than one hundred years. The prevailing strategy was one of forced assimilation, in which Iberian religion, language, and political organization were imposed on the surviving fragments of native society. In some areas, such as southern Mexico, Guatemala, Bolivia, and Peru, Amerindian cultures have shown remarkable resilience, as evidenced by the survival of Amerindian languages—Maya, Quechua, Aymará, and Guaraní. Later, other European, African, and Asian peoples, arriving as both forced and voluntary migrants, were added to the region's cultural mix. Yet, perhaps the single most important factor in the dominance of Iberian culture in Latin America was the demographic collapse of native populations in the first 150 years of settlement.

Native Population Decline

It is hard to grasp the enormity of human and cultural loss due to this cataclysmic encounter between Europe and the Americas. Throughout the region, archaeological sites are poignant reminders of the complexity of precontact (that is, pre–European arrival) civilizations. Dozens of stone temples found throughout Mexico and Central America attest to how Mayan and Aztec civilizations flourished in the area's tropical forests and upland plateaus. In the Andes, farmers still use stone terraces built by the Incas; earthen platforms for village sites and raised fields for agriculture are still being discovered and mapped. Ceremonial centers, such as Cuzco (the center of the great Incan Empire), and hundreds of miles of Incan roads are evidence of the complexity of Amerindian networks. The Spanish, too, were impressed by the sophistication and wealth they saw around them, especially in the incomparable Tenochtitlán, where Mexico City sits today. Tenochtitlán was the political and ceremonial center of the Aztecs, which supported a complex metropolitan area with some 300,000 residents. By comparison, the largest city in Spain at the time was considerably smaller. (See Map 2.3.)

The most telling figures of the impact of Iberian expansion are demographic. It is widely believed that precontact America (the Western Hemisphere) had 54 million inhabitants; in comparison, Western Europe in 1500 had a population of 42 million. Of the 54 million, about 50 million were in Latin America and the Caribbean (Denevan 1992). There were two major population centers: one in central Mexico, with 14 million people, and the other in the central Andes (highland Peru and Bolivia), with nearly 12 million. Nearly all of the estimated 3 million Amerindian people who inhabited the islands of the Caribbean were gone within fifty years of contact with Europeans. By 1650, after 150 years of colonization, the indigenous population was one-tenth its precontact size. The relentless elimination of 90 percent of the indigenous population was largely caused by epidemics of influenza and smallpox; however, warfare, forced labor, and starvation due to a collapse of food production systems also contributed to the death rate.

The tragedy of conquest did not end in 1650, the population low point for Amerindians, but continued throughout the colonial period and, to a much lesser extent, continues today. Even after the indigenous population began its slow recovery in the central Andes and central Mexico, there were small tribal bands in southern Chile (the Mapuche) and Patagonia (Araucania) that experienced the ravages of disease three centuries after Columbus landed. Even now, the isolation of some Amazonian tribes has made them vulnerable to disease.

At present, Mexico, Guatemala, Ecuador, Peru, and Bolivia have the largest indigenous populations. Not surprisingly, these are the areas that had the densest native populations at contact. Indigenous survival also occurs in isolated settings, where the workings of national and global economies are slow to penetrate. The Caribbean Coast of Panama, home to the Kuna, or the Gran Sabana of Venezuela, where the Pemon live, are two examples of relatively small groups that have managed to maintain a distinct indigenous way of life despite pressures to assimilate.

The Columbian Exchange

Historian Alfred Crosby likens the contact period between Europe (Old World) and the Americas (New World) to an immense biological swap,

Map 2.3
Indian Migration Routes and Empires

which he terms the Columbian exchange. According to Crosby (1972), Europeans benefited greatly from this exchange, and Amerindian peoples suffered terribly from it, most notably through the introduction of disease. The human ecology of both sides of the Atlantic, however, was forever changed through the introduction of new diseases, peoples, plants, and animals. Take, for example, the introduction of Old World crops. The Spanish, naturally, brought their staples of wheat, olives, and grapes to plant in the Americas. Wheat did surprisingly well in the highland tropics and became a widely consumed grain over time. Grapes and olive trees did not fare so well; eventually, grapes were produced commercially in the temperate zones of South America. The Spanish grew to appreciate the domestic skills of Amerindian agriculturalists, who had developed valuable starch crops such as corn, potatoes, and bitter manioc, as well as exotic condiments such as hot peppers, tomatoes, pineapple, cacao, and avocados.

Tropical crops transferred from Asia and Africa reconfigured the economic potential of Latin America. Sugarcane became the dominant cash crop of the Caribbean and the Atlantic tropical lowlands of South America. With labor-intensive sugar production, came the importation of millions of African slaves. Coffee, a later transfer from East Africa, emerged as one of the leading export crops throughout Central America, Colombia, Venezuela, and Brazil in the nineteenth century. And pasture grasses introduced from Africa enhanced the forage available to livestock.

The movement of Old World animals across the Atlantic had a profound impact on the Americas. Initially, these animals hastened indigenous decline by introducing animal-borne diseases and by producing feral offspring that consumed everything in their path. Over time, native survivors appreciated the utility of Old World animals. Draft animals were adopted, and so, too, was the plow, which facilitated the preparation of soil for planting. Wool became an important fiber for indigenous communities in the uplands. And slowly, pork, chicken, and eggs added protein and diversity to the staple diets of corn, potatoes, and cassava. Ironically, the horse, which was a feared and formidable weapon of the Europeans, became a tool of resistance in the hands of skilled indigenous riders who inhabited the plains of the Chaco and Patagonia. With the major exception of disease, many transfers of plants and animals ultimately benefited both sides of the Atlantic. Still, it is clear that the ecological and material basis for life in Latin America was completely reworked through this exchange process initiated by Columbus.

Repeopling the Americas

The dramatic and relatively rapid decline of Amerindian peoples simplified colonization in some ways. Spain and Portugal were able to refashion

Latin America into a European likeness. And as rival European powers vied for power in the Caribbean in the mid-sixteenth century, the islands they fought over were virtually uninhabited. Yet, instead of creating a tropical neo-Europe, a complex ethnic blend evolved. Beginning with the first years of contact, unions between European men and Amerindian women began the process of racial mixing that became a defining feature of the region over time. The Iberian courts officially discouraged racial mixing, but not much could be done about it. Spain, which had a far larger native population than the Portuguese in Brazil, became obsessed with the matter of race and maintaining racial purity among its colonists. Yet, after generations of intermarriage, four broad categories resulted: *blanco* (European ancestry), *mestizo* (mixed ancestry), *indio* (Amerindian ancestry), and *negro* (African ancestry). The *blancos* (or Europeans) are still well represented among the elites, yet the vast majority of the people are of mixed racial ancestry.

For the Caribbean islands and the Atlantic Coast of South America, the scarcity of indigenous labor hastened the development of the trans-Atlantic slave trade. Beginning in the sixteenth and lasting until the nineteenth century, at least 10 million Africans landed in the Americas, and an estimated 2 million perished en route. Nearly two-thirds of all African slaves were first sent to the islands of the Caribbean and Brazil, creating a neo-Africa in the Americas (Curtin 1969). In absolute numbers, more Africans landed in Latin America than Europeans in the first three centuries after contact. Yet, because Africans were brought in as slaves, their survival rates and life expectancy were much lower than those of Europeans, which undermined their overall demographic impact (Sánchez-Albornoz 1974).

When much of Latin America gained its independence in the nineteenth century, the new leaders of the region sought to develop their territories through immigration. Firmly believing in the dictum, "to govern is to populate," many countries set up immigration offices in Europe to attract hard-working peasants to till the land and "whiten" the *mestizo* population. Argentina, Chile, Uruguay, southern Brazil, and Cuba were the most successful in attracting European immigrants from the 1870s until the Depression of the 1930s. During this period, some 8 million Europeans arrived (more than came during the entire colonial period), with Italians, Portuguese, Spaniards, and Germans being the most numerous. Some of this immigration was state sponsored, such as the nearly 1 million laborers (including entire families) brought to the coffee estates surrounding São Paulo at the turn of the century. Other migrants came seasonally, especially the Italian peasants who left Europe in the winter for agricultural work in Argentina and were thus nicknamed "the swallows." Still others paid their own passage, intending to settle permanently and prosper in the growing commercial centers of Buenos Aires, São Paulo, Montevideo, and Santiago.

Less known are the Asian immigrants who arrived during this same period. Although considerably fewer in number, they established an important presence in the large cities of Brazil, Peru, and Paraguay, as well as throughout Guyana, Suriname, and Trinidad. Beginning in the mid-nineteenth century, most of the Chinese and Japanese who settled in Latin America were contracted laborers brought in to work on the coffee estates in southern Brazil and the sugar estates and guano (waste from seafowl used as fertilizer) mines of Peru. The Japanese in Brazil are the most studied Asian immigrant group. Between 1908 and 1978, a quarter million Japanese immigrated to Brazil; today the country is home to 1.3 million people of Japanese descent. Initially, most Japanese were landless laborers, yet by the 1940s they had accumulated enough capital so that three-quarters of the migrants had their own land in the peripheral areas of São Paulo and Paraná states. Increasingly, second- and third-generation Japanese have taken professional and commercial jobs in Brazilian cities; many of them have married outside their ethnic group and are losing their fluency in Japanese. South America's economic turmoil in the last two decades resulted in many ethnic Japanese emigrating to Japan in search of better opportunities. Nearly one-quarter of a million ethnic Japanese left South America in the 1990s (mostly from Brazil and Peru) and now reside in Japan.

In the Caribbean, sugar estate owners who feared labor shortages with the abolition of slavery in the nineteenth century sought indentured labor from South and Southeast Asia. As Guyana and Trinidad were British colonies, most of the contract labor came from India. Today, half of Guyana's population and 40 percent of Trinidad's claim South Asian ancestry. Hindu temples are found in the cities and villages, and many families speak Hindi in their homes. In Suriname, a former Dutch colony, more than one-third of the population is South Asian, and 16 percent are Javanese (from Indonesia).

Emigration and Transnational Networks

Movement within Latin America and between Latin America and North America has had a significant impact on Latino settlement patterns. Within Latin America, shifting economic and political realities have shaped immigrants' destinations. Venezuela's oil wealth, especially during the 1960s and 1970s, attracted between 1 and 2 million Colombian immigrants, who worked as domestic or agricultural laborers. Argentina has long been a destination for Bolivian and Paraguayan laborers. And sugar plantations in the Dominican Republic have relied on Haitian labor, just as farmers in the United States have depended on Mexican laborers. Political turmoil has also sparked waves of international migrants and refugees, such as the Cuban flight from Fidel Castro in the 1960s and the Chilean exodus during General Augusto Pinochet's reign in the 1970s.

One of the largest migrant flows continues to be Mexicans to the United States. Twenty-two million people claimed Mexican ancestry in the 2000 U.S. Census, of whom approximately 8 million were immigrants. Today, roughly 60 percent of the Hispanic population (both foreign born and native born) in the United States claim Mexican ancestry. Mexican immigrants are most concentrated in California and Texas, but increasingly they are found throughout the United States. Although Mexicans continue to have the greatest presence among Latinos in the United States, the number of immigrants from El Salvador, Guatemala, Cuba, the Dominican Republic, Nicaragua, Colombia, Ecuador, and Brazil has steadily grown. The 2000 Census counted 35 million Hispanics in the United States (both foreign and native born). Most of this population has ancestral ties with peoples from Latin America and the Caribbean.

Today, Latin America is seen as a region of emigration rather than one of immigration. Both skilled and unskilled workers from Latin America are an important source of labor in North America, Europe, and Japan. Many of these immigrants send monthly remittances to their home countries to sustain family members. In 2003, it was estimated that immigrants sent over $30 billion to Latin America. Most of this money came from workers in the United States, but Latino immigrants in Spain, Japan, Canada and Italy also sent money back to the region. Through remittances and technological advances that make communication faster and cheaper, immigrants maintain close contact with their home countries in ways that earlier generations could not. Scholars have labeled this ability to straddle livelihoods between two countries as transnationalism. A cultural and an economic outcome of globalization, transnationalism highlights the social and economic links that form between home and host countries. Declining economic opportunities within Latin America have forced many individuals to emigrate in order to sustain their families. In the process, a new human geography is being created, one that extends well beyond regional boundaries.

Language

Roughly two-thirds of Latin Americans are Spanish speakers, and one-third speak Portuguese. These colonial languages were so prevalent by the nineteenth century that they were the unquestioned languages of government and instruction for the newly independent Latin American republics. In fact, until recently many countries actively discouraged, even repressed, Amerindian languages. Because Spanish and Portuguese dominate, there is a tendency to overlook the persistence of native languages. In the central Andes of Peru, Bolivia, and southern Ecuador, over 10 million people still speak Quechua and Aymará. In Paraguay and lowland Bolivia, there are 4 million Guaraní speakers; in southern Mexico and Guatemala, at least 6–8 million speak Mayan languages. Small groups of native-language speakers are found scattered throughout the sparsely settled interior of South America and the more isolated forests of Central America, but many of these languages have fewer than ten thousand speakers.

Due to the more complex colonial history of the Caribbean, other languages are spoken there. Roughly 8 million people speak French (Haiti, French Guiana, and the islands of Martinique and Guadeloupe); 6 million speak English (Jamaica, Belize, Guyana, Trinidad, and other smaller islands of the Lesser Antilles); and there are about half a million Dutch speakers (Suriname and several small islands). Yet, these figures tell only part of the story. Typically, colloquial variants of the official language exist that can be difficult for a non-native speaker to understand. In some cases, completely new languages emerge; in the Dutch islands of Aruba, Curaçao, and Bonaire, Papiamento (a trading language that blends Dutch, Spanish, Portuguese, English, and African languages) is the *lingua franca,* with usage of Dutch declining. Similarly, French Creole or *patois* in Haiti has constitutional status as a distinct language. In practice, French is used in higher education, government, and the courts in Haiti, but *patois* (with clear African influences) is the language of the street, the home, and oral tradition.

Religion

Like language, the Roman Catholic faith appears to have been imposed upon the region without challenge. As Michael Fleet shows in Chapter 12, most countries report between 70 and 90 percent of their population as Catholic. Every major city has dozens of churches, and even the smallest hamlet maintains a graceful church on its central square. In countries like El Salvador and Uruguay, a sizable portion of the population attend Protestant evangelical churches, but the Catholic core of this region is still intact.

Yet, exactly what native peoples absorbed of the Christian faith is unclear. Throughout Latin America, syncretic religions—the blending of different belief systems—enabled animist practices to be folded into Christian worship. These blends took hold and endured, in part, because the Christian saints were easy surrogates for pre-Christian gods and because the Catholic Church tolerated local variations in worship as long as the process of conversion was under way. The Mayan practice of paying tribute to spirits of the underworld seems to be replicated today in Mexico and Guatemala via the practice of building small cave shrines to favorite Catholic saints and leaving offerings of fresh flowers and fruits. One of the most celebrated religious icons in Mexico is Guadalupe, a dark-skinned virgin seen by an Indian shepherd boy; thought to intercede on behalf of the poor, Guadalupe has become the patron saint of Mexico.

Syncretic religious practices also evolved and endured among African slaves. Millions of Brazilians practice the African-based religions of *umbanda, macumba,* and *candomblé* along with Catholicism. In many parts of southern Brazil, *umbanda* is as popular with people of European ancestry as with Afro-Brazilians. Typically, people become familiar with *umbanda* after falling victim to a magician's spell by having some object of black magic buried outside their home. In order to regain control of their life, they need the help of a priest or priestess. So accurate are some of these religious transfers that it is common to have Nigerian priests journey to Brazil to learn forgotten traditions. Likewise in the Caribbean, Afro-religious traditions have evolved into unique forms that have clear ties to West Africa. The most widely practiced are *vodou* in Haiti, *santería* in Cuba, and *obeah* in Jamaica.

Race and Inequality

There is much to admire about race relations in the Americas. The complex racial and ethnic mix that was created in Latin America fostered tolerance for diversity. Nevertheless, as Kevin A. Yelvington shows in Chapter 9, Amerindians and people of African ancestry are disproportionately represented among the poor of the region. More than ever, racial discrimination is a major political issue in Brazil. Reports of organized killings of street children, most of them Afro-Brazilian, make headlines. For decades, Brazil espoused its vision of a color-blind racial democracy that refused to address racism. Evidence from northeastern Brazil, where Afro-Brazilians are the majority, shows death rates approaching those of some of the world's poorest countries. Throughout Brazil, Afro-Brazilians suffer higher rates of homelessness, landlessness, illiteracy, and unemployment. The last few years have seen revolution in Brazilian society as affirmative action measures have been implemented. From federal ministries to public universities, various quota systems are being tried to improve the condition of Afro-Brazilians.

Similarly, in areas of Latin America where Indian cultures are strong, one also finds low socioeconomic indicators. In most countries, mapping areas where native languages are widely spoken invariably corresponds with areas of persistent poverty. In Mexico, the Indian south lags behind the booming north and Mexico City. Prejudice is embedded in the language; to call someone an *indio* (Indian) is an insult in Mexico. In Bolivia, women who dress in the Indian style of full pleated skirts and bowler hats are called *cholas*. This descriptive term, referring to the rural *mestizo* population, has negative connotations of backwardness and even cowardice. No one of high social standing, regardless of skin color, would ever be called a *chola* or *cholo*.

It is difficult to separate status divisions based on class from those based on race. From the days of conquest, being European meant an immediate elevation in status over the Indian, African, and *mestizo* populations. Class awareness is very strong. Race does not necessarily determine one's economic standing, but it certainly influences it. These class differences express themselves in the landscape. In the large cities and their handsome suburbs, country clubs and trendy shopping centers are found. High-rise luxury apartment buildings with beautiful terraces offer all the modern amenities, including maids' quarters. The elite and the middle class even show a preference for decentralized suburban living and dependence on automobiles, much like North Americans. Yet, near these same residences are shantytowns where urban squatters build their own homes, create their own economy, and eke out a living.

Geography of the Possible

Latin America was the first region in the developing world to be fully colonized by Europe. In the process, perhaps 90 percent of the native population died due to disease, cruelty, and forced resettlement. The slow demographic recovery of native peoples and the continual arrival of Europeans and Africans resulted in an unprecedented level of racial and cultural mixing. It took nearly 400 years for the population of Latin America to reach 50 million again, its precontact level. During this long period, European culture, technology, and political systems were transplanted and modified. Indigenous peoples integrated livestock and wheat into their agricultural practices but held true to their preference for native corn, potatoes, and cassava. In short, a syncretic process unfolded, in which many indigenous customs were preserved beneath the veneer of Iberian ones. Over time, a blending of indigenous, Iberian, and African influences gave distinction to this part of the world. The music, literature, and artistry of Latin America are widely acknowledged.

Compared with Asia or Europe, Latin America is relatively lightly populated yet still rich in natural resources. However, as population continues to grow along with economic expectations, there is considerable concern that much of this natural endowment could be squandered for short-term gains. In the midst of a boom in natural resource extraction, popular concern for the state of the environment is growing. Not only was Brazil the site of the 1992 United Nations Earth Summit, but hundreds of locally based environmental groups have formed to try to protect forests, grasslands, indigenous peoples, and freshwater supplies. This brand of environmentalism is pragmatic; it recognizes the need for economic development and aims to improve urban environmental quality and sustainable resource use.

In Latin America, the trend toward modernization began in the 1950s, and the pace of change has been rapid. Unlike people in other developing areas, most Latin Americans live in cities. This shift started early and reflects a cultural bias toward urban living, with roots in the colonial past. Not everyone who came to the city found employment; thus, the dynamics of the informal sector were set in place. Even though population growth rates have declined, the overall makeup of the population is young. Serious challenges lie ahead in educating and finding employment for the cohort under age fifteen. Those who cannot find work often consider emigrating to other parts of Latin America, North America, Europe, or Japan to seek better economic opportunities.

Latin America is one of the world regions that North Americans are most likely to visit. The trend, of course, is to visit the northern fringe of this region. Tourism is robust along Mexico's border and coastal resorts. Unfortunately, there is a tendency to visit one area in the region and generalize for all of it. Although it is historically sound to think of Latin America as a major world region, extreme variations in the physical environment, levels of social and economic development, and the influence of indigenous society exist. Therefore, underlying the unifying factors, these differences add much to the texture and complexity of Latin America, making it one of the world's most ecologically and culturally rich, diverse regions.

▓ Bibliography

Ardao, Arturo. *Genesis de la Idea y el Normbre de América Latina*. Caracas: Centro de Estudios Latinoamericanos Rómulo Gallegos, 1980.

Caviedes, César, and Gregory Knapp. *South America*. Englewood Cliffs, N.J.: Prentice Hall, 1995.

Christen, C., S. Herculano, K. Hochstetler, R. Prell, M. Price, and J. T. Roberts. "Latin American Environmentalism: Comparative Views." *Studies in Comparative International Development* 33, no. 2 (1998):58–87.

Clapp, Roger Alex. "Waiting for the Forest Law: Resource-Led Development and Environmental Politics in Chile." *Latin American Research Review* 33, no. 2 (1998):3–36.

Crosby, Alfred. *The Columbian Exchange: Biological and Cultural Consequences of 1492*. Westport, Conn.: Greenwood Press, 1972.

Curtin, Philip D. *The Atlantic Slave Trade: A Census*. Madison: University of Wisconsin Press, 1969.

Dean, Warren. *With Broadax and Firebrand: The Destruction of the Brazilian Atlantic Forest*. Berkeley: University of California Press, 1995.

Denevan, William M. *The Native Population of the Americas in 1492* (2d ed.). Madison: University of Wisconsin Press, 1992.

Ezcurra, Exequiel, Marisa Mazari-Hiriart, Irene Pisanty, and Adrián Guillermo Aguilar. *The Basin of Mexico: Critical Environmental Issues and Sustainability*. New York: United Nations University Press, 1999.

Gade, Daniel W. *Nature and Culture in the Andes.* Madison: University of Wisconsin Press, 1999.

Gilbert, Alan (ed.). *The Mega-City in Latin America.* New York: United Nations University Press, 1996.

Gwynne, Robert, and Kay Cristobal. *Latin America Transformed: Globalization and Modernity.* London: Arnold Press, 1999.

Hecht, Susanna, and Alexander Cockburn. *The Fate of the Forest: Developers, Destroyers and Defenders of the Amazon.* London and New York: Verso Press, 1989.

Klak, Thomas (ed.). *Globalization and Neoliberalism: The Caribbean Context.* Lanham, Md.: Rowman & Littlefield, 1998.

Knapp, Gregory (ed.). *Latin America in the 21st Century: Challenges and Solutions.* Conference of Latin Americanist Geographers, distributed by University of Texas Press, Austin, 2002.

Place, Susan E. (ed.). *Tropical Rainforests: Latin American Nature and Society in Transition,* (2d ed.). Wilmington, Del.: Scholarly Resources, 2001.

Population Reference Bureau. *World Population Data Sheet.* Washington, D.C.: Population Reference Bureau, 2003.

Preston, David. *Latin American Development, Geographical Perspectives* (2d ed.). Essex, England: Longman Scientific and Technical, 1996.

Roberts, J. Timmons, and Nikki Demetria Thanos. *Trouble in Paradise: Globalization and Environmental Crisis in Latin America.* New York and London: Routledge, 2003.

Sánchez-Albornoz, Nicolás. *The Population of Latin America: A History.* Berkeley and Los Angeles: University of California Press, 1974.

Wilkie, Richard. *Statistical Abstract of Latin America.* Vols. 35 and 38. Los Angeles: University of California Press, 1997, 2002.

Young, Kenneth R. "Threats to Biological Diversity Caused by Coca/Cocaine Deforestation in Peru." *Environmental Conservation* 23, no. 1 (1996):7–15.

3

The Historical Context

René de la Pedraja

The conquest and colonization of the Americas in the sixteenth and seventeenth centuries created the conditions for the exploitation of the vast territories described by Marie Price in the previous chapter. Beginning in the late fifteenth century, European imperialist expansion resulted in the defeat and subjugation of the native peoples of Latin America, the first non-European continental area to be westernized. It was not until the early nineteenth century that challenges to European domination unleashed the revolutionary forces that ended in independence. Therefore, an understanding of the enduring legacies of a colonial system that lasted three centuries is fundamental to the illumination of developments and issues in contemporary Latin America. In this chapter, I focus on the ways in which Europe imposed itself on the New World and how independence was achieved. Recent research has shown that the Indians were never passive victims. Despite the ultimate failures of armed resistance, the Indians were still able to decide what elements of the new Spanish civilization to incorporate into their daily lives.

■ The Conquest

Spanish colonization began after Christopher Columbus arrived in the Caribbean in 1492. Ineffective resistance in the islands allowed the Spaniards to exploit conquered Indians for forced labor. They did so initially through the brutal system of *repartimiento* (from the verb *repartir*, "to distribute") in which Indians were seized and enslaved. In 1503, the crown adopted the legal system of *encomienda* (from the verb *encomendar*, "to

41

entrust") to replace the earlier system. Henceforth, the conquerors were obliged to Christianize the Indians and treat them justly. Nevertheless, this "civilizing" role degenerated rapidly, given an economic imperative for free labor. Therefore, captured Indians remained in a state of virtual slavery.

European diseases ravaged the Indian populations of the Caribbean, leading to slave-hunting expeditions on the coasts of Florida, Venezuela, Central America, and the Yucatán. These expeditions also continued the avid search for mineral wealth, as the small gold deposits in the Caribbean became exhausted. The discovery of pearls off the island of Cubagua in 1510 led the Spaniards to occupy the northeastern part of Venezuela and expand into the interior in search of El Dorado (the legendary city of great wealth).

Hernán Cortés set out from Cuba in 1519 to pursue reports of a rich kingdom in the highlands of central Mexico. Cortés and his small force conquered the vast Aztec Empire—whose population of 20 million was defended by at least 100,000 warriors—by forming alliances with tribes that sought to end Aztec rule and by deceiving Montezuma, the powerful Aztec leader. By 1521, central Mexico was under Spanish control.

Indian laborers then leveled the Aztec capital, Tenochtitlán, and built Mexico City on the same site, which immediately became the wealthiest and largest colonial city in Latin America. From the central location of Mexico City, Spanish expeditions fanned out in all directions to subdue any pockets of Indian resistance. The march into Central America brought Spanish rule to Guatemala, El Salvador, and Honduras by 1525. The Yucatán Peninsula, however, was successfully defended by the militaristic city-states of the Maya until 1527, when Francisco de Montejo and his son began the conquest they finally completed in 1546.

Vasco Núñez de Balboa crossed Panama and discovered the Pacific Ocean in 1513, and Panama City was established in 1519. From this strategic location, Spanish explorers spread over the surrounding regions. The Indians of the highlands of Costa Rica had repulsed the sporadic Spanish expeditions until the 1570s, when the Spaniards were able to complete the conquest of the Pacific Coast and the highlands in Central America. Only on the Caribbean side of Central America did Spanish rule fail to take hold, not because of any major opposition but simply because the sparse Indian population, the lack of any immediately valuable resources, and the sweltering tropical climate combined to make the region unattractive to the Spaniards.

Rumors of a rich kingdom to the south along the Pacific Ocean led Ferdinand Magellan to discover the straits at the extreme southern tip of South America in 1520. In an attempt to find what lay between that point and Panama far to the north, Francisco Pizarro took two exploring expeditions south from Panama along the Pacific Coast of Colombia in the mid-1520s. Pizarro returned to the coast of Peru in 1532 with a force of roughly two hundred explorers and soon discovered the Inca Empire, the largest in the Americas. Rather than conducting a frontal attack, Pizarro entrapped the unsuspecting Inca emperor in 1533. The huge Inca armies could not be assembled in time to try to stop the advancing Spaniards. Hence, Cuzco was captured easily, and the capital of the Inca Empire—which had stretched from Quito, Ecuador, to Santiago, Chile—came under Spanish control. In 1535, Pizarro established the Spanish capital in Lima, which became—after Mexico City—the second most important urban center in colonial Latin America.

Expeditions fanned out from Peru in all directions in the hope of finding either precious metals or large numbers of Indians for free labor. To occupy the southernmost parts of the Inca Empire, Pizarro sent Pedro de Valdivia, who established Santiago, the capital of Chile, in 1541. South of Santiago, the Araucanians mastered European methods of warfare and successfully resisted Spanish control. But the region contained gold, and miners and settlers continued to clash with the Indians in almost continuous warfare until the late nineteenth century.

An expedition from Spain landed on the coast of Colombia, and Gonzalo Jiménez de Quesada took this force up the Magdalena River into the highland Indian kingdom of the Chibchas. After defeating the Chibchas, Jiménez de Quesada established the capital at Bogotá in 1537. Through a piecemeal process, Spanish colonizers gradually converged from the original pearl fisheries on the east coast of Venezuela and the trading routes on the west toward the central region in Caracas, founded in 1567. An expedition from Spain had established Buenos Aires in 1536, but the bitter hostility of the seminomadic Indians forced starving colonists to relocate in Asunción, Paraguay, where the friendly Guaraní Indians developed a uniquely harmonious relationship with the settlers. Only later, in 1580, did the Spanish colonists feel strong enough to reestablish Buenos Aires as a permanent settlement.

Spanish explorers continued to push into distant areas. Although the Indian civilizations were very advanced in aspects of astronomy and mathematics, they lacked basic elements of technology—in particular, the wheel and iron. Thus, hundreds of Spaniards could easily defeat tens of thousands of their opponents using steel swords, firearms, and cannons. Also, horses terrorized Indians, who were unfamiliar with them. Even though the conquerors were only slightly better than armed civilians, with very few professional soldiers among their ranks, the Spaniards' knowledge of tactics and strategy far surpassed the Indians' sometimes rudimentary conception of warfare. And the European diseases were the most terrifying weapon of all, decimating millions of Indians. Against such odds, the desperate Indian resistance against the invaders should evoke as much admiration as the boldness of the Spaniards in entering unknown regions.

The plight of the native peoples gave enemies of the Spanish crown ample reason to be extremely critical of the conquest and colonization of the Americas. For example, La Leyenda Negra (the Black Legend) attributed only great cruelty, evil, and exploitation to the Spaniards. Ironically, the Black Legend was based in part on information from missionaries such as Bartolomé de las Casas (1474–1566), who attempted to end the abuse and enslavement of the Indians. Later, leaders of the Latin American independence movements used the Black Legend—a mixture of fact and myth—to justify revolution against the crown. More objective interpretations of this history include references to the achievements and loftier purposes of the conquest, as well as to the negative impact of this encounter between cultures.

Although formal conquests had ended by 1580, the task of incorporating frontier regions was far from over. The Spanish Empire continued to grow until it reached its greatest extension in the eighteenth century.

The Colonial Period

The conquerors gave their colonies such names as "New Spain" and "New Granada," thus affirming their desire to reproduce Spanish civilization in the New World. Map 3.1 illustrates the colonial divisions. The colonies were treated as the personal possessions of the Spanish monarchs, who created structures for government, the church, and the economy that essentially transplanted their European institutions into the Western Hemisphere. Hence, social classes and cultural values, particularly Latin American ones, emerged very gradually—often with unexpected consequences.

Spain was able to duplicate its institutions and culture fairly closely in areas with scant numbers of Indians, such as the Rio de la Plata, as well as in areas where the Indian population rapidly disappeared, such as the islands of the Caribbean. Spanish became the sole language and Hispanic practices rapidly took root. However, in areas of dense Indian population, particularly central Mexico and the Peruvian highlands, the process of transmitting Hispanic structures and customs took much longer and was seldom ever completed. Where Indians survived the ravages of war, diseases, and exploitation, they aptly selected those Spanish objects or traits most suitable for their daily lives. Indians quickly adopted practical materials like iron, the wheel, and wool clothing, as well as the corresponding nomenclature. The Indians came to accept selected Spanish items, customs, and terminology as integral parts of their timeless traditions. The Indians readily accepted some new foods (particularly chicken, eggs, and sugar), but they steadfastly refused to accept the wheat the Spaniards so insistently imposed upon them.

Map 3.1
Eighteenth-Century Colonial Latin America

The Spanish *encomienda* succeeded only because the authorities based it on existing pre-Hispanic structures. Outwardly converted to Roman Catholicism, the Indians preserved many of their spiritist beliefs within the new Christian rituals. In spite of repeated orders to use only the Spanish language in official documents, not until the 1770s did the Mexican Indians finally adopt the language of the conquerors for paperwork. As Indian rebellions became infrequent after the sixteenth century, the Spanish crown no longer saw the Indians as a threat to Spanish rule and tolerated their failure to adopt all the new customs and official practices. As a result, Mexican and Peruvian Indians found themselves with a significant degree of control over precisely how they would coalesce with the Spanish world.

The Spanish government, which was an absolutist monarchy, relentlessly attempted to maintain its monopoly over political power in the newly conquered territories to prevent the rise of any group or rival institution that might challenge royal authority. The first urgent task of the royal government was to remove from power those men who had carried out the conquest of the New World under the sweeping authorizations the crown itself had granted. Asserting royal power in the Caribbean and marginal areas like Panama proved easier than on the mainland, where the conquerors were well entrenched. The opposition became so violent that in Peru the Pizarro family led an insurrection against Spain. The crown's obsession with absolute power triumphed in both Peru and Mexico largely because the government did not revoke the economic privileges of the original conquerors.

Throughout the colonial period, the Spanish government remained extremely reluctant to share any political power with the wealthy upper class. An unwieldy separation arose between political power and economic wealth, making colonial government ineffective and cumbersome at best, as government officials—who were generally short of funds—tried to impose official policies on the wealthy upper classes. This pattern of conflict between economic and political power has continued to plague Latin American countries in the modern era. Spain left Spanish America a legacy—not of open government and consensus building but of secrecy and absolutism.

The highest-ranking colonial official was the Spanish viceroy appointed by the crown, who, because of the slowness of communications with Spain, enjoyed powers almost comparable to those of the king. The viceroy in Mexico City had jurisdiction over North America, and the viceroy in Lima had jurisdiction over South America. The distances were too vast for the viceroys, so in the sixteenth century, Spain appointed captains general to rule over strategic regions such as Santiago, Caracas, and Havana. The captains general, who were also *peninsulares* (Spaniards) appointed by the crown, were soldiers whose military practices necessarily reinforced the authoritarian nature of colonial institutions. The decline of Peru and the increase in foreign threats convinced Spain of the need to create two new viceroyalties in the eighteenth century, one for Buenos Aires and another for Bogotá.

The colonial government was subject to much abuse and corruption.

Moreover, *peninsulares* looked down on *criollos* (Spanish Americans). Special privileges, called *fueros*, were granted to *peninsulares*, clergy, the military, and government officials. Although abolished in Spain in 1820, *fueros* were continued in Latin America even beyond independence. Membership in the *cabildo* (town council) usually remained the only form of political participation available to upper class *criollos*. In addition, the centralizing tendencies of the eighteenth century came to reduce the modest authority of the municipal bodies and aroused *criollo* resentment.

The viceroys and captains general formed the executive branch of government, yet they also possessed sweeping legislative and judicial powers. The highest courts in Spanish America were the *audiencias*, whose number fluctuated around eight and whose judges (*oidores*) were *peninsulares* appointed by the crown. In effect, the *audiencia* formed the main council of the viceroy or captain general, while functioning as the highest court of appeals in America (appeals later could be taken to Spain). Although most legislation came directly from the king's councils in Spain, the *audiencia* issued local laws and decrees. The principles of Roman law used in the *audiencia* simplified the application of laws at the personal level. Roman law, however, became one more vehicle through which to reinforce absolutism and impose authoritarian principles.

One of the most problematic legacies of the colonial period was the confusion among the three branches of government. The same officials, whether viceroys or judges, often performed legislative, executive, and judicial functions. By the twentieth century, Latin America was able to define the authority of the executive branch and, to a lesser degree, that of the judiciary. The failure to develop viable, independent legislatures, however, has often undermined attempts to practice democracy and has reinforced tendencies toward authoritarianism. The ongoing political implications of this colonial legacy are discussed in greater detail by Thomas J. D'Agostino in Chapter 4.

In pursuit of a policy of divide and rule, Spain created overlapping territorial jurisdictions for viceroys, captains general, and *audiencias* and also for the parallel structure of the Catholic Church. Spain successfully prevented any high royal or church official in the New World from ever challenging the authority of the crown, but it did so at the cost of increased inefficiency. The officials were more concerned with defending their power or spying on each other than with conducting government business. After independence, the vague lines separating the colonial jurisdictions led to conflicting territorial claims and border wars. Most had ended at the end of the twentieth century, but some—like the border between Peru and Ecuador—remain flash points for renewed conflict.

Spain justified its extraordinary authority over the Catholic Church on the grounds that civil and ecclesiastical officials had to function as one to carry out the vast undertaking of the military and spiritual conquest of the New World. The Catholic Church could do nothing without the approval of the crown, and the authority extended to matters of religious belief or dogma. Whatever doctrine the Pope proclaimed in Rome was only valid for the New World if the Spanish crown approved. But even after almost all of Latin America had been converted to Roman Catholicism, the government continued to preserve its authority over the church for the more blatantly political reason of allowing no rival power base to emerge. In Chapter 12, Michael Fleet shows how this affected the ongoing role of the church in Latin America.

Initially, the task of converting the large native populations to Catholicism was carried out with missionary zeal. The priests learned the Indian languages and established missions in remote areas. The idealism of the first generations of missionaries gradually waned, however, and in any case by the 1560s, few Indians remained to be converted. Unable to enter local politics, the clergy devoted itself to the profitable management of wealth.

The Catholic Church soon owned the largest percentage of the land in Latin America and received a vast income from the properties. The money reserves accumulated, and the church's institutions became the financial lenders of the colonial period (banks did not appear until the mid-nineteenth century). Land was the almost universal collateral, so the failure to repay loans meant the church added foreclosed property to its already enormous holdings.

The spiritual decay of the clergy caused the Spanish government, in part out of religious conviction but also to avoid any questioning of its authority, to attempt to revitalize the Catholic Church. Supported by the Spanish government, the Jesuits (members of the Roman Catholic Society of Jesus) entered Latin America in 1572. Although the Jesuits encouraged scholarship and independent thinking in their schools, the Inquisition (a special Spanish law court designed to identify heretics and "allow" them to repent or be put to death—at times by torture) severely limited intellectual activities. The Inquisition began its Latin American operations in 1569 in Lima and Mexico City and gradually opened branches in other major cities. Although staffed by clergy, the Inquisition was a governmental body that made its most valuable contribution by detecting and punishing sexual crimes by priests and other religious personnel.

This moralizing effect on the clergy, however, came at the high price of an unending series of witch-hunts against ordinary people. The inquisitors eagerly searched for any signs among the local population of unusual behavior that could fall under the broad definition of heresy or "crimes against the faith." The favorite investigative techniques of the Inquisition were anonymous accusations and torture, and its jail cells remained filled with supposed criminals. Although the Inquisition executed fewer than two hundred men and women, its most ruinous effect was to stifle free inquiry in the New World. As all Indians were considered minors and not fully responsible for their actions, they were, in principle, exempt from the Inquisition's jurisdiction. However, in Mexico, some unlucky Indians occasionally fell victim to it. The environment of fear made dissent dangerous, and the Inquisition reinforced the tendency toward absolutism. Spain accepted the Inquisition because, as an institution independent of the bishops and viceroys, it provided one more check on the government and the church in the New World. It could be argued that the Inquisition was the forerunner of the infamous secret police and intelligence services that emerged in Latin America in the early twentieth century.

Throughout colonial Latin America, both the Catholic Church and the Spanish government constructed extensive institutional structures that were supported by the material resources of the New World. The Spanish crown had not only expected the new institutions to be self-supporting but from the start had also demanded a major share of the wealth coming out of the New World. To extract the largest amount of wealth from the New World in the easiest way possible, the Spaniards established a colonial economy whose two foundations were the exploitation of local labor and the mining of precious metals—activities that often occurred simultaneously. In Chapter 6, Richard Harper and Alfred Cuzán analyze the negative impact of the colonial economy on future Latin American development.

Throughout the colonial period, gold and silver exports paid for imports from Europe and brought additional wealth to Spain. The apparently endless waves of precious metals leaving Latin America created the image of a rich paradise. Consequently, England, France, and Holland sent trading expeditions to the Caribbean from the 1530s until the 1620s. Gradually, a pattern of trade and smuggling with Europeans became an accepted practice for the Spanish American population, which sought to avoid high Spanish taxes on the imported merchandise.

The decline of the Spanish Empire in the seventeenth century gave Europeans the opportunity to establish bases in many of the deserted islands of the Spanish Caribbean, starting with the British island of Barbados in 1627 and the Dutch island of Curaçao in 1634. Seduced by tales of great wealth and aware of Spanish weakness, an English force tried to capture the entire West Indies, only to meet with dismal failure in its attack on Santo Domingo. This same expedition did capture Jamaica from Spain in 1655, and this island became the staging base for subsequent English penetration into Spanish America. France also began to occupy islands in the West Indies and by 1665 had gained control of the western part of Santo Domingo, which is now Haiti.

The islands occupied by the Dutch, French, and English served as excellent ports for an extensive smuggling trade with Spanish America, but by the second half of the seventeenth century the non-Spanish Caribbean had turned to plantation agriculture as the main source of its wealth. Examination of parallel events in Portuguese Brazil illuminates how the plantation system spread to the Caribbean.

■ Portuguese Brazil

During the same period when Spain conquered the West Indies, Mexico, and Central America, Portugal had barely a presence on the Brazilian coast. Pedro Cabral, leading a Portuguese fleet to India in 1500, was blown off course and landed on the coast of Brazil, which the king of Portugal decided to claim as a resupply base. Not until 1532 did the Portuguese establish the first permanent settlement at São Vicente (near present-day Santos on the coast). The two key elements of the Spanish American economy—precious metals and abundant Indian labor to exploit—appeared to be lacking in Brazil. Therefore, the Portuguese, who were driven by profit and commercial concerns even more than the Spanish, invested not in the Brazilian wilderness but rather in the lucrative spice trade between Europe and the Indian Ocean.

The reddish dyes drawn from brazilwood trees were in demand in Europe, however. This attracted the French, who poached on the forests the Portuguese crown considered its own private reserve. To repel both the French and expansionist Spanish expeditions, the Portuguese government sent the first royal governor to San Salvador in 1549. Ultimately, the Portuguese expelled the French from Rio de Janeiro. In the early seventeenth century, the French attempted to reestablish settlements on the north coast of Brazil, only to have the Portuguese push them into what is now French Guiana.

As brazilwoods became scarce due to excessive logging, expeditions called *bandeiras* set out for the interior of Brazil in search of precious metals and Indian slaves. Initially the *bandeiras* (whose members were called *bandeirantes*) found no precious metals and only a small number of slaves among the widely scattered Indian villages. Brazil found its economic salvation not in the interior but on the coast.

Sugarcane grew well in the hot, humid lands along the Brazilian coastline. Spanish America had neglected the agricultural potential of its tropical lowlands for the sake of mining, and prices for sugar remained high in Europe. Portugal had only to draw on its prior experience with sugarcane plantations in the Atlantic islands of the Madeiras and the Cape Verdes to introduce a proven and profitable economic model into Brazil. Essentially, to supply the European demand for tropical crops—sugar in particular—Portugal imported large numbers of slaves from Africa annually to work in the sugar plantations in Brazil. Sugar and slaves remained an inseparable link during the colonial period, and the profits from the sugar exports sustained Portuguese colonization in Brazil.

Slaves and sugar made Brazil very wealthy, and many Portuguese migrated to the new country in the hope of finding fortunes. Portuguese merchants enjoyed a monopoly (similar to Spain's in its empire) over Brazilian trade, and the Portuguese government taxed the European imports and the sugar that passed through Portugal. The rising revenues from Brazil were very important to the Portuguese government, whose commercial empire in Asia was collapsing in the early seventeenth century. Henceforth, Brazil replaced Asia as the source of most of Portugal's wealth.

The Dutch, who had attempted to take over Brazil in the mid-seventeenth century, abandoned the struggle in the face of armed local resistance. The Dutch instead introduced plantation agriculture in the Caribbean as a more profitable alternative to hostile Brazil. Other European powers followed this example. In fact, British Jamaica and French Haiti became the principal sugar producers in the world. Production outpaced European demand, however, and as sugar prices dropped, the sugar mills in Brazil entered a prolonged period of depression after 1680. Planters struggled to meet their loan payments in the face of rising production costs—in particular, the higher prices of imported slaves. Brazil stagnated, and Portugal suffered loss of income and revenue because of the colony's economic problems.

By 1700, the *bandeiras* had found gold deposits in the region of Minas Gerais (general mines). Mineral exports—mainly gold and, after 1729, diamonds—became the driving force behind the Brazilian economy as sugar sank to a secondary position. Plantation owners found the task of supplying their slave force much more difficult as the slave trade shifted to providing Africans for the mines.

Immigrants flocked from Portugal and other parts of Brazil to participate in the gold rushes, and the demand for food and goods in the new mining cities provided a powerful stimulus to agriculture and commerce. To supply the meat and leather, ranches pushed farther into the interior, thereby broadening the areas under effective Portuguese colonization. The gold fields were located primarily in the southern half of Brazil. In response, the Portuguese crown shifted the capital in 1763 from San Salvador in the north to Rio de Janeiro in the south.

The reliance on mineral wealth made Brazil resemble Spanish America but with the crucial difference that without a large Indian labor force, the Brazilians had to turn to African slaves and, to a lesser degree, *mestizos* (the offspring of Europeans and Indians) to work the gold deposits. By the eighteenth century, *mestizos* had become the largest racial element in the interior, whereas the *mulatos* (the offspring of blacks and Europeans) had gradually become the majority racial element in the coastal sugar regions. Because of the constant arrival of new African slaves, many *mulatos* eventually acquired their freedom. In Chapter 9, Kevin Yelvington analyzes patterns of ethnicity and class that were set into motion during the colonial era.

Brazil faced hardships as gold output fell after 1750. To try to save the Portuguese Empire from economic collapse, the marquis of Pombal—a virtual dictator because the king had lost all interest in ruling—undertook major initiatives from 1750 to 1777. Pombal tinkered with the bureaucratic structures of the Portuguese Empire, but the very nature of his personal rule precluded any fundamental change.

The imperial bureaucracy—although never as extensive as that of Spain—continued to suffer under the weight of corruption, slowness, overcentralization, and conflicting jurisdictions. To increase trade between Portugal and Brazil, Pombal attempted to improve the system of annual fleets (similar to Spain's) but without success. He abolished the annual fleets in 1765, allowing individual Portuguese vessels to sail between Brazil and Portugal at any time. Similar to the Caracas Company in Spanish America, Portuguese monopoly companies failed and were abolished by 1779.

With gold exports declining, both Brazil and Portugal attempted to grow crops and manufacture products that previously had been imported. Pombal encouraged the expansion of agricultural production to include new crops, such as rice, wheat, and coffee. This combination of import substitution and the development of new crops had restored Brazil to prosperity, although it always depended on the constant inflow of slaves from Africa.

During the second half of the eighteenth century, no serious challenge to Portuguese rule in Brazil appeared. To eliminate any possible rival power base, Pombal had expelled the Jesuits and confiscated their properties in 1759. In the more religious areas of Spanish America, the expulsion of the Jesuits had undermined royal authority, but this was not the case in Brazil, where planters and merchants eagerly purchased most of the Jesuit lands at bargain prices. Rather than sell the lands to peasants, the Portuguese government reinforced the overconcentration of wealth in less than 1 percent of the Brazilian population.

Brazil, which did not have a single university or printing press, appeared content to remain under Portuguese rule, and the few failed conspiracies did not disrupt the colonial peace. The first plot was that of Tiradentes (Joaquim José da Silva Xavier) in 1788–1789, but, like the others, it gathered conspirators only from the lower and middle classes. Without the support of the upper class, no challenge to Portuguese rule could have been successful. After the slaves revolted in the 1791 Haitian Revolution, no planters dared to suggest any political change for fear of provoking a similar uprising among the slaves in Brazil.

▨ The Bourbon Era

As the Spanish American empire faced a real danger of collapsing, during the eighteenth century its reforms were considerably more extensive than those in Brazil. When the last Spanish king of the Hapsburg dynasty died without leaving an heir, European powers fought the War of the Spanish Succession to determine which royal family would occupy the Spanish throne. Spain ultimately selected a member of the Bourbons (the royal family that also ruled France under Louis XIV), hoping to avoid French invasions. Spanish America, however, was left exposed to repeated English naval attacks during the rest of the Bourbon period (1700–1808).

Fear of English attacks gave a military urgency to reforms in Spanish America, a strategic concern less prevalent in the more economically driven reforms of Portuguese Brazil. The economic dimension was no less absent in Spanish America than in Brazil, however, because of the bankruptcy of the model based on the exploitation of Indian and *mestizo* labor and the export of precious metals. The Bourbon reformers thus faced the double task of creating effective defense forces for the many distant frontiers of the Spanish Empire and of finding new sources of economic wealth to support the vastly enlarged military establishment.

Before the Bourbon reformers could make any changes, they needed to establish an effective government structure to carry out their orders. New institutions and new taxes were the order of the day. Spain had ruled Spanish America with institutions largely unmodified since their creation in the early sixteenth century. The Bourbons in the eighteenth century attempted to replace the original institutions with new dynamic agencies staffed largely by *peninsulares* and with the minimum possible participation by *criollos*. The old bureaucracy proved remarkably resistant, however, and the Bourbons could often do little more than add another layer of bureaucracy to these decrepit institutions.

Beginning in 1763, the combination of newly formed royal monopolies and the presence of the new intendants disrupted the existing power relationships. The new intendants, independent of the viceroys and the captains general, aggressively began to collect taxes in 1763, thereby antagonizing both elite groups and the masses. Rather than binding Spain closer to Spanish America, the intendants further strained the imperial relationship.

The intendants, viceroys, and judges of the *audiencia* all continued to mix judicial, legislative, and executive functions. Accountable only to

Spain, each was, in effect, independent and could easily display despotic excesses of power. Secrecy remained the rule; only a few privileged insiders had access to information within the bureaucracy, and officials kept the public ignorant of deliberations and of many decisions. Therefore, the Bourbon reforms reinforced authoritarianism and the expectation that policies should flow from rulers rather than the people.

Although the local elites had always embraced the principle of keeping the masses out of government, the Bourbon challenge to the elites themselves engendered a struggle to preserve their influence. At the same time, the military began to function as a separate group and to feel superior to the rest of society in many ways. Ironically, the Bourbons trained the officers and soldiers who later gained great distinction in fighting against the Spaniards during the wars of independence. The role of the military in Latin America is analyzed further by Paul Zagorski in Chapter 5.

By 1800, it was clear that no further reforms were possible from the Bourbons, who desperately attempted to retain their eroding power over Spanish America. Because of the rigid class structure and fears of unleashing a popular uprising by the masses, the elites were reluctant to defy the established authority of Spain. When it became clear that the monarchy was endangering the established order, however, the resulting stress gave the local elites the opportunity to escape once and for all—not only from the stifling Spanish commercial system but also from the domineering royal bureaucracy.

■ Independence

Early Rebellions

Although the independence period formally began in 1808, in reality earlier colonial revolts and British attacks formed the opening acts of the struggle for independence. Indian rebellions had been frequent in the sixteenth century and had never totally ended, whereas urban riots had shaken even Mexico City at times. In the late eighteenth century, however, two revolts of a magnitude previously unknown threatened to overthrow the colonial order completely.

The first occurred in the highlands of Peru and Bolivia, where Indians and *mestizos* rose up in November 1780 to overthrow corrupt officials and abolish the new taxes of the Bourbons. The leader of the uprising was a *mestizo* merchant who, as a descendant of the last Incan emperor, took the name Tupac Amarú II. In an attempt to rally the Indian masses behind him, Tupac Amarú II declared himself king but never declared independence from Spain. This unclear position undermined his support among Spanish Americans and many *mestizos*. The fighting soon degenerated into a war of racial extermination against the white *criollos*, who joined with the Spanish forces to crush this bloody insurrection by the end of 1781.

In contrast with the huge number of casualties in Peru, the rebellion in Colombia was relatively bloodless and lacked the racial overtones that had generated so much hatred. As in Peru, the revolt in Colombia was caused by popular opposition to the tax policies of the Bourbons, but the Indian population was considerably smaller than that in Peru, so *mestizos* and *criollos* made up the bulk of the rebels, who called themselves *comuneros*. During mass rallies in March 1781, the townspeople chose leaders to call for repeal of the new taxes. The movement spread like wildfire, and soon a huge crowd was marching on the capital city of Bogotá.

The Spanish government kept almost all of its forces near the coast, especially in the fortress city of Cartagena, as a defense against foreign attack; thus, the military could not quell the revolt. Consequently, on June 4, 1781, the *audiencia* in Bogotá caved in and granted the *comuneros'* demand to repeal the taxes. The crowds dispersed, and with the exception of one rebel leader, who was later captured and executed, the movement was over.

Whereas in Colombia the revolt had taught the upper class how easily Spanish rule could be overthrown, in Peru the lesson learned was that any change in government released bitter class and racial hatreds. Thus, while the upper class in Colombia remained open-minded about exploring new political alternatives if the opportunity arose, the upper class in Peru was so obsessed with its very survival that it resisted any attempt to change the political status. These contrasting attitudes in Colombia and Peru later played a major role in shaping events during South America's struggle for independence.

External Influences

By 1800, Latin America had been overtaken economically by both Europe and the United States. Nevertheless, the promise of wealth and plenty persisted for the British, who maintained their designs of conquering the region's mineral wealth. The outbreak of the French Revolution in 1789 ended Spain's alliance with the French Bourbons, who were overthrown, and Spain joined England in a coalition that attempted to destroy revolutionary France. Fear of French armies compelled the Spanish government—foolishly—to switch sides and to return to an alliance with France in 1796. Once again, to safeguard Spain's frontiers, the government was willing to expose Spanish America to English attacks.

British warships began to raid many coastal ports, and old plans to capture Panama and other strategic points resurfaced. A British expedition captured the ill-defended island of Trinidad near the coast of Venezuela in

1797 but failed miserably against the determined opposition of the new militias in the fortress city of San Juan, Puerto Rico. The most significant British attack came in 1806, when a British force captured Buenos Aires after royal officials—including the viceroy—fled in panic rather than face the advancing British troops. The *criollos* were shocked by the disgraceful performance of the royal officials, and the local militias decided to avenge the dishonor by secretly organizing the expulsion of the British troops, who surrendered when surprised by the unexpected *criollo* attack. A second British expedition had come too late to save the garrison, but it did attempt to recapture Buenos Aires in 1807. The assault was unsuccessful, and determined resistance by well-prepared militias persuaded the British commanders to abandon the attack.

The British continental offensive had barely dented the outer defenses of Spanish America, whose protection depended not on the inefficient institutions of a corrupt empire but rather on the dedication and discipline of the new militia units. Military power had passed imperceptibly into the hands of the *criollos* under the Bourbons. Thus, the transfer of political power to the *criollos* who already dominated the economy could not be far away. It later came as no surprise that Buenos Aires was the first region to throw off Spanish rule permanently.

Moreover, news of events in other parts of the world filtered in, despite the attempts of the Inquisition and the Spanish government to keep subversive ideas out of the region. After 1783, U.S. ships engaged in smuggling brought news of U.S. independence and ideas about how to set up a constitutional republic, thereby destroying the myth that a country in the Western Hemisphere could not exist without support from Europe.

The 1789 French Revolution seemed to offer a compelling example for all of Latin America, although the upper classes quickly tempered their revolutionary enthusiasm when the slaves in Haiti rose up and eventually established the first black republic in the Western Hemisphere in 1804. The landholders and miners in Latin America would not rush into independence because of fear of triggering social revolts, but no lingering attachment to the old colonial order would deter them from taking advantage of a favorable opportunity to gain control over the political structures in their regions.

The decay of Spanish institutions was pervasive and reached right up to the king and the royal family, who foolishly allowed themselves to be taken prisoners by the French. Napoleon Bonaparte attempted to place his brother on the throne of Spain, but the Spanish people indignantly rejected the new French ruler and began popular uprisings on May 2, 1808. Meanwhile, throughout Spain a large number of regional juntas, or governing boards, appeared to rule in the name of the captive Spanish king, Ferdinand VII.

Loyalty to the crown, the last cement bonding the Spanish Empire together, dissolved, as competing groups attempted to fill the power vacuum left by the capture of the royal family. French armies continued their relentless advance through Spain, until only the junta in Cádiz was left to defy Napoleon. Spanish America had watched these incredible events closely, and finally, in summer 1810, the elites in Bogotá, Caracas, Buenos Aires, and Santiago decided to overthrow the royal officials and establish governing juntas of Spanish Americans. In other places, particularly Havana and Mexico City, elites had tried to establish their own juntas but had failed because of fear of unleashing revolts by the black slaves in Cuba or the Indian and *mestizo* masses in Mexico.

The Wars Against Spain

The independence of Spanish America began without bloodshed, but the struggle soon turned into bitter and constant warfare that devastated large areas for over a decade. These independence movements are illustrated on Maps 3.2 and 3.3. The juntas tried to ease the transition by not declaring independence immediately and maintaining the fiction that they, too, ruled in the name of the captive Ferdinand VII, but even this concession failed to calm diehard royalists, who soon started revolts against the juntas.

Caracas proclaimed itself a republic in 1811, but the next year it was recaptured by royalist forces. Simón Bolívar attempted to reestablish the republic, but a brutal royalist campaign ended Venezuelan independence in 1814. In Bogotá, Buenos Aires, and Santiago, internal quarrels and even civil wars divided the *criollos*, who wasted the opportunity to drive the *peninsulares* from their last strongholds in Peru, Bolivia, and Uruguay.

Meanwhile, in Mexico a very different type of independence struggle had erupted. When the elite in Mexico City threw away the opportunity to establish its own junta, the initiative passed to provincial groups. Without access to the levers of power in Mexico City, the plotters in the provinces counted on a movement of Indians and *mestizos* to overthrow Spanish rule. On September 16, 1810, Spanish American priest Miguel Hidalgo—a key plotter—sounded the church bells to urge his parishioners to join the rebellion, which spread rapidly throughout nearby provinces. At the last moment, however, Hidalgo turned his huge forces (more a mob than an army) away from Mexico City and toward Guadalajara. The failure to capture the capital gave the Spanish government time to regroup and to regain the full support of the upper-class Mexicans who had panicked when Hidalgo's forces engaged in wholesale slaughter of all whites, whether *criollos* or *peninsulares*.

Hidalgo was soon defeated, captured, and executed, but the insurrection continued under *mestizo* priest José María Morelos. Defeated in formal battles, the Mexicans adopted guerrilla warfare against the Spanish armies,

Map 3.2
Early Independence Movements

whose morale began to suffer under the constant campaigning and the effects of tropical diseases. The capture and execution of Morelos in 1815 did not end the popular insurrection, and Mexican guerrillas continued to harass the increasingly exhausted Spanish troops. Meanwhile, the efforts of

Map 3.3
Later Independence Movements

the royal government to collect more taxes to pay for the large counterinsurgency army only increased resentment of Spanish rule. The Spanish government appeared to have clung to power in Mexico, but its control rested on disintegrating foundations.

The defeat of Napoleon Bonaparte in 1814 brought Ferdinand VII back to the Spanish throne and also released large numbers of Spanish veterans for the campaign of reconquest. Spanish battalions had contributed to the defeat of Hidalgo in Mexico, but counterinsurgency campaigns did not seem very glamorous to the Spanish government, which decided instead to pursue a grand strategy against the independent countries of South America. First, an expedition sailed from Spain to the Caribbean to crush the last patriot strongholds in Venezuela and then to reoccupy Colombia. Afterward, this force would then join Spanish forces in Peru to make a final push down the Andes Mountains to press the forces in Buenos Aires from the north, which then would be struck from the sea by a second force sailing directly from Spain. Pablo Morillo, who imagined himself to be another Hernán Cortés, led this huge Spanish expedition that first subdued Venezuelan resistance and then sailed to Colombia and landed off the coast of Cartagena in 1815. In a supreme irony, the Spaniards, who had spent entire fortunes to build this fortress city, had to lay siege to Cartagena, which surrendered only because its defenders were starving. The Colombians, who were too divided among themselves, could put up no significant resistance, and Morillo had soon reestablished Spanish rule in Bogotá and throughout Colombia. Meanwhile, Spanish forces in Peru had managed on their own to reconquer Chile in 1814, so by 1816, of all of the original independent countries, only Buenos Aires remained under patriot control. It, too, expected land attacks from the Andes Mountains and a sea invasion from Spain at any moment.

Before Spain could complete the reconquest of Buenos Aires, Simón Bolívar returned from exile to Venezuela and raised a patriot army in the plains of the Orinoco River in 1816. Morillo was forced to postpone his plans to march against Buenos Aires until he could destroy Bolívar's forces. In Venezuela, Colombia, and Chile, the *criollos* had come to hate Spanish rule. The Spanish government, rather than seeking a reconciliation, had become more inflexible than ever. Ferdinand VII and Morillo not only refused to share any power with the *criollos* but also took economic and political reprisals against all those who had participated in the independent regimes.

Spanish control rested only on brute force. Both Simón Bolívar in Venezuela and José de San Martín in Argentina saw the chance to end Spanish rule once and for all through brilliant military moves. Bolívar left behind some troops to distract Spanish forces in Venezuela, while he marched with his main army westward across the plains into the Andes Mountains of Colombia. His flanking march came as a total surprise, and after several engagements he decisively defeated the Spanish army in the Battle of Boyacá in August 1819.

All of Colombia fell under patriot control, and with these larger resources Bolívar led an expedition to drive the Spaniards out of Venezuela. This more difficult task was completed only after his troops had defeated the Spaniards in the Battle of Carabobo in June 1821. Bolívar sent another force south to expel the Spaniards from Ecuador, which joined the union of Colombia and Venezuela proclaimed in 1821. Panama, the best transit point for moving troops from the Caribbean to the Pacific Coast, had also joined the new country.

The areas of South America still under Spanish control continued to shrink, not only because of Bolívar's actions but also because of a separate campaign conducted by the Argentine José de San Martín, who adopted a new strategy to protect Argentina from an expected Spanish invasion. Previous attempts to march north directly into Peru had failed. Instead, San Martín decided to march across the Andes to surprise the Spaniards in Chile before sailing by ship to attack the lightly defended coast of Peru.

After over a year of preparing an army on the Argentine side, San Martín crossed the Andes and defeated the Spaniards in several battles, until the last one at Maipú in 1818 ended Spanish rule in Chile. He formed a navy with English sailors and ships, and his new fleet took the army to Peru and captured Lima in 1821. The Spanish troops had merely withdrawn into the interior highlands, however, and Bolívar took over the task of destroying the last Spanish forces in South America. With the resources of Colombia, Venezuela, and Ecuador at his disposal, Bolívar arrived with a considerable force. Extensive fighting ensued, but finally, in December 1824, the patriot forces defeated the last Spanish army at Ayacucho. Spanish rule had completely ended throughout South America.

Mexican independence took place in a rather sudden but almost inevitable manner. In 1820, Ferdinand VII gathered a second expedition in Cádiz to attack Buenos Aires. A mutiny, however, forced the king to hand over power to a Liberal government in Spain. By then, the Spanish forces in Mexico had become thoroughly demoralized by the unceasing guerrilla war, and the Mexican population saw the coming to power of the Liberal government in Spain as an excuse to stop paying the large war taxes.

The royal government in Mexico was disintegrating, but unlike the case in 1810, when the elites missed an opportunity to take power, this time Agustín de Iturbide, the *criollo* commander of the army in Mexico, was the right person to achieve independence. The rebels who had fought against Spanish rule were brought into the movement, and without firing a shot, Iturbide was able to proclaim Mexico's independence on September 28, 1821. Only the Spanish garrison in the main fortress of Veracruz refused to obey Iturbide's orders and did not accept Mexican control until 1823.

Central America, which traditionally had enjoyed close links to Mexico, was sufficiently impressed to break its ties with Spain and join the new Mexican Empire in 1821. Thus, all of mainland Spanish America—

from Mexico to Argentina and including Chile, Peru, Colombia, Central America, and Venezuela—had gained permanent independence from Spain. All that remained of the Spanish Empire were the islands of Cuba and Puerto Rico in the Caribbean and the distant Philippine Islands in the extreme western Pacific. Spain retained these territories until 1898.

Brazilian Independence

Brazil, with its large slave masses toiling in the gold mines and sugar plantations, was the least likely candidate for independence. If Cuba— with the largest number of slaves in Spanish America—had remained under Spanish dominance, then fear of slave rebellions promised to keep Brazil under Portuguese rule for a long time. However, as in the case of Spanish America, actions in Europe unleashed a chain of events that finally culminated in Brazil's independence from Portugal. Although Napoleon Bonaparte was unable to capture the royal family as he had done in Spain, the entire Portuguese government had to flee to Brazil in November 1807, just a few days before French armies captured Lisbon, the Portuguese capital.

British warships escorted the Portuguese royal family to Brazil until it was safely established in Rio de Janeiro, which, in effect, became the capital of the Portuguese Empire. This was the only time in history a government in Latin America ruled over colonies—in this case, the Portuguese territories in Asia and Africa. The British wanted favors in return, and Portuguese ruler Dom João complied by opening Brazilian ports to direct trade with the British.

Dom João was so happy in Rio de Janeiro that he refused to return to Portugal, even after Napoleon had been decisively defeated in 1815. Furthermore, he formally ended Brazil's colonial status when he proclaimed the country to be a "coequal kingdom" with the same rank as Portugal.

The printing press finally came to Brazil, and for the first time the king established institutions such as academies and universities. The Brazilian elite was delighted to have its king nearby and shared enthusiastically in the prosperity and feeling of progress that existed during the 1810s.

The new government in Portugal, however, demanded that Dom João return, and in a vain attempt to preserve the political unity of the Portuguese Empire, the king agreed. He left his son, Dom Pedro, behind and told him to declare Brazil independent if the necessity arose. When Dom João arrived in Portugal, the government was outraged to find he had left his son behind and not only insisted on Dom Pedro's prompt return but also began to strip Brazil of many of the privileges Dom João had granted. Portugal was determined to reduce Brazil to colonial status, but the Brazilian elite was not about to surrender its newly gained influence.

With the full support of the Brazilian elite, on January 9, 1822, Dom Pedro refused to obey the order to return to Portugal. Events flowed forward with an air of inevitability, until the king proclaimed Brazil's independence on September 7, 1822. The Brazilian elite rallied behind Dom Pedro I, and only some isolated Portuguese garrisons briefly resisted the proclamation of the Brazilian Empire.

Troops from poverty-stricken Portugal deserted almost as soon as they landed, making any Portuguese reconquest of Brazil pointless. Unlike the rest of Spanish America, Brazil had achieved independence with almost no bloodshed, so the country escaped both the destruction of war and the legacy of a large military establishment. Unlike Spanish America, which disintegrated into many rival nations, Brazil—under the unifying force of a traditional monarchy—remained a single country in spite of repeated regional revolts. The Brazilian monarchy inherited the existing structure of government and retained the overwhelming majority of officials in their posts, unlike the countries in Spanish America, where Spain's more extensive colonial bureaucracy usually failed to survive independence. Clearly, Brazil enjoyed distinct advantages in the challenging task of creating a new government and, at the least, seemed to have escaped the worst ravages of its Spanish American neighbors.

Conclusion

The early-nineteenth-century independence of Spain's and Portugal's vast colonial territories carries great historical significance in the emergence and subsequent evolution of Latin American countries. Three centuries of dominance were followed by the elimination of two great colonial empires from the Western Hemisphere.

Although the *peninsulares* lost power to the *criollos*, independence did not result in democratic government. Indians, persons of African descent, and *mestizos* did not benefit; the successful slave revolt in Haiti and the Indian rebellion led by Hidalgo were exceptions. Liberation allowed for expanded U.S., British, and French trade and investment. Hence, the newly developing Latin American economies came increasingly under the control of foreign investors. *Caudillismo* (rule by military dictatorship), civil war, anarchy, and foreign intervention in the lengthy period immediately following independence and subsequent government instability reveal the perseverance of the strong colonial impact, as well as modern Latin America's difficulty in developing alternative stabilizing systems.

Conquest allowed European institutions to be transplanted in the distant territories of the New World. As in most experiments in colonial governance, political, economic, and social systems were modified by indigenous cultures, thereby producing innovative patterns. In the case of the Americas, Eurocentric societies were influenced by Indian and African traditions. Conditioned by both integrative and disintegrative forces, the resulting fusion became known as Latin America.

The absolutist and centralized political tradition Spain transferred to Latin America continues to be manifested, even during a period of supposed democratization, in a strong tendency toward authoritarianism. This tendency had been bolstered by moral and theoretical foundations provided through the church as an instrument of the state. The power of the church and the importance of land ownership continued after independence. In effect, the separation from Spain and Portugal, far from initiating a liberal social revolution, left intact the transplanted conservative triumvirate of power: the church, the military, and the *criollo* oligarchy.

Attempts to hold on to privilege and the status quo, however, produced great political instability in the absence of a unifying central authority, such as that previously provided by the crown. Rival *caudillos* and elite factions entered into open conflict. The institutions transferred through conquest and colonialism persevered but were highly problematic in light of changes set into motion by the new political, social, and economic imperatives of independence.

In Chapter 4, Thomas J. D'Agostino discusses the ongoing effects on politics of this historical background. In this context, it is important to remember the profound impact of the conquest and colonization periods in the evolution of contemporary Latin America.

Bibliography

Bethell, Leslie (ed.). *Cambridge History of Latin America* (8 vols.). Cambridge, England: Cambridge University Press, 1985–ongoing.

Brown, Jonathan C. *Latin America: A Social History of the Colonial Period.* Orlando, Fla.: Harcourt Publishers, 2000.

Burkholder, Mark A., and Lyman L. Johnson. *Colonial Latin America* (4th ed.). New York: Oxford University Press, 2001.

Burns, E. Bradford. *A History of Brazil* (3d ed.). New York: Columbia University Press, 1993.

Bushnell, David. *The Making of Modern Colombia: A Nation in Spite of Itself.* Berkeley: University of California Press, 1993.

Bushnell, David, and Neill Macaulay. *The Emergence of Latin America in the Nineteenth Century* (2d ed.). New York: Oxford University Press, 1994.

Haring, Clarence C. *The Spanish Empire in America*. New York: Harcourt, Brace, 1985.

Hillman, Richard S. *Democracy for the Privileged: Crisis and Transition in Venezuela*. Boulder, Colo.: Lynne Rienner Publishers, 1994.

Keen, Benjamin, and Keith Hayes. *A History of Latin America* (7th ed.). Boston: Houghton Mifflin, 2004.

Klein, Herbert S. *Bolivia: The Evolution of a Multi-Ethnic Society* (2d ed.). New York: Oxford University Press, 1992.

Knight, Allan. *Mexico: The Colonial Era.* New York: Cambridge University Press, 2002.

Knight, Franklin W. *The Caribbean: The Genesis of a Fragmented Nationalism* (2d ed.). New York: Oxford University Press, 1990.

Lockhart, James. *The Nahuas After the Conquest: A Social and Cultural History of the Indians of Central Mexico, Sixteenth Through Eighteenth Centuries.* Stanford: University of California Press, 1994.

Loveman, Brian. *Chile: The Legacy of Hispanic Capitalism* (3d ed.). New York: Oxford University Press, 2001.

Meyer, Michael C., William L. Sherman, and Susan M. Deeds. *The Course of Mexican History* (7th ed.). New York: Oxford University Press, 2003.

Pérez, Louis A., Jr. *Cuba: Between Reform and Revolution* (2d ed.). New York: Oxford University Press, 1995.

Woodward, Ralph Lee, Jr. *Central America: A Nation Divided* (3d ed.). New York: Oxford University Press, 2001.

4

Latin American Politics

Thomas J. D'Agostino

C ontemporary Latin America has experienced a profound transformation. Significant advances in industrialization, urbanization, education, health care, and per capita income have set the region apart from other developing areas. Whereas many proclaimed the emergence of a "new Latin America" at the advent of the twenty-first century (Kryzanek 1995; Wiarda 1995), we should not lose sight of the enduring legacy of Latin America's colonial past, described by René de la Pedraja in Chapter 3. The values and institutions transplanted by the European powers during more than three centuries of colonial rule have been remarkably resilient. As they have been adapted to fit new realities, the region's dual political currents of traditional authoritarianism and emerging democracy have been blended and partially reconciled. The recurring clashes between the old and the new, between tradition and modernity, have strongly influenced the course of Latin American political evolution. The countries of Latin America have now reached a critical point in the process of political change.

As Richard Harper and Alfred Cuzán show in Chapter 6, the dramatic economic changes engendered through rapid modernization have had far-reaching social and political implications. The region's political history has been characterized by governments of virtually every conceivable type: monarchies, *caudillo* rule ("man on horseback"; a strong leader, often a military figure, who dominates politics through the use of force), populist regimes, oligarchic democracy, civilian and military dictatorships, revolutionary systems, Westminster-style parliamentary democracy, and bureaucratic-authoritarian states. Today, there has been a near universal movement toward democratic civilian rule, with Cuba a significant exception to this trend. Despite the protracted socioeconomic crisis of the "lost decade of the

1980s," the transition from authoritarian rule has generated great expectations among observers and mass publics alike. Although support for democratic elections, civil liberties, and greater pluralism has increased, the prevailing optimism has given way to the realization that the task of regime consolidation is far from complete. Indeed, democracy is perceived by many to be "on trial" (Wiarda 1995), and the magnitude of the challenges confronting national governments is daunting (Von Mettenheim and Malloy 1998).

As a result, the sustainability of democracy in the region is questionable. Popularly elected civilian leaders throughout the region have faced mounting public discontent, as they attempt to introduce painful economic reforms mandated by international lenders. What will be the long-term political implications of neoliberal policies, and how can leaders hope to reconcile the conflicting demands of their internal and external constituencies? How will traditionally praetorian militaries respond to the frustration and anger that will build as democratic governments prove unable to ameliorate endemic problems and fulfill the heightened expectations of increasingly mobilized publics? What must be done to promote further consolidation and to avert yet another devolution to authoritarianism? Is the current era of democratization an indication of genuine maturation and political evolution or merely another phase in the historical alternation of democratic and authoritarian impulses?

Clearly, some countries have made greater strides than others in the process of democratic consolidation. In an area as diverse as Latin America, the experiences of and prospects for different countries vary considerably. Latin America is a region composed of disparate states (see Appendix 1 and Appendix 2) with divergent colonial heritages, constitutional and cultural traditions, institutional structures, and levels of socioeconomic modernization. However, such differences, which have contributed to the tendency in the literature to segregate analyses of subregions, defined largely by cultural and linguistic criteria, must not obscure common patterns of political evolution in the region (Hillman and D'Agostino 1992). Illuminating these commonalities as they pertain to contemporary politics and addressing the aforementioned questions is the dual focus of this chapter.

▓ The Postindependence Era

The three decades following the independence of the former Spanish colonies were characterized by economic stagnation and political turmoil. The break from Spain did not entail any fundamental socioeconomic or political transformation, as the wars for independence were essentially conservative movements intended to preserve the existing structure of society and to forestall radical change. Hence, the rigid two-class hierarchical structure remained in place, with the *criollos* replacing the *peninsulares*. In fact, many colonial institutions and practices endured, including authoritarian, centralized top-down rule, and in some cases flourished well into the postindependence era. Independence removed the crown, however, the only viable form of centralized political authority the area had known. Unlike Brazil, which retained the monarchy and its centralizing presence following independence in 1822, and the Caribbean region—most of which remained under European control for some time, including the Spanish colonies of Cuba and Puerto Rico—Spanish America was basically left to its own devices. In the absence of a strong, unifying central authority and given the economic devastation wrought by the wars, the nascent Latin American states were ill prepared for independence and the arduous process of nation building.

Among the most problematic challenges were determining how the newly independent countries were to be governed and, subsequently, establishing order and consolidating national authority. Although virtually all of the constitutions written after independence embraced democratic principles, such as the separation of powers, and called for representative government, they also included provisions for maintaining the power and privileges of traditional corporate groups, such as the church and the military, and for ensuring the dominance of the executive branch of government (Wiarda 1995:53). Early efforts to promote democracy were further constrained by the absence of a democratic tradition in the region and the dearth of viable democratic institutions. The failure of these efforts underscored the difficulty of grafting a democratic political framework onto societies with deeply rooted authoritarian heritages and rigid, bifurcated social structures. At the same time, efforts to promote other forms of governance and to maintain stability at the national level were largely ineffective. Notable exceptions included Brazil, with its centralized monarchy, and Chile, where the early development of a system of oligarchical rule paved the way for a long tradition of stable constitutional government.

Few other countries, however, were able to keep in check the powerful disintegrative forces brought on by the removal of the crown. A vacuum of power and legitimacy at the national level contributed to the devolution of power to rival regional *caudillos* or competing elite groups. In some countries, the early independence era was marked by an intense struggle for control over national resources among rival *caudillos* and elites who alternated in power. In other cases, virtual anarchy gave rise to the emergence of powerful national *caudillos*, who came to dominate their respective countries in the initial stages of independence. Among the most notorious of these figures was Antonio López de Santa Ana of Mexico, whose leadership exacerbated political turmoil and brought the country into a conflict with the United States that resulted in Mexico's humiliating military defeat and loss of substantial territory. Similarly, through a mix of *personalismo* (the dominance of the individual in politics), strong-arm rule, and repression, Juan Manuel de Rosas came to dominate Argentine politics from 1835 to 1852. Although Rosas provided some degree of order and unity in a deeply divided country plagued by regional disputes, his dictatorial style of rule failed to lay the groundwork for long-term stability. In fact, although often viewed as a "necessary evil" in societies characterized by disarray and fragmentation, *caudillo* rule perpetuated the institutional void by inhibiting the formation of new institutions. As Latin America embarked on the second half of the nineteenth century, the need for more permanent institutional arrangements was clear.

Although a modicum of order had been established by the mid-1800s, national politics throughout Latin America remained highly contentious. Loosely organized "political parties," typically called Conservatives and Liberals, emerged among the elite in the decades following independence. Beyond the primary distinctions that revolved around Liberal support for free trade, federalism, and the separation of church and state, as compared with Conservative support for trade protectionism, centralization of authority, and the maintenance of traditional church power and perquisites, little distinguished these groupings ideologically. The competition for power, however, was intense and often violent. At stake was access to national power and resources with which to reward supporters through patronage. Although the seemingly perpetual conflict greatly inhibited national development early on, by 1850, signs of economic growth were appearing within Latin America. Spurred by the ongoing Industrial Revolution in Western Europe and North America, an influx of foreign investment, primarily British, stimulated the expansion of national industries and economic infrastructure, all of which served to integrate Latin America into the emerging global economy as an exporter of raw materials and agricultural products. As the latter part of the nineteenth century reveals, socioeconomic modernization had profound political implications.

■ Early Modernization and Dictatorial Rule

As the international demand for primary products increased, Latin American leaders sought to establish governmental systems capable of providing the stability needed to sustain the export model of development. Howard Wiarda (1995:60) has identified two general patterns that emerged during the late nineteenth century. In certain countries, including Chile, Brazil, and Argentina, the conservative oligarchy consolidated an exclusionary system of rule designed to preserve its interests and privileges. The gradual merging of the commercial elite with the traditional landed elite enhanced their ability to confront the challenge posed by the rising middle sectors and working classes spawned by economic modernization and, in some cases, such as Argentina, by the massive influx of European immigrants. Ultimately, in each case, the system of oligarchic rule would give way under pressures for change engendered through rapid modernization.

Elsewhere, a second pattern of rule emerged that relied on a familiar method of maintaining stability: highly centralized, personalistic *caudillo* leadership. Often referred to as "order and progress dictators," leaders such as Juan Vicente Gómez of Venezuela, Ulises Heureaux of the Dominican Republic, and Porfirio Díaz of Mexico employed strict, repressive measures to promote an environment of passivity and stability that proved inviting to foreign investors eager to open Latin America to the world. These regimes stressed the application of science and the maintenance of stability as the keys to development and benefited from the transfer of capital and technology from countries such as Great Britain and, increasingly, the United States. The most successful of these regimes was that of Mexico's Díaz, who dominated national politics from 1876 to 1910.

The Case of Mexico

Following its bitter, protracted struggle for independence from Spain (1810–1822), Mexico endured decades of political strife and economic stagnation, as disputes between rival elite groups (Conservatives and Liberals) undermined efforts to forge a national consensus. The death in 1872 of popular Liberal reformer Benito Júarez paved the way for Porfirio Díaz to seize power in 1876. Determined to modernize the country, Díaz struck a resonant chord within a society weary of chronic conflict and instability. Through his policy of *pan o palo* (bread or the stick), Díaz rewarded those who accepted and supported his rule while harshly suppressing opponents. The federal army and the *rurales* (rural police) were used to enforce the regime's dictates, bringing the country under national control and enhancing the authority of the central government. Attracted by the promise of order and lucrative incentives offered by the Díaz regime, investors pumped more capital into Mexico, spurring economic growth and providing the government with additional resources to reward and co-opt its supporters or, conversely, to bolster the repressive capacity of the state.

Mexico under Díaz experienced both unprecedented political stability and extraordinary industrial and infrastructural development as railroads, ports, and electrification facilities were established. The successful promotion of "order and progress," however, which had eluded Mexico since independence, came at a great cost. Critics charged Díaz with compromising Mexico's sovereignty and hard-won independence by allowing foreign control of key sectors of the economy. Indeed, development came about largely under the auspices of European and U.S. investors, who reaped enormous profits by exploiting Mexican labor and natural resources, particularly oil. Thus, such "progress" was achieved mainly at the expense of the Mexican masses and served to exacerbate the inequality between, on the one hand, *campesinos* (peasants), whose land was often confiscated to boost export production, and laborers, whose wages were kept low to enhance profits, and, on the other, members of the domestic elite, who profited from their association with foreign investors (Meyer and Sherman 1995:487–488).

Development also occurred at the expense of basic freedoms that had been established under the progressive leadership of Benito Júarez during the era of La Reforma (the reform). Although many in Mexico initially embraced Díaz's authoritarian rule, his regime grew increasingly repressive and dictatorial. In a pattern that was replicated throughout the region in the early 1900s, socioeconomic development engendered enormous pressure for political change, most notably among the emerging middle sectors, whose newfound stature did not translate into meaningful political power. In an ironic twist (one that would plague other Latin American modernizers as well), the success with which Díaz was able to promote "order and progress" ultimately sowed the seeds of his regime's demise. His narrow, highly personalized, dictatorial style of rule grew increasingly anachronistic and untenable amid the profound changes brought on by rapid modernization.

By 1930, these changes had undermined the old oligarchic order and facilitated the rise of middle-class politics in Latin America. In some cases, such as in Argentina and Chile, this clash between the forces of tradition and modernity was resolved relatively peacefully, and the transition occurred through electoral means. In Mexico, however, Díaz's unwillingness to accommodate demands for political reform set the stage for the greatest upheaval in twentieth-century Latin America: the Mexican Revolution.

Although it began largely as an expression of middle-class disaffection with the Díaz regime, the conflict that engulfed Mexico from 1910 to 1917 soon evolved into a mass rebellion that claimed over 1 million lives. In the end, Mexico had experienced tumultuous change, yet a great deal of continuity with the past remained.

Despite a pledge to step down at the end of his term in 1910, Díaz was again fraudulently elected. His primary opposition, Francisco Madero, challenged Díaz's *continuismo* (the practice of extending one's term in office beyond constitutional limits) under the banner of "effective suffrage and no reelection." After failing to bring about political change through constitutional means, Madero fled to the United States, where in October 1910 he issued a call for Mexicans to rebel against the dictatorship. What followed was a broad-based rebellion composed of disparate groups united in their opposition to Díaz. The defeat of federal forces at the Battle of Ciudad Júarez and Díaz's subsequent resignation on May 25, 1911, marked the end of an era but not the end of the conflict in Mexico.

With Díaz gone, divisions soon appeared within the diverse revolutionary coalition. Although Madero won the 1911 election, he was immediately confronted by a host of powerful opponents, and his presidency was doomed to failure. Ironically, although Madero's call to arms against Díaz marked the beginning of the revolution, his objectives once he was in power were far from revolutionary. Madero set his sights on political reform and attempted to introduce a more open, democratic political system in Mexico. His reforms failed to address the primary concerns of the masses, however, most notably the Mexican peasants who, under the leadership of Emiliano Zapata, took up arms in the name of land reform. For the vast majority of Mexicans, "effective suffrage and no reelection" had little meaning (Meyer and Sherman 1995:536). Members of the conservative elites viewed Madero's intentions with suspicion, concerned that their power and privileges might be threatened. Madero's inability to appease either the masses or the elites led to a renewed outbreak of rebellion in late 1911, which culminated with a bloody uprising in Mexico City in February 1913, during which Madero was overthrown and subsequently executed.

The ascension of Victoriano Huerta, a supporter of Díaz who sought to reassert strict, centralized authoritarian rule, signified the failure of Madero's experiment with democratic reform and triggered further conflict. Huerta was faced with two separate rebellions—one in the north (the Constitutionalist rebellion), led by Venustiano Carranza and supported by General Álvaro Obregón and the legendary Francisco "Pancho" Villa, and another, the Zapatista revolt, in the southern state of Morelos. Huerta's attempt to consolidate his control over Mexico was complicated further by a depleted treasury, severe economic dislocations caused by the widespread conflict, and strong opposition from U.S. president Woodrow Wilson, who objected to Huerta's seizure of power (Meyer and Sherman 1995:528–529). U.S. support for the Constitutionalist cause and the subsequent military occupation of the key city of Veracruz contributed to the demise of Huerta's regime in July 1914.

Once again, the disparate revolutionary forces fragmented because of their divergent interests. Villa and Zapata broke with the Constitutionalists and dedicated their efforts to opposing Carranza. With the assistance of General Obregón, Carranza was eventually able to subdue the rebel forces and consolidate his control over the nation. The 1916 constitutional convention, designed to institutionalize the revolution, resulted in the 1917 Constitution (which remains in effect today). Radical for its time, the constitution strictly limited the power of the Catholic Church, restricted foreign corporations, granted extensive rights and benefits to labor, and called for agrarian reform.

Given the country's history of conflict and fragmentation, the 1917 Constitution was intended to forge a consensus by including provisions that would appeal to a variety of constituencies. Its proclamation, however, did not signal an end to the conflict, nor did it bring about unanimous agreement regarding Mexico's future direction. Carranza himself, although he accepted the constitution, did not agree with all of its provisions and ignored many of them after assuming the presidency in mid-1917. In fact, his attempt to circumvent the no-reelection stipulation by naming his successor led to his removal by General Obregón in 1920.

Despite his ignominious political demise, Carranza successfully laid the groundwork for the institutionalization of a new political system that has produced unprecedented stability over the past several decades. General Álvaro Obregón, who was elected to succeed Carranza in 1920, gradually implemented the 1917 Constitution and did much to enhance the power of the national government despite a period of economic decline, conflicts with the United States, and continued internal instability. Turmoil continued during the presidency of General Plutarco Elías Calles, whose implementation of the anticlerical provisions of the constitution exacerbated church-state tensions. Calles, however, helped to institutionalize Mexico's revolutionary government by establishing the broad-based, multiclass National Revolutionary Party (PNR) in 1929. Designed to integrate all relevant organized groups into the political arena, the PNR enabled the Mexican government to co-opt and control all major social groups that could threaten its control. By creating institutionalized mechanisms that both facilitated and controlled popular participation, Mexican leaders provided the stability with which to confront the changes brought on by modernization. Ironically, the violent Mexican Revolution resulted in a "modernized" version of the strong, centralized, authoritarian state that existed during both the Díaz era and the colonial past.

*   *   *

The demise of the order-and-progress dictatorship of Porfirio Díaz in the early 1900s paralleled the emergence of similar regimes in a number of Caribbean Basin countries. These regimes, however, were not established by individual *caudillo* leaders but rather by the United States as part of a series of direct military interventions and occupations. Thus, in the early twentieth century, a third pattern of governmental rule emerged in Latin

America designed to promote stability and to enhance the prospects for national development (Wiarda 1995).

As Cleveland Fraser describes in greater detail in Chapter 7, following the defeat of Spain in the Spanish-American War in 1898, the United States became a major force in the Caribbean region as well as a colonial power by acquiring control of Puerto Rico (among other territories) and establishing a protectorate over Cuba. Having surpassed Great Britain as the primary investor in the area, the United States had extensive economic interests to protect along with the long-standing security concerns articulated in the 1823 Monroe Doctrine. After the proclamation of the 1904 Roosevelt Corollary to the Monroe Doctrine, the United States embarked on a series of military interventions and occupations in such countries as Cuba, the Dominican Republic, Haiti, Nicaragua, and Panama. Ironically, whereas these interventions were designed to establish and maintain order, they ultimately sowed the seeds of future conflict.

The Modern Era

The inherent weaknesses of export-led development and the traditional elite's tenuous hold on power were evident in the early 1900s. Monocultural production and overreliance on the export of raw materials made Latin American economies vulnerable to market and price fluctuations and increasingly dependent on the importation of manufactured goods and technology. World War I and the Great Depression exacerbated the region's economic problems and further undermined the old oligarchic order, which had already been debilitated by the Mexican Revolution and electoral defeats in Argentina and Chile.

The 1930s were a "critical juncture" in the process of Latin American development (Wiarda 1995). As governments fell throughout the region—through elections, coups, or revolts—new national leaders turned to a new model of economic development that stressed industrialization. Modernization, the pace of which varied considerably by country, significantly altered the social structure, and with the emergence of new power contenders came mounting pressures for change.

With the shift from exportation of primary products to industrialization, which occurred initially in the larger, more economically advanced countries of South America and in Mexico, incipient modernization gave way to a more accelerated version of socioeconomic change. Known as import substitution industrialization (ISI), this new development strategy was designed to stimulate domestic production of industrial and manufactured goods that had previously been imported. Latin American leaders viewed ISI as a means of creating jobs and reducing external dependence.

Moreover, it was perceived as a symbol of progress, as evidence of Latin America's vast potential and its transition to modernity.

Accompanying rapid economic modernization were profound changes in Latin America's social structure, significant improvements in living standards, and heightened popular expectations. In addition to expanding an already sizable middle class in the larger, more advanced states, industrialization spawned a burgeoning urban working class whose organization into labor unions and, later, political parties marked the emergence of a new actor in the Latin American political arena. Over the next several decades, dealing with labor was one of the most pressing concerns confronting Latin American leaders.

Modernization generated substantial pressure for change in the traditional elitist political order. In confronting this pressure, Latin American political systems were flexible and innovative. Rather than disappear in the face of rapid change, traditional patterns, structures, and values were modified to reflect and conform to new conditions (Wiarda 1995:79). For example, the old landed elite gradually absorbed the nascent commercial elite, a relatively easy process, given the groups' limited numbers and generally compatible interests. Accommodating the middle sectors was more problematic because of their lack of cohesion and their divergent interests. In some countries, such as Mexico, accommodation occurred only after violent conflict, whereas in others, such as Chile, the process was relatively peaceful because the upper classes recognized that they shared a common interest in uniting against the masses. In both instances, the emerging groups were assimilated by expanding the traditional hierarchical power structure—composed of the oligarchy, the Catholic Church, and the military. In this manner, although the status quo was technically altered with the incorporation of new groups, the fact that these groups now had a stake in preserving the system ensured its perpetuation. In fact, their incorporation was contingent upon accepting the existing rules.

In contrast, less agreement existed regarding the most effective means of confronting the emergent urban working class. The initial reaction from those within the power structure was to exclude labor, as the strong Marxist and anarcho-syndicalist (a working-class political ideology that opposes all forms of exploitation and domination, i.e., anticapitalist and antiracist) influence within the trade union movement was perceived as threatening to the elites' control. This approach became less viable in countries where ongoing industrialization increased both the size and potential power of organized labor. Simply put, it became increasingly difficult to ignore or repress workers whose awareness and expectations had risen dramatically and who were effectively mobilized within the union movement. Ultimately, a variety of strategies were employed in addressing the labor challenge; some proved to be reasonably effective in mediating class conflicts, and others exacerbated tensions and eventually provoked radical challenges to the existing order. Clearly, responses to the emergence of labor profoundly affected political evolution.

Recognizing the need to accommodate union demands at least partially, most Latin American leaders struggled to integrate labor into the power structure. In Mexico, for example, emerging power contenders had been co-opted into a corporatist state structure under the control of a single dominant political party since 1929, called the Institutional Revolutionary Party (PRI) since 1946, until Vicente Fox's election as president in 2000, when the National Action Party (PAN) finally displaced the PRI. Through the PRI's unique sectoral structure, labor, along with the peasants and "popular sectors," had been accorded the status and concomitant privileges of major corporate groups. This arrangement facilitated the organization and representation of divergent interests, albeit within a corporatist framework under the firm, watchful eye of the state. Nevertheless, the PRI's innovative blend of modern institutional structures and traditional patterns, such as patron clientelism and centralized, authoritarian decisionmaking, had peacefully co-opted labor into the prevailing system. The relevance of this approach to the rest of Latin America is limited, however, as is the likelihood that it could ever be replicated elsewhere, because of the unique circumstances that confronted Mexico's postrevolution leaders and their idiosyncratic institutional arrangements.

In contrast with Mexico's "authoritarian democracy," a number of countries managed to incorporate labor within pluralist party systems. This strategy was employed with considerable success throughout much of the English-speaking Commonwealth Caribbean. By the early 1900s, labor organizations had proliferated in the region, and the working class gradually emerged as a political force (Knight and Palmer 1989:12). This became apparent when labor disturbances broke out in response to deteriorating socioeconomic conditions, first in St. Kitts (1935) and culminating in Jamaica and Guyana in 1938. In the aftermath of these disturbances, a strong linkage between political parties and workers' unions was established in most British colonies, with Trinidad a notable exception. Although this link provided workers with access to the political process, it was accomplished largely under elite tutelage. In fact, the formation of parties with links to labor unions has been viewed by some observers as a means of integrating the masses into the existing framework of power (Edie 1991; Stone 1985).

While workers throughout Latin America have enjoyed varying degrees of access to participatory institutions, the assimilation of labor has been a long, complicated process, even in countries widely viewed as among the most stable and democratic in the region. For instance, serious setbacks to democracy and to the inclusion of labor in power structures occurred during the 1970s and 1980s in Chile and Uruguay, when elected civilian governments were ousted by the military and replaced by brutal regimes that relied on repression in an attempt to demobilize the labor movement, among other goals. Democratic processes have also been impeded in the region by pervasive violence in Colombia, stemming from narcotics trafficking and ongoing guerrilla and paramilitary conflicts, as well as by massive discontent culminating in two coup attempts in 1992 against an elected civilian government in Venezuela. As these cases illustrate, labor incorporation can be reversed or constrained during periods of crisis and when rising demands go unfulfilled or are perceived as threatening.

The emergence of the labor movement elicited different responses in Argentina and Brazil, which saw the rise of populist dictators who appealed to urban workers as a means of consolidating their power. In both cases, rapid industrialization that began in the late nineteenth century had produced burgeoning working classes, which became influential political actors. Both Juan Perón in Argentina (in the 1940s) and Getulio Vargas in Brazil (in the 1930s) employed traditional practices, such as the creation of corporatist structures and the use of patronage through which labor would be integrated under state direction and control. But unlike Mexico's institutional framework, the processes in Argentina and Brazil depended primarily on the charisma of individual leaders. The dearth of viable institutions in Argentina and Brazil, exacerbated by the highly centralized, personalistic, authoritarian regimes of Perón and Vargas, became even more problematic after the leaders left power (Perón initially in 1955 and Vargas in 1954). By inhibiting institutional growth and the development of effective, long-term mechanisms for the peaceful incorporation of labor into their countries' power structures, both leaders left legacies of instability and conflict.

The relatively lower level of industrialization and modernization in some of the smaller, less socioeconomically developed countries of the region—where conditions differed substantially from those in Mexico, Chile, Argentina, and Brazil—precluded the formation of a sizable, highly mobilized urban working class. As a result, rather than seeking to co-opt labor, regimes such as those of Fulgéncio Batista in Cuba, Rafael Trujillo in the Dominican Republic, François Duvalier in Haiti, Anastasio Somoza García in Nicaragua, and Alfredo Stroessner in Paraguay found that brutally suppressing the labor movement was far more expedient. In fact, these personalist dictatorships—in which virtually absolute power and authority were concentrated in the hands of a single individual—were among the most violent, repressive, and long-lasting regimes in Latin America.

Although the use of repression effectively subdued the labor movement for a time, these regimes eventually faced mounting discontent and demands for change, as the pace of development and modernization accelerated. The response to increasingly vocal opposition, however, was frequently an even greater reliance on coercion and intimidation. For example, François (Papa Doc) Duvalier formed the dreaded Tonton Macoutes, a paramilitary force that terrorized the regime's opponents, and Rafael Trujillo transformed the Dominican Republic into a virtual police state. This type of state-sponsored, institutionalized repression, along with the continued domination of personalist dictators, greatly inhibited the process of institutional development in societies basically devoid of any viable channels through which the regimes' opponents could press for change. A persistently low level of institutionalization, coupled with the regimes' inflexibility in the face of modernization and their unwillingness to accommodate any demands for reform, diminished the likelihood of a peaceful transfer of power and set the stage for the most turbulent period in Latin American history.

Revolutionary Change

By the 1950s, industrialization had stimulated far-reaching change in Latin America. Urbanization and technological advances first necessitated, and later facilitated, improvements in both the transportation and communication infrastructure. The social structure grew more complex. Latin America was no longer semifeudal in nature, dominated by a rigid, two-class social hierarchy. Instead, it now exhibited a more differentiated structure with the emergence of urban-based groups—the commercial and industrial elites; the middle sectors, composed of white-collar professionals such as doctors, lawyers, teachers, and bureaucrats; and the industrial working classes—all of which had grown in numbers and political relevance. The size of the state had been expanding rapidly, as a result of these urban groups' increased demands for services and for greater roles in the economy. Moreover, following the collapse of the old oligarchic order around 1930, the middle sectors—despite a lack of unity and cohesion—had become the predominant force in the military officer corps, the clergy, and the government bureaucracy.

Yet, the emergence of new power contenders created problems, as the level of conflict among groups with divergent interests continued to escalate. In a number of cases, including El Salvador, societies became so polarized and disputes among groups so contentious that it was difficult for anyone to govern effectively. With political awareness and mobilization at unprecedented levels as a result of improvements in education and greater exposure to new ideas and values through the media, Latin America experienced a "revolution of rising expectations." National leaders' inability, because of fiscal constraints or political opposition, or unwillingness to accommodate mass demands and rising expectations, along with a growing disparity between the rich and the poor (as industrialization had exacerbated preexisting inequalities), significantly increased the level of popular discontent. This mounting frustration and the realization that, in many cases, genuine change would not come about through peaceful electoral means fueled numerous revolts and guerrilla insurgencies. Such revolutionary potential instilled fear in the upper classes, as well as in some middle-class elements, who sometimes allied against the perceived threat from below in an effort to forestall the outbreak of class conflict. In Argentina, Brazil, and Chile, among others, this fear led to calls for the military to restore order. In other cases, disaffected members of the middle class led movements to overthrow governments and to bring about radical change. Both Bolivia and Guatemala experienced attempts to promote profound social and political transformation that, although not sustained, served as a portent of further challenges to the established order.

The 1952 Bolivian Revolution, which brought the National Revolutionary Movement (MNR) to power, was the culmination of years of political conflict and economic decline that dated back to the Great Depression and the disastrous Chaco War with Paraguay (1932–1935). These events undermined the legitimacy and precipitated the downfall of the alliance between the traditional landed elite and the emerging mining elite that had dominated national politics and the economy. The MNR, a broad multiclass party founded in 1941, brought together a variety of groups opposed to the existing order. These included the urban working class—long excluded from the political process through literacy and property requirements and whose efforts to press demands were typically ignored or repressed—some disenchanted sectors of the military, and key sectors of the middle class whose demands went unfulfilled in the context of economic stagnation.

A series of revolts organized by the MNR in April 1952 helped to bring down a conservative government whose collapse reflected the inherent weakness of the Bolivian elite, which lacked sufficient resources to co-opt the emerging middle class as a result of Bolivia's low level of industrialization and a prolonged economic crisis. They also suffered from the lack of a strong, unified military that could suppress the challenge posed by the middle class (as in Peru, where the military prevented the American Popular Revolutionary Alliance [APRA] from taking power until 1985). After the revolution, the MNR came to include the Indian peasantry, who constitute the majority of Bolivia's population, yet had previously been excluded from national politics by discriminatory electoral requirements.

Led by Víctor Paz Estenssoro, the MNR pursued an ambitious agenda that emphasized economic development and social justice. The Bolivian Revolution accomplished the granting of citizenship, voting, and other rights to the Indians to facilitate their integration into national life for the first time in the country's history; the nationalization of the nation's largest tin mines and formation of a state mining corporation; and a program of agrarian reform. Factional strife within the MNR coalition, however, impeded efforts to sustain the revolution. The fragmentation of the MNR and a coup ousting Paz in 1964 ended Bolivia's revolutionary experiment and ushered in an extended period of military rule.

Guatemala's experiment with social revolution also began with disenchanted sectors of the middle class organizing demonstrations and strikes against a regime they perceived as obstructing change. The popular revolt that toppled the dictatorship of General Jorge Ubico in 1944 marked the beginning of a decade-long experiment in democracy, which led to substantial national development and reform, but which also provoked a strong response from the United States. Following the ouster of Ubico, Juan José Arévalo was elected to the presidency in 1945. The Arévalo government introduced a program of land and labor reforms, coupled with political reforms aimed at encouraging popular mobilization and the creation of trade unions, political parties, and interest groups. These measures, which were well received by the masses, engendered strong opposition from conservative elements within Guatemala, as evidenced by the more than twenty attempted coups during Arévalo's tenure.

A peaceful transfer of power brought Colonel Jacobo Arbenz Guzmán to power following the 1950 election. Arbenz maintained his predecessor's commitment to social welfare and national development, promoting infrastructure development to spur the economic growth needed to fulfill his agenda. To this end, Arbenz introduced the Agrarian Reform Law in 1952, designed to expropriate uncultivated land for distribution to the peasants. This measure soon brought Arbenz into conflict with the United Fruit Company (UFCO), a U.S.-based multinational with extensive landholdings and substantial political influence throughout Central America. The perceived "attack" on UFCO by the Arbenz government caused great concern in Washington, in part because of close personal ties between the company's executives and high-level U.S. government officials and in part because of a greatly exaggerated perception of communist influence within the Arbenz administration. Portraying Guatemala as a significant threat to its national security, the United States began efforts to destabilize and topple the Arbenz government. When diplomatic efforts proved insufficient, covert action was undertaken, with the Central Intelligence Agency (CIA) sponsoring an "invasion" by a small force of Guatemalan exiles that succeeded in overthrowing Arbenz in 1954.

The coup, which brought an end to the decade of democratic reform, marked a significant turning point in Guatemalan politics. The Arbenz government was followed by a series of military or military-dominated regimes that routinely violated civil liberties and committed human rights abuses, prevented institutional development, and heightened the degree of polarization in a society already deeply divided by race and ethnicity. In the decades following the coup, Guatemala experienced a protracted civil war that claimed the lives of over 100,000 people and displaced thousands more. This conflict pitted the government's security forces, along with a variety of right-wing paramilitary organizations and "death squads," against a left-wing guerrilla insurgency composed of numerous groups, some of which united to form the Guatemalan National Revolutionary Union (URNG) in 1982. Although political power was nominally returned to civilian authorities in 1986, hostilities between the government and the URNG officially did not come to an end until peace accords were signed in December 1996. For over four decades, Guatemala endured a level of violence and repression matched by few other countries in Latin America.

The events of 1954 were also significant for the entire hemisphere. The actions taken by the United States to oust a popularly elected leader were clear signals of U.S. resolve to confront "communism" and of the fact that any challenges to U.S. business or strategic interests would not be tolerated.

The Case of Cuba

The 1959 Cuban Revolution is one of the most significant events in Latin American history. Unlike the inability of the Bolivian and Guatemalan movements to sustain themselves over the long term, Cuba's revolutionary leadership—notwithstanding difficulties over the past decade or so—consolidated the revolution and brought about a complete social transformation.

Cuban independence, achieved only after the United States intervened in the revolt against Spain in 1898, and subsequently compromised as the United States established a protectorate over the island, was defined by a pattern of strongman rule and military intervention in politics through the 1950s. Following the overthrow of Gerardo Machado, who was popularly elected in 1924 but who maintained himself in power illegally until 1933, a brief revolutionary period under the leadership of Ramón Grau San Martín was thwarted by a military revolt led by Fulgéncio Batista. Batista dominated Cuban politics over the next decade, initially behind the scenes and later through direct rule from 1940 to 1944—a period in which U.S. economic and political ties to Cuba were strengthened. Two successive democratic governments, under the watchful eye of Batista, produced a variety of social and economic reforms, but their legitimacy (and that of the democratic alternative in general) was severely undermined by widespread corruption and endemic political violence. Finally, in March 1952, Batista launched another coup and reinstituted a system of authoritarian rule.

On the surface, Cuba during the late 1950s did not appear a likely candidate for a full-scale revolution. By Latin American standards, Cuba was relatively modernized and had reached a level of development comparable to that found in some of the larger countries in the region. Moreover, Batista cultivated close ties with the United States, which focused considerable attention on Cuban affairs, given its proximity and the extensive U.S. business interests on the island. Further analysis reveals, however, that Cuba's development was badly skewed, which produced enormous disparities between relatively modern urban areas and impoverished rural areas.

Batista's harsh rule and what was seen by many as an overly accommodating stance toward the United States provoked strong nationalist sentiments and engendered broad opposition to his regime. Among the various groups seeking to oust the dictator was the 26th of July Movement, named after the date in 1953 on which its leader, Fidel Castro, launched an ill-fated attack on the Moncada military barracks. After his release from prison, Castro went to Mexico, where he plotted to overthrow Batista. The struggle began in 1956, when Castro and his forces (numbering less than one hundred) returned to Cuba and waged a remarkably effective campaign of guerrilla warfare against Batista's well-equipped (by the United States) army of around 40,000 troops. With his forces unable to quell the rebellion, Batista increased repression against student and other groups that led urban-based opposition to the regime, as well as against those suspected of sympathizing with the rebels. Lacking any substantial popular support and having lost U.S. backing, Batista fled into exile on January 1, 1959.

Batista's sudden departure left a vacuum of power that Castro and his movement quickly moved to fill. As the broad revolutionary coalition began to splinter, Castro's faction, including his brother Raúl and the Argentine revolutionary Ernesto "Che" Guevara, became the dominant force. The ultimate direction the revolution would take was unclear at this time, largely because of uncertainty about Fidel's ideological orientation. Although Che Guevara, an avowed Marxist, maintained that Fidel was not a Marxist prior to the revolution, Fidel himself has given conflicting accounts as to the evolution of his political views over the years. He was not a member of the prerevolutionary Communist Party, focusing his appeal on the middle sectors as a nationalist reformer. Initial uncertainty over his intentions gave way to the realization that Castro was committed to a radical revolutionary program designed to transform Cuban society irrevocably and assert Cuban sovereignty and independence from U.S. influence.

The Castro regime established several mass organizations—including the Committees for the Defense of the Revolution (CDRs) and others geared toward labor, peasants, women, and students—along with a militia to mobilize popular support. Although these organizations helped to pro-

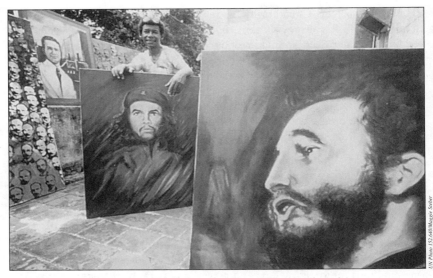

Julio Pérez Medina, a Cuban artist, displays his
portraits of Che Guevara and Fidel Castro.

vide the new regime with a type of institutional framework, the political
system was restructured around the charismatic leadership of Fidel. In fact,
it was his presence that did much to fill the institutional void that confronted revolutionary Cuba at the outset. Arguably the most charismatic figure
Latin America has ever known, Castro has come to personify the revolution. His highly personalistic, centralized style of rule is consistent with
Latin America's *caudillo* tradition and has allowed him to consolidate his
personal control over the country.

By late 1960, the country's dependent capitalist economy had been dismantled and a majority of the economy nationalized, including the property
of both domestic and foreign owners. This action, coupled with the movement toward an authoritarian single-party state, prompted the exodus of
thousands of upper- and middle-class Cubans. Ironically, this exodus and
subsequent ones, such as the Mariel Boatlift in 1980, have served as a kind
of "safety valve" for Castro, helping to defuse potential domestic opposition to his regime.

Another component of Cuba's revolutionary agenda was a program of
socioeconomic reform designed to improve the standard of living of its
masses. This program included educational reform, a literacy campaign,
and extensive efforts to improve health care and other social welfare services. These measures, along with plans to redistribute land and wealth,
sought to address the glaring inequalities that had characterized pre-1959

Cuban society and to ensure that the basic daily needs of all Cubans would be met.

Castro was keenly aware of the precedent set in Guatemala and recognized that revolutionary Cuba would inevitably face U.S. opposition. Two actions that ensured this were the seizure of U.S. businesses and properties and the reordering of Cuba's foreign policy, which resulted in close ties with the Soviet Union. Determined to reduce the pervasive U.S. role in Cuba's economy and to diversify economic relations, Castro entered into a trade agreement with the Soviets in February 1960. With this new source of technology (and, later, military assistance) and a market for Cuban sugar, Castro intensified his strident anti-U.S. rhetoric, and relations with the United States deteriorated rapidly.

The U.S. response came in April 1961. Alarmed by the increasingly radical tone of the Cuban Revolution, the John F. Kennedy administration, acting on a plan devised under Dwight Eisenhower, sponsored a Guatemala-style invasion by U.S.-trained and -equipped Cuban exiles at the Bay of Pigs. Intended to foment a counterrevolution within Cuba to topple Castro, the poorly organized operation failed miserably. A colossal U.S. foreign policy blunder, the Bay of Pigs represented a monumental victory for Castro, the young revolution, and Cuban nationalism. It provided definitive proof of Castro's contention that the United States was the mortal enemy of revolutionary Cuba and, according to many observers, pushed Cuba further into the embrace of the Soviet bloc.

Indeed, in December 1961, Castro formally declared himself, and hence the revolution, Marxist-Leninist. Within a matter of months, Soviet leader Nikita Khrushchev ordered the installation of missile bases on the island, thus transforming Cuba into a stage for a Cold War confrontation that literally brought the world's superpowers to the brink of nuclear war. The October 1962 Cuban missile crisis was resolved when Khrushchev, under pressure from the Kennedy administration, agreed to withdraw the Soviet missiles in exchange for a pledge from the United States that, among other things, it would not invade Cuba.

Over the next three decades, Cuba became a valuable Soviet ally in the Third World. The relationship gave the Soviets access to a critical strategic location in the Western Hemisphere just 90 miles from the United States, and Soviet efforts to assist communist movements in Africa were bolstered by Castro's desire to "export revolution" and his willingness to contribute troops and other personnel to missions in Angola and Ethiopia. In return, the Soviet Union provided the military protection and economic and technical assistance that facilitated the institutionalization of the revolution and enabled Cuba to survive the severe economic embargo imposed by the United States in 1962.

Critics of the revolution argue that despite all of Castro's rhetoric about

Cuban students. The one on the left wears a shirt proclaiming "I am a free man."

UN Photo 156020/Milton Grant

asserting Cuba's independence from foreign domination, he did little more than replace the country's dependence on the United States with dependence on the Soviet Union. Although supporters counter that since 1959 Cuba has belonged to Cubans rather than to foreign investors, Soviet influence became pervasive. Castro maintained a greater degree of autonomy than most other Soviet satellite states, but there can be no doubt that Soviet backing contributed much to his longevity in power.

Another factor contributing to Castro's longevity has been his style of leadership. He established a centralized authoritarian state in which dissent is severely repressed, democratic civil liberties are nonexistent, and human rights abuses have been widespread. Although Fidel Castro epitomizes the worst excesses of dictatorship and the brutality of Stalinist communism to many, he has remained immensely popular with much of the rural populace of Cuba. They point to the "achievements of the revolution"—the guarantee of education, health care, and other social services—as the rationale for their support. They maintain that under Castro inequality has been greatly reduced, and the dire poverty, malnutrition, and unemployment of the pre-revolutionary period have been eliminated. To be sure, Castro depended heavily on the Soviet Union to provide such benefits. But Castro's popularity has also been derived from his willingness to confront the United States, which has given Cubans an immense sense of national pride and dignity.

The course of the Cuban Revolution was influenced profoundly by the prevailing international context. For three decades, the bipolar global structure institutionalized during the Cold War enabled Castro to parlay his country's strategic geopolitical location into leverage in dealing with the

Soviet Union. The situation changed dramatically, however, with the emergence of President Mikhail Gorbachev and his introduction of reforms, such as *glasnost* (openness regarding shortcomings) and *perestroika* (restructuring of the economy and government). Soviet rapprochement with the West caused Cuba to become a costly burden, both economically and politically. As Cold War hostilities dissipated and the Soviet domestic crisis deepened, its diminished ability and willingness to continue subsidizing Cuba led to an appreciable reduction in assistance. Further, as Cuba's trade partners began to demand hard currency payments for imported goods, Cuba was forced to borrow from Western European banks to stay afloat, thereby accruing a substantial foreign debt (Kryzanek 1995:107).

The collapse of communist regimes throughout Eastern Europe and the dissolution of the Soviet Union deprived Cuba of its primary trading partners, its source of economic and technical assistance, and its long-time benefactor. As one observer has noted, Cuba faced a "double blockade"— besides the long-standing embargo imposed by the United States, the subsequent loss of Soviet-bloc assistance (Kryzanek 1995:108). Ironically, with Castro left to fend for himself, Cuba could be considered truly "independent" for the first time since formally gaining independence a century ago.

Despite his intense criticism of Gorbachev's reforms and his oft-heard refrain of "socialism or death," Castro gradually adopted a more pragmatic approach to maintaining the revolution. For example, in an effort to attract much-needed hard currency, Castro allowed for the "dollarization" of the Cuban economy, thus enabling people to trade in U.S. dollars. In 2004, in reaction to the Bush adminstration's stringent adherence to the embargo, Castro issued an edict forbidding U.S. dollars to be sent to Cuban citizens. He has also sought out foreign investment, establishing joint ventures with a variety of foreign firms to stimulate the economy. In particular, Cuba banked on a revitalization of the once-vibrant tourist industry to keep the economy, and possibly the regime itself, afloat. This approach had its drawbacks, however, as the influx of tourists (and their dollars, euros, and pounds) has no doubt exacerbated inequalities and the sense of deprivation felt by many Cubans. This proved especially troubling for Cuba's youth, who face bleak prospects with few opportunities and who lack the previous generation's strong emotional attachment to Castro and the revolution. The continued escape of Cubans to Florida and islands in the Caribbean and the increase of prostitution (sex tourism) among Cuban youth and even professionals trying to supplement meager incomes are equally disturbing.

Castro has already defied the odds by surviving amid the collapse of the Soviet Empire. As the Cuban people are asked to endure further austerity measures, however, other Latin American economies are showing signs of vitality. It seems apparent that Castro's future and that of the revolution will depend upon his ability to revive the economy and to generate resources to provide additional opportunities for the people.

Cuba's regional influence has declined dramatically as Castro struggles to maintain his grip over the country. Cuba's post-Soviet decline has, for the foreseeable future, discredited the Marxist alternative in Latin America. Nevertheless, for much of the past four-plus decades, Castro and Cuba have played an active role in the region. The idea that Cuba was obliged to "export the revolution" led to support for guerrilla movements in a variety of Latin American (and Third World) countries, including Argentina, Chile, Colombia, El Salvador, Grenada, Guatemala, Nicaragua, and Venezuela. The Cuban Revolution served as both inspiration and model to groups that viewed dependent capitalism and U.S. hegemony as the principal causes of Latin America's "underdevelopment."

*   *   *

Castro's relevance during the heyday of the Cuban Revolution is best illustrated by the response he provoked throughout the region. For example, U.S. policy toward Latin America after 1959 was focused primarily on preventing a "second Cuba." The Alliance for Progress was designed to stimulate development in an attempt to ameliorate conditions in which communist insurgency could flourish. After the death of John F. Kennedy, U.S. policy became more militaristic, and substantial assistance was provided to Latin American militaries to bolster their capacity to crush guerrilla movements.

The U.S. intervention in the Dominican Republic in 1965 is illustrative of this new approach. When a civil war broke out between "Constitutionalist" forces seeking to reinstate the popularly elected government of Juan Bosch, who had been ousted from power after winning the 1962 election, and "Loyalist" forces opposed to Bosch's reformist government, the Lyndon Johnson administration sent 23,000 U.S. Marines to Santo Domingo to aid the Loyalists, with the pretense that the Dominican Republic was in danger of falling under communist control. With the defeat of the pro-Bosch forces, the post-Trujillo experiment with democracy ended, and former Trujillo protégé Joaquín Balaguer took power and established a highly centralized authoritarian regime, which was friendly to the United States, that held power until 1978. Balaguer returned to the presidency in 1986, was reelected in 1990, and, as Kevin Yelvington discusses in Chapter 9, won again in 1994 amid charges of fraud.

Subsequent U.S. interventions in Chile in 1973, in Grenada in 1983, and in El Salvador and Nicaragua throughout the 1980s further reflected the U.S. preoccupation with containing leftist movements and regimes influenced by Castro and the Cuban Revolution. Whether through the CIA

Juan Bosch (center, with tie) appearing at the
Universidad Iberoamericana, Santo Domingo, in 1990.

(as in Chile); direct military intervention (as in Grenada); or providing technical assistance, military training and equipment, or economic aid to governments (as in El Salvador and Jamaica) or to counterrevolutionary groups (as in Nicaragua), the United States actively opposed efforts to promote radical change. A similar response came from Latin American elites who, when civilian regimes proved incapable, often turned to the military to confront the threat of Cuban-style revolution.

The Rise of Bureaucratic Authoritarianism

The Military Returns to Power

The Cuban Revolution alerted Latin American leaders and elites, as well as U.S. policymakers, to the potential for further radical change within the region. The Cuban example emboldened revolutionary movements, as Latin American societies became increasingly polarized. Civilian leaders were caught between powerful opposing forces: those on the left, frustrated by the slow pace of reform and demanding radical change, and those on the right, seeking to preserve order and forestall change. The fact that both sides were willing to utilize force to achieve their objectives was even more problematic, leading to an escalation in violence and a forceful response from national militaries. During the 1960s–1980s, many of the Spanish-speaking countries, as well as Brazil, endured further descents into authoritarianism. Among the more notable exceptions were Colombia, Costa Rica, and Venezuela, where democratically elected civilian leaders retained power and direct military rule was averted.

Even in the Commonwealth Caribbean, where most nations were attaining independence and establishing their own systems of Westminster-style parliamentary democracy during this period, democratic governments were imperiled or fell prey to authoritarianism. Increased political violence plagued St. Lucia and Jamaica, where several hundred people were killed prior to the 1980 election, and the collapse of liberal democracy led to military rule and the formation of one-party states in Guyana and Grenada, as well as in the former Dutch colony of Suriname (Stone 1985:15). An attempted coup launched by fundamentalist Muslim officers (the Jamaat-Al-Muslimeen) in Trinidad in 1990 suggests that although democracy has indeed "flourished" (Domínguez, Pastor, and Worrell 1993) in the Caribbean, significant threats remain.

A variety of factors contributed to the wave of military coups that occurred in Central and South America during this period. Most were precipitated, at least in part, by the military's perception that the existing civilian leadership was incapable of containing rising levels of violence. Economic stagnation was also a decisive factor in some coups, with a lack of development considered by many military leaders to be a catalyst of guerrilla insurgency and urban rebellion. Having received extensive military and academic instruction at institutions such as Brazil's Superior War College, Peru's Center for Higher Military Studies, and U.S. training centers, many officers were confident of their ability to preserve order and promote national development.

Actions taken by civilian leaders to mobilize the masses also provoked military interventions. In Brazil and Chile, leftist leaders appealed directly to the masses with promises of reform in attempts to build support. In the end, these actions stirred fears among the upper and middle classes of a "threat from below," leading them to appeal to the military to oust João Goulart in Brazil, as well as Salvador Allende in Chile, who was the first popularly elected socialist in Latin American history. In addition, these coups and a number of others can be attributed to threats, real or perceived, to the corporate interests of the military. Budget cuts, meddling in internal military affairs (such as promotions and the determination of strategies and missions), and plans to arm popular militias were viewed as detrimental to military interests.

The fact that many Latin American countries reverted to authoritarian military rule during the 1960s and 1970s should not surprise those familiar with the history of the area. The Iberian colonial powers imbued their New World possessions with a strong military tradition. Since independence, praetorianism (a form of militarism in which the armed forces consider their corporate interests to include control of the state) has been, in most cases, the rule rather than the exception. The 1964 Brazilian coup, however, introduced a new form of military government that was very different from previous periods of military rule. For example, in contrast to the pattern of *caudillo* rule characteristic of the early postindependence era, in which individual leaders ruled in a highly personalistic manner, the new "bureaucratic authoritarian" regimes were governed by the military institution with the assistance of key civilian technocrats, such as economists, on whose expertise the military relied (O'Donnell 1973). These new governments exhibited a much higher level of professionalization, as a result of extensive training and education, than the early *caudillo* dictatorships.

A New Pattern

Bureaucratic authoritarianism also differed from more recent instances of military rule. Whereas national militaries had previously played a more moderating role behind the scenes, intervening briefly to replace an unacceptable civilian government, bureaucratic authoritarian regimes pursued a much more ambitious agenda. Guided by the "national security doctrine" (analyzed by Paul Zagorski in Chapter 5), military leaders viewed internal leftist subversion—rather than external aggression—as the greatest security threat confronting their societies. Acting under the premise that such subversion was fueled by a lack of social, political, and economic development, military leaders, bolstered by increased professionalization and the policymaking expertise provided by civilian technocrats, adopted a greatly expanded role that entailed long-term institutional rule as opposed to the brief interventions of the past.

Military leaders called for wholesale restructuring of their countries' economies and particularly their political systems, which they deemed necessary to address the root causes of instability effectively. The technocrats advocated economic revitalization by attracting foreign investors who had the capital and technology Latin American countries needed. Both groups believed that foreign investment depended on military rulers' capacity to restore order and maintain an environment favorable to commercial interests.

The leaders of bureaucratic authoritarian regimes considered traditional politics to be one of the principal factors contributing to the high level of instability within Latin America. They viewed civilian leaders with disdain, judging most to be inefficient, corrupt, and absorbed in self-interest. Political parties were seen as divisive, with their actions mobilizing support for specific, narrow political agendas that served to polarize badly fragmented societies even further.

In their zeal to eliminate the causes of disorder and upheaval, bureaucratic authoritarian regimes curtailed political activity by banning political parties and many interest groups. As these regimes sought to demobilize society, student associations and other popular organizations were often targets of repression, and labor movements were suppressed to keep wages down, thereby appeasing foreign investors. With the exception of Peru, where the first phase of the military *docenio* (twelve-year period in power) was led by a reformist regime, most bureaucratic authoritarian governments were acting on behalf of elite interests in guarding against all challenges to the status quo.

The Cases of Brazil, Argentina, and Chile

This pattern is best illustrated by events in the three most conspicuous cases of bureaucratic authoritarian rule: Brazil, Argentina, and Chile. The 1964 Brazilian coup that ousted João Goulart introduced this new form of military rule to Latin America. Threatened by Goulart's proposed reforms, the elite and key sectors of the middle class supported the military, content to sacrifice certain freedoms to achieve an environment of stability needed for economic growth. For a time, the military regime delivered on its pledge of order and progress. Bolstered by intensive industrialization and expanding exports, the Brazilian economy soon began to experience remarkable growth. Between 1968 and 1974, average annual growth exceeded 10 percent, with a rate of 14 percent in 1973. During this period, referred to as the "Brazilian Miracle," foreign investment soared, and Brazil appeared to be emerging as an economic superpower.

Brazil's economic program, however, was undermined by several inherent weaknesses. First, the country was almost completely reliant on imported sources of energy. When the Organization of Petroleum Exporting Countries (OPEC) announced its sharp increase in oil prices in 1973, rather than scale back, Brazil's leaders forged ahead with their plans for large-scale industrialization and infrastructural development. They were, therefore, compelled to engage in massive borrowing to cover increased energy costs. The government expected the economic windfall to cover Brazil's outstanding loans, but the Miracle wore down under the burden of debt-led development. The second oil shock in the late 1970s further increased Brazil's energy costs and sparked a severe recession in the industrialized world that had devastating repercussions for Brazil. Although export markets contracted, rising interest rates sharply increased the country's debt payments, thus ending the Brazilian Miracle.

Concurrently, opposition to the military regime had mounted. The Miracle produced substantial growth, yet the distribution of this new wealth was skewed heavily toward foreign investors and the domestic elite. The vast majority of Brazil's population saw scant improvement in their standard of living. Hence, the Miracle exacerbated the already substantial gap between rich and poor and frustrated those who did not share in its benefits. The harsh treatment of the labor movement, which organized strikes and demonstrations to protest government policies, also heightened tensions and opposition to the regime. But most devastating to the military rulers was their inability to sustain the Miracle and counteract the economic decline of the late 1970s through the early 1980s. Popular protests shook the regime as spiraling inflation and an unmanageable debt eroded the support of the middle and upper classes—those who had initially sought military action to "save" the society. As opposition broadened, the military allowed a gradual political opening (*abertura*) that culminated in the transition to civilian rule through a military-supervised presidential election in 1985.

In contrast with Brazil's experience, the Argentine military was unable to maintain control of the transition process. Although it possesses one of the highest levels of socioeconomic development in Latin America, Argentina has experienced considerable economic and social instability and since 1930 has been subject to repeated military interventions in national politics. Much of this turmoil has revolved around the legacy of populist dictator Juan Perón and the influence of *peronismo*, which could not be eliminated despite his ouster in 1955. In fact, efforts to suppress *peronismo* only seemed to bolster its followers. After two civilian governments failed to eradicate *peronismo*, the military seized power in 1966 and established its version of Brazil's bureaucratic authoritarian regime.

Efforts to demobilize politicized groups, such as students and labor, the most ardent supporters of *peronismo*, failed, and violence escalated. The ineffectiveness of these efforts compelled the military to return power to civilians in 1973, a process that culminated in the return to power of Juan Perón after eighteen years of exile. With the Peronist movement deeply divided, however, even Perón was unable to stem the tide of violence and economic decline. His death in 1974 and the disastrous rule of his second wife and vice president, Isabel Perón, led the military to seize power again in 1976.

This time the military was determined to take forceful action to stabilize Argentina. In response to an increasing level of violence, the military embarked on a ruthless campaign of terror against urban guerrillas (Montoneros), suspected sympathizers, and the Argentine left in general. Matched in its intensity and brutality only by the actions of the Chilean security forces, Argentina's "war against subversion," as it was referred to by the military, resulted in the arrest, detention, torture, murder, or "disappearance" of tens of thousands of people. The "Dirty War," as it has been called by others, caused Argentina to be condemned by much of the world community and engendered widespread domestic opposition.

This opposition, coupled with the regime's inability to revive the economy, led Argentina's military leaders to search for alternative ways to legitimize their rule. In 1982, in an attempt to divert attention from domestic problems and appeal to the public's sense of nationalism, the military launched an invasion of the British-held Falkland (Malvinas) Islands, a small group of islands off its coast over which Argentina maintained a long-standing claim. Badly underestimating Britain's resolve to keep control of the islands and greatly overestimating the effectiveness of its own forces, the Argentine military was dealt a humiliating defeat that led it to relinquish power in 1983, with little control over the transition to civilian rule.

Chile's descent into bureaucratic authoritarianism began with the electoral victory of socialist Salvador Allende in 1970. By leading Chile down the "peaceful road to socialism," Allende introduced policies that engendered intense opposition and further polarized the deeply divided society. As the country fell into a period of severe economic and social crisis, the Chilean armed forces—with the backing of the upper and middle classes and a degree of U.S. support—overthrew Allende in 1973 in a bloody coup that cost Allende his life and led to around 5,000 additional deaths in its immediate aftermath.

This forceful military intervention, which was completely at odds with Chile's long tradition of stable, democratic, constitutional rule, led to the formation of a bureaucratic authoritarian regime under General Augusto Pinochet. Pinochet abolished political parties, closed the National Congress, and embarked on a brutal campaign to suppress the left. The Pinochet regime, with the assistance of civilian technocrats trained at the University of Chicago, adopted a free-market approach, which opened the Chilean economy to foreign investment and competition. The initial results were problematic for the working classes, because unemployment rose while wages and the overall standard of living fell. The national debt skyrocketed as Chile borrowed heavily to stimulate development and the restructuring of the economy. Ultimately, the program paid dividends, and Chile enjoyed steady growth after the early 1980s.

Despite Chile's impressive economic resurgence under Pinochet, opposition to his rule mounted. International criticism focused on the regime's dismal human rights record, including the pervasive use of torture and the "disappearances" of union officials, student leaders, and others deemed threatening to national security. On the domestic front, widespread protests and strikes led to a 1988 referendum to determine whether Pinochet would continue as Chile's president for another term. In a stunning turn of events, Pinochet suffered a decisive defeat, paving the way for a return to democratic civilian rule in 1990.

The Demise of Military Control

Military disengagement from power and the demise of bureaucratic authoritarian rule in Brazil, Argentina, and Chile can be attributed to three factors. First, the ruthlessness with which military regimes suppressed internal opposition generated substantial criticism and condemnation. Whereas international criticism at times proved troublesome for the regimes, internal domestic protests—which, in turn, tended to provoke even greater levels of repression—severely undermined regime support. For example, as Susan Tiano shows in Chapter 10, the Madres de la Plaza de Mayo have been influential in bringing international attention to human rights abuses in Argentina.

A second factor prompting the military's "return to the barracks" was the generally poor economic performance of their regimes. For example, despite intense criticism of its civilian predecessors, the Argentine military's performance was dismal. Even in Brazil, which experienced a remarkable period of growth, the economy's long-term performance was little better than that under civilian rule. Only Chile experienced much success, although critics maintain that it was the result of massive borrowing and that the social and political costs were enormous. In any case, the poor overall performance of the Argentine and Brazilian militaries led to their retreat from power, and even Chile's relative economic success was not enough for the public to prolong Pinochet's tenure.

A final factor contributing to the demise of bureaucratic authoritarianism was the perceived damage poor performance did to the military's reputation. Without question, the image of most militaries was tarnished, perhaps nowhere more severely than in Argentina. Not only did the regime there fail to revive the economy, but the level of repression during the Dirty War reached horrific levels. Moreover, the military thoroughly discredited itself during the Falklands debacle. In general, concerns that perpetuating its rule could spark the outbreak of civil strife or exacerbate factional disputes and potentially divide the military itself brought about the withdrawal of the military from power and the transition to civilian rule.

■ Democratization

Obstacles and Challenges

As military regimes throughout Latin America relinquished power, various attempts to promote the spread of democratic government were undertaken during the early 1980s. A decade later—following the U.S.-led overthrow of the People's Revolutionary Government in Grenada and of Panamanian dictator General Manuel Noriega, the election of Patricio Aylwin to succeed General Pinochet in Chile, and the election (and subsequent restoration to power) of Jean-Bertrand Aristide in Haiti—the Castro regime in Cuba stood as the sole remaining authoritarian dictatorship in the Americas. Clearly, movement toward more open, competitive, pluralistic forms of politics had taken place. The ultimate results of this transition, however, have been the subject of much debate. Whereas some observers have expressed optimism concerning the sustainability of "third wave" democratic regimes throughout Latin America, others counter that the current era is merely part of an ongoing cyclical alternation between democratic and authoritarian tendencies. An analysis of Latin American democracies over the past two decades reveals a decidedly mixed record, replete with examples of both "progress and decay" (Diamond et al. 1999:vii). Has sufficient progress been made to enable elected civilian leaders to surmount the considerable obstacles to the consolidation of democratic rule? If not, then what lies ahead?

The return to elected civilian rule was welcomed enthusiastically in societies weary of the harshness of authoritarian military rule. The opening of political systems, however, came precisely at the time national economies were experiencing great difficulties. The profound socioeconomic crisis that enveloped the region during the lost decade of the 1980s—the most severe since the time of the Great Depression—seriously hindered efforts to promote development and the ability of newly elected civilian leaders to meet popular expectations, which had risen to unprecedented levels. In addition, the authority and integrity of some national governments were severely undermined by their inability to maintain order, to enforce laws, and to curb political violence. The perceived "failure" of the new governments raised serious questions about the sustainability of democracy within highly mobilized yet frustrated societies.

One of the most daunting challenges that faced emerging democratic regimes across the region during the 1980s and 1990s was the explosion of illicit narcotics trafficking, fostering an environment of corruption and violence that compromised democratic institutions and legal systems in a number of societies. The drug trade has grown into a multibillion-dollar industry that generates more revenue than most legal exports and employs tens of thousands of people. No country can escape the expansive reach of the drug trade, serving as a producer (Peru, Mexico, Jamaica), a transshipment point (Central America, the Bahamas, and other Caribbean islands), a money laundering center (Panama, the Cayman Islands), or a source of drug consumers (the United States and Europe). Colombia, however, has been the undisputed center of the drug trade and has exhibited its most deleterious impact. The power of the Colombian cartels that have dominated the industry rivals that of the state. Corruption has become endemic, and at times violence has virtually paralyzed the country. Drug lords were implicated in the 1985 massacre of Supreme Court justices, as well as in the assassinations of presidential candidates, journalists, judges, and government officials who threaten their interests. The government's inability to curb narcotics-related violence and crime has had a devastating impact on Colombian society, severely undermining public confidence and eroding the legitimacy of its democratic system. Despite the massive infusion of U.S. aid to combat the narcotrafficking, drug eradication and interdiction efforts have met with limited long-term success. The failure of supply-side measures suggests that until the demand for illicit narcotics in major markets, including the United States and Europe, is significantly reduced, the war on drugs in Colombia and throughout the Americas is far from over.

Yet another challenge during the era of democratization has been the threat posed by guerrilla insurgencies. This threat was most pronounced in Central America, where governments in El Salvador and Guatemala faced left-wing movements and the Sandinista regime in Nicaragua battled a counterrevolutionary group, the Contras, supported by the United States. In neither El Salvador nor Guatemala were the rebels able to seize national power. In El Salvador, the Farabundo Martí National Liberation Front (FMLN) fought to a stalemate with U.S.-supported government forces during a twelve-year-long civil war that claimed some 75,000 lives. In El Salvador and Guatemala, the prolonged conflicts and allegations of widespread human rights violations—mainly, although not exclusively, attributed to government forces—did much to hinder national development and to polarize society. In Nicaragua, while the Contras lacked sufficient popular support to challenge the Sandinistas realistically for direct control, their presence did force the government to divert scarce resources away from the economy and badly needed social programs. Ongoing civil strife and the government's inability to fulfill popular expectations contributed to the Sandinistas' electoral defeat in 1990 and the end of the Nicaraguan Revolution.

Colombia and Peru have also faced significant guerrilla threats. Both the Revolutionary Armed Forces of Colombia (FARC) and the National Liberation Army (ELN) have violently opposed Colombia's civilian government and have forged alliances of convenience with narcotraffickers to fund their operations. Colombian leaders have struggled to address this dual threat, with little success. Large areas in southern Colombia have been under the de facto control of insurgent groups, and escalating violence and lawlessness have underscored the debility of the state. The threat of renewed conflict amid an on-again, off-again peace process has placed the country's prospects for future democratic consolidation in peril. In contrast, the government of former president Alberto Fujimori in Peru achieved considerable success in reducing political violence and containing guerrilla insurgency. Throughout the 1980s, the Maoist Sendero Luminoso (Shining

President Daniel Ortega of the ruling Sandinista Party
addressing crowds at a rally in Managua, Nicaragua, 1990.

Path), a group committed to the radical restructuring of Peruvian society
and the formation of a communist state, carried out a campaign of economic warfare and terrorism that did much to undermine the credibility of
Peru's civilian leadership. However, with the strong backing of the military,
Fujimori took the offensive and set out to crush the movement. Following
the capture of its top leader, Abimael Guzmán, in September 1992, and subsequently other top leaders, Sendero's once extensive power has been
reduced substantially, as has the threat it poses to the Peruvian state.
Similarly, Fujimori's decision to use force in ending a four-month hostage-
taking crisis at the residence of the Japanese ambassador in April 1997
demonstrated his firm resolve in dealing with the guerrilla threat and all but
eliminated the Tupac Amaru Revolutionary Movement (MRTA). Although
the threat posed by the Shining Path and other rebel groups in the region
has diminished considerably in the post–Cold War era, Latin American
leaders continue to struggle to ameliorate the socioeconomic conditions
that have sparked rebellion in the past.

As Richard Harper and Alfred Cuzán demonstrate in Chapter 6, the
precipitous economic decline experienced throughout the region during the
lost decade was a particularly difficult obstacle for democratic leaders to
overcome. In part, the region's economic malaise during the 1980s was the
result of ill-conceived policies pursued in the aftermath of OPEC's massive

oil price increases in 1973 and 1979, although other factors beyond the control of Latin American governments also were present. Rather than taking measures to slow the pace of industrialization and development, the region's governments, many under military control, pressed forward. To pay the rising costs of imported oil and to finance developmental projects, they began to borrow from abroad. Latin America's total foreign debt surpassed $400 billion during the 1980s; Brazil, followed by Mexico and Argentina, incurred the largest national debts. The level of indebtedness within some of the region's smaller countries, on a per capita basis, was also of great concern.

All sides had expected continued growth to enable the borrowers to meet debt payments without difficulty. Conditions deteriorated dramatically with the onset of global recession in the early 1980s, however, as the interest rates on outstanding loans rose sharply, and declining demand for traditional Latin American exports led to drops in commodity prices and export earnings. Ironically, in the early 1980s, falling oil prices created difficulties for some of the region's main oil exporters, including Venezuela, Trinidad and Tobago, and Mexico—with the latter announcing in the summer of 1982 ("the Mexico weekend") that it was unable to service its debt.

A number of other countries, including Brazil, Argentina, and Venezuela, soon followed Mexico's lead. To prevent countries from defaulting on their loans, the international financial community responded to the mounting debt crisis by renegotiating debts and extending additional loans. Countries fell further and further into debt, which underscored the weakness and vulnerability of Latin America's dependent economies and generated enormous pressure on the region's fledgling democratic governments.

With rising debt payments taking up a larger share of export earnings, Latin American leaders were faced with the difficult task of balancing debt payments and stimulating economic growth to provide basic services to increasingly frustrated domestic populations. As commercial lenders grew wary of extending further credit and both international and domestic investors became unwilling to sink capital into stagnant economies plagued by high inflation, Latin American leaders eventually found they lacked funds to repay loans or to spur growth. With more capital flowing out of their countries—through debt payments and capital flight—than was coming in, many leaders were compelled, however reluctantly, to negotiate with the International Monetary Fund (IMF) to receive emergency loans. However, such assistance often proved as onerous as the debt crisis itself because it was conditioned on the structural adjustment or "austerity" programs of the neoliberal economic agenda pursued as part of the "Washington Consensus."

Economic Restructuring

Structural adjustment programs were designed to stabilize Latin American economies by requiring measures to reduce inflation, including eliminating price controls and limiting wage increases; the privatization of state-owned firms; a reduction in state subsidies and public-sector spending and employment; and incentives to attract foreign investment. Although such austerity measures were deemed critical for the long-term development of Latin American economies, many elected leaders feared that imposing them would be tantamount to political suicide. "IMF riots" were commonplace during the 1980s and into the 1990s, as popular protests broke out in Brazil, the Dominican Republic, Guyana, and Jamaica, among others, in response to rising unemployment and price increases on basic goods that were mandated by austerity programs. In most cases, governments were unable to implement the programs fully because of public outrage over higher prices, job losses, and sharp declines in social spending. An explosion of demonstrations and violence in Venezuela in 1989, sparked by the unexpected implementation of austerity measures, revealed the depth of popular discontent (Hillman 1994). These actions also underscored the fact that even in one of Latin America's most affluent, stable countries, democracy was somewhat fragile and far from being fully consolidated.

The sense of crisis that pervaded the international financial community largely subsided amid indications of economic recovery during the 1990s. However, many countries remained deeply in debt, and this—coupled with declining export revenues, significant capital flight, and fiscal mismanagement—contributed to deteriorating economic conditions across the region into the early twenty-first century. The magnitude of the problems was best exemplified by the situation in Argentina, whose stunning default and economic collapse in 2001 sparked renewed concerns about the sustainability of fledgling democratic governments in Latin America. Argentina's plight was widely viewed as an indictment of the neoliberal policies zealously implemented under former president Carlos Menem. Although the policies initially achieved some short-term success in curbing inflation and stimulating growth, the country's debt continued to mount, unemployment skyrocketed, and the number of people living in poverty exceeded 50 percent.

Once viewed as a model of neoliberal reform, Argentina erupted in turmoil, as popular frustration with the unfulfilled promises of such reform (sometimes referred to as "reform fatigue") fed massive protests that led to the resignation of President Fernando de la Rua as well as three short-term successors. Bolivia's President Gonzalo Sánchez de Lozada resigned in October 2003, following protests against an IMF-mandated tax increase in February of that year and a plan to export valuable natural gas reserves in September and October 2003. The protests were violently suppressed by government forces. Although the turmoil that engulfed Argentina and

Bolivia did not spread to other parts of the region as some had feared, the experiences of both countries underscored the profound social and political repercussions of economic reform during the neoliberal era in Latin America.

The Fragility of Emerging Democracies

Over the past two decades, a number of peaceful transfers of power have occurred, and in most countries historically active militaries have largely avoided overt involvement in national politics. Nevertheless, the fragility of democratic civilian rule in Latin America has been evident. In many cases, popular perceptions of democracy and of democratic leaders have been severely undermined by deteriorating socioeconomic conditions and pervasive corruption and fraud. The deleterious impact of neoliberal economic policies also has served to debilitate key democratic institutions and to facilitate the emergence of populist leaders. Elsewhere, the region's strong authoritarian tradition and powerful opposition to democratic reforms among some conservative groups have been significant obstacles to the consolidation of emergent democratic regimes.

In Haiti, for example, President Jean-Bertrand Aristide was deposed just months into his first term by military forces acting on behalf of the nation's small but powerful elite. Thousands were killed or fled the country

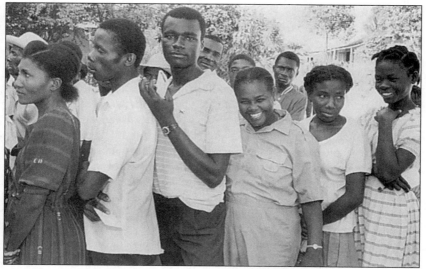

UN Photo 177243/Milton Grant

The people of Haiti vote in a democratic presidential election for the first time in their history on December 16, 1990.

in a wave of violence following the coup d'état, as the military and para-military "attachés" sought to rid Haiti of Aristide's supporters. Only after intense pressure and the threat of a U.S. invasion did the military relent, allowing Aristide to return to Haiti to complete his term. As Irwin Stotzky (1997:42) has observed, both Aristide and his successor, René Preval, "faced a multitude of seemingly intractable obstacles" that impeded efforts to institutionalize Haiti's nascent democratic system.

Among the most problematic of these obstacles were the deep divisions that continued to permeate Haitian society. Following disputed local and parliamentary elections in 1997, in which an estimated 5 percent of registered voters participated, the government was paralyzed by gridlock. Subsequent elections scheduled for late 1998 were delayed until May 2000. In the interim, legislators whose terms had officially expired were dismissed, and the president and prime minister ruled by decree. While turnout in May 2000 approached 60 percent, the credibility of the electoral process was compromised by irregularities that led all main opposition groups to boycott the November 26, 2000, presidential and Senate elections that were dominated by Aristide and his supporters. Aristide's return to power sparked an upsurge of political violence and disorder, and by late 2003 opposition protests had intensified and spread throughout the country. With much of Haiti no longer under government control, Aristide fled into exile on February 29, 2004. Although the circumstances surrounding Aristide's departure and U.S. involvement are in dispute, it is clear that Haitian society remains deeply polarized, and there is little to suggest that the institutional framework needed to sustain a democratic system is in place. Interim Prime Minister Gerard Latortue faces enormous challenges in trying to stabilize the country and prepare for new elections, which he has stated will allow for a new government to take office by early February 2006.

In Peru, Fujimori's frustration with what he perceived to be an inefficient, obstructionist legislature dominated by corrupt party leaders led to an *autogolpe* (self-coup) in April 1992, in which he suspended the constitution, closed the national congress, and began to rule by decree.[1] The election of a new combined legislature and constituent assembly, complete with a pro-Fujimori majority, resulted in a new constitution, approved in a national referendum, that allowed Fujimori to seek and win reelection in 1995. Although strongly supported by a public tired of violence and economic decline, this move toward "presidential authoritarianism" (Kryzanek 1995:84) demonstrated a disdain for democratic institutions and principles that was underscored by Fujimori's controversial pursuit of an unprecedented third consecutive term. On April 9, 2000, he defeated several opposition candidates led by Alejandro Toledo, whose decision to boycott the runoff election due to alleged irregularities in the first round enabled Fujimori to retain power. However, within months, Fujimori had resigned and fled to Japan in the wake of a bribery scandal involving his closest adviser and intelligence chief, Vladimiro Montesinos, and amid allegations of corruption and human rights violations under his rule.

The legacy of the Fujimori era has cast a long shadow over the current Peruvian government, led by Alejandro Toledo following his victory in the April 2001 election. In pursuing one of the most extensive privatization programs in Latin America, Fujimori used the proceeds to build support through clientelism, bolstering his populist credentials in the short term at the expense of long-term development. His personalist style and the increased centralization of power in the executive served to marginalize further key democratic institutions, including the legislature, the judiciary, and traditional political parties that had been in decline, dating back to Fujimori's surprising rise to the presidency as an independent. Within this context, Toledo has struggled to meet popular expectations and to build support both for his government and for the democratic alternative in general. His approval ratings have plummeted, however, and optimism that accompanied his victory has given way to cynicism and frustration with the slow pace of reforms and the campaign promises of more jobs and improved living conditions that remain largely unfulfilled.

Widespread corruption—at times reaching the highest levels of government—and electoral fraud have plagued some political systems, diminishing faith not only in individual leaders but in democracy itself. In Mexico, it is widely held that the ruling PRI rigged elections to maintain the monopoly on power it held from 1929 until 2000. For example, the 1988 presidential election has been cited as one of the dirtiest in Mexican history, when opposition candidate Cuauhtémoc Cárdenas was denied an apparent victory over the PRI's Carlos Salinas. Despite a 1995 agreement between the PRI and the main opposition parties "to guarantee the credibility of future elections," a number of subsequent state and local races were also marred by allegations of fraud by opposition parties as well as international observers (Peeler 1998:124). However, the PRI's hold on power came to an end in the aftermath of the July 2, 2000, election in which opposition presidential candidate Vicente Fox swept to victory, as did his National Action Party in the legislative contest, giving hope that a more open, competitive political system would evolve.

While some significant progress has been made in Mexico, widespread poverty and illiteracy, particularly in rural areas, have left fertile ground for clientelism, coercion, intimidation, and vote-buying that compromise efforts to institutionalize democratic procedures and values. Despite being deeply discredited by its defeat in 2000, as well as by criticism that it had become excessively centralized and exclusionary, the PRI remains the largest and best organized party organization in Mexico. While it has done little to modify its program or to "reinvent itself as a responsible party capable of providing Mexico with clean, innovative leadership" (Grayson 2004:81), the PRI reasserted its status as the dominant force in the Chamber of Deputies and has been able to obstruct a host of Fox's initiatives, after soundly defeating the PAN during the 2003 congressional midterm elections. With a series of gubernatorial and key state and municipal elections to be contested during the latter part of 2004 and 2005, the PRI has the opportunity to position itself to regain the presidency in 2006.[2] In light of the poor turnout for the 2003 elections (less than 42 percent) and a stagnant economy, the outcome of that election—and the credibility of the electoral process—will have a significant impact on the prospects for Mexico's democratic transition.

Similarly, the 1990 and 1994 presidential elections in the Dominican Republic, in which incumbent Joaquín Balaguer was narrowly reelected, were tainted by the dubious performance of electoral institutions and by charges of fraud. In fact, the manipulation was so blatant in 1994 that Balaguer agreed to hold new elections (in which he would not be eligible to run) roughly halfway through his term. Although the election of Leonel Fernández in 1996, followed by that of Hipólito Mejía in 2000, and Fernández's reelection in 2004, in what were widely regarded as free and fair contests, would appear to be causes for optimism, confidence in the institutions of democracy has been challenged by economic turmoil and remains tenuous in the Dominican Republic.

In Brazil and Venezuela, popular support for democracy and democratic institutions was shaken by the removal of popularly elected presidents in the early 1990s. Brazil's Fernando Collor de Mello, the country's first directly elected civilian leader since 1960, took office in 1990 pledging to fight corruption. By 1992, Collor de Mello had resigned after being impeached amid allegations of financial misconduct. Venezuela's long-standing democracy was challenged by two coup attempts against the government of Carlos Andrés Pérez in 1992. Popular opposition to Pérez, stemming from charges of corruption and the imposition of harsh austerity measures, had grown so great that the leaders (particularly the current president, Hugo Chávez) of the initial coup attempt on February 4 were widely supported. Pérez was removed from office in 1993, accused of misusing funds, and was ultimately tried and convicted. The demise of the Pérez government further undermined popular perceptions of democratic rule in a country where economic decline and elite domination have severely eroded support for traditional parties. Although the images of both the Brazilian and Venezuelan political systems were tarnished by these events, it is significant that in both instances democratic processes were employed successfully to remove the leaders (Hillman 1994:151).

Over the past decade, both Brazil and Venezuela have experienced significant political transitions that have attracted considerable regional and international interest. In Brazil, Fernando Henrique Cardoso was elected in October 1994, and introduced a package of neoliberal reforms that helped to stabilize the economy, drastically reducing inflation and sparking growth until the onset of the Asian crisis. However, crushing debt, widespread poverty, and deep inequities continued to plague the country, and in 2002 Brazilians turned to Luiz Inácio Lula da Silva, a former labor union leader and candidate of the Brazilian Workers' Party (PT), whose previous attempts at the presidency had been undermined by radical rhetoric that unnerved the domestic elite as well as potential foreign investors. However, since taking office, President da Silva has pursued a decidedly moderate, pragmatic approach to economic policymaking in seeking an alternative path between neoliberalism and statist development. While he has continued to advocate for change, da Silva clearly recognizes the need to balance Brazil's obligation to honor its international fiscal debt with his pledge to address its "social debt" at home. This latter objective has proved elusive thus far, as a stagnant economy has prevented the government from implementing the full range of antipoverty programs that were envisioned by policymakers and eagerly anticipated by the mass public. Nevertheless, the fact that da Silva has managed to avoid unduly provoking the elites and that, consequently, Brazilian society is not as deeply polarized as many had feared bodes well for the future.

Venezuela, in contrast, has grown increasingly polarized in recent

Courtesy of the Brazilian Chamber of Commerce, Great Britain

Luiz Inácio Lula da Silva, president of Brazil, exemplifies the new type of populist leader in Latin America.

years. In 1993, independent candidate Rafael Caldera was elected president, marking the demise of the traditional political party system and the "pacted" system of elite agreements that had dominated national politics for some thirty-five years. However, Caldera received a tenuous mandate, winning just over 30 percent of the vote in a contest marred by an abstention rate exceeding 40 percent, and his ability to govern was compromised by conflict with the opposition-controlled Congress (Coppedge 1996). This set the stage for the reemergence of Hugo Chávez, who seized upon popular frustration with the stagnant economy and what was widely perceived as a corrupt, exclusionary political system to win the 1998 election just six years after his attempt to oust the democratically elected Pérez government.

Chávez's rise to power is part of a much-discussed "leftward tilt" in Latin American politics, a trend that includes Lucio Gutiérrez in Ecuador, Néstor Kirchner in Argentina, and Lula da Silva in Brazil, among others. Unlike da Silva, who relied upon the well-established organizational apparatus of the PT to mobilize support, Chávez has eschewed political parties and other traditional intermediary organizations, in favor of direct populist appeals to build support among the disenfranchised masses. They see in Chávez someone who truly represents their interests, and with their support he was able to gain approval for the formation of a Constituent Assembly and subsequently for a new constitution that served to consolidate his

Hugo Chávez, president of Venezuela, uses the media in his television program "Aló presidente" to illustrate his "connection" with the general population of Venezuela.

power. In the process, Chávez has marginalized the traditional political elite and antagonized the middle and upper classes, deeply dividing Venezuelan society (Hillman 2004). The extent of this polarization was made apparent in April 2002, when a coalition of opposition groups temporarily ousted Chávez in a coup that many suggest had at least the tacit support of the United States. Although the coup was quickly reversed, the opposition continued its efforts to remove Chávez with a series of strikes and ultimately a recall referendum in August 2004, which was soundly defeated. While increased oil revenues have enabled Chávez to maintain his support, the lack of strong democratic institutions raises questions as to what form the Venezuelan political system will take if and when Chávez leaves office at the end of his term in 2006.

Despite the different leadership styles employed by da Silva and Chávez, numerous parallels have been drawn between the two, given their popularity among the masses, their pursuit of alternative developmental and political models, and the daunting challenges they face. In challenging the status quo, both they and their governments have been subject to intense regional and international scrutiny. The future of democracy in Brazil and in Venezuela may well have profound implications for the rest of Latin America.

For the current era of democratization to be sustained, some rather significant obstacles must be overcome. For example, elected civilian leaders throughout Latin America will have to deal with national military institutions that, despite generally inauspicious performances while in power, have traditionally enjoyed considerable autonomy, essentially comprising a "fourth branch" of government, and have played a very active political role. Democratic consolidation will require greater civilian control over the military, not an easy task given this traditional role. Moreover, civil-military relations have been tense in countries such as Argentina, where a number of barracks revolts have occurred since 1983; Chile, where General Pinochet remains a controversial and polarizing figure; Ecuador, where the current president, Lucio Gutiérrez, led a military coup ousting the elected president, Jamil Mahuad, in January 2000; Haiti, where past human rights abuses and the departure of Aristide in 2004 continue to be contentious issues; and Venezuela, where, despite reassignment, retirement, or resignation of high-ranking officials, divisions regarding assessment of the Chávez government continue in the middle ranks. Although few military leaders in the region are eager to return to power, the constitutional mandate to preserve order and stability and a long praetorian tradition raise the possibility of some form of military intervention if civilian leaders prove incapable of keeping the peace.

In many respects, Latin America will have to overcome its past to continue the process of democratic consolidation. Because of persistently low levels of institutionalization, many of the former Iberian colonies possess relatively weak foundations on which to establish stable, democratic political systems. A variety of factors have impeded institutional development, including the tradition of personalism, intense repression and demobilization practiced by bureaucratic authoritarian regimes, the imposition of neoliberal economic policies that have increased wealth among a few and increased poverty among many, the emergence of neopopulist leaders, and the inability of political parties and their leaders to fulfill popular expectations.

Even in the Commonwealth Caribbean, where strong political institutions and democratic structures were transplanted through British colonialism, the prospects for further consolidation are mixed. The Westminster model of parliamentary democracy, "Caribbeanized" to fit the regional context, now exhibits strong authoritarian features. Elitism and limited mass participation; pervasive patron clientelism; and the dominance of personalistic leaders such as Vere Bird (Antigua), Eugenia Charles (Dominica), Eric Gairy (Grenada), and Eric Williams (Trinidad) have limited democracy in practice (Payne 1993:71–72). Moreover, in a region where "democracy has been shown to be stable primarily where it is related to the establishment of concrete material gains for most of the population" (Grugel 1995:123), consolidation has been hindered by economic stagnation and deteriorating living standards. Popular confidence in democratic leaders and institutions has diminished, as evidenced by significant declines in electoral participation in a number of countries. A heightened sense of alienation and frustration pervades the region, particularly among the poor and the younger generation, contributing to rising levels of violence and emigration that threaten economic and political stability.

The emergence of leaders such as Fujimori and Chávez, who captured the imagination of frustrated electorates with direct, populist appeals independent of traditional parties, raises serious questions about the process of democratization in Latin America. The personalization and centralization of power, ostensibly as a means of addressing endemic socioeconomic and political problems more efficiently, has marginalized democratic institutions ranging from national legislatures to political parties, electoral agencies, and civic organizations. The tradition of powerful executives is deeply ingrained in Latin American political cultures, yet strengthening Latin American democracy will require measures to curtail the powers of the executive while bolstering those of the legislature and the judiciary as autonomous branches of government. Further, democracy must be deepened to transform the narrow, elitist rule that has long characterized Latin America.[3] This process may come about through the formation of increasing numbers of nongovernmental organizations, including neighborhood associations and peasant groups, to give voice to popular demands. Such demands also may be channeled through political parties and party systems, widely recognized as the key to stable, democratic rule.

Party Politics and Elections

The existence of formal democratic bodies, such as political parties and competitive elections, does not alone necessarily guarantee representative government (Edie 1991:48). Parties and elections perform critical functions, however, and are essential components of democratic systems. The resurgence of party politics and competitive elections during the 1980s, after sustained periods of repressive military rule throughout much of the region, engendered great optimism regarding the prospects for (re)democratization in Latin America.

However, recent trends have tempered such optimism. Declining rates of voter participation reflect mounting apathy and cynicism among electorates frustrated by the perceived ineffectiveness of democratically elected governments. Much of this anger has been directed toward traditional parties that have been viewed by many as corrupt, elite dominated, and unable or unwilling to address popular concerns. The precipitous drop in support experienced by such parties contributed to the rise of populist leaders such as Fujimori and Chávez and the formation of "delegative democracies," in which powerful executives dominate the political process (O'Donnell 1994). Constraints on institutional development, and particularly the marginalization of national legislative bodies and political parties, have led some to question the prospects for emerging democracies in Latin America, as well as those considered to be stable and well established. Indeed, Scott Mainwaring and Timothy Scully (1995:474) conclude that "without a reasonably institutionalized party system, the future of democracy is bleak, even if feckless democracies manage to stay in place."

Party politics in Latin America has its origin in the early postindependence era, when informal elite groups coalesced into Conservative and Liberal parties. Other types of parties began to appear in the more socioeconomically advanced Southern Cone countries during the late 1800s and early 1900s in response to the impact of modernization. The rise of an educated, politically aware middle class that sought access to the political process led to the formation of reformist parties, the most prominent being the Radical Civic Union in Argentina and the Colorado Party in Uruguay (McDonald and Ruhl 1989:6). As electorates diversified with industrialization, party systems expanded with the emergence of Marxist, nationalist-populist, and Christian Democratic organizations. In Jamaica and elsewhere in the British Caribbean, labor union activity during the tumultuous 1930s, coupled with the movement toward self-government, fostered the emergence of modern political party systems. The party-union bond was strong and represented "one pillar of the democratic order" in the

Anglophone Caribbean at the time of independence (Domínguez 1993:17).

Logically, there has been considerable diversity among Latin American parties in terms of ideological orientations, the structure of party systems, and the relative importance of parties in their respective systems. A significant degree of ideological variation was evident in the past, ranging from Marxism to fascism, although parties have become increasingly pragmatic as international relations have evolved in the aftermath of the Cold War. Latin American party systems have ranged from vibrant multiparty systems to stable two-party arrangements to authoritarian one-party states to cases where no viable parties exist.

Another area of divergence lies in the nature of the functions Latin American parties perform. While some may resemble those typically carried out by North American or Western European parties (recruit new members, aggregate and articulate interests, develop programs, and select candidates to compete for office), Latin American parties also serve a number of other purposes. For example, in authoritarian systems, such as Cuba under Castro and the Dominican Republic under Rafael Trujillo, parties were created as a means of mobilizing support for the regime and of maintaining social control. In the cases of Brazil during the military dictatorship (1964–1985) and Nicaragua during the Somoza dynasty, the existence of parties and elections was viewed as a method of legitimization. As noted earlier, many Latin American parties have served as electoral vehicles for personalistic leaders. Many also function predominantly as machines through which patronage and favors are dispensed in return for support. In this sense, party organizations have served to channel popular participation and, in the process, have facilitated the co-optation of the masses into the existing framework under elite tutelage.

Such diversity notwithstanding, there are a number of commonalities among Latin American parties that appear to transcend cultural, developmental, and regional distinctions (McDonald and Ruhl 1989). First, they tend to be elite dominated and exclusionary to the extent that there is minimal opportunity for genuine popular participation in decisionmaking. A second characteristic common to many Latin American parties has been the dominance of individual leaders and the importance of personalism in politics. As noted earlier, parties are frequently created to serve as electoral vehicles for those aspiring to power. Such parties typically lack any significant organizational apparatus or programmatic base, and it has been common for parties to appear around election time to support a particular individual and then to disappear when that leader passes from the scene.

Finally, while party politics in Latin America enjoyed a resurgence during the 1980s, incumbent parties across the region faced a common challenge: to govern effectively and maintain popular support amid the worst economic crisis in Latin American history. With the demise of statism and the ascendancy of the neoliberal economic agenda, democratically elected leaders were compelled to implement painful economic stabilization programs that aroused widespread—and often violent—opposition. The inability of those in power to promote sustained, broad-based economic growth and to improve visibly the quality of life for most citizens severely discredited the parties and their leaders.

In societies weary of socioeconomic decay, political corruption and violence, and elitism, support has grown for personalistic leaders who have distanced themselves from traditional parties and whose populist rhetoric has struck a chord of resonance among cynical and alienated publics. This trend has sparked concern as to the prospects for party politics and the consolidation of truly democratic governmental systems. Although it is apparent that political parties in some Latin American countries have seen their influence and role in the political process somewhat diminished, Mainwaring and Scully (1995:4) assert that "because parties control access to policy-making positions, the way they function is a key in affecting the performance and viability of Latin American democracy." Thus far, however, political parties and their leaders have been only partially effective in ameliorating endemic problems. As long as basic socioeconomic aspirations go unfulfilled, support for political parties will diminish further, the legitimacy of democratic governments will be called into question, and the stability of many Latin American states will remain precarious.

* * *

The current transition toward democratic rule in Latin America has been bolstered by an international environment in which Western-style democracy and free-market capitalism have prevailed. Domestic conditions have been less fortuitous, however, and in much of Latin America, democratic institutions and principles are not well rooted because of the lack of a long, successful democratic tradition and a corresponding "reservoir of legitimacy." Elected civilian leaders throughout the region, including Caribbean states in which democracy is perceived to be established and stable, are under great pressure because their ability to maintain support through the use of patronage and clientelist links has been constrained by stagnant economies or the imposition of economic restructuring programs (Weyland 2004). Although democratic values are spreading and, in theory, democracy is enjoying widespread support, Latin American publics are increasingly pragmatic and demand quick solutions to their problems. Clearly, the key to consolidating democracy and averting a devolution to authoritarian rule is for governments to perform effectively. Democracy is very much on trial in Latin America, and the verdict will ultimately rest on the degree to which mass publics can be satisfied without unduly provoking elites.

▣ Conclusion

Underlying the cultural, economic, and political diversity of the nearly fifty states that Latin America comprises are a number of similar patterns and experiences that facilitate (and indeed demand) a comprehensive analysis of the region. In this chapter, I have highlighted these similarities and provided an overview of the politics of this vital area. Those interested in a more detailed analysis of individual countries or of the themes discussed here are encouraged to begin by consulting the sources included in the bibliography.

Contemporary political systems in Latin America, whether they are in countries where the predominant language is Spanish, English, French, Dutch, Portuguese, or an indigenous variant, have been shaped by the legacies of the past, the pressures for change that accompany modernization, and the realities of the post–Cold War international system. These systems exhibit the impact of a process inherent in transitional Latin American societies, whereby traditional institutions and values derived from a protracted colonial experience endure and blend with emergent modern ones (Hillman and D'Agostino 1992). This blending of old and new has been evident in the patterns of leadership found within the region, as personalism has remained vitally important even for democratically elected civilian leaders. Blending or "hybridization" has also been apparent in party politics, where

Old and new forms of transportation in Costa Rica.

organizations that operate on the basis of patron-clientelism remain dominated by elites, serve in some cases as vehicles for personalistic leadership, and employ increasingly sophisticated campaign techniques to contest democratic elections. The durability of the authoritarian political culture alongside the emerging democratic one attests to the fact that the past weighs heavily on the present in Latin America.

The resilience, adaptability, and persistence of traditional patterns are remarkable, given the profound transformation that has occurred in recent decades. Latin American countries are increasingly urban, industrialized, and technologically advanced. As a result, their societies are more complex and diversified, and their populations are more literate, politically conscious, and politically active. Latin American leaders now recognize that political systems cannot remain static amid such change and have, therefore, been compelled continually to renovate the old and to devise new institutional arrangements.

Despite divergent constitutional traditions and structures, in practice, political systems throughout the region have appeared to converge (Hillman and D'Agostino 1992). Latin American systems have exhibited a high degree of formalism, as evidenced by the lack of congruity between basic constitutional precepts and formal structures on the one hand and actual political practice on the other. The countries of Latin America have been confronted by a number of common challenges, including severe poverty and inequality, dependent economies, a paucity of viable institutions, and conflicting demands of domestic and international constituencies. Despite structural differences, they have sought to address these problems in similar ways. Unfortunately, efforts to resolve such endemic problems and promote sustained economic development have proved largely ineffective.

Over the past two decades, since the transition from military rule began, there has been undeniable progress in the promotion of democratic values, processes, and institutions in Latin America. A greater respect for human rights and civil liberties has evolved, along with a growing consensus that democratic elections constitute the sole legitimate route to power, and more dynamic and robust civil societies have emerged. Nevertheless, the prospects for democratic consolidation remain uncertain. The demands and expectations among highly mobilized populations far exceed the capacities of most Latin American governments to fulfill them, engendering widespread cynicism and frustration. In some cases, this has facilitated the rise of neopopulist leaders, weakening traditional political parties and other intermediary organizations. In other cases, politics have grown increasingly contentious and volatile, as evidenced by the fact that since 2000 several leaders across the region have been forced from power amid turmoil and unrest. Such trends are worrisome and do not bode well for the near future, underscoring the reality that the "new Latin America" faces many of the same problems that have plagued the region in the past.

▨ Notes

1. A similar attempt by Guatemalan president Jorge Serrano to carry out an *autogolpe* in 1993 was thwarted, although it provided further evidence of the vulnerability of democracy in some societies.

2. Mexico's electoral landscape has changed considerably prior to the July 2006 presidential election. July 4, 2004 kicked off a busy electoral season with fourteen state-level elections, ten of which were for governorships (the remaining four were for local state legislators and municipalities). An additional seven gubernatorial elections were to take place in 2005. The PRI won two key mayoral races in 2004, in Cuidad Júarez and Tijuana, but lost control of the Veracruz state legislature for the first time ever. Polling data from Parametría (a Mexico City–based public opinion firm) showed four major characteristics of voting behavior in Mexico's state-level elections: (1) lack of national pattern, (2) party identification weaker than in federal elections, (3) increased number of independent voters or "switchers," and (4) low turnout. These results suggest that the race for the next presidential election in 2006 remains wide open.

3. This point is discussed in Hillman and Cardozo (1996) in great detail as it pertains to governability in Venezuela. See Peeler (1998) and Von Mettenheim and Malloy (1998) for a regional analysis.

▨ Bibliography

Agüero, Felipe, and Jeffrey Stark (eds.). *Fault Lines of Democracy in Post-Transition Latin America*. Coral Gables, Fla.: North-South Center Press at the University of Miami, 1998.

Coppedge, Michael. "Venezuela: The Rise and Fall of Partyarchy." In *Constructing Democratic Governance: South America in the 1990s*, edited by Jorge I. Domínguez and Abraham F. Lowenthal. Baltimore: Johns Hopkins University Press, 1996, pp. 3–19.

Diamond, Larry, Jonathan Hartlyn, Juan J. Linz, and Seymour Martin Lipset (eds.). *Democracy in Developing Countries: Latin America* (2d ed.). Boulder, Colo.: Lynne Rienner Publishers, 1999.

Domínguez, Jorge I. "The Caribbean Question: Why Has Liberal Democracy (Surprisingly) Flourished?" In *Democracy in the Caribbean: Political, Economic and Social Perspectives*, edited by Jorge I. Domínguez, Robert A. Pastor, and R. DeLisle Worrell. Baltimore: Johns Hopkins University Press, 1993, pp. 1–25.

Domínguez, Jorge I., Robert A. Pastor, and R. DeLisle Worrell. *Democracy in the Caribbean: Political, Economic, and Social Perspectives*. Baltimore: Johns Hopkins University Press, 1993.

Domínguez, Jorge I., and Abraham Lowenthal. *Constructing Democratic Governance: Latin America and the Caribbean in the 1990s—Themes and Issues*. Baltimore: Johns Hopkins University Press, 1996.

Edie, Carlene J. *Democracy by Default: Dependency and Clientelism in Jamaica.* Boulder, Colo.: Lynne Rienner Publishers, 1991.

Grayson, George W. "A Guide to the 2004 Mexican State Elections." Washington, D.C.: Center for Strategic and International Studies, July 2004.

Grugel, Jean. *Politics and Development in the Caribbean Basin: Central America and the Caribbean in the New World Order.* Bloomington: Indiana University Press, 1995.

Hillman, Richard S. *Democracy for the Privileged: Crisis and Transition in Venezuela.* Boulder, Colo.: Lynne Rienner Publishers, 1994.

———. "Intellectuals: An Elite Divided." In *The Unraveling of Representative Democracy in Venezuela,* edited by Jennifer McCoy and David Myers. Baltimore: Johns Hopkins University Press, 2004, pp. 115–129.

Hillman, Richard S., and Thomas J. D'Agostino. *Distant Neighbors in the Caribbean: The Dominican Republic and Jamaica in Comparative Perspective.* New York: Praeger Publishers, 1992.

Hillman, Richard S., and Elsa Cardozo Da Silva (Comp.). *La Democracia Desbordada: De Una a Otra Gobernabilidad en Venezuela.* Caracas: Fondo Editorial Tropykos/Comisión de Estudios de Postgrado, Facultad de Ciencias Económicas y Sociales, Universidad Central de Venezuela, 1996.

Knight, Franklin W., and Colin A. Palmer (eds.). *The Modern Caribbean.* Chapel Hill: University of North Carolina Press, 1989.

Kryzanek, Michael J. *Latin America: Change and Challenge.* New York: HarperCollins, 1995.

Mainwaring, Scott, and Timothy R. Scully (eds.). *Building Democratic Institutions: Party Systems in Latin America.* Stanford, Calif.: Stanford University Press, 1995.

Malloy, James M., and Mitchell A. Seligson (eds.). *Authoritarians and Democrats: Regime Transition in Latin America.* Pittsburgh: University of Pittsburgh Press, 1987.

McDonald, Ronald H., and J. Mark Ruhl. *Party Politics and Elections in Latin America.* Boulder, Colo.: Westview Press, 1989.

Meyer, Michael C., and William L. Sherman. *The Course of Mexican History* (5th ed.). New York: Oxford University Press, 1995.

Molineu, Harold. *U.S. Policy Toward Latin America* (2d ed.). Boulder, Colo.: Westview Press, 1990.

O'Donnell, Guillermo. *Modernization and Bureaucratic-Authoritarianism: Studies in South American Politics.* Berkeley: Institute of International Studies, University of California, 1973.

———. "Delegative Democracy." *Journal of Democracy* 5 (January 1994):55–69.

Payne, Anthony. "Westminster Adapted: The Political Order of the Commonwealth Caribbean." In *Democracy in the Caribbean: Political, Economic and Social Perspectives,* edited by Jorge I. Domínguez, Robert A. Pastor, and R. DeLisle Worrell. Baltimore: Johns Hopkins University Press, 1993, pp. 57–73.

Payne, Anthony, and Paul Sutton (eds.). *Modern Caribbean Politics.* Baltimore: Johns Hopkins University Press, 1993.

Peeler, John A. *Building Democracy in Latin America.* Boulder, Colo.: Lynne Rienner Publishers, 1998.

Stone, Carl. "A Political Profile of the Caribbean." In *Caribbean Contours,* edited by Sidney W. Mintz and Sally Price. Baltimore: Johns Hopkins University Press, 1985, pp. 13–53.

Stotzky, Irwin. *Silencing the Guns in Haiti: The Promise of Deliberative Democracy*. Chicago: University of Chicago Press, 1997.

Von Mettenheim, Kurt, and James Malloy. *Deepening Democracy in Latin America*. Pittsburgh: University of Pittsburgh Press, 1998.

Weyland, Kurt. "Neoliberalism and Democracy in Latin America: A Mixed Record." *Latin American Politics and Society* 46, no. 1 (Spring 2004):135–152.

Wiarda, Howard J. *Latin American Politics*. Belmont, Calif.: Wadsworth Publishing Company, 1995.

5

The Military

Paul W. Zagorski

The military, as Thomas J. D'Agostino shows in Chapter 4, has played an important and frequently pivotal role in most Latin American countries. This role, however, has evolved over time and continues to evolve today. The end of the Cold War, the need for economic structural adjustment, and reawakened domestic and international attention to human rights and democracy have all placed the Latin American armed forces once again in the spotlight. Whatever the long-term outcome of the current process of democratization, the armed forces are likely to be instrumental in establishing democratic stability or in facilitating a return of political instability or authoritarianism. Thus, civil-military relations constitute an important aspect of the evolving politics of the region.

What is the likely trajectory of this evolution? What options do civilian and military leaders have for furthering democratic consolidation and economic growth? What are the most important challenges the consolidation of democracy is likely to face? These questions cannot be adequately addressed without at least an elementary appreciation of the historical legacy embodied in current institutions and practices.

▪ The Historical Legacy of Civil-Military Relations in Latin America

The Latin American armed forces and their relations to civilian authority have adapted to changing political and social circumstances, much like a biological species adjusts to changes in its natural environment. As the environment changed, old practices and patterns were made to serve new purposes, and new structures and techniques were developed to meet old challenges. From the time of the European conquest, the military has played a key role in frontier security and, on occasion, in the maintenance of internal order. From colonial times, the armed forces have had a privileged corporate existence, whereby individual members gain status and rights by their group membership. Yet, there have been significant changes as well as continuity. The class origins of members of the officer corps, the military's doctrine and matériel, and the political orientation of the military have changed markedly even in the past century and a half.

The Conquest and Wars for Independence
The political role, the social prestige, and the privileges of the armed forces were an outgrowth of the Iberian tradition. This tradition, especially in the case of Spain, was heavily influenced by a strong military ethos. The transplantation of the tradition was no mere coincidence. In 1492, Spanish forces took Granada and completed the *reconquista* (the Christian reconquest of the Iberian Peninsula from the Muslims). With the destruction of the last Moorish stronghold in the peninsula, Spain and its military aristocracy were, quite literally, looking for new worlds to conquer. The fall of Granada freed resources to support Columbus's expedition to do just that. By chance rather than design, that New World, instead of India, turned out to be America, but in any event that world promised wealth in land and precious metals. Moreover, America was populated by "heathens," who in Mexico and the Andes were organized into empires with substantial military forces. The similarities between the Old World and the New World were unmistakable, and institutions and practices that had been successful in the Old World were transferred to the New World. Not the least among these was the fusion of military power, social prestige, and landed wealth. During the colonial period, military forces were required to extend European control against Indians yet unsubjugated, to suppress them when they revolted, and to defend the crown's possessions against depredations by European rivals.

Despite the role that they were meant to fulfill, imperial garrisons were relatively modest in size and capacity, compared with the expanse of territory they had to protect and the missions they were assigned. The New World could not be held in subjection to the Old World by force alone. Spanish and Portuguese rule was based on strong mutual interest, linking the mother country with the interests of the local European elite (*criollos*). Yet, local and imperial interests diverged in a variety of ways, most tellingly over trade and issues of local self-rule. The reforms of the late eighteenth century provided a glimpse of increased trade and expanded local economic activity without resolving these antagonisms. Thus, it was not surprising that when the Napoleonic Wars and their aftermath provided Spanish America and Brazil the opportunity to gain more control of their own affairs, they took it. The first quarter of the nineteenth century found the local population first asserting its own autonomy and finally demanding independence.

Brazil's declaration of independence was not contested by the mother country, thus paving the way for the continuance of the established social and political institutions (including the Portuguese monarchy). And, for a variety of reasons, even the wars of independence in Spanish America modified rather than displaced the existing military traditions. Not the least of the reasons was the fact that these conflicts were indeed wars for independence rather than social revolutions. Moreover, the revolutionary generals (*caudillos*) played the pivotal role, relegating other actors to essentially supporting positions. Although intellectuals could provide the rationale for independence by popularizing the rights of man, as proclaimed by the French Revolution, only military force could secure independence and establish a new government's authority.

In Spanish America, more than in the newly independent United States, the process of gaining independence and establishing government was fraught with problems. Social conditions in Latin America did not provide an adequate basis for establishing effective republican institutions that guaranteed equal rights to all citizens. Local loyalties provided rallying points against central authority. *Caudillo*-led military forces were both part of the solution and part of the problem. Only they could unify nations by force. However, reliance on force also promoted the region's divisive tendencies. Schemes for a nearly regionwide government for Spanish-speaking America (most notably Simón Bolívar's Gran Colombia) collapsed in a welter of factional infighting and local revolts. The lack of a professional, competent, and effective military institution and the personalistic character of military leadership made it easy for local leaders to rebel against national or transnational authority. Successful *caudillos* became presidents, who were threatened, in turn, by other *caudillos*. Moreover, the lack of a dominant independent small farmer class (the preponderant group in most parts of English-speaking America) meant that there was little civilian counterbalance to the militarization of politics. Thus, the process of mobilizing armies of the disenfranchised carried the danger of social instability without the promise of establishing stable republican institutions.

In sum, the nineteenth-century military inherited many characteristics from the periods of imperial rule and wars for independence. Military leadership brought prestige. Such leadership was personalistic and relied on a fusion of social, military, and political roles. The military continued to have certain institutional rights and privileges (*fueros*) that separated it from the rest of society and limited the jurisdiction of civilian courts over military officers. As a general rule, the military could not adequately fulfill its missions of frontier defense, internal pacification, and protection of the government against armed revolts. In fact, to speak of "the military" as if it were a unified, centrally organized institution entails an oversimplification at best. In Brazil, rivalries between the professional officer corps and the militia officers in the hinterland caused their interactions to be dysfunctional. In much of Spanish America, the weakness of national armies meant that ad hoc military forces under amateur generals remained a part of the system. Latin American countries continued to be plagued with problems of external and internal security that *caudillo*-led military forces could not address adequately: foreign threats to the territory of the state; military rebellion; and, in some cases, the need to subdue and pacify indigenous peoples.

Early Professionalization

Given the inadequacies of the military system in the nineteenth century, it is not surprising that modernizing administrations would seek to promote military reform. The rationale for the change is not hard to understand. The state needed to be modern if it were to survive and prosper. Military reform was one part of a complex of changes meant to modernize the state apparatus and provide the basis for economic development. Thus, by the end of the nineteenth century, this new element was added to the Latin American armed forces. And when governments and military reformers sought modern models on which to reorganize their own forces, they looked to Europe. Britain, France, and Germany sent military missions to Latin America to assist in the restructuring of both armies and navies; these European rivals were happy to provide both matériel and advice. Thus, as the twentieth century began, few countries believed they could afford to be without their own foreign experts, lest regional rivals gain a decisive advantage in acquiring or defending disputed territory. A modernization race had begun.

Modernization required professionalization. New equipment, new organizations designed to use the equipment effectively, and a reserve system capable of raising mass armies required an officer corps capable of managing such complex new elements of military power. The new demands of officership meant that officer recruitment and promotion practices also had to be changed. This transformation induced by professionalization, although gradual, was worldwide and thorough in scope. It occurred in the United States and Europe as well as in Latin America. For example, during the U.S. Civil War, many general officers were politicians or other members of the social elite. A division or regimental commander had to have certain military virtues: courage under fire and the ability to lead. Although professional military training was desirable, it could be dispensed with for lower-ranking commanders, provided the senior general in the field had the requisite background. Thus, political connections or the ability to raise troops personally provided alternate means of access to the officer corps for nonprofessionals. A half century later, by the time of World War I, nonprofessional credentials for advancement would no longer suffice. Military officers had become professional managers of military operations, who were charged with managing large numbers of specialized troops with new and complicated weapons systems over great distances. The age of amateur generalship was over. The age of modern warfare had begun.

Although the military modernization race did not lead to the sort of continental war that eventually occurred in Europe, changes in Latin America were no less dramatic. With more effective national military organizations, governments were able to suppress revolts by regional *caudillos* and indigenous peoples. Professional military staffs settled down to long-range planning to meet foreign threats. After the War of the Pacific (1879–1884), which helped spur professionalization, relatively few major regional wars were fought. The major large-scale exception was the Chaco War between Paraguay and Bolivia from 1932 to 1935. Yet, professionalism advanced, and the character of the officer corps itself was eventually transformed.

Professional officership entailed its own set of norms and habits—a military mentality that influenced the way in which officers addressed military and political issues. In the eyes of professional officers, international conflict was not simply a matter of personal ambition but the result of inexorable geopolitical forces. National strategy required professional analysis and direction. The issue of military power became much broader than the immediate size and condition of the armed forces. The military power of modern states rested on an economic and social base, the cultivation of which became a matter of military concern. Military decisionmaking specifically and governmental decisionmaking generally (if it were to be done properly) took on a technical cast. In addition, professionalization gave the armed forces yet another reason for asserting their traditional privileges against the political class: the technically proper direction of the military institution required that trained professionals make military decisions. At all costs, civilians must avoid the "politicization" of the armed forces that occurs when politicians interfere with personnel matters or questions of policy internal to the military.

Professionalization provided an additional basis for asserting military tutelage over politics. Many of the early-nineteenth-century constitutions had provided for military enforcement of law in emergency situations; others established the armed forces as guardians of the constitution, a virtual fourth branch of government. These legalisms had provided a pretext and legal cover for dictatorial rule by military *caudillos,* and such constitutional provisions continued to exist into the twentieth century. Whereas *caudillos* could use such provisions to support their personal ambitions, the new officer corps could cite them as the legal rationale for asserting its institutional interests. In short, changes brought about by professionalization made the military more than just a vehicle by which individuals sought power; it became an institutional actor in its own right. Members of the professional officer corps were socialized through a lifelong system of education and step-by-step promotions that gave them their own esprit de corps and tended to insulate them from the rest of society. Political policies and actions that affected individual officers often had an effect on the officer corps and armed forces as a whole. Collective perceptions were likely to induce collective action. The military had developed a new relationship with the rest of society.

What is the best shorthand characterization of this relationship? Were the armed forces progressive or conservative? Did they represent the middle class or their own distinct institutional interests? Scholars do not agree on answers to these questions. Military officers formed lodges of nationalist and even progressive orientations. Dissatisfied with the politics and policies of conservative cliques, military men applied pressure for political reform in a number of countries in the 1920s and 1930s. In fact, as late as 1968, leftist military coups overthrew civilian governments in Peru and Panama. Yet, the armed forces' commitment to political and social change was far from the norm by the late twentieth century. Although the armed forces might have challenged conservatives on policies that seemed to promote economic backwardness and threatened eventual social upheaval, the officer corps usually saw leftist activism as even more suspect. Thus, the armed forces often played an important role in "breakthrough" or "middle-class" coups that challenged the unilateral control of the entrenched elites early in the century. But as the twentieth century wore on, military officers more commonly led "veto" coups to defend their institution's autonomy or to prevent the adoption of leftist policies that seemed to threaten national unity through their class-based appeals. Today, yet another subtle shift back to the left may be beginning. Progressive elements of the armed forces have formed official or de facto alliances with social movements in such countries as Venezuela, Ecuador, and Paraguay.

The ambiguity of the military's political role has been more the result of officers' professional development than of their class origins. In fact, the class makeup of the officer corps had changed. The professional standards of merit and time-in-grade tended to discourage the scions of the social elite from choosing officership as a career; the sons of the elite could no longer step into high-ranking military positions commensurate with their social status. For the lower middle class, however, the promise of a free education and of career prospects that exceeded opportunities in civilian life more than offset the disadvantages. Thus, professionalization changed the class composition of the officer corps, but even more, it imbued professional officers with a mentality that distinguished them from other members of the middle or upper classes.

Professionalism also entailed a technocratic mentality that saw knowledge and technical skill as keys to problem solving. Professional military leadership, after all, required more than personal charisma; it demanded the mastery of technological and organizational skills. In military science, as in engineering and other technical fields, there were better and worse solutions to problems, as well as nonsolutions. Tactical and strategic doctrines (the principles for employing military force to fulfill military missions) were not matters of personal taste. Doctrine was to be grounded on an understanding of supposedly scientific principles. It was the product of disciplined investigation, not the product of majority vote.

Professionalism also meant discipline. Military organizations could not function effectively—and the nation itself would be put at risk—if personal interests and opinions were not ultimately subordinated to the authority of the command structure. Professionalism also meant loyalty to the nation above all else. Family, class, and party loyalties had to be subordinated to this higher good. Military officers were expected to set aside such extraneous loyalties, and they expected that governments would avoid anything but professional considerations in their governance of the military institution.

It is hard to imagine a worse match than that between the professional officer and the politician. Compromise, bargaining, and the satisfaction of factions and interests are the very substance of politics. To the professional officer, these activities seemed mildly unsavory at best or totally corrupt at worst—hence the ambivalence of the military's attitude toward politics and government. In professional terms, at least in theory, politics was something to be avoided. Yet, in practice, such an apolitical stance was out of harmony with the Latin American tradition and with what military officers themselves often saw as overriding national needs.

Thus, although professionalization did not mean the abolition of military intervention into politics, it did alter, by way of addition, the motivation for such intervention. Defense of military professionalism against the intrusion of politics, as well as the promotion of national power, became additional rationales for military involvement. Nonetheless, military involvement in politics rarely entailed the long-term displacement of civilian institutions. As individuals, officers could gain a political following because of their military careers, but when they became involved in long-term politics, they normally reverted legally to a civilian or retired status. As an institution, the armed forces served as a balancer or mediator or intervened to protect the autonomy of the institution from what it considered undue political control. After a coup, the armed forces often ruled the country for only a brief period until an acceptable version of the status quo ante could be reestablished, and then they returned to the barracks. But whether military rule was long or short term, political coups, like elections in consolidated democracies, were a widely accepted—almost normal—means of transferring power and ensuring a more general stability.

In sum, by the middle of the twentieth century, professionalization had changed the character of the armed forces in part but had not—as it had in leading countries of Western Europe and the United States—marginalized them as a political force. Latin American officers had ceased to be amateur military leaders drawn primarily from the upper class. Officers came much more frequently from the middle sectors and developed a distinct attitude toward modernization, class conflict, and national power. In Latin America, effective political power continued to be held primarily by a relatively narrow portion of the population, and coups usually were staged to preserve rather than threaten the ruling sectors. Military dictatorships replaced democracy and vice versa, but overall there were few substantial political or social changes.

The Emergence of the New Professionalism

Yet nothing remains stable forever. In fact, the image of a cycle of civilian governments and coups d'état, with the military always preserving an adjusted status quo, is part simplification and part wishful thinking. Dynamic forces underlay this apparently banal cyclical repetition. In actuality, politics as usual, as well as the armed forces' peculiar role in it, came under considerable pressure as the twentieth century wore on.

Problems of Political Development

Traditionally, political demands in Latin America had been accommodated by intraelite bargaining, and new social and economic groups had been co-opted by a process of adjustment that allowed for the gradual expansion of privileges to these new groups. In this manner, commercial interests and the middle sectors had managed to gain entry into the system that had originally excluded them. But with accelerated social and economic change, it became difficult to accommodate new groups successfully and still maintain practices that were essentially exclusionary in nature. Likewise, it was becoming less possible for the armed forces to carry out their balancing role—intervening for short periods and then returning to the barracks—because more than piecemeal changes in the political system seemed to be required. Something had to give, and it did. The military eventually moved from a moderating to a ruling role under the rubric of the new professionalism.

Events in Argentina, one of the socioeconomically most advanced countries in the region, illustrate the sorts of challenges that eventually faced most Latin American regimes and their armed forces. By the second decade of the twentieth century, the Radical Party, based on the support of the rising middle sectors, had finally broken the traditional elite's monopoly on political power. Political reforms enfranchised the middle sectors and allowed for effective political competition. Sectors of the armed forces were sympathetic to this development. But by 1930, the military was reacting defensively to what it saw as President Hipólito Irygoyen's attempt to make senior military appointments on the basis of political criteria. This political-military conflict led to a coup and a period in which the armed forces became more rather than less entrapped in politics. For a decade and a half, military presidents or civilian protégés of the armed forces ruled the country. The military aligned itself with conservatives and attempted to block an accession of Irygoyen's Radical Party to power. A pattern emerged that continued into the 1980s: no constitutionally elected president served a full term and handed over power to an elected successor.

In the 1940s, the Argentine armed forces' balancing act was complicated even more by the emergence of a labor movement and the appointment of military officers to normally civilian portfolios. Political and administrative issues became increasingly day-to-day concerns for the officer corps. The crisis occurred in 1946, when Colonel Juan Perón, the labor minister, was dismissed from his post and imprisoned by his military colleagues in the government. Perón and his wife, Eva, had cultivated the labor movement as a base of support, and Eva Perón helped mobilize masses of urban workers to demand Perón's release. Their success eventually culminated in a multiterm Perón presidency and the creation of a Peronist political party and labor federation. Even a successful coup that removed Perón from office in 1955 could not remove the newly awakened working class as an important political actor. Periodic bans on Perón himself, his party, and Peronist candidates handicapped and fragmented the movement but could not destroy it. The lower classes could no longer be ignored. In less industrialized countries and countries where political party development was different, the pattern by which the disenfranchised lower classes became a critical factor varied. Yet, in almost all instances, maintaining stability could not be achieved simply by buying off and incorporating relatively small and organized groups into the power structure.

By 1960, this social and political problem had assumed a military dimension. The victory of Cuban revolutionaries in January 1959 energized the radical left throughout the region. Whereas mainline communist parties had declared that revolution was impossible in the short term, Fidel Castro's guerrillas and the 26th of July Movement had demonstrated the opposite. The Cuban Revolution provided a model and Cuba itself provided a base of support for would-be revolutionaries in the whole of Latin America. The facts that the revolutionaries were overly optimistic, their opponents overly alarmist, and the initial analyses of the causes behind the revolutions wide of the mark are beside the point. The whole of Latin America seemed on the brink of violent left-wing revolution. A military response was inevitable.

This response came in the form of the national security doctrine, which was at the core of what came to be called the "new professionalism." Traditionally, professional armed forces focused on external threats. Strategy, tactics, organization, and the acquisition of matériel were premised on deterring and fighting against neighboring states or others that could effectively threaten the territorial integrity of the state by outright military invasion. In this vein, Latin American countries had developed military institutions designed to fight conventional wars. Involvement in domestic politics had been the by-product of Latin American constitutions and political traditions rather than of professionalism per se. The new national security doctrine changed all that. The primary enemy was now subversives—citizens of the country itself. This enemy's primary logistic and recruitment base was not the elaborate depot and training system of a foreign conventional armed force but was a portion of the country's citizens, who provided direct and indirect support as well as recruits for the guerrillas. Thus, military concepts for fighting wars (military doctrine) had to change.

Military theorists in many countries, inside and outside Latin America, had considered the problems associated with this sort of internal war.

A member of the
Farabundo Martí
National Liberation Front
in El Salvador, 1992.

UN Photo 159528J. Bleibtreu

Although significant differences existed in the strategy and tactics they recommended, a common thread ran throughout their analyses. Irregular forces—guerrillas who fought a hit-and-run war of attrition—were the direct military threat and would have to be defeated. However, an effective strategy would have to provide for defeating the logistic, intelligence, and recruitment bases as well; otherwise, no final victory would be possible. The defeat of the guerrillas would be tactical only, and armed conflict could easily reemerge. These analysts also went a step further, by stating that the underlying cause of subversion was the lack of social, economic, and political development. And, more ominously, they concluded that a proactive policy on all levels was likely to be more successful and much less costly than a simple reactive response.

Much of the expansion of the military's new role, as defined by this proactive new doctrine, took relatively benign forms: nation building and civic action—programs to develop physical and human infrastructure, supposedly in areas where the government's and the private sector's efforts were inadequate. More threatening were the expansion of military intelligence into the domestic arena and the possibility of the armed forces taking over ordinary police functions. The stage was set for a qualitatively and quantitatively different sort of military political involvement.

The militarization of politics did not emerge immediately. Initially, the altered threat perception gave impetus to such regionwide efforts as the Alliance for Progress, designed to address underlying social, economic, and political problems, as well as U.S.-induced and indigenous efforts to redirect military attention to the internal guerrilla threat. But as the Alliance and other reform efforts faltered, military attention became more fixed on internal threats. Thus, it was not surprising that the 1960s saw the renewal of another cycle of military governments throughout the region.

The National Security State

Most of the governments of this cycle were strikingly different from those of prior periods of military rule. Previously, the armed forces had functioned primarily as moderators. Their direct interventions were usually relatively brief and, on the whole, did not involve the armed forces as an institution assuming civilian administrative functions. Except at the most senior levels, military personnel tended to remain in military posts. Even long-term military presidents normally left active duty and developed civilian support as a foundation of their governments.

The national security doctrine changed this. The new national security state was meant to do something quite different from repairing and reestablishing the political status quo. Military governments assumed the mission of reforming the underlying social, economic, and political structure that had been the source of instability. Thus, the military took on a new long-term "ruler" role that rested on the national security doctrine and the well-established tradition of military intervention. The watershed between the old and new patterns of military was stark. Before the 1964 Brazilian coup, the armed forces in most countries played the more limited moderator role, whereas almost every intervention after the coup established military governments with much broader aspirations.

These new-style military governments generally went through a number of phases. The first was a stabilization phase, which generally took a year or two. Coups were normally induced by a variety of problems: subversive violence, political deadlock, economic difficulties, and threats to the viability of the armed forces. Stabilization was meant to suppress these threats. Coups frequently led to a political recess: the abrogation of political guarantees, the closing of Congress, and the banning of certain individuals and political parties. Military interveners took control of key civilian institutions, and security was tightened. Frequently, subversives or suspects were detained without trial, exiled, or sometimes executed. Where open combat occurred, the armed forces often assumed direct control of the civilian population, establishing curfews and sometimes moving whole villages and enlisting civilians in part-time paramilitary units. In almost all instances, armed resistance was negligible or it quickly collapsed. In the economic realm, governments took steps to control strikes and to curb inflation through stern fiscal measures.

As the initial crisis faded, the military government could turn its efforts to the second phase—constructing new institutions. If the country was to become economically progressive and politically stable, new social, economic, and political habits had to be developed. This phase was never more than sketched out by military doctrine, and the task of creating new institutions was much more complex than simply seizing power and imposing order. Militaries in various countries took different tacks, but a number of common themes emerged. The executive branch of government had to be strengthened. Political participation had to be restructured to prevent uncontrolled mass mobilizations and the undue influence of special interest pleading. Patriotism and duty had to be the dominant ideological themes; class struggle as a rallying point had to be eliminated. The economy had to be modernized to produce dynamic rates of growth. Institutional capacity to prevent and contain social turmoil was essential.

Yet, by the beginning of the 1980s—and in certain countries even earlier—when the construction of new institutions was far from complete, many military-sponsored reforms had miscarried. In addition, the armed forces' authoritarian rule had provoked widespread opposition, often involving such mainline sectors as the church, professionals, and segments of the business community. Moreover, the effort at national reconstruction eventually entangled the armed forces in a host of issues that were unfamiliar to them and that engendered factionalism within the institution itself. It was time to strategically retreat.

Thus, in most countries, the last phase of military government—transition to civilian successors—did not go as the armed forces had originally anticipated. The transfer of power was meant to maintain the achievements of the military regimes, including a major domestic role for the armed forces. It was to have been a gradually and carefully orchestrated process.

However, in actual practice, these transfers were driven to a greater or lesser degree by popular pressure and factions within the armed forces themselves. Patterns varied from country to country. Transitions ranged from forced exit to military-dominated transfer. The best example of the former is the Argentine military's exit in December 1983, which was spurred on by the disastrous Falklands/Malvinas War eighteen months earlier. The prestige of the military was at an all-time low, and the military government's amnesty law was revoked by its civilian successors.

The most nearly successful military-staged transition was that in Chile, where the military-inspired constitution of 1980 provided the vehicle for installing a new regime. Even in Chile, however, the transition did not go exactly as scripted. The military junta had hoped to have a single, regime-nominated candidate (the incumbent, General Augusto Pinochet) approved by the voters. However, in October 1988, the "no" vote against Pinochet gained the majority, and the regime was forced to use its fallback mechanism: a competitive election. In this contest, held one year later, proregime candidates lost as well. Nonetheless, the military's constitution largely held against popular pressure to change it. The military retained most of its prerogatives as spelled out in the document, including appointed senators, an additional eight-year term for incumbent service chiefs, and a fixed portion of the gross domestic product (GDP) for the military budget.

▨ The Postnational Security State: Real Change or the Same Old Thing?

As with earlier watersheds in Latin American politics, governments and citizens in the contemporary period still have to confront problems and practices inherited from the past. The armed forces have not disappeared and still possess considerable political influence. Even in Argentina, where the armed forces suffered their greatest loss of power and prestige, there has been no serious consideration of abolishing them or even undertaking a systematic purge of the institution. Even the attempt to punish those guilty of the most heinous human rights abuses during the Dirty War (by a conservative count, more than 9,000 extrajudicial killings of those in military custody) eventually collapsed after a series of military revolts. In short, the armed forces, even in their generally diminished political position, retain some capacity to challenge civilian governments.

The national security state is dead, but a postnational security state has emerged. In this new political environment, issues from the past—some as old as the Iberian tradition, some associated with the national security doctrine—remain on the Latin American political agenda along with new issues that have emerged in the post–Cold War era. At the core of all these issues stands one central question: Can the armed forces be made democratic instead and their tendencies toward political intervention contained and eroded? Solving this problem requires something more than simply amending the language of written documents; it entails changing deep-seated practices and attitudes. Establishing a democratic vocation for Latin America's armed forces involves two related tasks: engendering apolitical professionalism and protecting human rights.

Apolitical Professionalism

Advanced democracies have relied on a number of methods to protect against military authoritarianism. Among the most important of these is cultivating the norm of apolitical professionalism both within the military's own ranks and in the broader political community. Such apolitical professionalism grants the armed forces a significant degree of autonomy, but only within a rather narrowly defined field of competence. Military autonomy is generally limited to matters of organization and tactics, whereas decisions concerning missions and overall funding are the province of civilian policymakers. On such matters of high military policy, the senior officers are competent to give advice, but their advice alone does not determine policy. On all other matters of policy, military opinion is irrelevant; or, more accurately, professional military opinion is by definition nonexistent. Apolitical professionalism is clearly out of step with the Latin American tradition of military involvement in politics. The adoption of apolitical professionalism would mean the loss of the armed forces' role as a political balancer. It would lead to the abandonment of the new professionalism's claim that the armed forces have a broad professional competence in developmental and internal security matters. It would undermine their role as managers and administrators in a host of governmental and quasi-governmental institutions that are only loosely connected to military competency, as that term is narrowly understood.

Is such a change possible? Even though almost every newly reestablished civilian government has favored the adoption of standards of apolitical professionalism and almost every Latin American military force has announced that the armed forces are essentially nondeliberative, history would counsel caution. Latin American civilian governments have rarely succeeded in getting full control of the armed forces except in a revolutionary context, for only in such circumstances could the military institution be completely purged and restructured or even abolished.

Yet, it is altogether too rash to believe that the past will determine the future. The development of a military ethos, whether apolitical or highly politicized, depends in large measure on the context in which the military organization operates. Professional military officers—those specially recruited, trained, commissioned, and promoted within a bureaucratic system designed to manage the instruments of modern warfare—generally have two seemingly contradictory attitudes: conservatism and distaste for politics. They tend to be conservative because they are, by temperament and training, extremely nationalistic, skeptical of idealistic projects, and alarmist. They also believe in the necessity of using force to settle conflicts. Yet, they also find the naked self-interest, compromise, and bargaining of politics distasteful because it conflicts with the technical, engineer-like approach to problems that typifies the military professional. Hence, in stable regimes with no overriding constitutional conflicts that adversely affect the ability of the government actually to govern, a well-established professional ethos leads to apolitical armed forces. Only in the face of serious ideological and constitutional crises does the armed forces' inherent conservatism kick in. They are apt to step in to make their presence felt in promoting authoritarian and nationalistic solutions to the country's problems.

In Latin America, the professionalization of the armed forces that began a century ago never produced an apolitical force. Endemic political and social conflict has been sufficiently severe to induce repeated military involvement in politics. Yet, by the twenty-first century, Latin American circumstances have changed. The experiences of the national security state have taught all parties something about the limits of military competence, the dysfunctional nature of revolutionary and counterrevolutionary violence, and the value of the rule of law. So there are grounds for hope, although major stumbling blocks to establishing civilian control remain.

Human Rights

Not the least of the stumbling blocks to establishing civil control is the human rights issue. During and sometimes immediately preceding military rule, the armed forces of many countries fought what they believed was an ideological war of national survival. To be fair, in most instances, the threat of violent subversion was real, if exaggerated, and there was often widespread support or tolerance for the military's action at the time it was undertaken. Still, it is also unquestionable that the military's prosecution of such wars often involved glaring human rights violations.

Acts of torture, murder, rape, and detention without judicial sanction violated both national and international laws, and in some cases they occurred on a massive scale. The armed forces argued that their actions were absolutely necessary for the defense of the nation, and most military officers remained unrepentant long after they were removed from power. They argued that the guerrillas and their allies were foreign agents (combatants operating without color of legal belligerency or internationally required insignia and uniforms) and, hence, outside the protection of the law. The military viewed any attempt to punish violators as an attack on the armed forces as an institution and an effort by the losing subversives to carry on the war by other (psychological) means. Foreseeing the potential for legal sanctions, military governments often tried to ensure for themselves an amnesty before the transfer of power to civilians.

When elected governments first returned to office, the human rights issues posed a dilemma for them. If they ignored past violations, they risked creating a precedent for impunity that the armed forces or police could use to suppress civil commotion, a real possibility, or to engage illegally in domestic intelligence and covert actions, a less likely but still important avenue for military intervention. Moreover, the armed forces easily could have interpreted governmental tolerance for past abuses as a sign that the government was not really serious about establishing civilian control over the military. However, if civilian governments attempted to challenge the armed forces by trying a significant number of officers, they risked serious consequences as well. The armed forces had ample means to make the government pay a high price for its efforts, ranging from lobbying and the reliance on right-wing political allies to outright revolts. Thus, efforts to prosecute human rights violators seemed likely to be time consuming, to detract from other government reform efforts, and to require the expenditure of a good deal of political capital.

In Argentina, Raúl Alfonsín's attempt to escape this dilemma during the mid-1980s foundered. President Alfonsín tried to distinguish between the military as a necessary and valued institution and individual officers who had committed heinous crimes. Nonetheless, he could not induce the armed forces to prosecute their own, nor could he convince them of the validity of his distinction. Three military revolts were each followed by embarrassing government backdowns that seemed to indicate that the armed forces had won. Chile's Truth and Reconciliation Commission, established by the new civilian administration of Patricio Aylwin in 1990, was another attempt to find some sort of middle ground, but here, too, the armed forces are unwilling to express remorse for any excesses that took place under the Pinochet regime and remain adamantly opposed to any rights prosecution, although a number have gone forward. El Salvador in 1993 established a similar commission, as the result of the peace agreement that ended the war between the government and leftist rebels.

Although hardly a perfect fulfillment of national and international legal obligations, such half measures were useful in buttressing, however imperfectly, the principle of due process of law. Such actions are akin to locking the barn door after the horses are stolen, but the installation of locks in such cases is reasonable if one intends to buy more horses. In other words, any action against past abuse serves notice that future violations may carry significant risks. Moreover, the escalation of conflict over the rights issue by the military carries significant costs for the armed forces themselves. Military intransigence over the rights issue in Argentina cost the institution prestige, deprived it of financial resources, and sapped its will to resist reform in other areas.

Initially, rights violators in the Argentine military seemed to get the better of the justice system. Alfonsín's rights prosecutions came to naught when the succeeding president amnestied the convicted officers. A de facto understanding in Brazil has made prosecution of rights violators largely a nonissue. A referendum upheld the amnesty in Uruguay shortly after the return of civilian government there. But by the end of the 1990s, the situation had begun to change. Although a full reckoning remained highly unlikely, aggressive prosecutors found the political climate supportive of their actions. Military saber rattling no longer seemed to terrify civilian politicians and the general public. Despite amnesties in Chile and Argentina, a number of generals in both countries awaited trial for rights violations, and the head of Chile's notorious secret police was in prison. The chief of staff of the Argentine army has formally apologized for rights violations by his forces, and other service chiefs there have followed suit. Even self-congratulatory Chilean military leaders have finally admitted that errors were committed. Perhaps the most spectacular case is that of Augusto Pinochet, who was arrested in London in late 1998 to face trial in Spain. He too, in an open letter, apologized—although obliquely. Subsequently, protracted legal haggling blocked his extradition to Spain, and Pinochet returned to Chile. Although he escaped prosecution in Chile, he did so on the grounds of advanced age, poor health, and diminished mental capacity—hardly an edifying position for Pinochet personally or the Chilean military as an institution. More recent efforts to bring Pinochet to justice have been similarly unsuccessful, yet international attention on human rights abuses in Chile has resulted.

Other Opportunities and Traps

Most civilian governments appear to recognize the need for military reform, although efforts and results have varied. There is no magic wand to solve the problems involved in establishing effective democratic control of the military and securing the rule of law, but a number of changes have merit and require persistent oversight. The military code of justice should be reformed to remove the concept of "due obedience" and should establish in its place the principle that each soldier is responsible for obeying the law. Due obedience, at most, should be a mitigating rather than an exculpating argument. Civilians should assume the control of unified defense ministries and establish the mechanisms and develop a cadre of personnel with sufficient skills to make their formal control meaningful. Strategy and grand strategy, as well as the acquisition of major weapons systems, should be areas in which civilians have both the legal authority and knowledge to make ultimate decisions.

Even more important, civilians should no longer knock on the doors of the barracks during a political crisis in an effort to promote a coup. And in a lesser but related matter, civilian presidents must not rely on the armed forces as a substitute for civilian political support and administrative talent. The first temptation, although it has not disappeared entirely, was more characteristic of the past than the present, but the second—reliance on the armed forces for political and administrative support—is worrisome in the contemporary era.

Although the specific causes for the second phenomenon are quite diverse, they fall under two main headings. First, the armed forces often wish to retain at least a veto power over significant government policies outside the military sphere as strictly defined, or they may even seek to expand their role. The administration of state companies, civil construction, and environmental management provide jobs for military officers and a reason to expand the military budget. A second impulse toward overreliance on the armed forces comes from the other direction. Civilian presidents may seek out military officers to fill cabinet and other high-level positions. Latin American political parties are frequently factious and ill-disciplined, and civilian appointees may be more interested in dispensing patronage and preparing for the next election than in efficient administration. In such instances, a president of dubious popularity and legislative support may well do as Brazil's Itamar Franco did in the last year of his interim presidency and appoint military officers to his cabinet instead of civilian politicians and business-based experts, whom he labeled "birds of prey." In contrast to their civilian counterparts, military officers seemed more committed to strengthening the executive branch and achieving administrative efficiency and less prone to becoming involved in the worst aspects of interest group politics.

However, such reliance on the armed forces includes very real dangers. Using military officers in governmental posts in which civilians should have adequate expertise stifles democratic development, provides a military filter on the advice and information the president receives, and positions the armed forces to support a self-coup. Indeed, a self-coup—an executive maneuver supported by the military suspending the operation of the legislature and the courts—is a likely route for the armed forces to follow if they are to assume power again. In April 1992, President Alberto Fujimori of Peru successfully used such a move in the context of an ongoing guerrilla war and economic crisis. Pressure from the international community forced a partial retreat, and Peru held elections for a new constituent assembly/legislature by the end of the year. In June 1993, President Jorge Serrano of Guatemala tried the same thing. In the Guatemalan case, however, political protests forced Serrano's resignation, and human rights ombudsman Ramiro de León Carpio was elected by the legislature to fill the vacated presidential chair.

Peru and Guatemala illustrate the current posture of the armed forces high command in many Latin American countries. Military leaders are unwilling to take the lead in an outright coup in which all three branches of government would come under military supervision or be replaced, but they are deeply concerned about the maintenance of law and order and the so-called governability problem.

Political deadlock, the fiscal and administrative collapse of the state, widespread outbreaks of popular disorder, or worse, are not out of the question in much of Latin America as the new millennium begins. Whether the armed forces co-opt the president or the president co-opts them is largely irrelevant. The dynamics of executive dictatorships are not conducive to democratic development. When a similar self-coup occurred in Uruguay in 1973, the government felt impelled to be more and more repressive and exclusionary, until finally the civilian president was replaced with a general. There is a compelling need to restrict the sphere of military activity to areas in which their organization and expertise are essential and do not threaten democracy. Military skills, useful and necessary in dealing with defense matters, are often inappropriate in other fields. Thus, appointing generals to civilian posts is clearly a move in the wrong direction.

Instead of militarizing civil administration to consolidate democracy, governments should civilianize the upper levels of the military bureaucracy. This task is a politically and technically delicate one. There is no strict dividing line between responsibilities that are purely military and those that are simply at the discretion of the civilian political leadership. Rather, various sorts of activity each have a particular balance of civilian and military responsibility. The development of tactics, training, promotion, and internal discipline are largely, but not exclusively, matters of military concern; budgets, procurement of major weapons, the defining of military missions, and matters of war and peace are fundamentally the concern of civilians, although sound military advice is important.

Establishing civilian control requires the appointment of civilians to the posts of defense minister and other senior-level positions. It requires the establishment of legislative oversight committees. But at least as important is the development of civilian expertise in defense matters. Civilian authorities must be capable of evaluating the advice of their nominal military subordinates. Political leaders, academicians, and others must be capable of engaging in a technical dialogue with military officers. Without adequate knowledge, civilians will find it difficult to gain meaningful control over and real respect from the armed forces.

What Should Be the Role and Mission of the Armed Forces?

Regardless of who actually controls the armed forces—civilians or uniformed officers—these authorities have to decide what the military's purpose is. This is no longer as obvious as it used to be, because global and regional developments have radically undermined old assumptions. The 1980s saw the end of the national security state and the disappearance of revolutionary communism as a major ideological force. Thus, the collapse of the Soviet Union in 1991 capped a series of events that rendered obsolete most of the Cold War missions that had been integral to military planning in the Americas for decades.

Defense against external aggression?   One of the primary missions, if not *the* primary mission, of any state's military forces is the territorial defense of the country against external attack. Over the course of more than a century and a half of independent statehood, Latin American countries have seen this mission change considerably, although perceptions have frequently been slow in catching up with reality. In the nineteenth and early twentieth centuries, Latin American countries generally had more to fear from their immediate neighbors than from other powers. Thus, the adoption of modern professional forces that focused systematically on this mission made good sense. The military staffs of professional forces could simulate conflicts with neighboring states and could formulate contingency plans and organize and train forces in light of their results. But by the mid-twentieth century, wars between Latin American states were little more than border skirmishes, and the investment of significant public resources on external defense seemed a questionable investment. The U.S.-inspired mission of hemispheric defense against Soviet invasion seemed hardly less credible, as the Soviet Union, even at the height of its power, lacked the capacity for significant force projection into the Western Hemisphere. Its existence, however, did provide a pretext for defense spending and equipment acquisition.

The hypothesis of a major imminent external threat was further undermined by the movement to regional integration begun in the mid-1980s by newly returned civilian regimes. Economic and diplomatic cooperation became the watchword, and it made little sense to maintain the fiction that the country was threatened with conventional cross-border attack. Hence, a number of military prestige projects—most notably the nuclear weapons programs of Brazil and Argentina—came into question. Why maintain large forces, a mobilization base, and research and development programs to develop technologically advanced weaponry if national security could not justify the cost?

It has taken time, however, for logic to erode bureaucratic and intellectual inertia. Prestige projects are always hard to give up. Decreasing the size of military forces and changing their mission wreaks havoc with established career patterns and powerful institutional interests. Moreover, geopolitics is popular among military intellectuals. It propounds the notion that international politics is the struggle between states for territory and that states function as "living" organisms in this Darwinistic survival of the fittest. War or at least preparation for war with neighboring states is the natural (and sensible) order of things. Yet, the military has gradually shifted emphasis away from such war preparation and has cut the size of its forces.

In the beginning, this downsizing was more a result of financial exigency than clearly thought-out arguments or an explicit rejection of geopolitics. But as the 1990s progressed, military integration and the demilitarization of borders became increasingly a matter of policy rather than a response to tight budgets. For example, two old rivals who almost went to war in the early 1980s, Argentina and Chile, have undertaken joint military exercises. A peace treaty has resolved the border conflict between Peru and Ecuador that sparked a war as recently as 1995.

Internal defense and development? The traditional activities involved in internal defense—frontier security, the imposition of order in remote areas, and the use of military force to supplement police forces in times of internal disturbance—have their roots in preindependence times. The activities associated with the national security doctrine—domestic intelligence, civic action, and direct control of the population—are of more recent vintage and more controversial. Latin American states are attempting to strike a balance between restricting the armed forces entirely to external defense and simply allowing them to participate in internal defense operations in an unregulated fashion. Civilian governments have begun to address a variety of issues through constitutional change, statute, or decree.

Domestic intelligence? Modern states need some sort of mechanism to defend themselves and their citizens against those who would engage in political violence: bombings, assassinations, kidnappings, and other politically motivated common crimes. And Latin America has certainly not been immune from such outbreaks. The task is to protect the government and society without degenerating into a police state. Yet the Dirty War in Argentina, with its more than 9,000 extrajudicial murders, is an object lesson about what can happen when security forces, the military, or both are unrestrained by due process or any constitutional checks.

To correct these problems, a number of governments have downsized and restructured their intelligence services. Domestic intelligence is now largely restricted to gathering information rather than conducting covert operations. Military units responsible for the worst abuses, such as the infamous Honduran 3-16 Battalion, have been disbanded. In other cases, civilian structures have been erected to supervise the collection of intelligence information. The principle of habeas data (securing an individual's access to information collected on him or her by the government) has been legally established in a number of countries. The effectiveness of these measures in limiting the abuse has yet to be proved and will depend on the follow-through by governments and private associations. But the record is uneven. For example, in April 1998, a Guatemalan archbishop was murdered. Eventually, former members of the president's military staff were implicated, but the prosecutor and other key individuals were forced to flee the country.

Civic action, civil defense, and environmental protection? The participation of military engineers in civil construction dates back to the Napoleonic era. Yet in Latin America today, use of the armed forces in areas tangentially related to their primary competence is still a matter of some controversy. This controversy stems from a number of sources. One source is a kind of guilt by association of civic action projects with the national security doctrine, which, along with counterinsurgency strategy generally, sees the participation of military forces in projects that directly benefit the population as part of an integrated strategy. Civic action projects—such as construction of basic public facilities, especially in rural areas; immunization campaigns; and the distribution of relief supplies and other materials of immediate benefit to the population—can be adjuncts to repressive measures directed against guerrillas and other subversives. In the context of counterinsurgency strategy, such activities are meant to win support for the government and indirectly promote the gathering of intelligence information.

In peacetime, such activities have been justified by the inability of civilian agencies or the private sector to provide such services. Yet, civic action projects have been criticized for that very reason: they tend to displace civilians from technical and administrative activities that are essentially civilian in nature. Why should the armed forces instead of the public health service provide immunizations? Why should military engineers construct rural roads, schools, and wells, instead of other government agencies working through the private sector? Why should disaster relief and activities to preserve the environment, a new mission popular with some militaries, be a military mission when civilian government agencies can be reformed and restructured to handle those tasks?

An even more disturbing sort of displacement is political displacement. Patronage is a staple of electoral politics. Leaders who are able to deliver benefits to people are often able to deliver their votes as well. Both North American ward heelers and Latin American *caciques* (local political bosses) have always understood this. What happens to the prospects of party development and democratic consolidation if the local military commander is seen as a powerful patron?

Peacekeeping? With the end of the Cold War, more than 70,000 troops have been deployed on peacekeeping missions under United Nations (UN) auspices. In 1998 alone, there were 14,347 troops, police, and observers deployed in peace missions in Latin America (see Table 5.1). The use of UN "blue helmets" is no longer restricted to areas of limited superpower competition as it was during the Cold War. Today, restrictions on such deployment are essentially based on cost-benefit analysis rather than on ideological considerations. This changed environment has provided an increased opportunity for Latin American countries to participate in peacekeeping, and many of them have done so. Troops from Argentina, Chile, Brazil, Uruguay, and Venezuela have participated in operations in such places as Cambodia, the Persian Gulf, Iraq, El Salvador, Mozambique, Cyprus, Haiti, Congo, and Croatia. This participation provides more than

Table 5.1 Participation in Peace Missions in Latin America, 1998

	Police	Military Troops	Observers	Total
Total	2,718	10,708	921	14,347
Argentina	195	459	10	664
Brazil	11	2	6	19
Chile	29	0	9	38
El Salvador	0	0	2	2
Honduras	0	0	12	12
Uruguay	30	2	30	62
Venezuela	0	0	5	5
United States	208	345	30	583

Source: Operations Department of Peace Maintenance, Office of Military Adviser, updated December 11, 1999. This is not an official UN document.

UN financial support; it provides actual operational experience with multinational forces, some of whose elements come from technologically advanced forces. Such opportunities have been sorely lacking for most Latin American armies. These operations can also provide an environment to help induce change in the military's organizational culture. In an interview, Argentina's army chief of staff noted that army battalions deployed in Croatia not only had their geographic horizons expanded but also saw the beginning of a transformation of the army's traditional caste-like barriers between officers and enlisted personnel. UN peacekeeping also provides a rational immediate use for small, well-trained forces that most military and civilian leaders see as a hedge against future threats to the state's national security and territorial integrity.

Counternarcotics operations? Another nontraditional mission that has recently come into vogue, at least in the United States, is counternarcotics operations. Such operations involve the armed forces in surveillance and interdiction of shipments of drugs, their precursors, and chemicals needed for processing. Additionally, the armed forces are tasked to destroy drug laboratories and possibly coca and poppy plants used for the production of drugs. In the late 1980s, the first Bush administration saw military involvement in these endeavors as part of a comprehensive war on drugs. The military seemed suited for the mission in that it had personnel and technology that could be useful in the antidrug effort.

Many Latin American governments and armed forces were not so sure about engaging in counternarcotics efforts. To military officers, employing the armed forces in the counternarcotics struggle threatened to reduce their status. Given global conditions after the end of the Cold War, Latin American militaries were looking for advanced military missions, not ones that seemed to confuse their role with that of the police. Civilian governments, wary of the dangers in military role expansion, were often less than enthusiastic as well. Moreover, the temptation of corruption, when traffickers could offer bribes that far exceeded the value of military pay, threatened to put the institution's integrity at risk. After all, large-scale military involvement in drug trafficking was not unknown in Latin America during the 1980s.

Nonetheless, the United States was at times able to offer significant inducements. Little U.S. military assistance was available to Latin America outside the counternarcotics field, and acquiring sophisticated radars and sensors necessary for part of the effort was appealing. In addition, in the case of coca-producing countries like Bolivia and Peru, which provided most of the crop for Colombian-based drug cartels, the United States tied economic aid to the fulfillment of national coca-eradication targets.

Thus, in Peru, the armed forces became heavily involved in counternarcotics operations, although not without cost. At the height of the struggle against Sendero Luminoso guerrillas in the late 1980s, counterdrug operations threatened to undermine efforts to win over the coca-growing peasantry. And the influence of drug money was corrosive. In mid-1994, the commander in chief of the armed forces announced that one hundred officers were being tried for involvement in the drug trade. Despite the associated problems and little hope for a decisive victory, the United States has continued to push for military involvement in the so-called war against drugs. In Bolivia, where most of the antidrug effort had been carried out by a special civilian force rather than the army, the military has begun to take a more direct role. Overt military participation in counternarcotics operations is on the increase in other South American countries as well.

An Interim Balance Sheet

Today, the overall picture of civil-military relations is generally heartening. Although there continue to be areas of serious concern, democracy is more secure, and the armed forces are less politically influential than they were at the time of the transition from military to civilian governments. The 1990s eroded the influence of the armed forces on a number of fronts: attempted coups were infrequent and, except for one instance, unsuccessful; civilian control over the armed forces increased; impunity for rights offenders generally disappeared, as some former offenders were brought to trial; military budgets grew but not disproportionately; and nationalism took a back seat to regional and subregional integration.

The expansion of civilian control over the armed forces has continued in many countries of the region. For example, the Brazilian government has abolished the separate armed forces ministries and subordinated them to a single defense ministry headed by a civilian. By the same token, the president's military household, which included the three military ministers, has also been abolished. In Honduras, the government has abolished the draft, separated the police from the armed forces, and done away with the post of military commander in chief of the armed forces, stripping the military of much of its autonomy and establishing a defense ministry in its place. Argentina, too, has abolished conscription. Even in Peru, where the military played an important political role, President Fujimori was able to dismiss the commander of military forces without incident. Also, due to its unique historical evolution—in which its topography precluded the *latifundio* system that fostered *caudillo* rivalries—Costa Rica has no military forces.

Unlike earlier periods, challenges to democracy and to civilian control of the military today represent a disparate set of problems rather than a broadly based regional trend. Perhaps the most potentially unstable situation exists in Colombia. Whereas civil wars in Central America have been ended by negotiated settlements and Peru's civil war has seen the near collapse of the insurgents, Colombia's long-lived civil war with left-wing guerrillas continues. In Colombia, systematic violence associated with rampant drug trafficking, corruption, and continuing human rights abuses by the armed forces and their right-wing paramilitary allies provide a disturbing example of what can go wrong as countries attempt to deepen and consolidate democracy. The country's problems feed on one another. Guerrillas derive part of their resources by protecting the drug trade and part of their legitimacy from the defense of *campesino* coca and poppy growers. The military uses guerrilla success as a pretext for a no-holds-barred war in which the civilian population often becomes a target. And the paramilitary right has it both ways, attacking the left and their supposed supporters, as well as profiting from links with the drug trade themselves.

Aided by mass movements, military officers and former military officers have vied for power in a number of countries. In 1998, Lino Oviedo, a general cashiered for participation in a coup two years earlier, won the ruling party's nomination for president of Paraguay. And, in February 1999, Hugo Chávez Frías assumed office as Venezuela's elected president. Chávez, as a lieutenant colonel, had led an unsuccessful coup in 1992. A similar situation occurred in Ecuador, where another lieutenant colonel, Lucio Gutiérrez, who helped lead a coup in January 2000, was elected president less than two years later.

In Venezuela, Chávez's presidency has been divisive, to say the least. His cavalier attitude toward the rule of law and the political opposition has produced a backlash. A failed coup against him in April of 2002; a crippling months-long general strike at the end of 2002; and a recall election that, despite winning, Chávez and his supporters initially resisted have all contributed to polarizing Venezuelan politics. Events in Bolivia, where an unpopular president was removed from office after a prolonged mass strike, also send disturbing signals. Such popular revolts have helped cast the armed forces as the potential political kingmaker. In short, although institution building and the extension of civilian control over the military have advanced in some countries, economic and institutional weaknesses have propelled the armed forces back into the political thicket in others.

■ Conclusion

Contrary to the expectations of most analysts at the beginning of the 1990s, the military's political influence eroded considerably throughout Latin America during the decade. The military as an institution, which had been a pillar of authoritarianism for centuries, is changing as a result of a changed regional and global context. The national security state that existed from the 1960s through the 1980s represented the culmination of a number of trends in the evolution of Latin American military institutions. The national security state was authoritarian, statist, and stressed traditional values—as had the Latin American armed forces since the time of the conquest. It was modernizing, technocratic, and meritocratic, as the professional armed forces of the region had been, at least in aspiration, since the turn of the century. But the national security state could not last; it lacked a distinctive ideology to legitimize its institutions. And, in fact, it proclaimed itself to be transitional. Where it achieved a modicum of success, for example, in Chile, the regime's own rules, as well as its human rights transgressions, provided the legal basis and substantial motivations for a transfer to the opposition. Where it was an almost unqualified failure, for example, in Argentina, the experience of the national security state delegitimized military governance almost everywhere. As Thomas J. D'Agostino points out in Chapter 4, military governance, for the most part, performed poorly in the economic sphere.

Moreover, the political and social environment at the beginning of the twenty-first century differs substantially from that of the mid-1960s, when the national security state first arose, and new issues have emerged. The experience of repression has made the left realize the importance of competitive elections and due process. The end of the Cold War has meant muted ideological competition. Failure of state socialism globally and the foundering of state-led development in Latin America have both narrowed policy options and made Latin American countries more susceptible and receptive to international influence. The armed forces themselves fit into this general pattern. To be modern and professional means to follow Western European and North American institutional patterns. The armed forces must not only be technologically advanced, highly mobile, and capable of joint (air-land-sea) operations, but they must also be nondeliberative, obedient, and apolitical. The need to modernize, professionalize, and restructure the military is clear to both civilian and military leaders.

This is not to say that the process of reform is easy and free of contention. Economic difficulties limit the availability of funds for military modernization. The potential for social turmoil continues to provide a pretext for resurrecting an attenuated version of the national security doctrine. The armed forces in some countries, such as Venezuela, Peru, and, during the late 1980s, Argentina, have divided openly into factions over the issue of subordination to political authority. In most countries, the exact role of the military has yet to be defined and, more important, sincerely accepted by members of the armed forces themselves. Thus, despite epoch-making shifts, the armed forces' democratic vocation is still in the balance.

▓ Bibliography

Abrahamsson, Bengt. *Military Professionalization and Political Power.* Beverly Hills, Calif.: Sage Publications, 1972.

Alexander Rodríguez, Linda (ed.). *Rank and Privilege: The Military and Society in Latin America.* Washington, D.C.: SR Books, 1994.

Finer, S. E. *The Man on Horseback: The Role of the Military in Politics* (2d ed.). Boulder, Colo.: Westview Press, 1988.

Goodman, Louis W., J.S.R. Mendelson, and J. Rial (eds.). *The Military and Democracy: The Future of Civil-Military Relations in Latin America.* Lexington, Mass.: D.C. Heath, 1990.

Hunter, Wendy. *The Eroding Military Influence in Brazil: Politicians Against Soldiers.* Chapel Hill: University of North Carolina Press, 1997.

Huntington, Samuel. *The Soldier and the State: The Theory and Politics of Civil-Military Relations.* New York: Vantage Books, 1964.

Loveman, Brian. *For la Patria: Politics and the Armed Forces in Latin America.* Wilmington, Del.: SR Books, 1999.

Lowenthal, Abraham F., and J. Samuel Fitch (eds.). *Armies and Politics in Latin America.* New York: Holmes and Meier, 1976.

Nordlinger, Eric A. *Soldiers in Politics: Military Coups and Governments.* Englewood Cliffs, N.J.: Prentice Hall, 1977.

Pion-Berlin, David. *Through the Corridors of Power: Institutions and Civil-Military Relations in Argentina.* University Park: Pennsylvania State University Press, 1997.

Rouquié, Alain. *The Military and the State in Latin America* (translated by Paul E. Sigmund). Berkeley: University of California Press, 1987.

Stepan, Alfred. *The Military and Politics: New Patterns from Brazil.* Princeton, N.J.: Princeton University Press, 1971.

———. *Rethinking Military Politics: Brazil and the Southern Cone.* Princeton, N.J.: Princeton University Press, 1988.

Zagorski, Paul W. *Democracy Versus National Security: Civil Military Relations in Latin America.* Boulder, Colo.: Lynne Rienner Publishers, 1992.

The Economies
of Latin America

Richard K. Harper and Alfred G. Cuzán

P revious chapters have described how geography, history, and politics
have shaped patterns of sociopolitical evolution particular to Latin
America. In this chapter, we concentrate on the economies of the region.
We trace the contours of development before the conquest, during three
centuries of Iberian colonialism, and since independence. Present structures
of demand and production; problems of poverty, inflation, and external
debt; and renewed interest in privatization, lowering trade barriers, and
encouraging foreign investment can be understood in light of the historical
background. As we shall see, however, this background—particularly the
last half century—is subject to alternative interpretations.

■ The Pre-Columbian Economies

The economic basis of pre-Columbian societies ranged from the primitive
to the sophisticated: hunting and fishing by nomadic tribes in what is now
Argentina, slash-and-burn agriculture in Amazonian rain forests, and
intense cultivation of irrigated and terraced fields in central Mexico and the
highlands of Peru. The Aztecs and Incas built impressive aqueducts and
temples in cities as large as any found in Europe at the time; produced fine
textiles made of cotton (or, in the Andes, of llama wool) and exquisite jew-
elry; and were knowledgeable about anatomy and astronomy. Even these
advanced societies, however, were limited technologically. They were unfamiliar with the wheel, iron, and discursive writing, and they lacked draft
animals. Exchange was based not on money but on barter, as well as on
tributes extracted from subordinate states and tribes in the form of goods,

forced labor, and—in the case of the Aztecs—human sacrifices to their gods (Gruzinski 1992).

In the Aztec, Incan, and Mayan empires, economy and state were tightly interwoven in a rigid hierarchy of status. At the top, an oligarchy of nobles, other state officials, generals, and priests ruled. Only the elite could own land, wear luxury garments, and consume certain commodities such as cocoa. The mass of commoners tilled fields in kinship-based communities, such as the Mexican *calpulli* and the Incan *ayllu*, where heads of families were allocated plots for subsistence farming. Commoners were required to labor on the estates of the nobility and on state construction projects and to serve in the army. Between the peasants and the nobility was a middle class of craftspeople, merchants, and state functionaries.

The Colonial Economies

The conquest and colonization of the New World had a disastrous demographic impact on the native population, which fell in many places by as much as 50 to 90 percent following contact with Europeans. Susan Place and Jacqueline Chase describe the impact of these and subsequent demographic trends in Chapter 8. We have seen in Chapter 3 by René de la Pedraja that the causes for the decimation of native peoples were pandemics caused by European viruses to which they had no immunities, along with cruel treatment and economic exploitation by the conquerors and colonists. With time, the Indian population in the Spanish-controlled mainland began to recover, although in Mexico the *mestizos* (offspring of Europeans and Indians) came to dominate demographically. In the Caribbean islands and lowlands and in Portuguese Brazil, African slaves and *mulatos* (offspring of blacks and Europeans) supplanted the native population. The significance of these patterns of ethnicity and class is analyzed by Kevin Yelvington in Chapter 9.

Spaniards introduced to the New World cattle, horses, pigs, sheep, wheat, sugar, olive trees and grapevines, the sickle and the plow, oxen-drawn carts, and a new technology for processing silver by amalgamation with mercury (see the essay by Lempat in Halperin 1992; see also Crosby 1972). The Spaniards, many of whom were of humble origin, sought gold, land, and status. They preferred densely populated areas in Mexico and Peru to the interior of South America, where the scarcity of precious metals and fierce resistance by nomadic tribes resulted in a slow rate of colonization. In Brazil, the Portuguese initially settled along the Atlantic Coast. Hunting for Indians to enslave, and, after 1700, rushing to mine gold deposits discovered in the interior, the Portuguese penetrated the Amazon Basin, progressively moving the frontier westward with the Spaniards (Williamson 1992).

Initially, the Spanish crown rewarded conquerors with land grants and allotments of Indian labor, called *encomiendas*. Confined to their own communities, Indians were, as under the Aztecs and Incas, obligated to pay tribute—including forced labor—to their new rulers. Responsibility for the delivery of workers, called the *mita* in Peru after its Inca name, fell on Indian chieftains. Although descendants of the pre-Columbian nobility, who were entitled to receive labor tribute, became wealthy under the *encomienda*, the masses of Indians remained, as before, at the bottom of the socioeconomic ladder.

As the disease-ridden Indian population shrank, relative to Spaniards and *mestizos*, the consequent scarcity of workers created incentives to develop a market in Indian labor. Many Indians, who were unwilling to stay in communities where they were subjected to the *mita*, abandoned them for Spanish *haciendas*, where they hired themselves out as farmhands, and for urban areas, where they became apprentices, *obraje* (factory) workers, and domestic servants. Uprooted from their communities, many Indians fell into debt peonage.

The export of silver, especially from Mexico City and Lima, enabled Spaniards and *criollos* to purchase European goods and regionally produced foodstuffs and manufactured goods. Other exports from the colonies included gold, dyes, leather goods, sugar, cotton, tobacco, and cacao. Through a trans-Pacific link with the Philippines, silver was exchanged for silk, spices, and other luxuries from the Orient. Merchants who engaged in transoceanic trade acquired sufficient liquid capital to lend, so, in effect, they became bankers. Also, the Catholic Church owned vast real estate holdings, including profitable *haciendas* and mines, which it leased or managed directly. Hence, the church became a major lender, financing long-term mortgages and other investments. Revenues from economic activity and from tithes and bequests were devoted to cathedrals, churches, convents, seminaries, and other strictly religious purposes, as well as to schools, colleges, hospitals, orphanages, poorhouses, hospices, cemeteries, and other institutions that supplied social services for the lay population.

Spain sought to monopolize transatlantic trade in Seville and Cádiz, but its control was undermined by contraband trade with ships from England, France, and Holland. Lagging behind in the production of manufactures, both Spain and Portugal were progressively reduced to intermediaries between their respective American possessions and their European rivals. During the second half of the eighteenth century, both monarchies sought to regain mercantilistic control over their American possessions. Although trading monopolies were loosened, so that commerce no longer had to go through designated ports, each metropolis sought to prevent its respective colonies from competing with homemade products. For example, Spain prohibited the production of wine and olive oil in its colonies and decreed the closure of *obrajes* that turned out textiles in competition with those of Catalonia. However, tax and other incentives were implemented to boost the production of commodities for which there was a demand in the peninsula. Portugal stimulated the establishment of new plantations in Brazil dedicated to rice and cacao and exempted coffee from export taxes. Both monarchies also sought to reduce the economic power of the church, expelling and expropriating the properties of the Jesuits in 1767 (Williamson 1992).

■ From Independence to the Great Depression

For decades after Latin American independence, the new nations were torn asunder by civil wars between Liberals and Conservatives. One of the issues of contention was economic policy. Against bitter Conservative resistance, Liberals advocated a market economy, into which Indian communal lands and estates of the church would be incorporated. The Liberals also advocated international trade, European immigration, and foreign investment. When Liberals were in control of the national government, usually after a civil war or a revolution, they would expropriate and auction off church holdings and break up Indian lands into individually owned parcels. Much of this land ended up in the hands of *hacendados* (owners of large estates), and many Indians fell into peonage, particularly those who had fled from being forced laborers and were no longer rooted in their communities.

In Chapter 4, Thomas J. D'Agostino explained how the wars between Liberals and Conservatives plunged the new nations into an economically devastating morass of political instability and chaos that lasted into the second half of the nineteenth century. International trade was severely disrupted during this era. The new governments routinely defaulted on their foreign debts, occasionally provoking armed intervention by creditor countries. In Mexico in the mid-nineteenth century, such intervention led to a short-lived French protectorate.

However, beginning with Chile, where by 1840 a combination of constitutional government and British capital had made it the world's chief copper producer, the second half of the nineteenth century witnessed an economic resurgence throughout the region. The civil wars gave way to political stability under the rule of enlightened despots, as in Mexico, or under commercial oligarchies, as in Argentina and Peru. These regimes pursued economic policies prescribed by laissez-faire liberalism, encouraging and protecting free trade with and immigration primarily from Europe. Trade was further stimulated by a dramatic drop in the cost of transoceanic crossings. Foreign capital—mainly flowing from Britain into South America and from the United States into Mexico and Central America and the Caribbean—poured into resurgent economies. As during colonial days, the economic basis of prosperity in the late 1800s was the large-scale export of primary products, except that silver and gold were superseded by industrial minerals, such as copper, lead, nitrates, petroleum, tin, and zinc, and agricultural commodities, including bananas, coffee, refrigerated beef, rubber, wheat, and wool. Population swelled through renewed immigration from Spain and Portugal, as well as from new sources of labor, especially Italy. Many immigrants found employment in budding industrial enterprises that processed surplus export commodities for domestic consumption. There was a general improvement in the standards of housing, public health, education, communication, and transportation, as well as a flourishing of the arts (Williamson 1992).

The most successful case of export-led growth was Argentina. Chile, Uruguay, and Cuba were also relatively successful. However, the region as a whole did not fare nearly as well. Although most economies expanded, their growth rates were generally not high enough to lift many countries from poverty, let alone catch up with the United States or Europe—due to a combination of unlucky commodity specialization, inadequate physical and financial infrastructures, labor shortages and labor market rigidities born of social inequalities, obstacles to horizontal and vertical economic integration, dissipation of profits in consumption, inefficient public administration, untimely public policies, and underinvestment in public health and education (Bulmer-Thomas 1994; Coatsworth 1998). Moreover, resting on the export of primary commodities, early-twentieth-century Latin America was vulnerable to external shocks. The Great Depression significantly reduced external demand for exports, and World Wars I and II cut off the supply of imported manufactures. As a result of these crises, Great Britain, long a major source of capital and destination of exports for Latin America, faded in economic importance. With the fall of external demand, the region's external trade shrank. By 1932, the dollar value of exports from the largest countries—Argentina, Brazil, Chile, Colombia, and Mexico— had fallen by 50 percent or more. Defaulting on public debt became generalized. World War II proved a boon for exports of raw materials, however, which allowed countries to accumulate enough foreign exchange to retire the old public debt. Import substitution industrialization (ISI) also gave the region's economies a large boost: unable to buy many consumer goods from its traditional suppliers, Latin America undertook production of its own substitutes (see the article by Thorpe in Halperin 1992).

ISI, Economic Nationalism, and Populism

At first largely a market response to scarcity, ISI increasingly became an objective of public policy after World War II. Economists associated with the Economic Commission for Latin America (ECLA, known as CEPAL in Spanish), founded by the United Nations in 1948 in Santiago, Chile, provided the theoretical rationale for ISI (Palma 1989a, 1989b). These economists shared the view of "export pessimism." That is, they forecast that the price of Latin American exports—which, as we have seen, were largely primary products—would continue to decline relative to the price of imports, which tended to require more sophisticated production technology. If this were true, Latin American countries would fall farther and farther behind their technologically more advanced trading partners, leading to a permanent state of underdevelopment. The fear was that Latin America would fall into a permanent state of dependency on foreign capital and would fail to grow. This idea was a radical departure from mainstream economic thinking, which suggests that international trade is a positive-sum game, in which all nations gain over time by specializing in the production of those items most suited to their resources and expertise.

A number of observations and assumptions led ECLA economists to conclude that the traditionally benign view of international trade would not work for Latin America. The region's export sectors used highly capital-intensive production techniques (for example, in mining), which allowed workers employed in these industries to be highly productive and, hence, relatively well paid. The downside was that these sectors existed only as exceptional enclaves, independent of the larger domestic economy—much of which was still engaged in subsistence farming and generated very low incomes. The economists' theory postulated that this situation would become permanent because the traditional sector had nothing to offer that could not be better provided to the enclave by its developed country trading partners.

This view rested on two more pessimistic assumptions. One is that as the demand for skilled labor could grow only with additional capital investment, the capital-intensive sector was generally too small to create quality jobs for the growing population and for traditional workers, whose sources of employment would be progressively displaced by imported goods. The latter phenomenon has begun to occur in Mexico, as low-cost producers from the United States acquire wider entry into that nation's markets as a result of the North American Free Trade Agreement (NAFTA), which is discussed later. The other assumption is that whereas Latin America's export-oriented enclaves would continue to demand modern, mostly imported goods, the reciprocal demand in developed countries for primary commodities exported from Latin America would be likely to decline over time, as technology developed substitutes. This would cause Latin American currencies to depreciate (people would not need pesos if they were not buying Latin American products) or would cause increasing trade deficits (if central banks did not allow pesos to depreciate, as discussed later). Were this to happen, Latin America would have to work harder just to maintain the status quo.

In brief, ECLA economists and their successors—the dependency theorists, or *dependistas*—thought the expected path of world economic development would cause Latin American incomes to stagnate. Unless it restructured its economy away from reliance on the export of primary commodities, Latin America would be relegated to permanent underdevelopment on the periphery of the world economic system.

ECLA's analysis reached the political process, where it was appropriated and used to justify the promotion of ISI by the state (Halperin 1992). Latin American developmentalist administrations used tariffs, preferential exchange rates, low-interest loans, tax incentives and subsidies, regulation, and outright nationalizations of enterprises to promote domestic industrialization through its various stages, from light manufacturing to heavy industry. Over time, these measures became essentially integrated into national plans, with governments attempting to direct substantial resources toward what they believed to be their best uses—namely, in industry. This did not constitute socialism, as the economies were still mostly privately owned and largely market-driven. The governments, however, intervened as owner, lender, or regulator over what might be called the pressure points of their economies: energy, railroads, communications, banking, and foreign trade. In short, after World War II *dirigismo* (state economic intervention) sought to alter export-oriented production and trade in favor of domestic industrialization—what we call "economic nationalism."

For a time, economic nationalism was relatively successful, especially in the largest economies of Brazil and Mexico. The most spectacular results were obtained in Brazil, which for three decades prior to 1980 grew at a rate fast enough to be called a "star" and a "miracle" (see the article by Cardoso and Fishlow in Halperin 1992). During this time, a policy of limiting imports of manufactured goods whenever a domestic substitute could be produced (the so-called law of similars) was maintained. Previously, prices in international markets were such that Brazilian businesses produced and exported crops and basic commodities, and more sophisticated goods were often imported. The law of similars, combined with export taxes on agricultural goods and an overvalued exchange rate, shifted market incentives so that Brazilian businesses found it more profitable to produce manufactured goods (Madisson, Angus, and Associates 1992).

Under ISI, Brazil succeeded in increasing the productivity of its resources, including capital and labor, at least until the 1960s. When more production can be obtained from resources by improving the efficiency and technology with which they are used, higher wages can be paid without the risk of inflation, because workers are producing more output and becoming more valuable to businesses. Rapid wage growth and improvement in the standard of living thus characterized this period, although the gains were spread unevenly. Smaller nations probably could not have been successful in pursuing import-substitution policies, but the size of Brazilian markets and the amount of available resources allowed state-favored sectors of the country's economy to prosper through several decades of relative closure to the international marketplace.

The turn toward economic nationalism was not all a matter of analysis of international terms of trade and the advantages of industrialization, however; politics played an important part as well. Turn-of-the-century governments had failed to incorporate new constituencies, including an expanded middle class and unionized industrial workers. They had been indifferent to, or actually collaborated in, the displacements of peasants, squatters, and sharecroppers caused by the expansion of commercial agriculture. And imbued with the laissez-faire doctrine of free trade, they had made it possible for foreign interests to wield economic and political power on a scale that offended nationalist sentiments. In fact, during the heyday of economic liberalism, foreign influence in the region was so great that a leading Latin American historian has characterized the entire period from 1850 to 1930 as "the neocolonial order" (Halperin 1992).

The political factors associated with the repudiation of laissez-faire liberalism first came to the fore in Mexico. In 1910—that is, before World War I—a revolution whose scope had initially been limited to political democracy expanded to encompass much wider aims, including land redistribution. This threw the country into a state of violence and turmoil that took a frightful toll of lives and property. From the cauldron of civil war emerged a regime that espoused economic nationalism and populism. Vast tracts of land were seized from the *hacendados* and converted into *ejidos* (the Aztec term for communal landholdings); foreign enterprises, including the oil industry, were nationalized; labor unions and business organizations were brought under ministerial supervision; foreign trade and investment came under strict controls; and the rhetoric of populism became part of the political folklore. Once the new regime was stabilized, the government placed a high priority on promoting industrialization. As in Brazil, this strategy seemed to work in Mexico: between 1940 and 1970, the economy grew at an average annual rate of over 6 percent per year (Cothran 1994).

In time, Bolivia, Cuba, and Nicaragua also experienced revolutions. Elsewhere, personalistic leaders—some in civilian clothes, others in military uniform—built up a mass of popular support for greater state intervention in the economy relative to foreign ownership and trade. They expropriated foreign-owned banks, utilities, railroads, and mining enterprises (in some cases, nationals also lost their properties), which came under the direct management of the state. They also pursued populist programs of income redistribution through mandated wage increases and public spend-

The Puerto Nuevo thermal power plant in Buenos Aires, Argentina.

ing (Dornbusch and Edwards 1991). Although generally a force for conservatism or reaction, the military as an institution, which, as Paul Zagorski showed in Chapter 5, became an all too familiar protagonist in most countries, was not immune to populism. In Peru during the 1970s, the generals carried out a program of expropriations and nationalizations that was exceeded only by revolutionary regimes aiming at socialism in Cuba and Nicaragua.

From the 1950s through the 1970s, economic nationalism became increasingly linked with populism—the implementation of economic policies aiming to redistribute income and wealth from domestic and foreign-based economic elites to organized labor and lower-middle-class groups. Populist policies generally take the form of large-scale expropriations of property, government-mandated increases in wages and benefits, and substantial increases in public employment and spending, all of which fuel an inflationary spiral, which is discussed later. Although no necessary logical connection exists between the two, economic nationalism and populism in the political process tend to become mutually reinforcing. If nothing else, state-promoted industrialization contributes to the creation of organized groups—namely unionized industrial labor and public employees located in urban centers—who can be readily mobilized to support populist policies (see the chapter by Kaufman and Stallings in Dornbusch and Edwards 1991). Another reason for the mutual reinforcement of economic nationalism and populism may be that as opportunities for ISI become exhausted, the momentum of government intervention shifts from growth toward redistribution. This seems to have happened in Mexico (Cothran 1994).

Whatever the reasons, as economic nationalism mutates into populism, redistribution takes precedence over growth. However well-intentioned, the results of this policy shift tend to have deleterious economic consequences and end up reducing the real income of its intended beneficiaries. This occurs because the inflation and shortages spawned by populist policies most strongly affect the lower-income groups (see introduction in Dornbusch and Edwards 1991).

The Lost Decade

Ironically, state-fostered or state-managed industrialization, intended to promote economic nationalism and a populist redistribution of wealth, was associated with external dependencies and domestic inequalities (Todaro 1989). Too often the beneficiaries of the policy were foreign industrialists who were providing the technology required for the new domestic firms, which in some cases amounted to mere subsidiaries of multinational corporations and remitted profits abroad while importing inputs for production. Thus, dependency on foreign-finished goods gave way to dependency on both intermediate goods and the international lenders who financed their importation.

Also, the overvalued exchange rates maintained to subsidize the purchase of foreign inputs for manufacturing contributed to perennial balance-of-payments problems. However, the agricultural sector—the fountain of foreign exchange and employer of millions of peasants—was fiscally penalized through export taxes and price controls, which contributed to large-scale migration to the cities. Only a minority of the urban labor force, however, could find employment in the state-favored industrial sector. Newly arrived city residents ended up eking out a living in the service and so-called informal sectors, in street vending and through employment in unlicensed shops. Squalid shantytowns sprang up almost overnight on the outskirts of the large cities, their residents marginally employed in the underground economy.

State intervention also failed to shelter economies from external shocks. The 1973 oil price hike was overcome only through increased indebtedness. In the 1980s, a second round of oil price hikes, accompanied by a rise in international interest rates and another cycle of political violence at the tail end of the Cold War, threw most countries into recession or depression and wreaked havoc with government finances. Inflation, which had been creeping up since the 1960s, skyrocketed (Roxborough 1992). All countries except Chile and Colombia experienced stagnation or negative growth, and much of the gain of the previous two decades was wiped out. It is easy to see why these years are called the lost decade of the 1980s (see the chapter by Cardoso and Fishlow in Halperin 1992).

Mexico notified the international banking community in August 1982 that it could no longer make payments on its debt. Within the next few years, most Latin American countries followed suit. During the 1970s, dollar earnings of the Organization of Petroleum Exporting Countries (OPEC) had been recycled through Western banks to many developing countries, including those in Latin America. Many state-owned enterprises took large loans on very favorable terms. This arrangement fell apart in the 1980s, when Latin America was squeezed financially by both rising interest rates, which increased the cost of making payments on existing loans, and falling prices for several major exports, which—along with the rising value of the U.S. dollar—made it more difficult to earn sufficient revenues to service the existing debt.

The initial response of most Latin American governments to this financial squeeze was to take out new loans to pay back the old ones that were coming due. Instead of cutting spending or increasing tax revenues, governments continued to spend more than they took in, resulting in larger and larger budget deficits. In Mexico, for example, the fiscal deficit reached 17 percent of gross domestic product (GDP) in 1982 (U.S. GAO 1994). (By way of comparison, U.S. federal budget deficits have not exceeded 6 percent of GDP in peacetime, although the U.S. deficit has vastly expanded during the war with Iraq.) The financing of such deficit spending could be achieved in the short run through selling additional government bonds.

Alarmed at the increasing deficits, however, investors outside and inside Latin America began to balk at buying additional bonds. Again refusing to face fiscal reality, Latin American governments simply directed their central banks to purchase the bonds. Thus, one branch of government (the Central Bank) ended up purchasing bonds sold by another branch of government (the Treasury). The wherewithal came from printing new money, pesos in Mexico and cruzeiros and later cruzados in Brazil.

With the quantity of money in circulation increasing rapidly and factories and farms producing no more than before, both domestic prices and the ratio of the national currency relative to the dollar began to climb. Thus began a vicious inflationary cycle. As the peso lost value, more were printed with which to purchase the bonds necessary to permit the government to continue to spend. As more pesos were printed, they became even less valuable, buying fewer and fewer dollars. By 1990, Argentina, Brazil, Nicaragua, and Peru had annual hyperinflation rates in excess of 10,000 percent. Although less severe, inflation also took a toll in Bolivia, Mexico, and Uruguay (see Table 6.1). In Mexico, the exchange rate fell from around

Table 6.1 Economic "Freedom," Corruption Index, Risk Rating, Trade Openness, and Development Indicators: Latin America, North America, and Iberia, 2002

Country	Population (millions)	Life Expectancy	Literacy	Calories Per Capita	GNI[a] Per Capita	HDI,[b] 2001	Average Annual GDP Growth, 1998–2002	Average Annual Inflation Rate, 1998–2002	IEF,[c] 2004	IEF Change, 1994–1999, 2000–2004	TI[d] Index 2003	TOI,[e] 1980–1982	TOI, 1998	Risk Rating,[f] 12/2003
Argentina	36	74	97	3,171	4,220	0.85	-3.126	5.4	3.48	0.12	2.5	1.5	7.3	64
Bolivia	9	64	87	2,267	900	0.67	2.4	3.6	2.59	-0.17	2.3	2.4	7.8	66
Brazil	174	69	86	3,003	2,830	0.78	1.64	6.9	3.1	-0.20	3.9	2.9	4.7	66
Chile	16	76	96	2,868	4,250	0.83	2.4	4.5	1.91	-0.37	7.4	5.9	6.8	77
Colombia	44	72	92	2,580	1,820	0.78	0.5	10.3	3.13	-0.07	3.7	3.4	6.0	64
Costa Rica	4	78	96	2,761	4,070	0.83	4.5	4.5	2.71	-0.24	4.3	2.6	8.3	72
Cuba	11	77	97	2,643		0.81			4.08	-0.31	4.6			60
Dominican Republic	13	67	84	2,333	2,140	0.74	5.9	6.9	3.51	-0.13	3.3	2.0	6.9	60
Ecuador	13	70	91	2,792	1,490	0.73	1.4	0.6	3.6	0.26	2.2	2.9	7.1	63
El Salvador	6	70	80	2,512	2,110	0.72	2.6	2.4	2.24	-0.42	3.7	2.2	6.6	70
Guatemala	12	65	70	2,203	1,760	0.65	3.4	7.4	3.16	-0.05	2.4	3.2	7.0	67
Haiti	8	52	52	2,045	440	0.47	0.8	11.5	3.78	-0.46	1.5			52
Honduras	7	66	80	2,406	930	0.67	2.4	9.4	3.53	-0.18	2.3	3.1	7.4	62
Mexico	100	74	91	3,160	5,920	0.80	3.2	10.8	2.9	-0.32	3.6	1.8	7.9	72
Nicaragua	5	69	77	2,256	710	0.64	5.6	20.7	2.94	-0.50	2.6	1.5	8.2	54
Panama	3	75	92	2,386	4,020	0.79	3.5	1.3	2.83	0.10	3.4	9.0	8.0	72
Paraguay	6	71	92	2,576	1,170	0.75	0.0	8.6	3.39	0.34	1.6	2.6	7.8	63
Peru	27	70	85	2,610	2,020	0.75	1.6	3.11	2.83	-0.29	3.7	4.0	7.5	68
Uruguay	3	75	98	2,848	4,340	0.83	-2.8	8.3	2.55	-0.27	5.5	6.2	7.4	65
Venezuela	25	73	93	2,376	4,080	0.78	-1.8	22.9	4.18	0.32	2.4	7.9	6.6	58

(continues)

Table 6.1 continued

Country	Population (millions)	Life Expectancy	Literacy	Calories Per Capita	GNI[a] Per Capita	HDI[b] 2001	Average Annual GDP Growth, 1998–2002	Average Annual Inflation Rate, 1998–2002	IEF[c] 2004	IEF Change, 1994–1999, 2000–2004	TI[d] Index 2003	TOI,[e] 1980–1982	TOI, 1998	Risk Rating,[f] 12/2003
Average Middle-income countries[g]	26	70 70	87 90	2,590	2,591 3,147	0.75	1.80 3.1	7.8	3.12	–0.14	3.3	3.6	7.2	65
Portugal	10	76	93	3,752	10,720	0.89	2.8	3.9	2.38	–0.16	6.6	5.9	7.8	79
Spain	41	78	98	3,422	14,580	0.92	3.5	3.4	2.31	–0.11	6.9	6.6	8.1	80
Canada	31	79		3,172	22,390	0.94	3.8	1.4	1.98	–0.09	8.7	7.5	7.5	86
United States	289	77		3,766	35,400	0.97	2.98	1.7	1.85		7.5	7.9	7.7	76

Sources: Unless otherwise noted, the sources are World Bank, *2004 World Development Indicators* (Washington, D.C.: World Bank, 2004), available online at http://devdata.worldbank.org/data-query/.

Notes: a. GNI: gross national income.

b. HDI: Human Development Index. United Nations, available online at http://hdr.undp.org/reports/global/2003/pdf/hdr03_HDI.pdf.

c. IEF: Economic Freedom Index. Heritage Foundation, Washington, D.C., available online at http://www.heritage.org/research/features/index/.

d. TI Index: Transparency International, Corruption Perception Index., available online at http://www.transparency.org.

e. TOI: Trade Openness Index, from James Gwartney, Chuck Skipton, and Kurt Shuler, *Openness, Growth, and Trade Policy* (U.S. Congress, Joint Economic Staff Report, 2000).

f. Risk rating: Updated monthly, the Composite International Country Risk Guide risk rating is computed from twenty-two risk economic, financial, and political components. It ranges from 0 to 100, where 0 represents the most risk and 100 the least. A rating below 50 is considered "very high" risk and one above 80 is regarded as "very low" risk.

g. Middle-income countries: those countries in which 2002 GNI per capita was between $735 and $9,075. This includes all Latin American countries except Haiti and Nicaragua.

20 pesos per dollar in 1980 to over 3,000 pesos to the dollar at the end of the decade.

High rates of inflation make it difficult for businesses to plan beyond the next week. Not surprisingly, then, in Latin America as a whole, investment spending fell from 25 percent of GDP in the late 1970s to 17 percent by the late 1980s. In some countries, the situation was much worse: by the late 1980s, investment spending in Argentina had dropped so much that it was insufficient to replace worn-out capital (that is, to cover depreciation expense), much less provide for any net growth in the capital stock. Yet such investment—in tools, factories, roads, bridges, buildings, and other plant and equipment—has a profound impact on the future productivity of the workforce, which is the source of sustained, noninflationary wage increases. In effect, the seed corn of the economy was being consumed.

Wages, too, rarely keep up with such extreme rates of inflation, and the ordinary worker usually loses ground. As the purchasing power of wages in Latin America was eroded by inflation, minimum-wage workers fell even further behind industrial workers, increasing the gap between skilled and unskilled members of the workforce. By 1990, only in Colombia, Costa Rica, and Paraguay were inflation-adjusted minimum wages higher than they had been in 1980. In contrast, by 1990, El Salvador, Guatemala, Mexico, and Peru experienced a fall in inflation-adjusted minimum wages to less than half the level of 1980.

Among those most affected by the crisis have been the very poor and their children. When spending could no longer be sustained, governments cut back on health and education programs. The United Nations Children's

UN Photo 72917

A low-income housing development in Caracas, Venezuela.

Fund (UNICEF) found that health spending cuts were particularly severe during the 1980s and that the proportion of six- to eleven-year-olds attending school dropped as well. These spending cuts may aggravate income inequality in Latin America. The proportion of total income going to the poorest classes in the region is lower, and that to the richest is higher, than is the case in the United States or Canada (Milanovic and Yitzhaki 2002). Greater equality will probably have to await further growth, as the middle and upper classes are unlikely to tolerate additional taxes to finance redistributive programs until incomes are growing rapidly.

Turning the Corner—the 1990s

The legacy of the lost decade of the 1980s—in the form of overall economic stagnation; deterioration of living standards; and reduced spending on health, education, and investment programs—will take years of strong economic performance to erase. Recovery is already under way, however. Since 1990, a combination of continued debt repayments, lower interest rates, and a cheaper U.S. dollar has turned the region as a whole, though not every country, around (see Table 6.2). Latin America has once again begun to appear to be a favorable credit risk to potential investors: capital has returned to the region to finance badly needed factories, equipment, and infrastructure.

The economic turnaround of the 1990s was at least in part the result of a change in attitudes on the part of Latin American governments and their creditors. Fearing major banks would become insolvent if they had to write off the Latin American debt, lenders insisted at first that all principal and interest payments be made on time. The International Monetary Fund (IMF) weighed in as well. The IMF assists governments in financial difficulty by making loans that are contingent on the design and implementation of an austerity plan of monetary and fiscal restraint. The accumulated debt was so large, however, and the ability of governments to pay it back in the short run was so inadequate, that only a certain amount of debt relief (in which lenders must write off part of the debt) could alleviate the situation. Thus, the U.S. government also became involved. First the Baker and then the Brady plans (named after successive U.S. secretaries of the treasury) offered some level of debt relief. The 1985 Baker Plan emphasized full repayment but with debt rescheduling, so as to shift some of the burden into the future. The 1989 Brady Plan contained elements of actual debt relief, so that some of the scheduled repayments were forgiven (Edwards 1994).

Perhaps even more important than debt relief was the radical change in public attitudes and policy regarding economic matters that took place

Table 6.2 Income Quintiles by Nation

Nation	Lowest 20 Percent	Second Quintile	Third Quintile	Fourth Quintile	Highest 20 Percent	Highest 10 Percent
Bolivia, 1990–1991	5.6	9.7	14.5	22.0	48.2	31.7
Brazil, 1989	2.1	4.9	8.9	16.8	67.5	51.3
Chile, 1989	3.7	6.8	10.3	16.2	62.9	48.9
Colombia, 1991	3.6	7.6	12.6	20.4	55.8	39.5
Costa Rica, 1989	4.0	9.1	14.3	21.9	50.8	34.1
Dominican Rep., 1989	4.2	7.9	12.5	19.7	55.6	39.6
Guatemala, 1989	2.1	5.8	10.5	18.6	63.0	46.6
Honduras, 1989	2.7	6.0	10.2	17.6	63.5	47.9
Mexico, 1984	4.1	7.8	12.3	19.9	55.9	39.5
Panama, 1989	2.0	6.3	11.6	20.3	59.8	42.1
Peru, 1985–1986	4.9	9.2	13.7	21.0	51.4	35.4
Venezuela, 1989	4.8	9.5	14.4	21.9	55.9	39.5
United States, 1985	4.7	11.0	17.4	25.0	41.9	25.0
Canada, 1987	5.7	11.8	17.7	24.6	40.2	24.1

Sources: World Bank, *World Development Report 1994. Infrastructure for Development* (New York: Oxford University Press, 1994); United Nations Development Programme, *Human Development Report, 1994* (New York: Oxford University Press, 1994).

Note: Data was not available for Argentina, Ecuador, El Salvador, Haiti, Nicaragua, Paraguay, or Uruguay.

(Hojman 1994). Backed into a corner by, on the one hand, the deteriorating domestic economy and, on the other, external demands from creditors, Latin American governments shifted away from economic nationalism. At first gingerly and then with increasing momentum, Latin America embraced what external observers call "neoliberalism." Tariffs came down, exports were promoted, foreign investors were invited to bid on state enterprises put up for auction, and customs unions and free-trade agreements were implemented both within the region and—as in the case of the North American Free Trade Agreement—with the United States and Canada.

This time the political sponsors of the market economy did have a mass following. A new generation of elected presidents redefined populism, seemingly ending its identification with state regulation of the economy (Weyland 1994). The new populism argues that the mass of the poor and the marginalized, who heretofore have had to manage on their own in the informal sector, do better in an economy that is unburdened by government regulations and restrictions. Neoliberals call for a government that does not do any of the following: intervene on behalf of one industry or labor union at the expense of another, choke off economic enterprise with a maze of regulations, and penalize economic success with taxes allegedly raised for redistribution to the poor, which in the past often ended up feeding inefficient bureaucracies and corrupt public officials. Free entrepreneurship, secure titles to property, more foreign investment, less bureaucracy, lower taxes, fewer regulations, greater transparency, and less corruption in government transactions are seen as the keys to raising living standards for larger numbers of people. In short, the market rather than the government is seen as the means for producing the greatest good for the greatest number, according to neoliberal practitioners.

The new economic liberalism was and continues to be resisted by unionized labor, tainted by highly publicized corruption cases, and criticized by Latin American and U.S. intellectuals and academics (Baer and Conroy 1994). However, at least for a time, it enjoyed a measure of popularity in most countries of the region (Philip 1994). In Mexico, the heirs to the revolution that first ushered economic nationalism into Latin America progressively dismantled the policies of their predecessors, embracing freer trade with the United States. The populist alternative to and defector from the ruling party (the PRI), Cuauhtémoc Cárdenas, son of former president Lázaro Cárdenas (who was famous for nationalizing the oil industry and redistributing vast tracts of land in the 1930s), peaked in popularity in the 1988 presidential election, dropped to third place in the 1994 election, and lost again in 2000. Mexico's current president, Vicente Fox, of the traditionally conservative National Action Party (PAN), has continued a policy of increased trade and more open borders with the United States.

Brazil's President Fernando Henrique Cardoso implemented economic policies based on freer trade. In Argentina, Presidents Carlos Menem and Fernando de la Rua attempted to resolve Argentina's economic problems through privatization of state enterprises. Víctor Paz Estenssoro, elected president of Bolivia for the second time, almost twenty years after he was ousted in a military coup, renounced his previous policies—which had emphasized nationalizations and redistributions—and steered the country toward a market economy, a policy his successors, all from different parties, accelerated. The restoration of democracy in Chile under Christian Democratic presidents resulted in the continuation of the neoliberalism instituted under the military dictatorship of General Augusto Pinochet, albeit with increased spending on social services. Following the ousting of the socialist Sandinistas in the 1990 election, Nicaragua made an about-face in economic policy. There, as in El Salvador and Guatemala, the left has been rejected at the polls time and again.

The collapse of the Soviet Union, the associated implosion of Cuba's socialist economy, and the global trend toward freer and larger markets undoubtedly contributed to this revolution in Latin American economic attitudes. But apart from these largely external influences, the painful experience of the lost decade no doubt made its independent contribution, exposing large-scale failures in public sector management. This is not to say that neoliberalism achieved an irreversible victory. The new millennium ushered leftist parties or candidates into office in Argentina and Brazil. In 2004, a wave of violent protests forced the resignation of a neoliberal president in Bolivia. Neoliberalism suffered its most serious defeat in Venezuela, where President Hugo Chávez, a former colonel once imprisoned for his participation in a failed coup, breathed new life into fiery antiliberal rhetoric and leftist economic and foreign policies following his landslide victory in 1998 (with economic consequences made evident in Table 6.1).

Nevertheless, as measured by the Heritage Foundation/*Wall Street Journal*'s "index of economic freedom" (IEF), a measure of neoliberalism in economic policy, the general trend during the last decade in Latin America has been toward less government intervention in the economy. The IEF ranges from 1 to 5, where 1 represents the most "economic freedom" and 5 the least. A "free economy" scores between 1 and 1.99 and a "mostly free" one between 2 and 2.99. An IEF value of between 3 and 3.99 indicates a "mostly unfree" economy and one 4.0 or above a "repressed" economy. The Latin American IEF average over the 1999–2004 period is 3.1 (2.99 if Cuba is excluded). In other words, Latin American economies are located right in the middle of the "economic freedom" continuum. Only Chile has a "free" economy. Another eight economies are "mostly free": Bolivia, Costa Rica, El Salvador, Mexico, Nicaragua, Panama, Peru, and Uruguay. The rest are "mostly unfree" or, in the case of Cuba, "repressed." The trend, though, is toward greater "economic freedom": between the first and second half of the 1995–2004 decade, the average Latin American IEF score dropped 0.14 (about the same as it did in Spain and Portugal). The exceptions to the trend were Argentina, Ecuador, Panama, and Venezuela. Interestingly, empirically there is in Latin America a moderate tendency toward faster economic growth in the 1998–2002 period, the greater the change toward "economic freedom" between the first and second halves of the 1995–2004 decade (Pearson's $r = -0.41$, $r = -0.47$ when Haiti is excluded).

■ Indicators of Economic Development

Assessing Latin American economic development must take into consideration the considerable variation that exists among countries (see Table 6.1). In 2002, gross national income (GNI) per capita ranged from less than $1,000 in Bolivia, Haiti, Honduras, and Nicaragua to more than four or even five times as much in Chile, Costa Rica, Mexico (the richest in 2004), Panama, and Venezuela. In fact, as measured by the Gini index, in Latin

America within-country inequality is the highest in the world (Milanovic and Yitzhaki 2002). (The Gini index measures the extent to which the distribution of income or consumption among individuals or households within a country deviates from a perfectly equal distribution.) The contrasts can be striking: modern skyscrapers and subways situated within walking distance of shantytowns and horse-drawn carts. Brazil, for example, seems like two countries, a modern one grafted onto a developing one.

Compared with the United States, where GNI per capita was $37,610 in 2003, many Latin Americans live in what North Americans would consider abject poverty. Even Spain and Portugal top every Latin American country on income per capita. Nevertheless, by world standards most countries in the region are not poor. All but two Latin American countries (Haiti and Nicaragua) are classified as "middle income" by the World Bank. As Table 6.1 shows, seven Latin American countries (Argentina, Chile, Costa Rica, Mexico, Panama, Uruguay, and Venezuela) have a GNI per capita that is higher than the world average for middle-income countries. And when other indicators of development are examined, the picture becomes even brighter. Half rank higher than the median out of 175 countries on the United Nations Human Development Index, and four (Argentina, Chile, Costa Rica, and Uruguay) rank in the upper quartile. People in more than half of all Latin American countries have a life expectancy exceeding 70 years. Remarkably, on this indicator, tiny Costa Rica not only ranks highest in the region but with not much more than one-tenth the per capita income of the United States. Costa Ricans have a higher average life expectancy than people in the United States. On literacy, Latin America also does well: the average for the region is only three points below that for the world's middle-income countries.

The region's rate of development is also worth examining. Between 1950 and 1980, per capita output in Latin America grew at an average rate of 2.7 percent per year. This compares favorably with historical growth rates in Europe and the United States (see the article by Cardoso and Fishlow in Halperin 1992). However, more recently the region's growth rate has lagged behind that of the middle-income countries (see Table 6.1). And compared with the success cases in East Asia, Latin America has done poorly. During the lost decade, while the region was undergoing the worst economic contraction since the Great Depression, with output per capita declining almost 1 percent per year, the so-called Little Dragons of Asia (Hong Kong, Singapore, South Korea, and Taiwan) continued to grow at average rates of between 6 percent and 9 percent per year. Another comparison is revealing: Japan and Chile, a relatively successful Latin American case, began the post–Great Depression period with roughly similar per capita incomes, but despite the devastation it suffered during World War II, the Japanese economy is now one of the richest in the world, whereas Chile is still no better than a middle-income country. Clearly, Latin America has underperformed economically vis-à-vis the Pacific Rim. Perhaps not coincidentally, in 1999–2004 the average IEF for Hong Kong, Singapore, Taiwan, Japan, and South Korea was 2.12 (vs. 2.99 for Latin America excluding Cuba), and every one of the Pacific Rim countries is ranked as either having a "free" or "mostly free" economy.

Valid assessment of Latin American development obviously requires the use of multiple measures of development, several points of reference, and an appreciation of the range of development within a single Latin American country. It is hard to escape the conclusion, however, that although the record is far from disastrous, by and large Latin America has underperformed economically since independence (Bulmer-Thomas 1994).

Structure of Production and Demand

For a region that historically has earned most of its foreign exchange by selling products extracted from the land (minerals or crops), relatively few of Latin America's inhabitants derive their livelihoods directly from the soil any more. Only about 25 percent of the Latin American labor force is employed in agriculture. Approximately another 25 percent is employed in manufacturing and the rest in services. Also, on average, agriculture contributes only 10 percent of value added to gross domestic product (see Table 6.3). Nevertheless, agriculture, processed foodstuffs, fishing, and mining continue to dominate the export sector. Latin America's primary exports include bananas, beef, cereals, coffee, cotton, seeds and fruits, shrimp and lobster, soybeans and soya, sugar, tobacco, vegetable oils, and wool; and minerals (gold and other precious metals, copper, nickel, tin), natural gas, and petroleum and its derivatives. Not to be overlooked are two illegal products, marijuana and cocaine, which generate substantial export revenues even as they insidiously corrupt society and state.

Due to weather changes and cycles of over- and under-production, these commodities are subject to wide price swings, both absolutely and relative to imported finished products. This is one reason why, as we have seen, Latin American policymakers wanted to shift their economies away from agriculture and mining toward government-sponsored industrialization. Today, industry contributes an average of a little over 25 percent of value added to GDP, or more than twice the contribution of agriculture. The proportion is about one-third or more in Argentina, Bolivia, Chile, Colombia, Cuba, the Dominican Republic, El Salvador, and Venezuela. The products of state-sponsored industrialization, however, have been largely disappointing—of lower quality and costing more to produce than imports from the United States, Europe, or Japan. Many Latin American manufactures could be produced only with tax breaks or subsidies and sold mostly

An outdoor market in Solola, Guatemala.

to nationals behind a protective wall of tariffs and other impediments to foreign competition. Some industrial products that Latin America does produce competitively enough to export include vehicles (Argentina), transport equipment and parts (Brazil), paper and printing (Chile), textiles (Costa Rica), apparel (Guatemala), leather products (Uruguay), and chemicals (Venezuela). As Table 6.3 shows, compared to middle-income countries around the world, Latin America's structure of production is somewhat skewed toward services at the expense of industry. Also, compared to middle-income countries, Latin America exports less (and out of what it exports, a larger share is devoted to servicing debt), imports more, and accumulates less capital, which means it consumes more.

Finally, although there are no comparable data for "middle-income countries," compared with the United States, governments in Latin America spend and consume less of their GDP. This difference is partly accounted for by the difference in per capita incomes (generally the richer the country, the more the government spends of GDP). Actually, given the middle income of the region, it could very well be that Latin American governments are spending and consuming too much. Nevertheless, the burden of government on Latin American economies may be not so much fiscal as regulatory and bureaucratic. Official corruption, too, no doubt exacts a toll: on the Transparency International "Corruption Perceptions Index," where 10 represents a "highly clean" state and 0 a "highly corrupt one," the Latin American average in 2003 was 3.3. (A score of 5.0 is the number Transparency International considers the borderline figure distinguishing countries that do and do not have a serious corruption problem.)

Table 6.3   Structures of Output and Demand, 2002 (as a percentage of gross domestic product)

Country	Agriculture	Industry	Services	Exports	Imports	Capital[a]	GDFI,[b] 1990	GDFI, 2002	Government Spending	Government Consumption	Trade Growth Minus GDP Growth,[c] 1990–2002	Debt Service (% of Exports)
Argentina	11	32	57	28	13	12	1.3	9.0	26.6	12.2	5.1	18
Bolivia	15	33	52	22	27	14	0.7	8.7	31.9	14.8	1.3	28
Brazil	6	21	73	16	14	20	0.4	4.4	26.5	19.3	4.8	69
Chile	9	34	57	36	39	23	2.2	5.5	23.7	12.6	3.2	33
Colombia	14	30	56	20	21	15	1.3	3.6	20.4	20.8	3.3	40
Costa Rica	8	29	62	42	47	22	2.9	4.8	21.1	14.4	3.8	9
Cuba	7	46	47	16	18	10			54.2	23		
Dominican Republic	12	33	55	26	35	23	1.9	4.6	16.3	9	-0.3	6
Ecuador	9	28	63	24	31	28	1.2	5.2	22.1	10	2.0	29
El Salvador	9	30	61	27	41	16	0.8	1.6	17.6	10	6.9	8
Guatemala	22	19	58	16	28	19	0.6	9.8	12.9	7.7	3.2	7
Haiti				13	36	21	0.3		10.1	7	5.4	
Honduras	13	31	56	37	53	28	1.4	2.2	26	13.9	-0.4	12
Mexico	4	27	69	27	29	20	1.0	2.4	23.7	11.6	9.2	23
Nicaragua	18	25	57	23	49	32		4.3	45.1	20.1		12
Panama	6	14	80	28	29	25	2.6	7.4	28	15.1	-2.0	20
Paraguay	22	29	49	31	43	20	1.5	8.3	18.5	9.1	-3.8	10
Peru	8	28	64	16	17	18	0.2	4.2	18.3	11.2	2.9	33
Uruguay	9	27	64	22	20	12	0.0	1.7	33.3	13.4	3.1	40
Venezuela	3	43	54	29	17	1.7	3.1	25.1	8	26		

(continues)

Table 6.3 continued

Country	Agriculture	Industry	Services	Exports	Imports	Capital[a]	GDFI,[b] 1990	GDFI, 2002	Government Spending	Government Consumption	Trade Growth Minus GDP Growth,[c] 1990–2002	Debt Service (% of Exports)
Average	11	29	60	25	30	20	1.2	5.0	25	13	2.9	24
Middle-income countries[d]	9	34	57	32	28	23						18
Portugal	4	30	66	31	41	28	3.9	7.1	46.1	20	3.7	
Spain	3	30	66	28	30	26	3.4	6.2	39.8	17.57	6.5	
Canada	3	32	66	44	39	20	2.7	7.3	40.6	21.3	4.2	
United States	2	23	75	10	14	18	2.8	2.4	35.6	15.5	2.9	

Sources: All data except for Government Spending and Government Consumption from World Bank 2004, available online at http://devdata.world-bank.org/data-query/; Government Spending and Government Consumption from Heritage Foundation, Washington, D.C., available online at http://www.heritage.org/research/features/index/.

Notes: a. Capital: gross capital formation.
b. GDFI: gross direct foreign investment.
c. Trade Growth Minus GDP Growth is a measure of a country's integration with the world economy.
d. Middle-income countries: those countries in which 2002 GNI per capita was between $735 and $9,075. This includes all Latin American countries except Haiti and Nicaragua.

Out of 133 countries included, only Chile and Uruguay ranked in the upper quartile.

Money and Stocks

Like other emerging markets around the world, Latin America has had its share of volatility in the prices of financial assets (stocks and bonds) and foreign exchange. Also, between 1970 and 1998, the region experienced almost half of the world's seventy-nine currency crises and twenty-five of the world's sixty-four banking crises included in a study by Gary Hufbauer and Erika Wada (1999). Investment spending is a necessary ingredient for economic growth, funding construction of new infrastructure and workplaces and other improvements to the production process. The essential element of investment spending is the choice to give up opportunities to have more consumer goods and services today and, instead, to opt to buy or build assets that will yield a payback in the future. By their decisions to spend on these assets today, people and businesses hope to generate additional returns down the road, over the productive life of the asset.

The funds that are necessary to build these new assets come from savers, both domestic and foreign. Nations that have high saving rates tend to finance most of their investment spending using domestic funds, while nations with low saving rates tend to import the necessary savings from abroad. In the United States, for example, a low national saving rate has led to capital flowing in from abroad, particularly from Asia, as foreign savers see opportunities for profitable investments in the United States. To make the most out of savings, that is, for capital to be most efficiently allocated, an economy needs to have mature financial markets. Maturity comes about from a combination of government supervision, regulation, reporting and auditing requirements, strong credit assessment, openness to foreign competition, and relatively free financial markets. While the United States is a world leader in this area, Latin America as a whole lags way behind. Only Chile has made good, if incomplete, progress on this front.

Despite their ups and downs since the 1990s, Latin American stock markets have been good performers more recently. In 2003, Argentina and Brazil substantially outpaced U.S. stock markets, and Mexico's market performed somewhat better than the U.S. market, earning good returns for investors willing to risk the historic volatility of these markets. However, from the perspective of the international investor, some of these markets are difficult to get involved with simply because there are very few traded firms compared to other nations (there are thirteen companies listed in Argentina's Merval index) or because there are capital controls in place that limit the amount of money that can be changed out of the local currency into dollars, as in Venezuela.

Brazil has done particularly well in 2003 and 2004. This is largely due to the fact that fears of default associated with the election of President Luiz Inácio Lula da Silva have not become a reality. Even as they have risen in value, share prices of Brazilian companies seem cheap relative to those of companies in more developed countries. According to *The Economist*, Brazilian companies traded in 2003 at prices per share that were about $7 per dollar of expected earnings. This was still cheaper than most emerging markets, where prices were about $11 per dollar of expected annual earnings, and much cheaper than markets in developed countries. Investors in the U.S. stock market—the Standard & Poor's (S&P) 500 is a broad cross-section of the market—had to pay as much as $24 to purchase $1 of expected earnings.

When Brazilian companies' shares sell relatively cheaply, capital is more expensive to obtain for them. This is because they must pledge a larger amount of their expected future earnings in order to raise the same amount of capital via stock offerings as their counterparts in, say, the United States. Again, in 2003 on average, a Brazilian company could only raise $7 in new funding by offering $1 of future earnings. This is about a 14 percent expected return for the investor (earning $1 on an investment of $7 is a 14.3 percent return). In contrast, a U.S. company could raise $24 by offering $1 of future earnings for a 4.2 percent expected rate of return to the investor.

Why must Brazilian firms offer more of their future earnings than U.S. firms in order to raise money? The primary reason is that investing in these firms is perceived as riskier than investing in U.S. firms. The Brazilian currency has historically been volatile, gaining and losing (mostly losing) value against major world currencies due to inflation and financial crises. If a Brazilian investment were to increase in value by, say, 20 percent, at the same time as the Brazilian currency fell against other major currencies at the same rate, the net gain would be zero. President Lula da Silva's threats to default on Brazilian debt added an element of politically induced uncertainty to the mix. Further, most Brazilian companies have made use of a law that permits them to restrict voting rights on certain types of stock, so that a small group of stockholders can effectively control the decisions of the company. This can deter foreign and domestic investors.

Generally, Chilean and Mexican stock markets are the most open to foreign investors. The Chilean market is heavily influenced by factors related to the world price of copper, as this is a major Chilean export. The Mexican market is much more closely tied to the health of the U.S. economy than are other Latin American markets, because of the high degree of integration of Mexican manufacturing facilities in the U.S. industrial process.

Investors can usually move their funds in and out of Latin American nations at will and do so in response to perceived changes in the profitability of their investments in a particular country. The availability of these funds should improve living standards in Latin America to the extent that they are used to invest in assets that make the nation more productive. Thus, capital flows are beneficial. However, at the same time, the presence of international investors can contribute to the periodic boom-and-bust crash cycles that plague the region, as money flows into areas that are perceived as "hot" destinations for investment but flows out just as rapidly from areas that fall out of favor. The consequences can have wide repercussions. For example, international investors tend to provide funding in dollars to Latin American financial institutions, which then make loans to a variety of local, regional, and national businesses. These loans are made in the local currency. This creates a mismatch, since the banks' assets (the expected loan repayments) are denominated in the local currency, for example, pesos, while their liabilities (money owed to international investors) are in dollars. If the peso were to fall against the dollar because the international investor community lost confidence in the central government's policies and sold pesos, then the local bank would be left with obligations to pay out dollars, but with a diminished ability to buy dollars due to the weakness of the peso.

To the extent that Latin American nations suffer disproportionately from perceptions of weak systems of governance and corporate control born of their immature financial systems, then they will likely have more of these disruptive capital flows, bidding up asset prices when the country is "hot," but falling precipitously when an event causes the investment community to flee the local market. In sum, due to immature financial systems and the extra risk imposed by political uncertainty, Latin America has to pay a higher cost for capital, which retards its rate of growth.

■ Latin America in the World Economy

On a trade openness index (TOI) ranging from 1 to 10, the Latin American average over the 1980–1998 period was 5.2. This contrasts with an average of 7.5 for the Little Dragons (Hong Kong, Singapore, South Korea, and Taiwan) and was below that of Canada or even Portugal or Spain (see Table 6.3 for figures on net exports as percent of GDP). Why have the Latin American economies not followed the example of the Little Dragons or their Iberian sisters? This question has no simple answer. Historical and cultural, as well as economic and political, factors are undoubtedly at work. Whatever the explanation, it is encouraging to note that average TOI in Latin America doubled between the early 1980s and the late 1990s, and in most countries, it is now on a par with that of Canada or the United States. (We say "encouraging" because TOI is associated with higher incomes around the world and, in Latin America, excluding Haiti, there is a moderate correlation between average TOI 1980–1998 openness and GNI per capita, Pearson's r = 0.46.) Relatedly, Latin America has also become more open to gross direct foreign investment (GDFI). As a share of GDP, on average, GDFI quadrupled between 1990 and 2002 (see Table 6.3).

Increasingly, then, Latin American countries are returning to the economic liberalism under which they had prospered in the nineteenth century. Perhaps the most dramatic change is that of Mexico, which dropped its previous policy of economic nationalism born of the 1910 Revolution. In 1980–1982, Mexico ranked third lowest in trade openness in Latin America, but by 1998 it was the third most open. In fact, in 1998 Mexico's TOI was higher than Taiwan's and only half a point lower than South Korea's. Between 1990 and 2002, in Mexico, trade growth exceeded GDP growth by a whopping 9.2 percentage points, a margin exceeded only by six other countries in the world, all formerly under communist rule. Also, in 1994, Mexico joined the United States and Canada in the North American Free Trade Agreement. Between 1995 and 2002, trade within NAFTA relative to the total exports of its three members was up 11 percentage points (56 percent vs. 45 percent). Also, Mexico signed a free-trade pact with Chile, joined the General Agreement on Tariffs and Trade (GATT) and the Asia-Pacific Economic Cooperation group (APEC), and became the twenty-fifth member of the Organization for Economic Cooperation and Development (OECD), whose membership to that point had been limited to the developed economies of the North Atlantic, Europe, and Japan. Also, once a leader in nationalization and expropriations of property, Mexico has become investor-friendly: in 2003 it tied with Costa Rica and Panama for the second most secure country in which to invest.

In Central and South America, regional trade blocs have also been established or revived, although they have not been as successful as NAFTA. As a percentage of their total exports, trade among Mercosur members (Argentina, Brazil, Paraguay, and Uruguay) nearly tripled between 1990 and 1998, from 9 percent to 25 percent, but fell back to a more modest 11 percent by 2002. During the same decade, the Andean group (Bolivia, Colombia, Ecuador, Peru, and Venezuela) did better; trade among member countries relative to their total exports more than doubled, from 4.1 percent in 1990 to 9.5 percent in 2002. But despite efforts to revive it, trade within the Central American Common Market relative to total exports—a temporary upswing in the late 1990s notwithstanding—remains stagnant at about 13 percent. Nevertheless, in most Latin American countries, the rate of trade growth exceeds that of GDP. Thus, the trend is clear: whether functioning within trade blocs or individually, most Latin American countries have turned away from an import-substitution toward an export-oriented developmental strategy. After a long detour down the dead end of economic nationalism, Latin America is back on a freer trade road, as it had taken before World War I.

▓ Conclusion

As the nineteenth century was coming to a close, most of Latin America lived under a liberal, export-oriented economic regime, at the core of which were free trade and foreign investment. Temporary recessions apart, this was an era of prosperity and rising living standards for the region, even if the benefits were far from evenly distributed. One hundred years later, Latin America—having taken a detour into economic nationalism, with its panoply of government controls and ownership of enterprises—is moving back to a more liberal regime. Tariffs are coming down, import and export controls are being relaxed, government ownership and regulation of economic enterprises has been cut—in short, the entire structure of *dirigismo* is being dismantled. Led by Chile, this process has gone further in some countries—notably Costa Rica, El Salvador, Mexico, Nicaragua, and Peru—than in others. This general change in policy has gone hand in hand with a fairly robust economic recovery. In most countries, inflation, unemployment, and government deficits are down, and growth is up.

The neoliberal path to prosperity is still rocky, however. The problem with neoliberalism is that in the short run it promotes income inequality. Even as unemployment goes up, a few people become rich or richer. Unemployment rises because privatization and the competition that comes with tariff reduction force a reallocation of resources, including labor, from uses the domestic and international markets value less to those they value more, thus allowing consumers' and investors' choices to determine more directly which businesses will be successful and which will fail. Firms merge, streamline, or go out of business. Thus, a period of higher unemployment is unavoidable, as both labor and capital adjust to a more competitive economic environment. Also, the price of some previously subsidized commodities—such as electricity, gasoline, and bus fares—may rise steeply with the ending of government subsidies, further squeezing the ordinary worker. At the same time, only the fastest learners and the best-positioned entrepreneurs and firms initially make the most of the new opportunities made available by freeing markets.

The spectacle of thousands of workers thrown out of work while a few millionaires flout their new wealth in conspicuous consumption runs against the populist grain embedded in Latin America's political culture. Also relevant is the opposition to neoliberalism by vested interests that had grown around state-sponsored industrialization, such as some labor unions and manufacturers. Moreover, the public's attention generally focuses on the short-run costs of unemployment and the unequal distribution of the gains from renewed economic growth. Ideally, in the long run the economic growth made possible by neoliberalist policies can raise living standards across all classes, swelling the middle class in particular. But in the short run, economic development is associated with relative, if not absolute, losses of income for the lower classes (Branco and Williamson 1988).

We close with cautious optimism. Latin America is well endowed with natural resources. It also possesses a good supply of productive workers and entrepreneurs whose energies will be released and channeled in unforeseen ways, provided the fruits of labor, investment, and savings do not run a high risk of confiscation by expropriation, taxation, arbitrary regulations, corruption, or inflation. Latin America has long had a shortage of good managers of the public's money. It has lacked governments that will not spend more than their revenues and prudent borrowing will allow, while acting as responsible stewards of the nation's currency. But if present trends toward freer markets, export-oriented growth, more secure and widely distributed property rights, a better climate for foreign investment, and fiscal and economic restraint continue and if the governments implement social services reforms to target those most in need, Latin America will, in short order, continue to recover from the ravages of the disastrous lost decade and once again enjoy a long period of rising living standards.

In short, Latin America's economic problems during the past several decades have largely been self-inflicted, the consequence, for the most part, of wrongheaded policies. Part of the solution, then, has to be political. Above all, old-fashioned populism, in which the state intervened at will to redistribute wealth and favor some economic activities or some groups or classes over others, must be eliminated permanently from the Latin American political culture. Ironically, to grow and prosper, Latin American economies require governments whose first rule is, like the physician's, to do no harm.

▨ Note

Many thanks to Teresa Tetrault, M.A. in political science candidate and graduate assistant in the Department of Government, University of West Florida, Pensacola, for her assistance.

▨ Bibliography

Angell, Alan, and Carol Graham. "Can Social Sector Reform Make Adjustment Sustainable and Equitable? Lessons from Chile and Venezuela." *Journal of Latin American Studies* 27 (1995):189–219.

Baer, M. Delal. "Profiles in Transition in Latin America and the Caribbean." *Annals of the American Academy of Political and Social Science* 526 (1993):47–57.

Baer, Werner, and Michael E. Conroy (eds.). "Latin America: Privatization, Property Rights, and Deregulation." Proceedings of the first conference of Latin America 2000. In *Quarterly Review of Economics and Finance* 34 (special issue) (1994).

Branco, Kenneth J., and John B. Williamson. "Economic Development and Income Distribution: A Cross-National Analysis." *American Journal of Economics and Sociology* 47, no. 3 (1988):277–297.

Bulmer-Thomas, Victor. *The Economic History of Latin America Since Independence.* Cambridge, UK: Cambridge University Press, 1994.

Coatsworth, John H. "Economic and Institutional Trajectories in Nineteenth-Century Latin America." In *Latin America and the World Economy Since 1800*, edited by John H. Coatsworth and Alan M. Taylor. Cambridge, Mass.: Harvard University Press, 1998.

Cothran, Dan A. "Mexican Economic and Fiscal Policies to Sustain Political Stability." *Public Budgeting and Finance* 4, no. 4 (1994):98–119.

Crosby, Alfred W., Jr. *The Columbian Exchange: Biological and Cultural Consequences of 1492.* Westport, Conn.: Greenwood Press, 1972.

Dornbusch, Rudiger, and Sebastian Edwards (eds.). *The Macroeconomics of Populism in Latin America.* Chicago: University of Chicago Press, 1991.

Edwards, Sebastian. *The Latin American Debt Crisis.* Washington, D.C.: World Bank, 1994.

Fishlow, Albert. "The Latin American State." *Journal of Economic Perspectives* 4, no. 3 (1990):61–74.

Gruzinski, Serge. *The Aztecs: Rise and Fall of an Empire* (translated from the French by Paul G. Bahn). New York: Harry N. Abrams, 1992.

Gwartney, James, Chuck Skipton, and Kurt Shuler. *Openness, Growth, and Trade Policy.* U.S. Congress, Joint Economic Staff Report, 2000. Available online at http://garnet.acns.fsu.edu/~cskipton/JEC_reports.htm.

Halperin Donghi, Tulio (ed.). *The Colonial and Postcolonial Experience: Five Centuries of Spanish and Portuguese America. Quincentenary Supplement of the Journal of Latin American Studies* 24. New York: Cambridge University Press, 1992.

Hojman, David E. "The Political Economy of Recent Conversions to Market Economics in Latin America." *Journal of Latin American Studies* 26 (1994):191–219.

Hufbauer, Gary Clyde, and Erika Wada. *Hazards and Precautions: Tales of International Finance.* Institute for International Economics, September 1999.

Lustig, Nora. *Mexico: The Remaking of an Economy.* Washington, D.C.: Brookings Institution, 1992.

Madisson, Angus, and associates. *Brazil and Mexico.* A World Bank Comparative Study. New York: Published for the World Bank by Oxford University Press, 1992.

Milanovic, Branko, and Shlomo Yitzhaki. "Decomposing World Income Distribution: Does the World Have a Middle Class?" *Review of Income and Wealth* 48, no. 2 (June 2002):155–178. Available online at http://www.worldbank.org/research/inequality/pdf/milshlomo.pdf.

Palma, J. G. "Dependency." In *The New Palgrave: Economic Development*, edited by John Eatwell et al. London: Macmillan Press, 1989a.

———. "Structuralism." In *The New Palgrave: Economic Development*, edited by John Eatwell et al. London: Macmillan Press, 1989b.

Philip, George. "New Economic Liberalism and Democracy in Spanish America." *Government and Opposition* 29, no. 3 (1994):362–377.

Roxborough, Ian. "Inflation and Social Pacts in Brazil and Mexico." *Journal of Latin American Studies* 24 (1992):639–664.

Todaro, Michael P. *Economic Development in the Third World* (4th ed.). London: Longman, 1989.

U.S. GAO (United States General Accounting Office). *Deficit Reduction Experiences of Other Nations.* Washington, D.C.: GAO/AIMD-95-30 Deficit Reduction, December 1994.

Williamson, Edwin. *The Penguin History of Latin America.* New York: Penguin Books, 1992.

Weyland, Kurt. "Neo-Populism and Neo-Liberalism in Latin America: Unexpected Affinities." Paper presented at the 90th Annual Meeting of the American Political Science Association, New York, September 1–4, 1994.

7

International Relations

Cleveland Fraser

Even though world attention has been focused more recently on events in the Middle East and South Asia, one has only to read the newspaper, pick up a magazine, watch television, or "surf" the Internet to discover various examples of continuity and change in Latin America's international relations. Bolivia's long-standing claim against Chile for "free, useful, and sovereign" access to the Pacific Ocean, for example, played a role in the resignation of Bolivia's President Gonzalo Sanchez de Lozada in October 2003 and strained relations between the two countries. Moreover, the 1995 conflict between Ecuador and Peru is the latest chapter in a territorial dispute over access to oil, dating back to the last outbreak in 1981. Tensions continue to flare up intermittently between Venezuela and Colombia, Guyana and Venezuela, Chile and Peru, Argentina and Brazil, Nicaragua and Costa Rica, and elsewhere over long-standing boundary issues. Map 7.1 shows the origins of territorial disputes since independence (for an enlightening discussion of this topic, see Dominguez et al. 2003). Additionally, the 1982 Falklands/Malvinas Islands War demonstrated the involvement of a European state, the United Kingdom, in armed conflict with Argentina. U.S. intervention in Caribbean and Central American affairs and in those of many other countries in the region seems to be another constant in Latin American international relations. U.S. involvements in Venezuela (2002), Guatemala (1995), Haiti (2004, 1994), and Grenada (1983) are powerful examples.

We have also witnessed profound changes in Latin America's orientation toward both the wider world and the United States. Indeed, it is worth remembering that movement in the Western Hemisphere toward more open political and economic systems predated the momentous changes in the for-

Map 7.1
Boundary Disputes Since Independence

mer Soviet Union and Eastern Europe. And just as these seismic political and economic tremors have shaped the way we look at the world, they have also influenced Latin American perceptions of it. Certainly, reverberations of the events of September 11, 2001, have altered perceptions and policies related to the issues of security and international terrorism and have brought home the point that the current international environment is extremely complex and challenging.

Yet, we must not forget that it is a world filled with new opportunities. Who would have thought, for example, that Mexico would seek greater integration with the U.S. economy? With the signing of the North American Free Trade Agreement (NAFTA), Mexico signaled just such an objective. Who would have believed that three Latin American countries (Chile, Mexico, and Peru), along with Canada and the United States, would participate as full members at annual Asia-Pacific Economic Cooperation (APEC) summits? In fact, two of the last three APEC meetings have been hosted by Latin American countries, Mexico in 2002 and Chile in 2004. And, who would have thought that the democratically elected heads of thirty-four nations in the hemisphere would meet in Miami in 1994 to discuss the opportunities and challenges in the region and that the success of this session would result in a succession of hemispheric summits (Santiago in 1998; Quebec in 2001; and Monterrey in 2004), including the World Trade Organization summit in Cancún, Mexico, in 2003 to construct the framework and a timetable for negotiating a Free Trade Area of the Americas (FTAA) by the middle of this decade? Nevertheless, negotiations broke down during the 2003 Cancún summit where a group of poor countries protested against U.S. intransigence.

As Thomas D'Agostino pointed out in Chapter 4, the region's political challenges are great. A number of countries struggle with ongoing threats to their domestic as well as their external security. Domestically, the governments of Peru and Colombia continue to grapple with low-level insurgencies of long duration. Mexico has had to deal with a rebellion in the southern state of Chiapas, where a group known as the Zapatista National Liberation Army (EZLN) has called for democratic reform and social justice. The activities of narcotraffickers also pose increasingly important threats to the stability of such countries as Colombia, Ecuador, Peru, and those used as transit points in the Caribbean. These examples highlight the fragility of the process of democratization in Latin America. Even Venezuela, a country with relatively long-standing democratic practices, has had to cope with challenges to its constitutional order. Indeed, its current president, Hugo Chávez Frías, led a failed coup attempt in 1992, was elected in 1998, reelected in 2001, became the target of an abortive effort to oust him in April 2002, and survived a recall referendum in August 2004.

Venezuela's recent tribulations reflect another set of daunting challenges: those posed by the widening gap between rich and poor within and between countries in the hemisphere. Richard Harper and Alfred Cuzán detailed many of these challenges in Chapter 6 and also analyzed various approaches to international economic relations. Clearly, economic growth per se offers an incomplete picture of development. Therefore, for international comparisons, other indicators of development are required.

A common method for comparing relative wealth between countries is to look at their gross national income (GNI) per capita. In Latin America, the disparity between rich and poor is striking. In Honduras, for example, per capita GNI is $920. In contrast, it is $4,060 in Argentina and $35,060 in the United States (World Bank 2003:252–253). Figures that relate the relative distribution of wealth and income within Latin American societies are just as stark. To use Venezuela as an illustration, the top 20 percent of the society consumes 51.8 percent of the national income; those in the bottom quintile consume a mere 4.3 percent (World Bank 1999:199). And Venezuela is by no means the most extreme Latin American case.

Other factors that have had the practical effect of diminishing wealth and income are inflation and debt, which have been severe problems in many Latin American countries. For example, between 1980 and 1992, inflation in Argentina and Brazil averaged 402.3 and 370.2 percent, respectively (World Bank 1994:163). Inflation erodes the purchasing power of everyone in a society, but we can assume that it has a more direct and negative impact on the poorer segments. Debt and monetary issues were prime contributors in Argentina's rapid turnover in presidents—five in a two-week period in December 2001—and to the largest debt default in the history of the International Monetary Fund (IMF).

These challenges have several important implications for Latin American international relations. The failure of governments to control economic and political turmoil creates conditions that might lead to the reversal of the trend toward more open markets and political systems. These types of political and economic problems also tend to limit the capacity of Latin American countries to pursue their foreign policy objectives. Finally, they might also induce governments to embark upon dangerous foreign policy adventures to deflect domestic attention from hard times at home or, alternatively, to withdraw from active participation in international affairs.

■ Organizing Concepts

A systematic understanding of these considerations helps to put Latin American international relations in perspective. Latin America is usually depicted as a subsystem in the international system. The elemental characteristics explored by Marie Price in Chapter 2—including geographic contiguity and regularized patterns of political, economic, and social interaction—have resulted in general recognition among the countries themselves that they constitute a distinctive area in the international environment. This regional system has also typically been divided into subsystems (Atkins 1999:25–57). Although analysts may define each element slightly different-ly, we identify four regional subsystems in Latin America: Mexico and Central America, the Caribbean, the Andean countries, and the Southern Cone.

In this context, we seek to address several questions. What is Latin America's role in the international system? More specifically, where has Latin America been, and where is it going? Are there identifiable continu-ities in Latin American relations with the wider world? How have the changes in the post–Cold War era affected Latin America? A number of analytic perspectives may be employed to describe and analyze Latin America's position in international affairs. Although it is beyond the scope of this chapter to catalog and amplify each potentially useful viewpoint, three merit consideration because of their particular relevance to Latin American affairs: realism, dependency, and interdependence.

Realism

This approach views international relations as a struggle among nations for power and influence (Morgenthau and Thompson 1985). Governments for-mulate their national interests in terms of power, usually defined as eco-nomic or military capability. This is clearly demonstrated in the analysis contained in Chapter 5 by Paul Zagorski. Moreover, nations are assumed to be unitary actors—that is, foreign policy results from decisions taken by top-level leadership. The role of popular opinion in formulating external policy is assumed to be minimal, because the public is deemed to be, at best, ill-informed and little interested in foreign affairs and, at worst, sus-ceptible to the "conventional wisdom" of the moment. Given the emphasis among nations on expanding their power and influence, the most salient international issues are those dealing with politico-military affairs. "High politics," therefore, tends to dominate the international agenda. Other issues—such as developing the economy, fostering social justice, and pro-tecting the environment—are considered secondary to the overarching goal of national security.

International politics is viewed as a very serious game that involves winners and losers. In this zero-sum environment, an adversary's gain, by definition, diminishes one's own capacity for action. Hence, a central diplomatic objective of realism is to balance and to check power and to acquire and protect spheres of influence. Whereas power politics does not foreclose reliance on instruments of diplomacy designed to foster coopera-tion, force and the threat of its use are also fairly common diplomatic weapons in the realist's arsenal, as are alliances and collective security arrangements.

From this perspective, Latin America has been viewed as a venue for great-power rivalry; as such, realism may serve as a framework for understanding Latin America in the nineteenth and early twentieth centuries. It may also provide greater insights into the actions of the United States in Central America and the Circum-Caribbean. Latin America has, of course, been characterized in the United States as "our own backyard." And in a stratified, hierarchical series of international systems and subsystems, the foreign policy latitude of smaller, weaker powers is constrained by the activities and interests of the larger regional and global powers.

Dependency

One of the most powerful prisms for viewing Latin America is that of *dependencia* (dependency) theory, which is based on economic relationships between developing and developed countries. There are many variations of this complex theory. One is André Gunder Frank's thesis that underdeveloped nations are "satellites" of developed metropolitan centers. Another is Immanuel Wallerstein's vision of a capitalist international economy divided into "core" states that extract cheap labor and resources from "peripheral" states (see Cockcroft, Frank, and Johnson 1972).

Some dependency theorists offer empirical evidence that the structure of the international trade and monetary systems has disadvantaged many Latin American nations. They show how the raw materials and semiprocessed goods on which many countries rely for generating foreign exchange fluctuate in price or have actually declined, relative to the prices of industrial products the region requires for development. Many of these theorists contend that Latin American nations are dependent on the decisions of multinational corporations (MNCs), the IMF, and the U.S. government. Therefore, it is easy to understand why they criticize modernization and development approaches as ethnocentrically derived from U.S. and Western European models. Basically, the argument holds that Latin America has been constrained in its ability to participate in world affairs because of external manipulation and exploitation by Western capitalist countries in general and the United States in particular.

Radical dependency theory argues that in its quest for markets, capital, and labor, the West had knowingly "stacked the deck" in its favor and deprived the nations of the region of resources necessary for industrialization, diversification, and a rising standard of living. The operation of MNCs is cited as a manifestation of this concerted effort. MNCs are portrayed as international vampires, draining the economic lifeblood out of their "hosts" by siphoning off profits, depleting resources, and dominating domestic markets. There are also nefarious political implications. These dependency theorists claim that the operation of this asymmetrical relationship creates and maintains client political and economic elites who identify more with the West than they do with their own countries. This, in turn, creates a propensity for governments to favor capitalist development and to accede to the norms and principles embodied in the international monetary and trading regimes. It also offers an explanation for development failures based on external rather than internal causes.

Interdependence

Dependency theorists emphasize the one-way effects of dependence. Other observers of international relations (Keohane and Nye 1977), however, have recognized that mutual dependence exists in many relationships. It is almost a cliché to say that the world is rapidly shrinking. It is only a few hours from the United States by airplane to virtually any point in Latin America. The fall in the value of the Mexican or Argentine peso roils stock markets and currencies around the globe. Many who are reading this are probably wearing Brazilian shoes or have flown in a Brazilian-made airplane or had Brazilian orange juice for breakfast. Some of the most popular beers in the United States are brewed and bottled in Mexico. Many of you are probably wearing clothing made in Central America or the Caribbean.

Therefore, some observers have maintained that contemporary Latin American relations can also be placed in the context of an increasingly globalized and interdependent world. What are some of the basic characteristics and assumptions of interdependence? First, this approach argues that although the primary actors in Latin America and the world are still sovereign nation-states, other governmental and nongovernmental actors are increasingly playing greater roles in shaping foreign policy and international relations. For example, as Michael Fleet shows in Chapter 12, the Catholic Church has not only influenced political life in each country, but it also transcends boundaries. Globe-girding corporations have also reduced the power and influence of nations. Political parties, especially those affiliated with international movements, such as Christian Democracy or socialism, have ties that bind them to both the region and the greater world. And, of course, the ability of terrorist organizations to operate across national frontiers has also posed profound challenges to the sovereignty and security of states. This view also stresses that changes in the distribution of power in the international system have provided opportunities for smaller powers to define their interests more broadly and to emphasize issues other than those of national security.

In an interdependent world, economic issues have taken center stage, with development, debt, and integration increasing in salience. Other issues—such as social justice, immigration, human rights, and ecological preservation—have also risen to the fore. In terms of diplomatic strategies, greater emphasis is placed on bargaining and compromise, persuading, and using regional and international institutions as venues for discussing issues and resolving disputes. Recall that realism assumes that countries with greater economic and military capabilities will tend to have greater success in achieving their foreign policy objectives. The interdependence approach suggests an answer to the question, "If bigger is better, why don't great powers 'win' all of the time?" Under these circumstances, less powerful states and nongovernmental actors may be able to mobilize and use different types of power resources effectively, such as persuasion or terror, which can offset or neutralize the advantages of larger states. From an interdependence point of view, bigger is not necessarily better or best.

These three perspectives can be viewed from another one. Let us consider realism, dependency, and interdependence to be needles we can use to pull historical threads together to form a tapestry of Latin American international relations. Although space precludes an exhaustive examination of each thread, we will strive to be selective in rendering the patterns and designs to highlight what an interesting, vibrant, and colorful tapestry it is.

▪ Historical Legacies

Although it is beyond the scope of this chapter to outline comprehensively the history of the region, we can point out some of the signposts along Latin America's road to increasing international prominence. Generally, the realist perspective, with its emphasis on international conflict and cooperation, will aid in this task. Both dependency theory and the concept of interdependence, however, illuminate important historical developments as well.

René de la Pedraja shows in Chapter 3 how most Spanish colonial possessions in Latin America gained their independence in the first two decades of the nineteenth century. Their attempts to free themselves from colonial control were in part "insulated" by the 1823 Monroe Doctrine, which asserted that the time for colonization in the Western Hemisphere had passed and that the United States would view any attempt by a European power to interfere in the area with grave concern. Of course, the United States was hardly in a position to enforce such a sweeping edict; as the doctrine also served the national interests of the United Kingdom, with its very powerful navy, it did provide a sort of deterrent to foreign adventures. Nevertheless, the doctrine evolved as a basis upon which the United States carved out its own sphere of influence in the Western Hemisphere.

Virtually all countries in Latin America struggled to foster internal unity and external security. During the first half-century of independence, a number of countries in the region sought to establish a hierarchy and extend their influence. In Central America, Mexico aspired to the role of regional hegemon. In response, the five Central American provinces attempted to amalgamate into the United Provinces of Central America in 1823. It was not to be; as the result of internal squabbling, this attempt to offset Mexico's power and authority disintegrated in 1838. Each of the five remaining states was left to deal with Mexico and, later, the United States in its own way. The Andean region also disintegrated in 1830, as the Bolívarian vision of an integrated Gran Colombia (encompassing Ecuador, Colombia, and Venezuela) faltered in the wake of economic malaise and political turmoil.

In the Southern Cone, the system was also hierarchical, as Brazil, Argentina, and Chile aspired to regional hegemony. Other, smaller countries were often drawn into the struggle for power. Indeed, issues of boundaries sparked conflicts throughout the nineteenth century. To cite two of the most important examples, in the War of the Triple Alliance (1864–1870), Brazil, Argentina, and Uruguay combined to crush Paraguay, which lost about one-half of its territory and all but 28,000 of its male inhabitants (Kolinski 1965:198). Brazil and Argentina gained control over territory and resources that could (and would) be used in their rivalry for regional power and influence. Both Paraguay and Uruguay served as buffers between the two great powers in the region. Less than a decade later, Peru and Bolivia were defeated by Chile in a dispute involving access to minerals and fertilizer. In the War of the Pacific (1879–1884), Bolivia lost its only outlet to the Pacific Ocean.

The nineteenth century was also an era of increasing economic dependence. Great Britain in particular provided much of the investment capital and technology necessary for rapid economic development. In many countries, British firms built the rail, telegraph, and telephone systems; invested in resource extraction; and established the manufacturing base. Especially in the century's later decades—as worldwide demands for commodities such as rubber, petroleum, coffee, sugar, beef, and wheat increased—countries such as Brazil, Mexico, Venezuela, and Argentina enjoyed economic "boom" times. But this came at a price. Although Latin American economies grew, they were fueled primarily by foreign rather than domestic or indigenous investments and by a reliance on exporting single crops or commodities to markets in Europe and, increasingly, the United States.

There was another interesting consequence of increased dependence during this period. Some countries, especially in the Southern Cone, lacked the population required to sustain the increased demand for skilled and unskilled labor. They, therefore, encouraged migration from Western and Southern Europe. The ethnic and class implications of these policies are analyzed by Kevin Yelvington in Chapter 9. These new immigrants to Argentina and Uruguay, for example, influenced not only domestic political alignments but also the general foreign policy orientation of these countries toward Europe and the United States.

Latin America was not immune to foreign influence of another sort. In spite of the Monroe Doctrine, European powers periodically sought to expand their influence in the Western Hemisphere. One of the most notable examples was an unsuccessful French attempt in the 1860s to establish a monarchy in Mexico, with Prince Maximillian of Austria on the throne. Nevertheless, of all the external actors seeking to expand their power and influence in the region, none exerted such a profound and lasting influence as the United States. In 1904, President Theodore Roosevelt enunciated a corollary to the Monroe Doctrine that held that the United States reserved the right to intervene in the internal affairs of Latin American countries in the event of their misbehavior, especially related to the collection of customs duties. Roosevelt's view of Latin America was portrayed at the time as "speaking softly but carrying a big stick."

The United States, particularly active in Central America and the Circum-Caribbean, was establishing its own sphere of influence through the acquisition of Puerto Rico and Cuba from Spain in the wake of the latter's defeat in the 1898 Spanish-American War. Appended to the new Cuban Constitution (1901) was the Platt Amendment, which, among other provisions, explicitly gave Cuba's consent that the United States reserved the right to intervene in Cuba's internal affairs if the United Stated deemed intervention was required. In 1903, the United States also had a hand in accelerating the separation of Panama from Colombia, which had balked at a planned trans-isthmian canal project proposed by the Americans and the French.

In a precursor to more recent events, Haiti was occupied by U.S. Marines in 1914 to stabilize the political situation and to "clean up" the society. The U.S. troops remained until 1930. Nicaragua was also a venue for U.S. troops (1912–1925; 1926–1933), as was the Dominican Republic, which was occupied from 1916 until 1930. Mexico's revolution, which spanned the first two decades of the twentieth century, provided more immediate examples of U.S. activism in its sphere of influence. U.S. forces occupied the port of Veracruz in 1914, and U.S. troops spent the better part of a year in futile pursuit of General Francisco "Pancho" Villa in northern Mexico. He was considered to be an outlaw who would have had a destabilizing effect in the region.

This is not to say, however, that conflict was the dominant pattern of interaction between the United States and Latin America. Diplomatic instruments were also used to foster greater inter-American cooperation and understanding. The United States was largely responsible for reinitiating what would become known as pan-Americanism based on the Bolívarian ideal. Beginning in 1889 with the first inter-American conference in Washington, D.C., the United States and Latin America sought to establish more frequent and institutionalized bases for communication. This and subsequent conferences spawned a number of regional institutions and agencies designed to address issues ranging from regional security and conflict resolution to the concerns of children, women, and indigenous peoples. It must be noted, however, that the United States viewed this process as another means of expanding its commercial interests in the area, especially in the Circum-Caribbean. "Dollar diplomacy," coupled with overt military intervention, dramatically expanded U.S. ascendancy in the Western Hemisphere. Concomitantly, European influence and power dramatically declined.

The first three decades of the twentieth century marked ferment and change in Latin America, similar in many ways to most other parts of the world. Latin American societies had been transformed by immigration and accelerating industrialization. One of the most important implications of this social and economic metamorphosis was the rise of a more complex class structure. Working- and middle-class sectors agitated increasingly for greater participation in political and economic decisionmaking. Between 1910 and 1920, Mexico underwent a profound political, economic, and social revolution. Farther south, in the early 1930s, economic depression precipitated the rise of various forms of authoritarian regimes, as well as economic experiments. Socialism and communism vied for support among various segments of Latin American society. Fascism also appeared to be an attractive political option to some, especially in those countries (for example, Argentina) with populations swollen by recent arrivals from Spain, Portugal, Italy, and Germany. Intraregional conflicts over territory were also evident. In 1932, a simmering dispute between Paraguay and Bolivia over an area known as the Chaco Boreal flared into a war that lasted three years and claimed 85,000 lives (Garner 1966:107).

The 1920s and 1930s spanned an era of regional attempts to establish a more equitable framework for the conduct of international relations. For instance, Latin America was initially enthusiastic about participating in the newly established League of Nations. And Latin American jurists and diplomats were in the forefront of reaffirming the international legal principles of the sovereign equality of states and of nonintervention in the internal affairs of sovereign nations. One prime example, the Estrada Doctrine (1930), enunciated by Mexico's Foreign Minister Genaro Estrada, held that if a particular government controlled population and territory, it deserved to be accorded diplomatic recognition. No normative evaluation or criteria should be applied. Obviously, this and other contributions to international law reflected historical memories in Mexico in particular, and in Latin America more generally, of external intervention and economic domination.

The Good Neighbor Policy of Franklin D. Roosevelt (1933–1945) marked a shift in U.S. policy away from the interventionism and power politics of previous administrations. Accordingly, the United States refrained from intervening in Cuban affairs in 1933 and abrogated the Platt Amendment in 1934. Moreover, Roosevelt did not retaliate when Mexico nationalized its primarily U.S.-owned oil industry in 1938. One of the questions posed by students of inter-American relations is whether the era of the Good Neighbor was an aberration or the beginning of a movement toward a more cooperative and less conflictual relationship between mature partners.

With the outbreak of World War II, Latin American nations were compelled to define their objectives in the context of global conflict. Many— such as Brazil, the Central American countries, and Mexico—supported the Allied cause, led by the United States, the United Kingdom, and the Soviet Union. Some, most notably Argentina, sympathized with Germany, Italy, and Japan. The war disrupted markets, exacerbated development problems, and set into motion a new set of international forces that dramatically altered Latin American external relations.

In sum, Latin America's international role in the pre-1945 period was constrained by its relative lack of economic and military resources necessary to project power and influence on a global scale. Europe remained the fulcrum around which international relations revolved; Latin America was a secondary arena for European rivalry. In one sense, this insularity from the wider world provided opportunities for aspirants to regional and subregional hegemony to extend their influence, many times by force.

Latin America's international role was also limited by other factors. The capacity for international action of Mexico, the Central American states, and such Caribbean states as Cuba, the Dominican Republic, and Haiti was severely limited by U.S. activism and interventionism in their internal affairs. Within the region as a whole, U.S. interventionism also increased the sensitivity of Latin American states toward external meddling in their internal affairs. Additionally, the disruption of markets and investment by two world wars and a prolonged economic depression also tended to reduce the propensity of Latin American nations to take a leading role in international affairs and to heighten the region's awareness of its economic dependency and vulnerability.

▪ The Cold War Era

With the end of World War II, Latin America faced a twofold challenge. First, the United States had emerged from the conflict as one of the world's two superpowers. Economically predominant and militarily preeminent, the United States was busily attempting to establish a world order based on free trade, stable currencies, and collective security. Second, the United States and the Western world were becoming increasingly aware that its wartime ally, the Soviet Union, did not share the same vision of the postwar world. Indeed, the Soviet Union seemed intent on establishing its own sphere of influence in Eastern Europe and expanding its global reach. Thus, with the movement toward confrontation between these two superpowers, the Soviet Union and the United States, the world system was transformed into a bipolar one. The implications of this reality for Latin American countries were largely negative: a highly conflictual, zero-sum international system dominated by the "high politics" of the emerging Cold War. Latin America's international role would be defined in terms of its importance as an anticommunist bastion in the U.S. sphere of influence. As one might suspect, this was not generally a period of intense foreign policy activism on the part of Latin American states.

In the years following World War II, two important regional institutions were established. The first was a collective security arrangement signed in Rio de Janeiro in 1947. Known formally as the Inter-American Treaty of Reciprocal Assistance and less formally as the Rio Pact, it declared that any attack by an outside power would be viewed by the signatories as an attack on them all. In 1948, the Ninth Inter-American Conference, held in Bogotá, Colombia, marked the creation of a forum for discussion among the nations of the hemisphere, the Organization of American States (OAS). This body was intended to foster cooperation and communication among member states, especially in the areas of crisis management, election monitoring, and human rights. As time went on, the OAS became increasingly perceived by many in Latin America as an instrument of U.S. control in its struggle to contain communist influence in the region. For example, the OAS was the forum used to denounce a reformist government in Guatemala as communist and to legitimate its overthrow in 1954. The OAS was also used to isolate Fidel Castro after he had begun receiving assistance from the Soviet Union in the early 1960s.

The 1950s and 1960s underscored the difficulties associated with fostering economic growth and political stability. Latin American nations such as Argentina, Mexico, and Brazil had enjoyed some success in sustaining economic growth through import substitution industrialization (ISI), a strategy intended to reduce dependence on foreign markets and investment through the creation of an industrial base capable of both satisfying domestic demand for consumer durables and other manufactured goods and providing a strong base for exports. This orientation created incentives to formalize closer economic linkages among Latin American countries themselves.

In 1960, for example, eleven countries formed the Latin American Free Trade Area (LAFTA). Intended to be the basis for a Latin American common market, LAFTA was reconstituted in 1980 as the Latin American Integration Association (LAIA). This period also marked the creation of the Central American Common Market (CACM) in 1960 and the Caribbean Free Trade Association (CARIFTA) in 1965, which was renamed the Caribbean Community and Common Market (CARICOM) in 1973. Both organizations were designed to accelerate economic growth and cooperation in these subsystems.

The United States, too, had an interest in ensuring that Latin American countries were improving the quality of life for their citizens. Under the Alliance for Progress, the John F. Kennedy administration (1961–1963) hoped to achieve the twofold goal of strengthening Central and South America against the threat of communism through accelerated capitalist development and of opening markets for U.S. producers.

The 1960s were also a period of ideological and political conflict. Ideologically, the 1959 victory of Fidel Castro in Cuba offered an alternative model of development for Latin America. Hence, the Cuban government was perceived as having an active interest in fostering socialism throughout the hemisphere. It is clear, however, that only certain elements of the revolutionary movement sought to accelerate the diffusion of the new Cuban model to other Latin American countries. Venezuela, which was in the process of institutionalizing a transition to democratic government, was the target of Cuban-inspired insurgents. Revolutionaries such as the Argentine Ernesto "Che" Guevara (who fought with Castro) took this one step further by seeking to replicate the success of the Cuban experience in Bolivia. Guevara's attempt to export revolution ended in dismal failure and death in 1967 at the hands of U.S.-trained Bolivian counterinsurgency teams.

The rise of a perceived communist threat in the hemisphere marked the demise of a period of political reformism, as Latin American militaries, concerned about communism and economic growth, replaced civilians with generals. In Chapter 5, Paul Zagorski analyzes the changing role of the military and the fact that approximately 85 percent of military conflicts in the postwar world have been intrastate rather than traditional interstate conflicts. Additionally, the abortive attempt to replace the Cuban government embodied in the Bay of Pigs invasion (1961), the Marine operation in the Dominican Republic (1965), and the overthrow of Salvador Allende (1970–1973) in Chile (1973) can be seen in terms of the legacies of the Cuban Revolution and as manifestations of realpolitik on the part of the United States.

The rise of bureaucratic authoritarian systems intent on protecting the state from subversion led to increased levels of domestic tension and international friction (O'Donnell 1979). The ideological ferment of the 1960s also yielded a social movement that was religious in conception but political in practice. As Michael Fleet details in Chapter 12, in the wake of the

Second Vatican Council (Vatican II) in 1964, the Catholic Church reexamined its relevance in the modern world. One of its most important legacies was to change the way many priests and laity looked at the church's mission and purpose. Many within the church began to advocate that it become a champion of the less privileged in Latin American society. They rejected the view that the church should only tend to the spiritual needs of its followers; they believed that it needed to further the economic and social aspirations of the least powerful. Whereas in the past the church had generally supported and justified the status quo, it could be a positive force for change in the present and in the future by advocating a theology of liberation.

Liberation theology differed dramatically from traditional Roman Catholic interpretations in its views of sin, the relationship between spiritual and secular activity, and the causes of poverty and social injustice in Latin America. The analysis of social conditions was based in part on Marxist analysis of capitalism and dependency. To some of the more radical adherents of liberation theology, armed struggle against an unjust state was justified under certain conditions.

As one might expect, elements in the church hierarchy, as well as the increasingly authoritarian governments of many Latin American nations, viewed the proponents of liberation theology as threats to national security and, therefore, as legitimate targets of repression by the state. Many governments viewed liberation theology as nothing more than Marxism and communism cloaked in spiritual dress. Moreover, although Pope John Paul II called on governments to respect the human rights of all their citizens, the Vatican took steps to silence the more outspoken liberation theologians.

Two significant implications for Latin American external relations resulted from the interaction between church and state. First, military authoritarian governments, seeking to ensure political stability and economic advances, tended to cooperate with one another on such issues as counterinsurgency and antiterrorism. Militaries also collaborated in providing a societal justification for establishing national security states. Second, the ferocity and alacrity with which many governments rooted out suspected subversives and communists focused both domestic and international attention on the issue of human rights. Nongovernmental organizations, such as Amnesty International and Americas Watch, as well as the administration of U.S. president Jimmy Carter (1977–1981), began to pressure Latin American governments to end the abuse of their citizens.

▓ Dependency and Debt

With the first oil price shock in the early 1970s, nations that controlled oil or other commodities possessed a great advantage. It was an era of global inflation, but it was also an era of developmental opportunity. This was especially true for those countries fortunate enough to possess lakes of oil or vast reserves of copper or tin or even those who were efficient producers of bananas or other primary resources and commodities. The high price of oil also created pressure for all countries to finance their energy bills.

What was the solution to this dilemma? For many, it was to borrow from Western banks. The international balance of economic power seemed to be shifting from the developed countries of North America, Europe, and Japan to the oil-producing cartel. Arab countries, such as Saudi Arabia and Kuwait, were receiving large infusions of cash, and they could not spend it fast enough. There was a limit to the number of airports, ports, hotels, and Mercedes Benzes individuals and governments could build or buy. Thus, they began to deposit the surplus into U.S. and European banks. This recycling of petrodollars created an incentive among bankers to lend the money to earn interest that would positively affect the bottom line.

From the perspective of both parties, the solution was obvious. Latin American countries needed investment capital to accelerate their development and, presumably, to reduce disparities in wealth and income. Bankers needed new opportunities to make money. And at the time, governments seemed to be very good credit risks. They controlled commodities that seemed to be continually rising in price, so there was no question that the borrowers would be able to pay back their loans. Also, governments would not go bankrupt. Thus, Mexico, Brazil, Venezuela, and Argentina, among others, borrowed millions of dollars during this period. Another round of oil price increases in the late 1970s induced another round of borrowing.

The increased sensitivity of the developed world to the demands of the less developed world provided an impetus for calls for a dialogue to be conducted under UN auspices between the North and South regarding a new international economic order (NIEO). Latin American nations, especially Mexico and Venezuela, were in the forefront of this dialogue, calling for reforms to the trade and monetary regimes and for greater restrictions on the operation of MNCs. Although the negotiations met with mixed success from the point of view of the Latin American states, one enduring legacy of the process was an increased assertiveness and activism on the part of resource-rich countries. In this era of expanding mutual dependence, the range of foreign policy maneuvers was also expanding, as were the economic and diplomatic capabilities of those countries aspiring to regional— and indeed global—leadership.

The boom went bust in the early 1980s, as international economic conditions conspired to send the global economy into recession. Suddenly, prices began to fall. Between 1980 and 1985, the price of oil declined from a high of almost $40 per fifty-five-gallon barrel, to under $12 per barrel. To cite one example, it was estimated that Mexico lost $.5 billion for every $1 drop in the price of oil. Suddenly, countries that had seemed like good risks were signaling that they could not pay their debts. This precipitated a crisis in the international monetary system, for if Latin American countries began defaulting on their debts, this might hasten the collapse of the system and bring economic hardship to the developed world.

Increasingly, many Latin American countries were forced to turn to the IMF for assistance. The IMF insisted, however, that before it would make loans to cover shortfalls, a certain set of reforms, called structural adjustment programs (SAPs), had to be implemented. Many countries viewed these SAPs as constituting undue interference in their sovereign ability to determine their own economic and political destinies. SAPs usually involved currency devaluations to stimulate exports and reduce demand for imported goods, as well as cuts in government spending to balance budgets and reduce inflation. As one might expect, such spending reductions sometimes adversely affected subsidies for food, energy, transportation, housing, and health care. Thus, the burden of economic stabilization was placed not only on Latin American governments but on the people as well. In many instances, these burdens were painful and politically unsettling.

To stabilize the system, the international community adopted plans put forward by two U.S. secretaries of the treasury. The first, proposed in 1985 by James Baker, secretary under President Ronald Reagan (1981–1989), called for the IMF and the World Bank to make more capital available to debtor nations. The second, unveiled in 1989 by President George H.W. Bush's secretary Nicholas Brady, expanded on the Baker Plan by calling for renegotiations and for sophisticated debt for equity swaps. These programs—which were discussed in detail by Richard Harper and Alfred Cuzán in Chapter 6—as well as an upswing in the global economy, eased the crisis. It is not over, however, and Latin Americans lament the 1980s as a lost decade of economic growth and development.

▩ The 1980s

Latin America was at the forefront of a surprising trend in international politics in the 1980s: the movement away from authoritarian political rule and state-directed economic development and toward democratic politics and free-market economics. The trend began with Argentina and Brazil and accelerated until almost every country in the hemisphere became "democratic," with notable exceptions. This process took different forms in different countries. In some, the military gave up power in an incremental fashion, as in Brazil during the process of *abertura democrática* (democratic opening). In others, longtime leaders were removed or voted out of office. A 1989 coup against Paraguay's seven-time president, Alfredo Stroessner

(1954–1989), is a good example of the former, and the Chilean electorate's emphatic "no" in a 1988 referendum on General Augusto Pinochet's (1973–1989) continuation in power illustrates the latter.

In Central America, civil unrest and violence characterized the process. In Nicaragua, the Sandinista National Liberation Front (FSLN) seized power in 1979, after ridding the country of Anastasio Somoza Debayle, the last in a line of dynastic dictators. In El Salvador, the Faribundo Martí National Liberation Front (FMLN) began struggling to depose a government controlled by the military and supported by the United States.

In both cases, the international system intruded on the internal politics of the area. The Reagan administration erroneously viewed both conflicts as inspired by outside forces. According to this analysis, the FMLN was aided and abetted by the Soviets, who were funneling arms and supplies through Cuba and Nicaragua. The Sandinistas were perceived to be instruments of Soviet attempts to expand Soviet influence in the Western Hemisphere. And from the perspective of the international system, it appeared that the Soviets were "on the march." They had made gains in the Horn of Africa, were engaged in Afghanistan, and had aided—with the assistance of Cuban proxies—the ascent to power of Afro-Marxist leaders and groups in Angola and Mozambique. Their military strength, particularly in the area of strategic weaponry, seemed to equal or perhaps even surpass that of the United States.

As enunciated by the Reagan Doctrine, the United States undertook to

UN Photo 157590/S. Johansen

UN soldiers (seated) document the Nicaraguan resistance forces as part of the overall peace process in Central America, 1990.

"roll back" communism by supporting groups and individuals supposedly struggling for freedom against tyranny. In the context of Central America, this meant increasing support in the form of arms and matériel for groups of Nicaraguan exiles in Honduras and Costa Rica. The Contras began operations in 1982 and carried on a low-level guerrilla campaign in Nicaragua for the next eight years. The United States also spent millions of dollars over a ten-year period to aid the Salvadoran government in its struggle against leftist insurgents.

The trouble in Central America and the Caribbean galvanized Latin America in opposition to another instance of external intervention into the region's affairs and energized the search for Latin American solutions to Latin American problems. In 1983, Mexico, Venezuela, Colombia, and Panama met on the island of Contadora to begin discussing a regional plan to end hostilities in Central America. This group was expanded in July 1985 to include a support group that included Argentina, Brazil, and Uruguay.

Central America was not the only arena for conflict in the early 1980s. A long-simmering dispute between Argentina and Great Britain over control of the Falkland Islands, or the Islas Malvinas, flared into war. Asserting that the United Kingdom had no right to control these specks of land off the coast of Argentina, the Argentine government sent troops in March 1982 to reassert sovereignty over the islands. The military government had taken this action in part to deflect attention from the worsening economic and social conditions in Argentina itself. It assumed that Britain's Prime Minister Margaret Thatcher (1979–1990) would not have the resolve or the money to mount a military operation to recapture the islands. They were wrong. Thatcher ordered a task force to sail south to engage Argentine forces. After a fruitless round of shuttle diplomacy by U.S. secretary of state Alexander Haig, the battle was joined, and in June 1982, victory for the British was assured. The Falklands War illustrated to Latin America that the United States could not be counted on to support one of its own in a conflict with a European power.

The Reagan administration's anticommunist orientation again manifested itself in the Caribbean with the October 1983 intervention in Grenada. Twenty-five thousand U.S. troops were dispatched to protect U.S. lives and property and to rescue a group of medical students attending an offshore medical school who were trapped by events. The administration feared the leftist government was becoming too friendly with Fidel Castro, with whose aid the Grenadians were building an airport capable of accommodating military aircraft. When a more radical faction seized power and ultimately purged the previous leadership in Grenada, the United States, at the invitation of a group of Caribbean nations, intervened. The message seemed clear: the United States would take action against instability in the region, especially if it appeared to be communist inspired, and it would not stand by and watch the Cubans attempt to expand their influence in the Caribbean. The invasion was denounced by many countries in Latin America as yet another example of wrongful U.S. interventionism.

The drug trade and the rise of very powerful cartels of narcotraffickers also constituted a new threat to the internal and external security of a host of Latin American countries—especially the Andean nations of Peru, Ecuador, and Colombia. Mexico, Panama, and Jamaica fit into this group as well. The drug trade provided an incentive for individuals, cartels, and governments to generate revenue. Trade in narcotics such as cocaine and marijuana had profound impacts on the domestic political climates of many countries. In Colombia, powerful cartels based in Cali and Medellín in effect declared war on the government, assassinating judges, prosecutors, and legislators who attempted to thwart their efforts. In Peru, drugs and ideology combined in a witches' brew of guerrilla terror, as a group known as Sendero Luminoso (Shining Path) sought to create a climate of fear and instability among the people and, more important, to provoke the government into taking action that went against its pledge to respect human rights and democratic freedoms.

The drug trade also influenced foreign policy issues. For example, much debate occurred between these Latin American countries and the United States regarding the importance of eliminating the supply or whether the United States had to do more to cut demand for the product. Sensitivities were also raised regarding the dispatch of U.S. drug enforcement agents and military advisers to aid in the struggle.

Finally, drugs also led to another instance of U.S. intervention in Central America with the December 1989 invasion of Panama. The ostensible justification for this operation was to take General Manuel Noriega into custody, which was accomplished. It was alleged that Noriega, the leader of Panama, had personally been involved in drug trafficking, as well as having sanctioned the laundering of drug profits through Panamanian banks. Moreover, Noriega—reputed to have been on the CIA payroll—had overturned the will of the people by negating national election results that would have transferred power to moderate, reformist civilians. From the Latin American perspective, this event was an outrageous violation of national sovereignty, as well as of human rights. And, tellingly, it went against earlier attempts to forge closer ties with Panama and the region as a whole through the 1977 signing of the Panama Canal treaties, which established Panamanian sovereignty over the waterway as of 2000.

■ The Post–Cold War Era

Stunning changes in the political and economic landscapes have given rise to new sets of issues on national, regional, and international agendas. Issues relating to regional security have obviously not disappeared, especially in the wake of the September 11, 2001, attacks on the United States, but those relating to trade and investment, immigration, and the environment have risen in importance on regional and international agendas. For instance, one major trend has been the formation of arrangements designed to foster integration or, at the least, to manage increased interdependence and globalization. The precursor of many of these attempts was the 1989 Free Trade Agreement (FTA) between the United States and Canada. In the wake of this treaty, U.S. president George H.W. Bush began to speak of an arrangement that would encompass all of North America. In response, Mexican president Carlos Salinas de Gortari (1988–1994) also affirmed that perhaps this proposal was one whose time had come.

Interestingly, for both Canada and Mexico, a movement toward greater economic integration with the United States represented a sharp break from traditional foreign policy orientations. Mexico in particular had taken many measures designed to guarantee less economic influence from the United States. It had nationalized its oil industry in 1938, as well as others over the years. Mexico had passed legislation in the 1970s, protecting its market by limiting the level and sectors of foreign investment. It had not joined the major trading regime, the General Agreement on Tariffs and Trade (GATT), until 1985. But in the early 1990s, all three countries began a round of negotiations that culminated in the December 1993 signing of the North American Free Trade Agreement. Proponents of NAFTA argued that it would accelerate the development of the Mexican economy, serve as a basis for a transition from authoritarian to more democratic political processes, and, by providing jobs for Mexicans, staunch the flow of immigration northward to the United States. Stock markets were buoyed by the prospects, and the peso was stabilized and pegged to the dollar.

In January 1994, however, a group of dissatisfied citizens began staging protests in the southern Mexican state of Chiapas. One of the poorest states in the country, and represented primarily by descendants of the Aztecs and the Mayan Indians, Chiapas had not benefited from previous attempts at reform, and some felt NAFTA would only widen the gap between the rich and poor in Mexico and Chiapas. The movement, known as the Zapatista National Liberation Army and led by a mysterious, charismatic leader known as Subcomandante Marcos, began to gain headway. The Mexican government's response was to send in the army to quell the unrest. The situation developed into a stalemate, with each side accusing the other of human rights abuses and a lack of good faith at the bargaining table. The Chiapas uprising demonstrated to many that Mexico still has some way to go before it can be considered a developed country worthy of membership in economic "clubs" such as the Organization for Economic Cooperation and Development (OECD). Hence, President Vicente Fox, who was elected in 2000, has initiated a dialogue with the Zapatistas.

This has also been an era in which the issue of international immigration has risen to the fore and has certainly become an important issue for the United States. During the civil war era in Central America, thousands of refugees fled from Guatemala, El Salvador, and Nicaragua into neighboring countries and northward through Mexico to the United States. With the collapse of the Cuban economy, Cuban refugees have also fled to the sanctuary of the United States. Many of these immigrants were returned to the U.S. base at Guantánamo Bay, where they have languished and, occasionally, rioted. Haiti is another example of the trend for economic and political refugees to seek refuge and mobility by entering the United States legally or otherwise.

The increased salience of immigration as an issue of Latin American international relations can be illustrated by two sensational examples. One involved Elián González, a six-year-old Cuban refugee plucked from the sea off the coast of Florida in November 1999, who became the focus of an international tug-of-war between the United States and Cuba over where he should live and who should have guardianship over him. Given that his mother died in her attempt to make it to the United States, should Elián have been granted asylum and permitted to live with relatives in Miami, or should he have been returned to his father, who had divorced his mother two years earlier and continued to live in Cuba? The answer was the boy's forcible removal from his Miami relatives and his repatriation to his father in Cuba. This issue engendered passionate debate in both countries and is an indication of how "new" international issues can be amplified by "old" antagonisms.

A similar observation could be made regarding the saga of General Augusto Pinochet, a former Chilean head of state who was arrested at the behest of a Spanish judge in October 1998, during a private visit to the United Kingdom. The judge requested that General Pinochet be extradited to Spain to stand trial for human rights abuses against Spanish citizens committed by the military regime Pinochet headed from 1973–1989. The judge based his claim on the allegation that Pinochet had violated international human rights covenants and that these conventions provided the legal basis to prosecute violators even if they were not nationals of the prosecuting countries. The issue raised some very interesting legal and political questions. For example, if the precedent were set, would it mean that a U.S. president could be tried for human rights violations in, say, the former Yugoslavia? As one would expect, this episode enflamed passions in Spain, the United Kingdom, and especially in Chile. Ultimately, after a series of judicial and administrative gyrations, the British and Spanish governments decided to declare General Pinochet medically unfit to stand trial, which permitted him to return to his homeland in March 2000. Since his return to Chile, he has given up his life seat in the Senate and has avoided prosecution due to his fragile health, though there have been several attempts to prosecute him for human rights violations during his dictatorship.

Environmental issues, such as those analyzed by Susan Place and Jacqueline Chase in Chapter 8, have also generated great interest. Perhaps the most striking example of this issue is the concern over the degradation of the rain forest in Brazil. Brazil faces the same dilemma as many countries in the developing world. On the one hand, the Amazon Basin contains vast stores of minerals, some oil, and valuable hardwoods. When cleared, the land provides fertile soil to grow crops or to sustain herds of livestock. This area has resources that can accelerate the process of economic development in Brazil. On the other hand, the "Wild West" atmosphere has led to the disruption of traditional ways of life among the indigenous peoples living there, the murder of those opposed to development, and the degradation of the land itself. An estimated 5,800 square miles of Amazonian rain forest are lost every year, and varieties of species become extinct annually.

Does Brazil have a duty to protect and conserve a resource that is crucial to the world's atmosphere? Is the rain forest a global human resource even though it is located within the sovereign territory of Brazil? These questions are very difficult to resolve. The nations of the hemisphere, however, did undertake to discuss these issues at an Earth Summit held in Rio de Janeiro in June 1992. The outcome was the Treaty on Preserving Biodiversity. Although hailed as a useful first step toward greater ecological responsibility, the treaty was not ratified initially by the United States. In Kyoto, Japan, in 1997, industrialized nations (except the United States) agreed to cut their emissions of greenhouse gases by an average of 5 percent below 1990 levels during the years 2008–2012. Developing countries adamantly refused any limits on emissions. Countries agreed in principle to create an international emission trading system that would let firms and countries trade emission credits; such a system could sharply reduce the cost of limiting emissions, but diplomats are making slow progress in working out the myriad of rules and procedures that are needed to make the system function.

Since the creation of the Kyoto Protocol, few nations have done much to limit their emissions. Many observers think that it is now impossible to put major economies such as the United States on track to meet the Kyoto limits without causing severe economic harm. In the United States, robust economic growth has placed emissions on a track to be perhaps one-third higher than 1990 levels by 2008–2012; yet, the Kyoto obligation for the United States would have been a 7 percent cut had the United States ratified the accord.

Another environmental concern involves the proliferation of nuclear weapons and the issue of technology transfer. Almost forty years ago, Latin American nations sought to create a nuclear-free zone. Although the Treaty

of Tlatelolco (1967) was hailed as a useful initial step, the specter of proliferation darkened the Southern Cone region, as Argentina and Brazil were
each assumed to be attempting to acquire a nuclear weapon before the other
did. This shadowy arms race was all the more likely because neither country had signed the 1968 Nuclear Non-Proliferation Treaty (NPT). In 1990,
however, President Carlos Menem (1989–1999) of Argentina and President
Fernando Collor de Mello (1990–1992) of Brazil met and acknowledged
the existence of their nuclear programs. (For a pithy overview of this
important bilateral relationship, consult Oxford Analytica 1991.) In 1991,
the two countries agreed to establish an Argentine-Brazilian Accounting
and Control Commission (ABACC) to verify by mutual inspection the
peaceful nature of their nuclear programs. Three years later, Brazil signed
the Treaty for the Prohibition of Nuclear Weapons in Latin America and the
Caribbean, which called for certification by the UN International Atomic
Energy Agency (IAEA) that nuclear facilities were not capable of producing nuclear weapons. Some concern was expressed by the international
community that Brazil had balked at permitting IAEA inspectors to tour a
uranium enrichment facility under construction in Resende, 70 miles from
Rio de Janeiro, in March 2004; in January 2005, inspectors were allowed
inside. Brazil notes that the plant will be used to provide low-enriched uranium fuel for nuclear reactors in its Angra I and Angra II nuclear plants.
International observers note that Brazil theoretically could produce highly
enriched material for nuclear weapons.

Although Brazil has ratified but not signed the NPT, it has committed
itself to follow the Missile Technology Control Regime. This has cleared
the way for Brazil to undertake commercial development of launchers
capable of hurling satellites and other payloads into space. By mid-1997,
Brazil became a fourth-tier missile producer. Today, Brazil's nuclear capabilities are the most advanced in Latin America; only Argentina has provided serious competition. Brazil is also a competitor in the area of civilian
space "delivery services," an excellent example of accelerating interdependence.

A profoundly different illustration of accelerating globalization was the
tragic and devastating September 11, 2001, attack on the United States by
elements of Al-Qaeda, a militant Islamic terrorist group led by a shadowy
Saudi multimillionaire named Osama bin Ladin. The organization was
responsible for a number of spectacular attacks against Western targets over
the years, but no one could imagine the shock associated with this attack. In
the aftermath of the disaster, there was an outpouring of sympathy from
around the globe. Indeed, even Cuba noted its profound sadness and rejection of terrorism. But there were those in certain quarters of Latin American
society who murmured the opinion that the United States in some perverse
way had gotten what it deserved (or had reaped what it had sown). The

immediate response of the administration of George W. Bush (2001–) was to attempt to track down bin Ladin and to root out and destroy the networks and support bases of Al-Qaeda. One of the most important supporters of bin Ladin seemed to be the Taliban government in Afghanistan, a group that had ruled the country since 1996 under harsh interpretation of Islamic law, and had provided training bases and sanctuary for Al-Qaeda fighters. The United States—along with a Northern Alliance of anti-Taliban forces and with support from its North Atlantic Treaty Organization (NATO) allies and countries such as Pakistan and Russia—was able to effect regime change in Afghanistan in the fall of 2001 but was not able to capture bin Ladin.

Declaring that an "Axis of Evil" (North Korea, Iran, and Iraq) were prime suspects supporting international terrorism, George W. Bush and his administration in early 2002 targeted Iraq and Saddam Hussein as the principal threats to the security of the United States and Western civilization. Arguing that Saddam possessed chemical, biological, and nuclear weapons of mass destruction (WMDs) and that he had continually flouted the requirements of a number of UN resolutions to dismantle his weapons programs and to permit international monitoring and verification of the process, the United States convinced the UN Security Council to adopt Resolution 1441. Passed unanimously (Latin American representatives Colombia and Mexico voting in favor) on November 9, 2002, this resolution mandated the return of UN arms inspectors to Iraq (they had been withdrawn in 1998); called on Iraq to account for all WMDs within ninety days; and promised "serious consequences" in the event of Iraqi noncooperation.

In late January 2003, reports of UN monitors from the IAEA and the Monitoring, Verification and Inspection Commission (UNMOVIC) suggested that Iraq had not restarted its nuclear program but had not fully complied with UN mandates regarding the destruction of chemical and biological stockpiles, and the monitors' reports recommended that a full accounting would require additional time. The reports raised the question of what course of action should be taken next, and there were divisions within the fifteen-member Security Council. Among the permanent members—France, the People's Republic of China, Russia, the United Kingdom, and the United States—all of whom possess the ability to block any proposed action, France, Russia, and China argued for more time for the inspectors to complete their tasks. The United States and the United Kingdom argued that the threat to international security was clear and present and pressed for a second resolution authorizing the use of force to disarm (and perhaps to change) the Iraqi regime. Among the ten nonpermanent representatives, Germany tended to support the French position, while Spain was more supportive of the Anglo-American view. The two Latin American representatives on the Security Council, Mexico and Chile

(Colombia had rotated off the Council at the end of the year), fell into the "undecided" camp, and both were the focus of an intense lobbying campaign between February 24, the date the draft resolution was submitted by the United States, the United Kingdom, and Spain, and March 17, the stipulated deadline for a vote. Both Chile and Mexico tended to be skeptical of the rationale for using force and argued that a second resolution would foreclose a successful outcome of the inspection process. In the end, on March 17, the United States and the United Kingdom withdrew the resolution for lack of votes and the threat of a veto by France; two days later, the United States, supported by a "coalition of the willing," including Colombia, El Salvador, Nicaragua, Costa Rica, the Dominican Republic, Honduras, and Panama, attacked Iraq, and Baghdad fell on April 9, 2003. In the intervening months, it has been very difficult for U.S. troops and the newly established Iraqi government to ensure security necessary for nation-building. The August 2003 truck bombing of UN headquarters in Baghdad, which caused the deaths of twenty-three UN staff members, including Sergio Vieira de Mello, Brazil's distinguished representative to the United Nations, who was charged with creating a working relationship between the occupation authorities and the UN, is a poignant case in point. No WMDs were found in Iraq. Elections took place on January 30, 2005.

The situation in Iraq illuminates continuities in Latin America's international orientation. First, it underscores a long-standing bias against the interventionism and unilateralism of the United States. Although there has been much debate in the United States and other parts of the world over the "preemptive unilateralism" of the Bush Doctrine, for many in Latin America, there is a certain sense of déjà vu. Second, it illustrates Latin America's differing definitions and perceptions of threats to national security, in that political and economic stability and narcoterrorism, rather than the more amorphous war on terror, tend to be higher on the region's agenda. Finally, given the U.S. preoccupation with nation-building in the Middle East and South Asia, Latin America may have to search for more cooperative regional means for dealing with perceived threats to security.

▓ The Future

Let us use our analytic needles once again in the attempt to weave a sampler of Latin American futures. From the perspective of realism, the post–September 11 environment has again placed politico-security issues high on the international agenda. However, the United States has never considered Latin America to be a central arena in its foreign policy activities. This was true during the Cold War, when the United States defined international problems in East-West terms; during the immediate post–Cold War era, when the United States had an interest in continuing the process of democratization and liberalization to foster regional stability; and in the post–September 11 era, when U.S. policymakers consider other areas of the world, such as South Asia and the Middle East, to be more immediate and problematic foreign policy issues than Latin America.

Cast in the light of realism, Cuba, even in its relatively weakened condition, is viewed as a threat by the United States. Over the past few years, the United States has jailed five Cubans for espionage and roundly denounced the Castro government's jailing of scores of dissidents during a time most of the world's attention was focused on events in Iraq. More recently, it has put in place more stringent restrictions on monetary remittances, travel, and other forms of societal interaction. For its part, Cuba claims the "Five Heroes" were assisting in the war on international terror and are, therefore, being held unjustly; that the writers, journalists, and intellectuals Cuba rounded up were "mercenaries" financed and controlled by the U.S. Interest Section in Havana; and it continues to rail against El Bloqueo (the embargo).

President Fidel Castro also seems to be playing a game of realpolitik with Mexico, one of Cuba's staunchest long-standing supporters. Castro has been critical of Mexican president Vicente Fox's close relationship with the United States and President George W. Bush. In 2002, Castro made public taped telephone conversations between himself and Fox that suggested that the latter had been disingenuous when he publicly denied encouraging Castro not to attend a UN-sponsored summit in Monterrey. More recently, Castro has opined that Mexico's standing within the Western Hemisphere has turned to "ashes," and Mexico has accused Cuba of interfering in its internal affairs, which has led to the lowest point in bilateral relations in decades.

The attack on the World Trade Center in New York has accelerated a redefinition of nonstate actors and movements as terrorist organizations by the United States and Latin American states. A number of groups in Latin America, ranging from the Zapatistas in Mexico to the Revolutionary Armed Forces of Colombia (FARC), are defined as terrorist organizations by the United States. Moreover, the rise of sophisticated and ruthless drug cartels may constitute a new hemispheric threat worthy of containment. At this juncture, however, there is little consensus on how to reduce or eliminate the cartels' influence. One approach might be to implement programs designed to reduce the attractiveness of cultivating coca plants through more effective and lucrative crop substitution. Another might be through greater efforts to capture and prosecute to the fullest extent of the law the kingpins of the underground empire.

To date, the emphasis has been on reducing the supply of narcotics and on interdiction. Perhaps the archetype of this approach is embodied in Plan

Colombia, a joint venture between Colombia and the United States. Begun in August 2000 and funded in part with $1.3 billion in U.S. assistance, this ambitious, controversial military and social development program is intended to root out Colombia's drug trade and end its decades-old armed conflict. Some argue that Plan Colombia might have the unintended effect of increasing conflict. The guerrillas are funded by drug money, and military action might increase tensions between Colombia and its neighbors, Venezuela and Brazil, as the struggle expands into guerrilla sanctuaries outside the boundaries of Colombia. Not surprisingly, Latin Americans themselves tend to favor an opposite approach: reduce the demand for drugs in the United States and other countries in the developed world.

From the viewpoint that emphasizes the consequences of accelerating interdependence and globalization, economic issues will remain high on the regional agenda. Although the Latin American debt crisis has subsided somewhat, this is not to say it will not pose a challenge in the future. For example, Mexico and Brazil collectively owe approximately $234 billion to Western banks and international lending institutions. The region as a whole owes about $430 billion. Progress has been made in renegotiating the terms of debt agreements. Many Latin American countries have made progress in servicing their debts through a movement toward more open economies. In Argentina, Brazil, Chile, Mexico, and other countries, governments have privatized literally thousands of public-sector businesses and industries. Are there downsides to increasing economic interdependence? You might wonder how a decision by the government of Thailand to devalue its currency in the summer of 1997 would have any impact on the value of the Brazilian real, or the Argentine peso, but it did. Over the next two years, the "Asian contagion" spread to Eastern Europe and Russia and then to Latin America, leading to decisions by Brazil in late 1999 to devalue the real and to implement austerity measures to mitigate the effects of a severe economic recession. And we have already alluded to the effects of the ongoing economic crisis in Argentina.

Another characteristic of contemporary Latin American relations is a movement toward greater interregional and intraregional trade. With respect to the latter, the rise of Japan, China, and the Pacific Rim, as well as the expanding European Union (EU), offer competitive challenges and opportunities for innovative approaches to development and trade. Many Caribbean states have been participants in the various Lomé conventions, which are intended to provide less developed countries with preferential access to European markets. The European Community/European Union has signed economic and commercial and cooperation agreements with numerous Central and South American states. And the momentum toward greater cooperation between the EU and the countries of Latin America and the Caribbean has accelerated as the result of a series of summits. In terms of fostering broader cooperation with Iberian Europe, from the early 1990s through 2004, nineteen Latin American countries, along with Spain and Portugal, have participated in annual Ibero-American summits. One very interesting proposal that emerged from a recent gathering was to establish an association along the lines of the British Commonwealth.

Perhaps it would be useful to introduce a final perspective—one that is not recent and that has been applied more frequently in the study of European affairs: integration. Integration theory is concerned with the process through which nations can increase cooperation and minimize conflict in their relationships. This approach has been centrally concerned with the role economic cooperation plays not only in fostering greater economic efficiency but also in expanding amity in other functional areas of activity, such as politics and defense. It is assumed that as transactions such as trade and investment increase, governments and societies will begin to attempt to institutionalize and regularize these patterns of communication. Cooperation will begin to spill over into other areas of endeavor, and with this proliferation of activity will come a desire to establish institutional mechanisms that are not just national but supranational in scope. Common strategies for fostering economic cooperation involve establishing common markets, customs unions, and regional institutions.

In fact, this is precisely what appears to be happening in Latin America. One of the most important trends in the contemporary period is the movement toward free-trade zones. In our view, this trend provides an emerging infrastructure for facilitating greater hemispheric integration. Consider the following list of economic associations (and countries) in sub-regions of Latin America:

- Andean Community: Bolivia, Colombia, Ecuador, Peru, and Venezuela
- Caribbean Common Market (CARICOM): Antigua, the Bahamas, Barbados, Belize, Dominica, Grenada, Guyana, Jamaica, Montserrat, St. Kitts and Nevis, St. Lucia, St. Vincent, Suriname, and Trinidad and Tobago
- Central American Common Market (CACM): Costa Rica, El Salvador, Guatemala, Honduras, and Nicaragua
- Latin American Integration Association (LAIA): Argentina, Bolivia, Brazil, Chile, Colombia, Cuba, Ecuador, Mexico, Paraguay, Peru, Uruguay, and Venezuela
- North American Free Trade Agreement (NAFTA): Canada, Mexico, and the United States
- Southern Common Market (Mercosur/Mercosul): Argentina, Brazil, Paraguay, and Uruguay; Bolivia and Chile (associate members); Venezuela (observer)

Some of these groupings have been in existence longer than others. CACM was formed in 1960, the Andean Community was amalgamated in 1969, and CARICOM has existed since 1973. Mercosur and NAFTA, in contrast, have existed around a decade. That being said, all are energized to promote the process of economic cooperation. For example, the members of Mercosur have committed themselves to establish a "viable" common market by 2006.

Moreover, a veritable "alphabet soup" of new amalgamations has emerged over the past few years:

- Association of Caribbean States: CARICOM members, Colombia, Costa Rica, Cuba, Dominican Republic, El Salvador, Guatemala, Haiti, Honduras, Mexico, Panama, Suriname, and Venezuela
- Central American Free Trade Agreement (CAFTA): CACM members, Dominican Republic, the United States
- Free Trade Area of the Americas: all states except Cuba
- Group of Three: Colombia, Mexico, and Venezuela

The Free Trade Area of the Americas is a proposal emanating from the December 1994 Summit of the Americas. Heads of state of the thirty-four nations attending (only Cuba was not represented) committed their countries to participate in forming a hemispheric free-trade area by the year 2005. The numbers boggle the mind: a potential market of 850 million people and a combined gross domestic product of $13 trillion. One also might mention what could be called a "group of two." In June 2003, the United States and Chile signed a free-trade accord that had been nine years in the making, which had been delayed by the rift in bilateral relations engendered by Chile's refusal to support the U.S. position vis-à-vis Iraq in the UN Security Council.

Clearly, one of the global trends in the post–Cold War era is a movement toward a reduction of trade and investment barriers within regions. This is not to say, however, that the potential for conflict does not exist, because protectionist orientations and policies between trading blocs have been tenacious. And of course, integration in the form of free-trade areas raises a host of challenging questions. How will environmental standards be "harmonized"? Will these cooperative efforts encompass the free movement not only of goods and services but also of labor?

Latin America is in the first stages of the process of integration. It is interesting to speculate as to the extent of the desire of its members to continue the process. Perhaps this is an opportunity for increased cooperation in the political and defense realms. There have been proposals for restructuring the OAS and rethinking its role in fostering regional security. Increased opportunities also exist for participation in the United Nations.

Argentina, Brazil, Chile, Uruguay, and Venezuela have contributed personnel to UN peacekeeping missions in such distant areas as Angola and the former Yugoslavia, and representatives of El Salvador's military, for example, are in Iraq.

Wherever these trends lead, it is clear that the region's vast natural resources, expanding markets, and great potential make Latin America a vital part of an increasingly interrelated world. International relations within the region and with countries throughout the world will be affected by the success with which Latin America deals with its own problems.

■ Bibliography

Atkins, G. Pope. *Latin America and the Caribbean in the International System* (4th ed.). Boulder, Colo.: Westview Press, 1999.

———. *Handbook of Research on the International Relations of Latin America and the Caribbean*. Boulder, Colo.: Westview Press, 2001.

Bulmer-Thomas, Victor, and James Dunkerley (eds.). *The United States and Latin America: The New Agenda*. Exeter, UK: Short Run Press, 1999.

Calvert, Peter. *The International Politics of Latin America*. Manchester, UK: Manchester University Press, 1994.

Cockcroft, James D., André Gunder Frank, and Dale L. Johnson. *Dependence and Underdevelopment: Latin America's Political Economy*. New York: Doubleday, 1972.

Dominguez, Jorge (ed.). *The Future of Inter-American Relations*. New York: Routledge, 2000.

Dominguez, Jorge, with David Mares, et al. *Boundary Disputes in Latin America*. Washington, D.C.: U.S. Institute of Peace, 2003. Available online at http://www.usip.org/pubs/peaceworks/pwks50.pdf.

Garner, William R. *The Chaco Dispute: A Study in Prestige Diplomacy*. Washington, D.C.: Public Affairs Press, 1966.

Keohane, Robert O., and Joseph S. Nye. *Power and Interdependence: World Politics in Transition*. Boston: Little, Brown and Co., 1977.

Kolinski, Charles J. *Independence or Death! The Story of the Paraguayan War*. Gainesville, Fla.: University of Florida Press, 1965.

Morgenthau, Hans J., and Kenneth R. Thompson. *Politics Among Nations: The Struggle for Power and Peace* (6th ed.). New York: Knopf, 1985.

O'Donnell, Guillermo. "Tensions in the Bureaucratic-Authoritarian State and the Question of Democracy," In *The New Authoritarianism in Latin America*, edited by David Collier. Princeton, N.J.: Princeton University Press, 1979, pp. 285–318.

Oxford Analytica. *Latin America in Perspective*. Boston: Houghton Mifflin, 1991.

Roett, Riordan, and Guadalupe Paz (eds.). *Latin America in a Changing Global Environment*. Boulder, Colo.: Lynne Rienner Publishers, 2003.

Smith, Peter H. *Talons of the Eagle: Dynamics of U.S.–Latin American Relations* (2d ed.). New York: Oxford University Press, 2000.

South America, Central America, and the Caribbean 2003 (11th ed.). London: Europa Publishers, 2002.

Tulchin, Joseph S., and Ralph S. Espach (eds.). *Latin America in the New International System*. Boulder, Colo.: Lynne Rienner Publishers, 2000.

World Bank. *World Development Report 1994: Infrastructure for Development*. New York: Oxford University Press, 1994.

———. *World Development Report 1998/99: Knowledge for Development*. New York: Oxford University Press, 1999.

———. *World Development Report 2004: Making Services Work for Poor People*. New York: Oxford University Press, 2003.

The Environment, Population, and Urbanization

Susan E. Place and Jacqueline Chase

I n Latin America, as elsewhere, the environment is a product of interactions between human society and the biophysical world. These interactions change over time as a result of technological, cultural, and demographic changes within societies. This chapter provides an overview of the relationships between society and the environment in Latin America since pre-Columbian times. It considers pre-Columbian environmental relations and the dramatic changes imposed by European conquerors. It also addresses the contemporary process of globalization and its impacts on the region's environments, populations, and urbanization.

The effects of globalization in Latin America filter through inequitable socioeconomic hierarchies that benefit the wealthy few—large landholders and well-connected entrepreneurs—while the people in the poor majority bear the brunt of the negative environmental and social consequences of articulation with global markets. As Richard Harper and Alfred Cuzán show in Chapter 6, foreign debt and dependence on the export of a limited range of commodities force Latin American nations to overexploit their natural resources, and more people are migrating to overcrowded urban areas in search of jobs, where pollution and other environmental problems await them.

Latin America's environmental challenges are primarily social problems, the result of huge economic disparities and traditional lack of truly democratic political institutions in much of the region. The key to understanding the relationship between nature and society in Latin America lies in identifying who controls the region's natural resources, especially the land itself. This, in turn, relates to the quest for political and economic stability that has engaged the region for almost two hundred years. As Thomas

D'Agostino shows in Chapter 4, competition for access to resources underlies much of the region's legendary political instability. The components of population change—births, deaths, and migration—have responded to conflicts over resources since the colonial period and should not be considered simply the cause of environmental problems.

■ Pre-Columbian Cultures and Latin America's Environments

Humans have occupied the Americas for at least 20,000 years. By 1500 A.D., they were living in every ecosystem from the Arctic to Tierra del Fuego, at the southernmost tip of South America. Their livelihood strategies ranged from foraging (hunting-gathering) to shifting cultivation in patches of tropical forest to highly intensive farming systems. These subsistence systems supported varying population densities, from sparse nomadic populations in the interior deserts of northern Mexico and Patagonia in southern Argentina to extremely dense populations in Mesoamerica (central and southern Mexico and northern Central America) and the Andes Mountains and adjacent lowlands. Awareness of the sophistication and variety of indigenous agricultural techniques and technology should help to dispel the commonly held stereotype of Latin America as more "natural" and "uncivilized" than Europe and the United States.

The high productivity of pre-Columbian Latin American agriculture supported a large population at the time of the European invasion. Estimates of the total population of the Western Hemisphere in 1500 A.D. range from 40 to 100 million, with a substantial majority living in what is today Latin America. The densest populations were found in Mesoamerica and the central Andes, where highly sophisticated empires had arisen well before the arrival of the Spanish. These civilizations were supported by intensive agricultural systems and regional trade that moved products across ecological zones. Indigenous agricultural systems were based upon the creativity of the ancestors who had domesticated many crop plants over several thousand years. The most important crops were maize, beans, squashes, manioc (cassava), peanuts, tomatoes, potatoes, and several grains, such as quinoa, that grow at high elevations in the Andes.

Over the centuries, indigenous people modified the environment as they devised innovative methods for increasing food production to keep pace with population growth. These included irrigation systems, terracing, raised fields, sunken fields, drainage systems, and an ingenious system of creating raised cultivation beds (*chinampas*) in the shallow, brackish lakes in the Valley of Mexico. There were an estimated 30,000 acres of *chinampas* around Tenochtitlan, the Aztec capital. The high productivity of the *chinampas* contributed to the support of Tenochtitlan's pre-Columbian population of over a quarter of a million. A few remnant *chinampas* can be seen in suburban Mexico City today, where they are marketed for tourists as "The Floating Gardens of Xochimilco." Other evidence of complex environmental modification exists in many parts of Latin America. For example, some 1.5 million acres of agricultural terraces have been discovered in the central Andes. Over 1.25 million acres of abandoned raised fields have been identified in northern Colombia.

"Simple" village farmers of the tropical lowlands also manipulated nature in ingenious ways. These farmers practiced shifting cultivation, a seminomadic system of farming the tropical forest without destroying it. They cleared and planted in scattered patches within the forest. After a few seasons, they abandoned a given field and allowed the forest to regrow. They planted a wide variety of crops, including many fruit and nut trees, from which they could continue harvesting even after abandoning a given field. They managed the regrowth of the forest, selecting for useful species, including trees whose ash provided nutrients to the soil when burned. Thus, they planned for the future even as they abandoned a given plot. Thousands of years of human management, including long-term mulching and selection of useful wild species, have modified the tropical forests of Latin America. Some scientists believe that such human activities have contributed to the legendary biodiversity of the Amazon Basin. Humans have actually created new soils in the Amazon Basin, where extensive areas of rich black soils, created by indigenous agricultural systems and household refuse, have been found amidst the infertile red soils that are natural to the region.

The Columbian Exchange

The arrival of the Spanish and Portuguese, with their diseases, domesticated plants and animals, weapons, religion, and European ways of organizing society, instigated a massive transformation of the region that would become Latin America. The Spanish, firmly believing in their own superiority, generally rejected indigenous agricultural systems and imposed their own on the land. In contrast, in some places Europeans adopted indigenous or African knowledge systems or blended elements of them into their own practices.

Europeans introduced domesticated animals that inflicted ecological damage on ecosystems that had evolved without heavy grazing pressure. Livestock—cattle, sheep, goats, horses, and mules—overgrazed, denuded the land, and accelerated soil erosion in the predominantly mountainous regions where the Spanish first settled. Pigs, especially on the Caribbean islands, became feral and damaged native vegetation and soils. European farming systems were based on the plow, which also caused accelerated soil erosion, especially when used on slopes. One of the most serious consequences of the insertion of Spanish agricultural systems was the introduction of "Old World" weeds. Today, exotic weeds have displaced native species throughout Latin America and constitute a major threat to biodiversity in the region.

Europeans introduced diseases that decimated the indigenous population. Whole zones were nearly depopulated, and the remaining native inhabitants were relocated, were forced to labor for the conquerors, or fled into the hinterlands. Large areas that were remote from the centers of Spanish and Portuguese settlement reverted to forest, leading to the "pristine myth" that the Americas were unpopulated and ripe for colonization by Europeans. As Marie Price asserts in Chapter 2, the most direct and profound impact of the conquest on the Americas was demographic. In addition to the destruction of up to 90 percent of the region's preconquest population, displacement, as well as changes in racial and ethnic identities, redefined both the daily life and the course of history and society in the colonies.

▪ Demographic and Environmental Change in the Colonial Era

European colonialism introduced into Latin America an economic system based on the export of commodities to Europe. The Spanish colonial system was oriented toward the extraction of mineral wealth, gold and silver, and its importation to Europe. Mining zones spawned a number of environmental impacts. Forests were quickly decimated to provide timbers for the mines, housing for workers, and charcoal for fuel. Around each mining zone grew one or more agricultural areas to supply the mines and miners with necessities such as food, hides (for ore sacks and pulleys), tallow (to illuminate mines), and grazing for the thousands of mules needed to transport the ore. The desertification created by these activities in the semiarid and mountainous environments in which the mines were located persists today.

The Portuguese, not finding precious metals and large Indian populations in Brazil, began extracting brazilwood for the reddish resin used in dyes. Soon, however, they introduced an Asian crop that was destined to change the face of Latin America—sugarcane. Sugarcane's environmental impacts included deforestation and degradation of the soil. The expansion of sugar plantations and logging into Brazil's Atlantic coastal forest led to the forest's virtual disappearance by the late nineteenth century. Sugar is also associated with the invention of a new economic institution, the plantation, which dramatically transformed nature and society in Latin America. The plantation was a commercial agricultural venture designed to specialize in the production of a tropical crop for export to Europe. Its high demand for labor stimulated the African slave trade, forcing at least 10 million Africans into Latin America and the Caribbean. Slave-based plantations caused northeast Brazil and many Caribbean islands to be populated far beyond their carrying capacities. Haiti, where a desperately poor population struggles to survive in a denuded landscape, exemplifies the end result of centuries of sugar production and slave labor.

High mortality robbed native peoples and slaves of future generations, and the reorientation of resource extraction and agriculture in the service of Europeans forced Indians to leave their homelands and to discontinue their traditional livelihoods. Attempts to survive and live ordinary lives in the framework of coerced labor and displacement ranged from resistance through flight to strategic alliances with Europeans through marriage and reciprocity. Whatever the specific strategy, they often implied mobility, displacement, and resettlement.

In Spanish America, colonial settlers and administrators achieved control over Indian labor by controlling their land. Indian communal lands were converted to Spanish dominion, and Indians were often forced onto marginal lands. By the end of the sixteenth century, Spaniards had appropriated most of the good land in the region. They established enormous *haciendas* (estates), some as large as European principalities, relegating the remaining Indian population to virtual serfdom. The indigenous populations in the uplands of Spanish America eventually returned to growth, even as the colonial economy deprived them of resources. Poverty, rural livelihoods, and the influence of Catholicism have conspired to keep fertility high in these areas. They are among the most densely populated regions of Latin America, despite high mortality and persistent out-migration in the twentieth century.

In the tropical lowlands of Brazil and the Caribbean islands, the plantation economies' dependence on African slave labor contributed to the racial diversity and complex social hierarchy of Latin America. As with the Indian populations of Spanish America, slaves were allowed to practice subsistence farming, and their agriculture was pushed to hilly, rocky, or dry areas. This pattern repeated itself in postslave society in areas that continued to produce tropical plantation crops. The *morador* (tenant farming) system in northeastern Brazil, for example, thrived until the late twentieth century. In this arrangement, sugarcane workers lived on designated areas of plantations, tending subsistence crops and working seasonally in the cane harvest and sugar production.

During the colonial period, Portuguese settlers' rising demand for Indian labor, land, and forest resources led natives to flee to the interior. Hence, evasion became the natives' primary means of resisting forced labor, disease, and disruption of their cultures. Meanwhile, from the southeastern flank of the Portuguese colony, organized bands of explorers (*bandeirantes*) went as far as the Amazon River in search of Indian slaves and gold. Intermarriage and trade with indigenous people led to the rise of a mixed *caboclo* (Indian and European) culture that has been influential in preserving many aspects of indigenous life in rural Brazil. Throughout Spanish and Portuguese America, the quest by the Catholic Church to convert souls reached far into the interior. The Jesuits formed an extended system of communities among the Guaraní Indians in the Paraguay and Paraná basins and chains of missions in Baja California and along the Amazon River. In these contexts of contact and exploitation, many Indians chose to flee upland, inland, and upstream. Legendary accounts of great Indian migrations in search of the "land without evil" in South America took place even before European contact, driving home the notion that Indian history has never been static, but the conquest gave new urgency to mobility.

Settlements of escaped slaves—maroons (*quilombos* in Portuguese)—challenged the authority and security of plantation societies all over the Americas. A group of *quilombos* formed the Independent Republic of Palmares, which endured for almost one hundred years in the northeast area of Portuguese America. It was eventually overcome by military force at the end of the seventeenth century. Maroons had occasionally developed trading relationships with plantations and towns, and others are known to have both battled with and cooperated with tribal people. In the Guianas, political accords between maroons and the Dutch led to the "Bush Negroes" working as slave hunters in exchange for being left alone. In Brazil and elsewhere, the descendants of maroons possess unique cultures but remain among the poorest people of their countries, as they continue to struggle for recognition and land rights.

For the seminomadic Indians in what later became northwestern Mexico, the colonial frontier yielded opportunities to live largely outside Spanish institutions until the mid-nineteenth century. Some people turned to nomadic life as a means to flee and resist the conditions of mission life. Interior areas of Latin America—the savannas and tropical forests of non-Andean South America, and the deserts and scrublands of northern Mexico—were left sparsely populated. Thus, throughout later years, these areas became vulnerable to resource extraction, peasant migration, and commercial agriculture; those who advocated the use and, more often, overuse of these sparsely populated areas declared them "empty."

▨ Independence and the Neoliberal Era

As explained by René de la Pedraja in Chapter 3, Latin America's independence from Spain and Portugal did not necessarily mark the beginning of democracy and equality. It merely opened the region up to investment and intervention by other European powers, especially the British and French, and eventually by North Americans. Latin America continued to export a limited range of commodities. The landed elite retained their power, and a rising entrepreneurial class benefited from its ties to foreign investors. In the second half of the nineteenth century, the first neoliberal era took hold in the region, and foreign investment in export commodities grew rapidly. The export boom was accompanied by an expansion of the agricultural frontier into many of Latin America's wildlands.

Technological innovations stimulated the production of new commodities for growing European markets. Just as in the United States, barbed wire, windmills, and railroads contributed to the opening up of the pampas (plains) in Argentina and Uruguay and the disappearance of wild grassland ecosystems. As wool and wheat production expanded, the largest economic boom, the meat industry, was made possible by the advent of refrigerated steamships. By the end of the nineteenth century, refrigerated shipping also transformed tropical countries, such as Guatemala, Honduras, Costa Rica, and some of the Caribbean islands. For the first time, perishable tropical crops could be sold in Europe and North America, and a major surge in banana production began. The burgeoning urban populations of the industrial cities of North America also created demands for tropical commodities, such as coffee and cocoa, which had previously been consumed only by the wealthy. As large commercial estates formed to produce the new export commodities—coffee, cotton, bananas, and cocoa—they expanded beyond existing farmlands and continued the process of deforestation that is in its final stages today.

Expansion of export production during the era of laissez-faire liberalism was accompanied by changes in land tenure. Much of the region's best farmland, which generally lies in plains and valleys, was concentrated in large commercial farms. At the same time, many indigenous communities lost their traditional communal land rights and swelled the ranks of the landless rural poor. The landless population sought to survive by clearing plots on marginal land, often hillsides, contributing to deforestation and accelerating erosion.

▨ Globalization and the Environment

As Richard Harper and Alfred Cuzán discuss in Chapter 6, the mid-twentieth century saw many Latin American governments embrace economic nationalism and import substitution industrialization. These policies led to accelerated urbanization and pollution in industrial zones. They also contributed to Latin America's foreign debt crises, along with international events such as the oil crises of the 1970s and 1980s. By the late twentieth century, a neoliberal era had overtaken Latin America, and a new era of privatization, foreign investment, and export-led economies reigned supreme in the region. Export production expanded into areas previously oriented toward self-sufficient small farms and domestic production, as well as into land that was not integrated into the national and global economy, including remote areas of tropical rain forest.

During the "lost decade of the 1980s," Latin America experienced a rash of debt crises that led to the imposition of structural adjustment policies by the World Bank, the International Monetary Fund (IMF), and the Inter-American Development Bank (IDB). In return for a restructuring of their crushing foreign debts, a number of Latin American countries were obligated to diversify and expand export production, open their economies to foreign investment, privatize state-owned industries and infrastructure, reduce the size of their government budgets, and raise prices for previously subsidized basic goods. These structural adjustments resulted in significant environmental impacts—including expansion of commercial agricultural production, mineral and petroleum extraction, growth of industrial production and concomitant pollution, and a reduction in protection of the environment and public health due to "downsizing" of governments.

The environmental aspects of the debt crisis and the neoliberal response are closely intertwined with social issues. The expansion of agribusiness into previously remote areas has displaced subsistence farming and generated internal migration in three directions, all with environmental consequences. Many displaced peasant farmers have headed for urban slums, hoping to find employment. Others have pushed farther into frontier areas, usually marginal land of low agricultural potential but highly vulnerable to ecological degradation. In some cases, new urban centers in agricultural regions have grown as a result of rural unemployment and opportunities in agricultural processing, transportation, and services. The challenges posed by these types of migration will be discussed in relevant subsections of this chapter.

Throughout Latin America, the last two decades of the twentieth century witnessed the resurgence of democracy. As authoritarian governments were forced out of office and democratic structures became established, civil society began to assert itself. New social movements arose throughout the region. Grassroots organizations focusing on local environmental issues sprang up all over Latin America, sometimes successfully pressuring governments for amelioration of environmental hazards. These successes suggest a connection between democratization and both the empowerment of civil society and environmental improvements. Some of the hundreds of local civil society organizations in Latin America have linked up with international organizations to protest globalization in its many manifestations, thus demonstrating the links between the local and the global under economic globalization. They also reveal the uneven nature of globalization. Economic activity has become globalized, while social and environmental issues remain primarily local or national—or are perceived as such. Environmental regulation remains confined almost entirely to the national level, limiting its effectiveness in confronting global capital.

Deforestation: Causes and Consequences

Despite several decades of worldwide concern over "saving the rain forest," Latin America's forests continue to disappear at a rapid rate. The causes are structural: expansion of commercial agricultural production, mineral and petroleum extraction (largely to supply increasing consumer demand in the affluent global North), inequitable domestic economic and social systems, and moderate to high rates of population growth, especially between 1950 and 1980. On the surface, the most obvious threat to forests appears to be the stream of poor migrants following newly built roads into the remaining wild areas in the tropical lowlands of southern Mexico, Central America, and the Amazon Basin (including parts of Brazil, Bolivia, Peru, Ecuador, Colombia, and Venezuela). Large-scale commercial farmers and ranchers often follow closely behind, consolidating the small farms cleared by the pioneers. Although the forests may be cleared by the rural poor, the land often ultimately goes into commercial production, following a decline in soil fertility after the first few years of traditional farming. The poor farmers move on, clearing more forest on the new agricultural frontier, while the commercial farms that replace them apply agrochemicals to compensate for the loss of soil fertility. Forest clearance serves the interests of multiple constituencies, including the landless poor; commercial timber, ranching, and agriculture; the politicians who need constituents' votes; and the international lending institutions that demand export production to repay the foreign debt. It is not surprising that environmentalists' dire warnings about the consequences of deforestation have had such limited effects.

Scientists have identified a number of important ecological problems caused by the destruction of tropical rain forests. These include loss of biodiversity, degradation of the soil, climatic change, and changes in the local (and possibly regional) water cycle. Studies in the Amazon Basin have shown that precipitation has declined in areas downwind of large deforested areas. Areas that have been denuded also experience troubling increases in flooding during the rainy season and drought stress during the dry sea-

A rally in Rio Branco, Brazil, protesting destruction
of the Amazon rain forests by cattle ranchers. The rally
was organized by the church and the rubber tappers.

son. Deforestation further affects the rural poor by eliminating subsistence resources, including construction materials, firewood, medicinal plants, and protein from wild game upon which they depend. Furthermore, previously isolated Indian tribes now find themselves under pressure from development interests, settlers, and miners, and land conflicts between the tribes and these groups and among the development interests are escalating.

Using a different strategy, some Indian tribes have been working with environmental and cultural preservation organizations to protect their forested homelands. In Brazil, Peru, Ecuador, and Colombia, Amazonian Indians have succeeded in gaining some legal autonomy and protection of their territories. In Brazil, large expanses of rain forest have been set aside as extractive reserves to protect the resource base of traditional Amazonian populations, such as rubber tappers and Brazil nut harvesters.

Expansion of Export Agriculture
The environmental and social consequences of large-scale commercial agriculture include deforestation and accelerated erosion, as well as degradation of the soil; pollution of the soil, waterways, and surrounding ecosystems by agricultural chemicals; declining biodiversity of both wild and agroecosystems; and the spread of genetically modified organisms

(GMOs). The spread of chemical farming has not occurred without controversy and resistance by the people suffering its negative consequences. Chemicals banned from use in the United States are routinely exported and used in Latin American fields. Pesticide poisoning of farm workers has been widely publicized, and a few cases have actually gone to the courts. For example, DBCP (dibromochloropropane) was banned in the United States because it caused sterility in Dow Chemical company workers but continued to be used on bananas in Central America and Ecuador in the 1970s and early 1980s. Eventually, 16,000 workers who became sterile (out of an estimated 100,000 worldwide) signed on to a lawsuit that was heard in Texas courts. About 1,000 Costa Rican workers received monetary settlements, and other workers' cases continued to be litigated throughout the 1990s.

By the end of the twentieth century, biotechnology was being applied to crops—in part to reduce the need to use dangerous pesticides. GMOs are created by the transfer of genetic material from one plant species to another, thereby conferring preferred traits, such as enriched nutritional value or herbicide resistance. However, the introduction of GMOs has been very controversial for a number of reasons, including their potential contamination of traditional crops.

In 2001, GMO-contaminated maize (corn) was discovered in a remote area of Mexico. This region is an important center of biodiversity, as it was one of the places where maize was domesticated and is still a zone of traditional peasant farming that is based on the cultivation of a wide range of maize varieties. The large maize gene pool found in this area is considered an ecological treasure, but its future is uncertain. If peasant fields become contaminated with GMOs, traditional varieties may be lost forever and, with them, unique genetic material that humans may need in the future. Peasant farmers, indigenous communities, and civil society organizations in Mexico joined forces in 2003 to test fields throughout the country, and they discovered transgenic maize in many regions of Mexico. The GMO controversy has become a worldwide concern and is part of the antiglobalization movement of the early twenty-first century, demonstrating the linkage of local civil society organizations with global movements.

Resource Extraction: Mining and Petroleum Production

Latin America has supplied valuable minerals to the world since the Spanish discovered gold and silver there in the sixteenth century. With the advent of the Industrial Revolution in Europe, markets for industrial minerals began to grow. In the nineteenth century, Chile became the world's leading copper exporter. In turn, other Latin American countries began to export tin, bauxite (aluminum ore), iron, nitrates, and phosphates. The methods of extraction, production, and transport of these commodities in the past were usually controlled by foreign companies that paid little attention to the environmental consequences of their actions. And now, where environmental regulations exist, governments frequently choose not to enforce them. This situation continues to the present day, even though most countries have asserted ownership of their natural resources and, in many cases, of the corresponding corporations that control them.

In the twentieth century, petroleum was discovered in Mexico, Venezuela, and some time later in the Ecuadorian Amazon. The exploration and extraction of petroleum in Latin America has been associated with environmental damage and disruption of the lives of indigenous communities. First, the roads built by exploration teams opened up previously remote rain forest regions to colonization by land-hungry peasants. The resulting deforestation destroyed the livelihoods of indigenous populations. Second, oil drilling inevitably led to oil spills that have contaminated the land and waters of the area. Accidents such as blowouts have occurred, releasing large quantities of crude oil into the environment, and the oil destroys everything in its path. Fires have raged out of control for weeks, causing serious air pollution as well as destruction of any remaining forest near the burning well. In 1979, an enormous blowout of an exploratory well in the southern Gulf of Mexico emitted an estimated 140 million gallons of oil, creating a river of petroleum that flowed for many months. It moved up the Mexican coast, wreaking havoc on both aquatic and coastal ecosystems and even contaminating the coast of Texas. The transport of oil by pipeline and tankers has inevitably entailed leakage that pollutes aquatic and terrestrial ecosystems on a regular, albeit less spectacular, basis.

Latin American governments, eager for the employment and foreign exchange provided by resource extraction companies, hesitate to impose environmental regulations. Foreign corporations may seek to locate companies in Latin America because environmental controls are less stringent than in the United States or Europe, thus reducing production costs. Nationalized companies, such as Mexico's PEMEX, have been notorious for corruption and inefficiency, which has extended to their environmental policies. All of these factors have conspired to create a dismal record of environmental degradation and public health nightmares in oil- and mineral-rich parts of Latin America.

Nontraditional Exports: Shrimp

Shrimp became the number one seafood in the United States in 2001, surpassing tuna. Rapidly escalating demand from North America and Japan, in conjunction with Latin America's need to diversify and expand exports, gave rise to a new industry in the 1980s and 1990s: shrimp farming. Shrimp farming destroys mangroves, which are tropical wetland forests found in sheltered coastal areas. Mangroves play an extremely important role in coastal ecosystems. They prevent erosion of shorelines and provide important protection during hurricanes and tropical storms. They help to break down organic matter deposited by rivers, serving as a sort of natural "sewage treatment plant." They also provide a necessary habitat for marine organisms that spawn in estuaries, thus playing an important role in sustaining offshore fisheries.

Traditionally, shrimp fishing was a small-scale activity of coastal residents in the American tropics. It was often part of a varied livelihood strategy, based on the productivity of natural ecosystems and including other types of fishing and farming on coastal plains. Such livelihood strategies helped preserve the mangrove forests and the health of the aquatic ecosystems of estuaries in Latin America.

Industrial shrimp farming, usually funded by foreign investors, requires the removal of the mangrove forests. The natural ecosystem is replaced by ponds and canals. Intensive shrimp farming requires large amounts of artificial nutrients, pesticides, antibiotics, and fresh water, in addition to the natural salt water. Shrimp excrement joins these substances in the outflow from the shrimp farms. Ponds eventually choke on their own waste and go out of production after a decade or so. They leave behind a devastated environment that is unable to produce wild shrimp. Small-scale traditional fishermen do not fit into this system, which destroys virtually all aspects of their livelihoods. Therefore, many fishing villages have mobilized to oppose the development of shrimp farms. Conflicts with the authorities in Guatemala and Honduras over shrimp farming have been less successful and more violent than in southern Mexico, where traditional small-scale fishermen have kept shrimp farms out of some villages.

Urbanization in Latin America

Environmental issues in Latin America have been increasingly tied to industrialization and accompanying urbanization. Industrialization is not new in Latin America. Countries such as Argentina, Chile, Colombia, Brazil, and Mexico have had a substantial industrial sector since the 1930s. During the import-substitution era (1930s to 1970s), they developed heavy industries that created negative environmental impacts such as air and water pollution. Authoritarian governments ignored the environmental and public health costs of industrialization, and ordinary people lacked the political influence to change the situation. Cubatão, an industrial city near São Paulo, Brazil, is one of the most polluted places on earth. It has been dubbed the "Valley of Death" due to the concentration of chemical industries there. Toxic emissions from Cubatão's industries led to elevated incidences of cancers, birth defects, and other health problems among its population. Poorly regulated industries also make residents of industrial cities vulnerable to disasters. For example, in 1984 a large petrochemical plant exploded in the densely populated Mexico City metropolitan area, killing over 1,000, injuring 4,200, and displacing over 200,000 people.

Latin America has become one of the most urbanized of all the world's regions, not only due to urban industrialization, but also because standards of living in rural areas increasingly have lagged behind urban areas. Agricultural strategies favoring exports and land monopolies that date back to the colonial period were instrumental in forcing landless people to leave the countryside from the early twentieth century on. Later, modern industrialization of agriculture dispossessed large numbers of peasant farmers, and many migrated to urban areas in search of employment. Industrial programs provided a "pull" factor toward the primate cities that received most investment. The population of São Paulo almost doubled between 1950 and 1960, growing from 2.3 million to 4.4 million, at a time when wealth generated by coffee in the surrounding region was subsidizing industry and commerce.

Although the rate of urbanization varies from country to country, the shift from a rural-based to an overwhelmingly urban society has been swift. Fifty years ago, the majority of Latin Americans lived in the countryside. Today, only about one-quarter do. The speed of this transition has made the "urban problem" a key theme in Latin American society. However, the rural conditions that spurred this growth and the inability or lack of interest by urban elites to address urban poverty have made this much more than a demographic problem. The tendency to perceive rapid urbanization as an invasion by impoverished migrants has deep historical roots dating back to the colonial period.

The demographic marginality of towns through most of Latin American history belied their importance as political, military, religious, and economic centers during and after colonialism. With the blessing of their rulers back home, the colonial elite quickly sought to establish towns as bases from which they could obtain resources from their rural hinterlands. In Spanish America, the location of colonial towns was closely tied to mineral sources and to pre-Columbian settlements. In Portuguese America and the Caribbean, coastal settlements supported the plantation economies, whereas the deep interior of Portuguese America remained relatively devoid of European settlement for the first century of the conquest. In contrast with the Spanish, Portuguese colonists settled into vast rural dominions, mostly within a few hundred miles of the coast, until the eighteenth century when the discovery of gold and diamonds gave rise to distant mining towns, such as Vila Rica (Ouro Preto) and Diamantina, both in the state of Minas Gerais. As noted earlier, the *bandeirantes* penetrated the interior from the southeast edge of the Portuguese colony, but they did not urbanize that region.

Although still predominant across Latin America, rural-urban migration has been joined by many other variations that have presented and are leading to unexpected urban patterns and problems. Before we discuss these, we will turn to a trademark outcome of rapid urban growth in Latin America since the 1950s: the squatter settlement. Migration rates from the 1950s onward made it almost impossible for urban authorities and the housing market to keep up with population growth. Between 1950 and 1960, over 1 million new people moved to Mexico City. The following decade, the population rose by 3.5 million, and by 2000, the city was gaining about 6 million more people per decade. Zoning, affordable housing, and infrastructure have lagged miserably behind this movement of people, despite decreasing population growth rates in many cities. As a result, poor people often resort to self-built shelters or doubling up with relatives.

In many Latin American cities, one-third of the people live in settlements with makeshift housing and substandard services. It is estimated that 60 percent of the population in Mexico City live in some form of substandard or squatter settlement. One of its barrios, Netzahualcoyotl, now a veritable city of some 2 million inhabitants, began with squatters occupying the

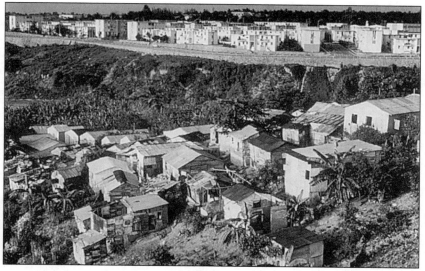

Large numbers of people live in squalid conditions in the urban areas of Latin America. This is a shantytown on the periphery of Santo Domingo, Dominican Republic.

dry lake bed surrounding Mexico City some fifty years ago. The residents themselves gradually transformed makeshift shacks into concrete block and stucco homes and successfully fought for basic city services. Many peripheral settlements support extremely high population densities because low-income families may be unable to afford their own homes. In Brazil, about 10 percent of the population—many adults with their own children—live "by favor" with relatives or friends, creating overcrowding and tension in the country's poorest neighborhoods.

Squatter settlements are not only a reflection of governments' inability to address urbanization, but emblematic of people's self-reliance and determination to survive. While many people are too poor to pay rent or buy a home, they quickly develop collective and individual strategies for survival. Squatter settlements have been incredibly innovative in devising collective strategies for education, recreation, and job creation. Second- and third-generation squatters have transformed their shantytowns into veritable cities within cities, with a mix of public and private infrastructure, permanent and improved housing, commerce, and social differentiation.

Urban officials and politicians approached the enormous population influx in different ways. One response was outright slum removal, an approach that held sway among military dictatorships. These forced evictions largely ended with the return of democracy across Latin America. With such a huge constituency of voting citizens, politicians feared the

UN Photo 153594/J. Frank

A *favela* (squatter town) in Rio de Janeiro, Brazil.

UN Photo 97369

Children in a *población* (slum) in Santiago, Chile.

results of direct confrontation. Self-help housing also subsidized the provision of housing and services in the region's exploding cities through "sweat equity." Because squatter settlements were often on government-owned land, they did not typically set off a confrontation over private property. In the last fifteen years, governments have quickened the provision of basic amenities to squatters, but they also put in place more rigorous environmental zoning. These two tendencies have led to a more restrictive governmental attitude toward urban squatters as well as a limited market for very low-income housing.

Although elites blame the poor for their urban problems, from crime to pollution, the poor are the first to be victimized by urban ecological disasters, such as toxic spills, explosions, landslides, and flooding, as well as by chronic urban environmental problems, such as water, air, and soil pollution.

Illegal economies, rooted in the international drug trade, quasi-governmental structures, and "police" forces, have emerged in the sprawling slums of all Latin American cities. These have become staging grounds for violent rivalries between powerful drug lords and sometimes corrupt police forces, while the majority of the people who live in them attempt to go about their daily lives in peace.

In search of security and comfort, the upper and middle classes have turned to high-rise security towers in the city or gated communities on the rural-urban fringe. Tangled traffic, overburdened sewage systems, noise, and loss of sunlight are some of the outcomes of the spread of the urban core into first-tier suburbs. Consequently, the urban elite has begun to "sprawl" into rural zones for its residential needs. Insufficient environmental oversight has allowed speculators to create notoriously illegal subdivisions that attract rich and middle-income squatters, whose ability to manipulate the judicial systems virtually guarantees the endorsement of their property claims. The elite's search for security has also produced luxurious shopping centers that have replaced the town plaza as the icon of Latin American leisure and public life.

Within individual countries, the trend has been for already large cities to grow larger and for medium-sized cities to become metropolitan cities. Metropolitan areas absorb the largest share of urban people. In Mexico, one-third of the country's population and about one-half of the urban population live in just six metropolitan areas. Mexico City alone, with 18 million people, holds about 18 percent of the country's total population and 25 percent of its urban population. The population of Argentina is almost 90 percent urbanized, about 40 percent of which live in the Buenos Aires metropolitan region. The growth of these areas has led to metropolitan sprawls that continue to swallow up towns, rural open space, and farms in their paths. Today, the cultural, economic, and political resources of these cities have a strong grip on elites, who often prefer to live in them despite the by-products of size, such as pollution, commuting time, and crime.

Jobs (even if informal), government infrastructure, schools, and family networks built up over time through previous migrations continue to draw

Latin American cities have grown rapidly. This view of Caracas, Venezuela, shows extensive urbanization in the eastern sector.

the poor to major cities. Unemployment and the struggle for urban liveli-hoods are associated with many urban environmental problems. Poverty and the informal economy (estimated at 70 percent of jobs by the International Labour Organization) send people into dangerous environ-ments, such as trash heaps and flood zones, that operate below the radar of environmental regulation. Lackadaisical waste disposal standards tragically introduced urban trash pickers to the atomic age in the Brazilian city of Goiania in 1987. People who made a living recycling trash took an x-ray cylinder containing cesium 137 from an abandoned hospital and dismantled it at home. Fascinated by its glow, they showed the cesium off, passing it around and playing with it. Four people died one month later, many hun-dreds became ill, and some died years later from cancer. Investigators found waste from the accident over one thousand miles away.

In order to reduce environmental and political pressures on the largest cities, government officials and planners have tried to decentralize urban growth by encouraging the growth of smaller cities. Other motivations, such as occupation of the interior and political symbolism, have also come into play in these efforts. The construction of Brasília, Brazil, and Ciudad Guyana, Venezuela, were bold attempts to build cities from the ground up. While these efforts succeeded in creating new pockets of urbanization out-side established cities, this has not slowed the galloping growth of cities that were already large when these new towns were constructed. Built in the late 1950s, Brasília has graduated to a metropolitan area with over 2

An abandoned street child picking garbage in a dump near São Paulo, Brazil.

UN Photo 154979/Claudio Edinger

Brazilian youth passing
time in the heart of
São Paulo, the second-
largest city in Latin
America. (Mexico City
is the largest.)

UN Photo 133592/J. Frank

million people. In the same period of time, however, São Paulo's population grew from 4.4 million to 24 million. Even though the new cities were built with strong planning ideals, they have succumbed to many of the same problems of older cities, such as squatters living in shantytowns, chronic pollution, high levels of crime, and heavy traffic.

Some urban decentralization has occurred as an unintended consequence of regional economic policies, such as export processing zones in the Caribbean Basin, border industrialization in Mexico, frontier occupation in the Amazonian portion of various countries, and rural development based on nontraditional export crops. During the neoliberal era, previously less industrialized countries, such as those of Central America and the Caribbean Basin, became the target of foreign investment in assembly industries such as clothing and electronics. One of the most spectacular sites of this type of industrialization is along the U.S.-Mexican border. In the last two decades of the twentieth century, thousands of assembly plants, called *maquiladoras*, moved to this zone to take advantage of its unique spatial characteristics. The United States represents the largest consumer market in the world, while Mexico represents a huge pool of cheap labor and lax environmental regulations. Hundreds of foreign companies were attracted to the close proximity of these factors.

The *maquiladora* phenomenon stimulated migration to Mexico's border area, where rapid urbanization occurred. By 1990, there were 3.5 million people in eighteen border cities, 6 percent of the country's total urban population that year. Urban infrastructure along the border is inadequate to meet the needs of the rapidly growing population, where high rates of poverty and the various types of pollution generated by the *maquiladoras* contribute to a host of environmental problems. Mexico's unaddressed environmental problems are finally getting attention from people across the border, as smog and raw sewage make their way into the United States. In recent decades, cities on both sides of the Rio Grande in Texas have experienced a significant increase in birth defects, most notably anencephaly (lack of brain development in a fetus). Many scientists and public health experts believe this to be the result of pollution from Mexico's *maquiladoras*.

Another facet of urban growth taking place outside countries' primate cities is boomtown growth in frontier regions. The drug trade, peasant migration, mining, and logging have led to the growth of boomtowns throughout the Amazon Basin. With little infrastructure and sudden increases in an impoverished population, these towns have become troubling sites of diseases such as malaria, yellow fever, dengue, and cholera. As a crossroads for sex workers, these towns also tend to have high rates of sexually transmitted diseases.

Export-oriented agriculture has expanded into the rural hinterlands in virtually all countries, as noted above. Since the 1980s, this expansion has rested on a whole new set of nontraditional export crops, such as soybeans, flowers, oranges for frozen concentrate, and forest products for pulp and paper mills. In most cases, profound changes come to regions that are swept into these new activities. In some contexts, this development attracts former peasants to local towns where some find work in the service sector and agroprocessing. But modern agriculture can also be a factor in population loss. The mechanization of cotton and other crops that were essential to rural livelihoods in Argentina's Chaco province destroyed thousands of jobs, leaving people with no alternative but to migrate to Buenos Aires or to other regional centers.

Urban decentralization of the kind described above has had a minimal effect on the urban system as a whole. More often, the same kinds of urban environmental problems spring up in all cities and towns that are growing rapidly, regardless of their size. Smaller towns, in fact, may have a less active and empowered citizenry to address urban pollution and environmental justice. Creative solutions to these problems are indeed coming from some of the region's largest cities. Mexico City, São Paulo, and Santiago all inaugurated programs to reduce automobile use, based on license plate numbers. During the economic crisis in Argentina in the late 1990s, people opened community-based factories and restaurants for the unemployed. In the southern Brazilian city of Curitiba, longtime mayor and architect Jaime Lerner took a series of measures to ease the pressures of urban life on people and the environment, leading to its being dubbed throughout the world as the "Ecological City." Lerner and colleagues sought to create a more livable environment around the reality of people's

This sign in Santo Tomé de Guayana, Venezuela,
indicates a green zone in which construction is
prohibited. The area is reserved for a park.

lives, offering, for instance, free bus passes in exchange for recyclables. They sought simple solutions to traffic circulation by creating an integrated bus system and bike paths and to downtown revitalization with a walkable central business district restricted to vehicles. Green spaces evolved through decades of tree planting, and new public parks and lakes double as diversion ponds for floods that had plagued squatter settlements in the past.

Population: Distribution, Fertility, and Mortality

Misinformation and emotional responses abound when dealing with the subject of population and the environment. Intuitively, people often blame the environmental and social problems of cities on overcrowding and on overpopulation in Latin America more generally. Resource destruction, however, is often spearheaded by commercial interests and has less to do with population. Urban environmental problems are primarily the result of highly distorted urbanization patterns and poverty. In fact, Latin America as a whole is less densely populated, at twenty-five people per square mile, than the United States, at thirty. In addition, Latin American women are taking the lead among women in the developing world, as they dramatically reverse historically high fertility rates.

Demographic Transition

Latin American mortality and fertility have both fallen to a point where the rate of natural growth is in decline. The annual growth rate peaked in the 1960s at 2.8 percent. Recent estimates show the annual growth rate at 1.4 percent. There is considerable variation among countries, however. Some countries still have growth rates that exceed 2 percent, whereas Uruguay, Cuba, and several English-speaking Caribbean nations have rates of less than 1 percent. Rates of more than 2.5 percent are found in Guatemala, Belize, Honduras, El Salvador, Nicaragua, Bolivia, and Paraguay.

Together, these numbers suggest that Latin America is undergoing a demographic transition toward low birth and death rates. The demographic transition model implies that the interplay between numbers of deaths and births and growth rates roughly follows a predictable path as societies modernize and urbanize. Even though Latin America as a whole appears to be following the model, each country and subregion does so in a unique way, and there is no guarantee that present patterns will hold. Under impoverished circumstances, people may choose to have fewer children out of desperation rather than because they have arrived at a new level of well-being. Many of the region's poorest people, in fact, suffer from diseases that are completely preventable, and women still suffer from lack of access to family planning.

In Latin America, death rates have declined dramatically with twentieth-century urbanization and accompanying advances in water and sewage treatment and vaccination for childhood diseases. Polluted water can be traced to many diseases or conditions that often kill young children, such as

Installing water lines in São Paulo, Brazil.

diarrhea. The percentage of people with access to potable water is now over 85 percent in the region as a whole, with higher rates in cities than in rural areas. Although 94 percent of urban Latin Americans have access to clean water, 24 million people living in cities still have none. Construction of sewage treatment facilities lags far behind the delivery of clean water.

As cities become megacities, the effects on water supply are contradictory. Population increase, urban sprawl, and industrial water use and pollution place huge stresses on water supplies and waste treatment. At the same time, because governments concentrate infrastructure in cities, urban people tend to have better access to safe drinking water. These improvements, however, often do not reach the most precarious urban settlements, where extreme population densities contribute to high levels of water contamination.

Because of these inequities, the decline of many chronic diseases of environmental origin has been inconsistent. Some recent epidemics can be traced to deteriorating conditions in cities together with precarious settlement in frontier areas and increased international and national mobility. The persistence of tropical diseases, like cholera, Chagas' disease, malaria, yellow fever, and dengue are dependent on environmental conditions close to home, such as poor drainage, lack of sewage treatment, polluted water supplies, inadequate trash collection, lack of window screens and mosquito netting, and building materials that harbor insect vectors. Migration into tropical lowland areas and the environmental consequences of settlement in makeshift boomtowns with little medical assistance, public health education, or planning have led to the resurgence of malaria, especially among those without the resources to purchase individual protection (screens, netting, and quinine treatment).

According to the Joint United Nations Program on AIDS, over 2 million Latin Americans are infected with HIV, and 100,000 died of the disease in 2003. Risk of exposure to AIDS is environmental, in the sense that certain behaviors associated with it have tended to cluster in large urban areas. Its spread to smaller towns and rural areas has accompanied an increase in heterosexual transmission and its presence among women. Drug injection and unsafe sex are the primary modes of transmission, but in Haiti the epidemic has carried over widely into the general population. Although until now AIDS has been concentrated in cities, rural areas face increasing rates. One mechanism for transmission in rural Mexico is temporary migration to the United States. Rural people with HIV are four times more likely than their urban counterparts to have acquired the virus after traveling to the United States. The narcotics trafficking in remote rural areas also leads to a rise in rural rates of infection. Other endemic diseases such as malaria and a chronic lack of medical services combine to produce an even more devastating profile of the epidemic.

Another prominent cause of death that varies by where and how people live is violence. Youth homicide deaths rank highest in the world for five Latin American and Caribbean nations, according to the United Nations Educational, Scientific, and Cultural Organization (UNESCO). Brazil is at the top of this list, with an average annual rate of fifty-five violent deaths per 100,000 people between the ages of 15 and 24, followed by Colombia, the Virgin Islands, El Salvador, and Venezuela. California gangs have appeared among El Salvador's repatriated population, contributing to that country's high rates of youth homicide. Turf wars over the drug trade in urban squatter settlements take a disproportionate share of young lives in all countries.

Fertility Change

As Susan Tiano shows in Chapter 10, Latin America has experienced spectacular declines in fertility in the last twenty years. Fertility is the average number of children a woman will bear throughout her lifetime. Fertility in Latin America fell from six to 2.5 children per woman between 1960 and 2000. Several countries are approaching replacement levels (two children per woman), and Cuba is below replacement at an average of 1.5 children per woman.

A combination of factors worked together to make the fertility decline one of the most extreme examples of social change in the last two generations. These included the women's movement, reproductive technologies, urbanization, and expectations by ordinary working people for a better life. International organizations such as Zero Population Growth and Planned Parenthood have been active in Latin America, although official policy on population growth is ambiguous, in part because of the enduring influence of the Catholic Church in most countries. Despite opposition from the church, sterilization has become the most sought-after form of birth control by women, to the point where supply of this procedure runs far behind demand in many countries. Abortion, although illegal in every country except Cuba and Guyana, has played an important role in the collapse of fertility in Latin America. Current estimates indicate about 4 million abortions are performed each year in Latin America.

The rise of urban middle-class consumerism, promoted by the mass media, has given Latin Americans the sense that only small families are compatible with wealth. *Telenovelas* (soap operas) typically place beautiful, small, rich families at the center of their plot lines. Fewer children may earn a working family the ability to reach a more humane standard of living; however, rising standards of living put mounting pressures on resources, as people come to expect private vehicles, electronic gadgets, better housing, and a diet high in exotic and processed foods. Most people, however, do not attain middle-class status as a result of lowering their fertility. Rather, as the lives of female breadwinners become a complex quilt of part-time, short-term, and irregular employment, having fewer children is a strategy for women who must work harder and longer to survive.

Conclusion

For Latin America as a whole, with a population of 540 million in 2003, there is nothing that guarantees that the recent drop in fertility will bring improvements to the environment and society. Alternatively, no one can predict with certainty that a stable population, at 700 or 900 million, will bring calamity beyond that which many people already suffer in their everyday lives. Social and environmental problems persist due to a legacy of grossly unequal distribution of land and wealth and the unsustainable consumption and production that have become synonymous with "development." As population grows, agricultural, forest, and aquatic systems struggle to keep up with demands. At the same time, demands increase with affluence, urbanization, and globalization, making sustainability a moving target. Pressures on uses of the land, air, and water are indeed at a breaking point in many cities. Assuming a commitment to sustainable practices by everyone, including the rich, the policymakers, and the poor, slower urban growth could reduce uncertainty and improve the chances for these practices to take hold.

The region's colossal size, divergent histories, and unique physical environments make generalizations dangerous. Nonetheless, given the finite nature of the earth's air, water, and land resources, Latin Americans will need to find ways to accommodate the basic needs of the poor alongside production for the affluent. Each country will devise its own solution to this conundrum, reflecting its unique history and physical endowments.

Bibliography

Blouet, Brian W., and Olwyn M. Blouet. *Latin America and the Caribbean: A Systematic and Regional Survey* (4th ed.). New York: John Wiley and Sons, 2002.

Chase, Jacqueline (ed.). *The Spaces of Neoliberalism: Land, Place and Family in Latin America*. Bloomfield, Conn.: Kumarian Press, 2002.

Clawson, David L. *Latin American and the Caribbean: A Systematic and Regional Survey* (2d ed.). New York: McGraw Hill, 2000.

Crosby, Alfred. *The Columbian Exchange: Biological and Cultural Consequences of 1492*. Westport, Conn.: Greenwood Press, 1972.

Denevan, William. *The Native Population of the Americas in 1492* (2d ed.). Madison: University of Wisconsin, 1992.

Gilbert, Alan. *The Latin American City*. New York: Monthly Review Books, 1994.

Guzman, Jose Miguel (ed.). *The Fertility Transition in Latin America*. Oxford, UK: Clarendon Press, 1996.

Hardoy, Jorge E., Diana Mitlin, and David Satterthwaite. *Environmental Problems in Third World Cities*. London: Earthscan, 1995.

Hardoy, Jorge E., and David Satterthwaite. *Squatter Citizen*. London: Earthscan, 1995.

Hemming, John. *Red Gold: The Conquest of the Brazilian Indians, 1500–1760*. Cambridge, Mass.: Harvard University Press, 1978.

Loker, William (ed.). *Globalization and the Rural Poor in Latin America*. Boulder, Colo.: Lynne Rienner Publishers, 1999.

Mann, Charles C. "1491." *Atlantic Monthly* (March 2002):41–53.

Perlman, Janice. *The Myth of Marginality*. Berkeley: University of California Press, 1977.

Pezzoli, Keith. *Human Settlements and Planning for Ecological Sustainability: The Case of Mexico City*. Cambridge, Mass.: MIT Press, Urban and Industrial Environment Series, 1998.

Place, Susan E. (ed.). *Tropical Rainforests: Latin American Nature and Society in Transition*. Wilmington, Del.: Scholarly Resources, 2001.

Population Reference Bureau. *World Population Data Sheet*. 2003. Available online at http://www.prb.org/.

Price, Richard. *Maroon Societies: Rebel Slave Communities in the Americas* (3d ed.). Baltimore: Johns Hopkins University Press, 1996.

Roberts, J. Timmons, and Nikki Demetria Thanos. *Trouble in Paradise: Globalization and Environmental Crises in Latin America*. New York: Routledge, 2003.

Zimmerer, Karl S., and Eric P. Carter. *Conservation and Sustainability in Latin America and the Caribbean: Latin America in the 21st Century*. 27th Yearbook of the Conference of Latin Americanist Geographers. Austin: University of Texas Press, 2002.

9

Patterns of "Race," Ethnicity, Class, and Nationalism

Kevin A. Yelvington

Identity politics in Latin America are often revealed, not to mention constituted, animated, and given form, in the context of the formal political process. One infamous episode occurred in the 1994 presidential election in the Dominican Republic. Joaquín Balaguer—the frail, blind, partially deaf 87-year-old incumbent—branded as a "Haitian" his strongest challenger, José Francisco Peña Gómez, the former mayor of Santo Domingo. Balaguer (1906–2002), who came to power in 1960 as a puppet of the notorious dictator, Rafael Trujillo, subsequently served six terms as president. In a country where the entrenched members of the political and economic elite are of light complexion, Balaguer was considered "white." In contrast, Peña Gómez (1937–1998) once described himself as "a humble man, the color of the night." Balaguer's campaign appealed to national fears and disdain for black Haitian immigrants and culture and reflected a keen awareness that Dominicans identify with their putative Spanish origins and cultural traditions and are in denial of their African heritage.

Whereas Balaguer portrayed himself as a *patrón* (benefactor) who was above dirty politics, because he inaugurated public works projects and took personal credit for every new road and apartment building, his supporters in the right-leaning Social Christian Reform Party produced television commercials showing a videotape of Peña Gómez attending a faith-healing ceremony they claimed was a *vodou* ritual. As Michael Fleet shows in Chapter 12, *vodou* is a syncretized Afro-Christian form of worship, sometimes called voodoo in English, which combines the worship of West African deities and Catholic saints. In this context, the reference to *vodou* was intended to contrast Euro-Dominican with Afro-Haitian culture.

Balaguer's supporters also left anonymous leaflets and sent fax mes-

237

Joaquín Balaguer in 1990. The longtime president of the
Dominican Republic was a protégé of the dictator Rafael Trujillo.

José Francisco Peña
Gómez in 1994. The
presidential candidate
was branded "Haitian"
by Balaguer's followers.

sages that warned of Peña Gómez's supposed sinister intentions for the
future of the country's cultural and political sovereignty. They claimed he
would give the country away to neighboring Haiti if elected. A pamphlet
was published in the campaign's final weeks that characterized Peña

Gómez's candidacy as the fulfillment of a centuries-old Haitian plot to re-conquer the Dominican Republic.

Forced to confront these charges, Peña Gómez and his left-of-center Dominican Revolutionary Party countered by charging the Balaguer regime with corruption, political repression, cronyism, and incompetence. Throughout the campaign, Peña Gómez consistently led in public opinion polls. Many Dominicans were apparently rejecting Balaguer's racist appeals. Nevertheless, amid charges of fraud, after three months of deliber-ation, the Central Elections Board (three of whose five members were appointed by Balaguer) finally announced that Balaguer had won by a slim margin of 22,181 votes.[1]

*   *   *

It is revealing to study the historical context within which labeling some-one as "Haitian" is viewed as socially and politically damaging. With a few exceptions in Latin America, European culture has been valued over indigenous or African culture, and a group's phenotypical features have often been conflated with "culture," understood not only as a way of life but also as a set of significant accomplishments. This value structure has been reflected in Haitian-Dominican relations. As René de la Pedraja shows in Chapter 3, the French sugar-producing colony of Saint-Domingue became the independent country of Haiti in 1804, after a massive and hero-ic slave revolt killed or forced into exile white slaveholders and colonial officials. Haiti became the first black republic and only the second inde-pendent country in the hemisphere (after the United States). At a time when African slavery was prevalent throughout the Americas, the Haitian Revolution caused slave owners elsewhere to fear similar insurrections. Moreover, Haiti invaded and occupied the Dominican Republic from 1822 to 1844. Although it occurred more than a century and a half ago, this occu-pation still burns in the Dominican national consciousness.

Haiti's subsequent isolation and impoverishment caused many Haitians to migrate in search of menial jobs. They found brutal work in the sugar-cane fields of the Dominican Republic, where they received low pay and suffered under poor working conditions. When he came to power in 1930, President Trujillo began a paranoid and prejudicial anti-Haitian campaign that preoccupied him until his assassination in 1961. Although considered a *mulato* (a mixture of African and European ancestry) himself, Trujillo sought to emphasize supposed "white" civilization and culture. He institut-ed a policy of *hispanidad* (Spanishness), by which the national identity and culture of the Dominican Republic were depicted as rooted in a glorious European past. Roman Catholicism, Spanish literature, the *conquistadores*, and even the bullfight were upheld as the true legacy of the country.

Trujillo's machinations were more than rhetorical. In the depths of the Great Depression, with sugar prices low, unemployment high, and declining government revenues, he ordered his police force to murder Haitian sugarcane workers. Between October 2 and 4, 1937, an estimated 20,000 to 30,000 Haitians were stabbed and beaten to death. In the Haitian Kreyòl language, a hard "r" is not pronounced. Consequently, Haitians were known to have difficulty pronouncing *perejil* (parsley), and it was based on this criterion that they were identified and killed. Although nothing like this atrocity has occurred since, in the intervening years Haitian workers have often been intimidated and forcibly deported when sugar prices have fallen.

Today, Haitian sugarcane workers in the Dominican Republic are still subjected to squalid living and working conditions. Of the Dominican Republic's 8.7 million people, more than 1 million are Haitians, and over 80 percent of the workers in the Dominican sugar fields are Haitian. A 1983 International Labor Office report outlined labor practices on the plantations that were tantamount to slavery: the workers are cheated out of their meager wages, are forced to work twelve-hour days with no lunch break, are confined to their camps by armed guards and the military, and live in sparse, overcrowded compounds with virtually no running water or electricity (Latortue 1985). There is evidence that these conditions still persist. But Haitians are encouraged to continue their migration because of poor economic and political conditions in their own country and the demand for their labor in jobs Dominicans regard as beneath them.

In his book, *La isla al revés: Haití y el destino dominicano* (*The Island Turned on Its Head: Haiti and Dominican Destiny*, 1990), Balaguer proved he was at least Trujillo's equal as a racist ideologist. Given Balaguer's dominance over Dominican political and public life for such a long period, his thoughts in this book are very revealing of a widespread political and class ideology. The Dominican Republic, he claimed, has always been a "white and Christian" country that is witnessing "progressive ethnic decadence" that threatens the country's "Spanish physiognomy." Except for a "minuscule" and unrepresentative number, any "black" presence in the Dominican Republic, he argued, is an alien "Haitian" incursion. "Haitian imperialism is now an even greater threat to our country than before [when it was military] for biological reasons."

Balaguer warned that the evil consequences of miscegenation are racial and cultural decay concomitant with the subsequent "vegetative increase of the African race." He feared that "the white race will eventually be absorbed by the African." Haitian culture is described in the book as "instinct-governed, vegetally fertile heathen." Haitians are "generators of indolence" and "of primitive mentality." As a remedy, Balaguer proposed tightening the national borders, increasing Catholic instruction, and promoting the immigration of white capitalists—a plan to be directed by the *raza selecta* (select race). Despite currents of opposition, these ideas continue to have popular currency, as well as elite justification, in the Dominican Republic. Ironically, at the end of *La isla al revés*, Balaguer—not Peña Gómez—proposed a confederation of the Dominican and Haitian states that would guarantee the independence of each and would improve relations after 150 years of conflict.

*   *   *

The consequences of *hispanidad*, repression, and apologist attempts at scientific justification demonstrate the convoluted interrelationship of "race," ethnicity, class, and nationalism. In the Dominican Republic, if one is considered black, one is a Haitian; if one is Dominican, one is not considered black. "Dominican" and "black" are mutually exclusive categories; therefore, it is impossible for one to be both. Haitians are those black people who come to the country to work in poorly paid, low-status jobs. They have few or no political or economic rights. While in recent years dissenting voices have developed, and a Dominican movement that embraces positive images of blackness can be identified, these voices continue to be drowned out by the dominant ideological representations.

Although some aspects of the Dominican case are clearly country specific, others illustrate patterns of ethnicity and class in Latin America. The complexity and diversity of these patterns prohibit an exhaustive study in one chapter. Similarly complex are the relative class positions of *jíbaros*, *guajiros*, and *campesinos* (as peasants and rural workers are called in Puerto Rico, Cuba, and South America, respectively) and their relation to *hacendados* (owners of large rural estates), as well as the economic conditions of urban *trabajadores* (workers), their *sindicatos* (trade unions), the *jefes* (bosses), and *dueños* (business owners). These factors are also beyond the scope of this chapter, which focuses on the impact of "race," ethnicity, and class on social relations and nationalism in contemporary Latin America through selected historical and ethnographic examples that provide a point of departure for further investigation of this vast topic.

▪ Defining Key Terms

Ethnic identities in Latin America, as elsewhere, are cultural constructs, that is, definitions and meanings that are enforced and enacted and become taken for granted and assented to, for the most part. Popular notions of "race" and ethnicity, by their very nature, however, are reified—spuriously considered biological absolutes. Such stereotyping is derived from a distinctly European perspective that sought to impose order on a world

consider abstractions as material object

A resident of
San Mateo, Guatemala.

UN Photo 152275/A. Jongen

expanding through the conquest and colonial domination of people held to
be fundamentally different and inferior.

"Racial" differentiation in terms of traits that became "racialized"
(observable phenotypical features such as skin color, shape of the nose,
type of hair, and so on) was linked with assumptions regarding mental and
behavioral capacities and characteristics. Even on its own terms, however,
this view does not stand up to close scrutiny. The world's population displays a panorama of genetic traits that belie popular stereotypes and the traditional, supposedly scientific view of "the three races." Infinite genetic
combinations have rendered impossible neat classification of specific traits
pertaining exclusively to Caucasoid, Negroid, or Mongoloid categories. No
absolute divisions exist in reality.

A cross-cultural perspective reveals other ways of thinking about
"race" and ethnicity. For example, many North Americans are incredulous
when very dark-skinned Latin Americans distinguish themselves from
African Americans. In North America, traditionally at least, "racial
accounting" through the lens of the concept of hypodescent regards the offspring of a black and a white as black. Throughout Latin America, in contrast, a number of "racial terms" are deduced from an individual's color,
ideas about ancestry, and social status in a system typified by ambiguity
and negotiation in assigning individuals to "racial" categories but where,
nevertheless, higher status is accorded to those who approach the European
ideal.[2]

"Racial" terms found in the Dominican Republic have parallels elsewhere. The term *indio* (Indian), with various modifiers, appears on official

forms that ask for "race." An *indio* may be a black person with wavy, rather than kinky, hair. *Indio claro* (light-colored Indian) may refer to light-skinned *mulatos*, whereas the term *indio oscuro* (dark Indian) refers to very dark-skinned people. Some people find themselves described as *de color medio* (of medium color), a distinction that refers to someone who is neither white nor black. Conversely, *bajo de color* (low in color) refers to skin color but also to the low social status of blacks. Often, physical features like an individual's hair are pointed out and used to make value judgments. *Pelo bueno* (good hair) refers to straight or wavy hair, for example, whereas *pasa* (raisin) refers to people with kinky hair in a deprecatory way.

There are two terms that are ostensibly about economic class and social status but that at the same time allude to a person's color. *Gente de primera* (first-class people) implies whiteness, whereas *gente de segunda* (second-class people) refers to people of lower status social or ethnic groups. Although the boundaries between identities are in some ways permeable, those who are seen attempting to transcend those boundaries overtly are derided as *blanco de la barranca* (white from the gutter) and *blanquito* (little white person), referring to nonwhite people who pretend to be white. The worst epithets, however, are reserved for those seen to be manifestly of African heritage. *Negro como una paila* (black as a frying pan) refers to a person with very dark skin, and *morejón* is a derogatory word for a black person considered ordinary or ugly.

Similarly, in the Anglo-Caribbean, distinctions made among those considered white, colored, and black are only partially derived from an interpretation of what are taken to be markers of ancestry. This contrast in "racial" reckoning is apparent when individuals with these identities migrate to North America. In their Anglo-Caribbean societies, people who are *mulatos* and colored are thought of, and think of themselves, as "racially" distinct from both whites and blacks. When they migrate to the United States, however, they are categorized as black—much to their regret in many instances. This phenomenon does not indicate that the people so described are "really" black but that through a combination of social position and psychological denial they are unable to shrug off an identity that is so liability ridden in the United States. It does indicate that "race" is a culturally constructed entity rather than something rooted in biological facts.

Latin American and Caribbean peoples possess a highly developed system of "racial" accounting, a system of ideas that is properly understood under the rubric of ethnicity. Ethnicity is a particular social and cultural identity typified by a reference to ancestors who are presumed to have had a shared culture.[3] Central to the concept of ethnicity is culture—the learned, patterned behaviors and systems of meanings of a given human group.[4] Here, a key concept is that of "ethnogenesis," the process of the creation and transformation of an ethnic group, including their "ethnonyms," the name of the group. This concept even holds out the possibility of the eventual dissolution of that group and its absorption into another group. From this perspective, ethnic identity and ethnic groups do not simply exist in nature, nor do they preexist sociohistorical processes. The intimately interesting but perplexing paradox is that, by contrast, in the discourse of "racial" and ethnic identity, the origins of the group are said to be outside history and to reside in nature.

Every country in Latin America is divided into elites and masses. The relative distribution of these basic classes varies in different countries. The concept of class is based in economic relations, the relation to the means of production as either an owner of those means or as one who is forced to sell their labor, but it is also cultural in the sense that in practice, it is based not only on an individual's position in the production process but also on various criteria such as ethnicity, gender, credentials, education, language, membership in certain families, wealth, status, and so on. Certain cultural aspects of class—for instance, a particular way of speaking or an accent— are more highly regarded than others. Highly valued cultural aspects of class tend to coincide with and facilitate higher positions in the economic class structure. However, these two aspects of class do not completely correspond. This allows us to conceive of a society's class structure as having not only cultural differences within classes but also cross-class alliances based on a number of different criteria. These can and often do include issues of "culture"—the possession of certain linguistic styles and accents, family ties, education, senses of aesthetics, and, of course, "race" and ethnicity.

Nationalism is an ideology or belief system in which the ethnicity and culture within a geographically defined territory is, or ought to be, congruent with its political boundaries. Latin American and Caribbean nationalism draws on the European nationalism that began to take its present form at the end of the eighteenth century. Nationalism of this kind involves a process that often identifies a homogeneous national type, sometimes referred to locally as a "race." In colonial Latin America, the process of homogenization occurred in a context in which ethnic differences were constructed and cultivated to divide and rule. As we shall see in this chapter, in the postcolonial era, local elites have ingeniously crafted discourses of national identity that, while departing somewhat from the colonial discourses they replace, nevertheless guarantee the ascendancy of Western and European ethnic identity and cultural forms, which are seen to be embodied in the elite. There is even some doubt as to whether the past was colonial per se or whether the present can be seen as postcolonial, especially for native communities and identities (Klor de Alva 1992).

Therefore, ethnicity, class, and nationalism are interrelated in a number of ways. Determining who one is and where one fits in Latin American or

Caribbean society depends on a number of factors. Physical appearance counts, but it can be overridden. Perhaps more profoundly, one's class position and status in society are determining factors. The reverse is also true; one's class and status are determined, at least in part, by one's "race" and ethnicity. Furthermore, conceptions of nationalism and the destiny of the nation are infused with notions of whose culture and whose "racial" and ethnic identity are most representative of the nation and, in turn, those to whom the nation really belongs. Obviously, the most powerful groups have strongly influenced the creation and enforcement of these cultural determinations. They purport to define and proclaim who is "authentically" Venezuelan, Dominican, Argentine, Guatemalan, Mexican, and so on, and who is deemed unworthy.

Foundations of Ethnicity, Class, and Nationalism

In the history of ideas pertaining to ethnicity in Latin America, "races" were presumed to be pure until after the arrival of the *conquistadores* in the New World. European interaction with "Indians," the indigenous people so misnamed by Columbus, and later with Africans began a process called *mestizaje* (miscegenation), supposed "racial" mixing. Despite the crown's attempts at legal separation, cultural mixing was a natural concomitant of the conquest. Sexual relations of dominance between Spanish men and Indian women—given the prerogatives of conquest and the male-female imbalance of early colonization—resulted in unions that were characterized by rape, concubinage, and occasionally marriage. *Mestizo* progeny of whites and Indians were often defined as "half-breeds." In Brazil, such mixtures were called *mamelucos* as well as *mestiços*. *Mestizos* would have been less conspicuous if Indians had not died in huge numbers as a result of contact with European diseases and poor treatment.

Mestizaje was seen to proceed apace with the arrival of African slaves from the early 1500s to the mid-1800s. It is estimated that more than 10 million Africans reached the New World, and another 10 million died en route. Brazil received the largest portion, about 40 percent, and now has the largest African population outside of Africa. The Caribbean as a whole received about 40 percent, Spanish Latin America received about 16 percent, and British North America—including what is now the United States—received about 4 percent of the enslaved Africans.

Racial Categories and Social Standing
All "race mixtures" were not deemed to be of the same type. On the contrary, the Spanish concern with *limpieza de sangre* (purity of blood) was

transferred to the New World. *Limpieza de sangre*, which had diverse meanings in Spain, was the principle used in consolidating the *reconquista* (the reconquering of Spain from the Moors) and in the expulsion of Spain's Jews in 1492. In the Americas, this principle was used to determine not only racial origins but also social and legal status.

Elaborate systems and nomenclatures emphasizing supposed degrees away from whiteness were established by Spaniards and *criollos*, whites born in Latin America. *Mulatos* and *pardos* were the general terms for non-whites. *Mestizos*, blacks, and Indians constituted the other general groupings. Magnus Mörner (1967:58) provided an example from eighteenth-century New Spain (Mexico):

1. Spaniard and Indian beget *mestizo*.
2. *Mestizo* and Spanish woman beget *castizo*.
3. *Castizo* woman and Spaniard beget Spaniard.
4. Spanish woman and black man beget *mulato*.
5. Spaniard and *mulato* woman beget *morisco*.
6. *Morisco* woman and Spaniard beget *albino*.
7. Spaniard and *albino* woman beget *torna atrás* ("turn away," as in "from white").
8. Indian man and *torna atrás* woman beget *lobo*.
9. *Lobo* and Indian woman beget *zambaigo*.
10. *Zambaigo* and Indian woman beget *cambujo*.
11. *Cambujo* and *mulato* woman beget *albarazado*.
12. *Albarazado* and *mulato* woman beget *barcino*.
13. *Barcino* and *mulato* woman beget *coyote*.
14. *Coyote* woman and Indian man beget *chamiso*.
15. *Chamiso* woman and *mestizo* beget *coyote mestizo*.
16. *Coyote mestizo* and *mulato* woman beget *ahí te estás* ("there you are").

This is but one example of the attempt to assign certain parts of a person's "racial" genealogy. For example, an *albarazado* was deemed to be 30.86 percent white, 43.75 percent Indian, and 25.39 percent black (Stephens 1989:18). A *barcino* was 40.43 percent white, 21.87 percent Indian, and 37.7 percent black (Stephens 1989:30). Ad infinitum absurdum.

Almost every territory in Spanish America had its own system, and only some of the terms overlapped. This kind of descent and "racial" reckoning had counterparts in non-Spanish-speaking areas as well. The terminology in Brazil seems to have been more vague, whereas in French colonial possessions, nonwhites were calibrated even more minutely than occurred in Spanish-speaking territories. This system was part of a rigidly stratified *sociedad de castas*, or society of castes. Caste came from the term the Portuguese applied to the complex social structure they encountered in India. *Casta* came to refer to all nonwhites. The *sociedad de castas* was characterized by social and legal discrimination based on ethnicity that was blatant and direct, as well as condescending and patronizing, on the part of the white elites.

Racial Discrimination

Legal and social discrimination largely coincided. Whites were at the top of the legal order, but Spaniards enjoyed more social status than local whites. Indians received special legal protection, as the Spanish crown attempted to separate them from the rest of colonial society in autonomous communities. In practice, Indians were relegated to the bottom of the social structure. The rest of the society was legally and socially accorded rights and prestige basically with respect to conformity to whiteness: *mestizos*, *mulatos*, and black slaves, in that order.

Even nonslaves among the *castas* were severely limited in almost every aspect of civil life, from prohibitions on holding municipal positions to bans on entering universities to being prevented from marrying whites. Sexual relations became contested terrain, as white men fanatically tried to prevent white women from marrying *castas*. As Susan Tiano explains in Chapter 10, women were made to serve as the boundaries of the group, and ideas about women's sexual "purity" were tied to "racial purity." A sexual double standard generally existed, however. White men from the upper classes typically had liaisons with *casta* women of lesser social status. The men rarely officially recognized any offspring from these unions, although some of these men did informally assist their progeny, who also in some contexts received the benefits accruing to what was seen as an approximation of whiteness.

The advent of independence movements in continental Latin America in the late eighteenth century featured the incipient nationalism of the *criollos* in their increasing conflicts with the *peninsulares*, as those born in the Iberian Peninsula were called. Whereas both groups—despite their growing differences—formed the upper stratum of their respective societies, by this time some mobility was experienced by a small but growing number of *mestizos* and *pardos*, although these latter individuals still encountered the obstacles of social and legal racism. Through the *cédula de gracias al sacar*, a decree of "thank you for the exception," though, high-status and wealthy nonwhites were able to buy a dispensation that made them legally white. With these royal *cédulas*, Spain was able to gain allies among these new whites, could ensure that the allegiance of these well-placed individuals would be not with *pardos* or *mestizos* but with the white minority, and, at the same time, was able to bypass local estimations of racial worth and, therefore, counterbalance the power and prestige of the *criollo* elite. This elite, which just a few years later would proclaim the Rights of Man and the French revolutionary motto of *"liberté, egalité,* and *fraternité,"* protested the *cédulas,* which allowed such personal mobility. Relatively few, however, were able to "advance" in this way. Even if nonwhites had the means, many were denied the opportunity by whites to buy into the privileges the whites were trying so desperately to hold onto themselves.

The rigidity of the *sociedad de castas* came to be undermined by the recognition that precise designations were increasingly meaningless, as *mestizaje,* with its phenotypical and cultural consequences, was seen to proceed from generation to generation, and the phenomenon of passing from one category to another became common.[5] As the definitional lines blurred, ethnic designations generally became more vague. Differences between *mestizos* and Indians were seen by contemporary observers to be based increasingly on social and cultural attributes, such as dress, manners, and language, rather than on ascribed racial ones. When the largely *criollo,* elite-led independence movements began in earnest, *pardo* and *mestizo* frustrations with the arrangements and limitations of the *sociedad de castas* led a great many motivated leaders to shift their allegiance to the *criollo* elites—when it suited them and their causes.

For example, in Venezuela's wars for independence in the early 1800s, *pardos,* long frustrated by the white elite's attempts to gain legal and social parity, fought with the royalists against Simón Bolívar's *criollo*-led forces in 1813—only to join with "the Liberator" in 1816, after he appealed to *llaneros* (rural *mestizos* who lived on the plains), *pardos,* blacks, and *zambos* (the offspring of blacks and Indians) and promised to end African slavery if he and his troops were successful. Ethnic tensions permeated the armies fighting for independence. And despite Bolívar's ostensible aims to create a society free of prejudice and class distinctions, he was equivocal on the issue of ethnicity after independence, expressing the *criollo* elite's fear and suspicion of nonwhites. Those deemed black were especially the objects of persecution. Despite Bolívar's promises, slavery lingered on in Venezuela, ending only in 1854.

Ethnicity, Class, and Nationalism After Independence

The wars for independence in Latin America ended the legal discrimination of the *sociedad de castas,* but its practices and the ideas surrounding it reflected, even if more loosely, the state of the social structure after independence. Systems of social stratification, based on ethnicity and class, in which skin becomes lighter in color as one goes up the class ladder, were further reinforced despite individual exceptions. The elite culturally absorbed nonwhites who climbed into the upper stratum.

By about the 1870s, a common thread was running through the discourse of nationalism in several continental Latin American countries. Elites imagined themselves as part of a European legacy of "civilization." They were influenced by the political, cultural, philosophical, and scientific strains of positivism—a belief in science and progress. Social Darwinism explained the relative economic and political development of countries through deterministic racial theories ("scientific" racism). According to this theory, the northern European countries and the United States were relatively prosperous because of the inherent physical and mental superiority of the Anglo-Saxon and Teutonic "races."

Latin American elites selected parts of these intellectual movements and applied them to what they saw as the reality of their societies.[6] Brazilian elites, for example—most of whom were white—reflected on their "racial" topography: The 1872 census listed only 38 percent as white, 20 percent as black, and the rest as *pardo*.

African slavery ended only in 1888 in Brazil, the last holdout in the Americas—even later than Cuba in 1886 and the United States in 1865. In Brazil, free *pardos* had been a large and powerful group during slavery and had struck a strategic alliance with whites versus blacks and slaves. As slavery ended, Brazilian elites worried publicly about the "racial" makeup of the country and, thus, about the country's fate. They accepted ideas of white superiority but, contradictorily, denied the immutability and absoluteness of "race." They believed the solution to the country's problems lay in the whitening of the population, "racially" and culturally.

These elites pointed to the supposed low fertility among *pardos* and blacks. They believed miscegenation would gradually whiten and consequently improve the population, ignoring contemporary mainstream "racial" theory, which held that hybrids were degenerate. Toward this end, European immigration was officially encouraged, and immigration laws— although not publicly acknowledged—were structured so that blacks, Jews, and others were barred from settling in Brazil. Some of these laws, codified from the 1890s until the 1940s, have never been changed. By the 1920s, racist thinkers in Brazil and the rest of Latin America even became involved in a "science of racial improvement" called eugenics. As Nancy Leys Stepan (1991) has shown, eugenics provided a scientific defense of whitening.

Brazilian elites were further consoled by nationalist myths generated by an emerging social science and a regional intellectualist tradition. Cultural nationalist Gilberto Freyre gained prominence for his historical studies of the plantation society in Brazil, *Casa grande e senzala* (*The Masters and the Slaves*, 1933) and *Sobrados e mucambos* (*The Mansions and the Shanties*, 1936). Although Freyre attacked scientific racism, he celebrated miscegenation and cultural diversity and proclaimed the creation of a new "luso-tropical" civilization, characterized by a *democracia racial* (racial democracy) in which, unlike the harsh racism of the United States, "the races" intermingled freely. This discourse—and the political dispensation it was part of—had the intention and effect of precluding mobilization of disempowered groups based on ethnic identity (and labeled them racist if they did so), allowing the white elite to avoid addressing claims of ethnic discrimination. *Democracia racial* was particularly effective for the elite when combined with *mestizaje*, a discourse of mixing and, therefore, dilution of racial and cultural "purity." Logically, the disempowered did have space to appeal to the elite to live up to their own democratic proclamations, but this was severely circumscribed.

In these conflicting ideological positions, Brazil had counterparts in the rest of Latin America. In Venezuela, for example, throughout history blacks and *pardos* had played a more important role in social and political institutions than they had in any other Latin American country and had gained access to political power at the regional and national levels. As Winthrop R. Wright (1990) has shown, however, Venezuelan elites simultaneously argued that theirs was a "racially" mixed country, where 70 percent of the population were *pardos*, and that racism had been eliminated. They described themselves as a *café con leche* (coffee with milk) people, while promoting a *blanqueamiento* (whitening) process by encouraging European migration, prohibiting blacks from entering the country, and calling for cultural and "racial" miscegenation to reduce the "pure" black minority. Despite their other nefarious functions, *democracia racial* and *café con leche* can be seen as a kind of moral resistance against the more technologically advanced and wealthy United States and Europe by claiming that Brazil and Venezuela were actually more advanced than their more powerful counterparts because they had already solved the "race" problem.

Immigration and Indigenous Movements

Immigration laws have been used throughout the Americas—including by the United States—to sort out the "desirable" and "undesirable" "racial" stock that will make up the nation. In Argentina, a country that set up an immigration program and received more than 3 million immigrants from Europe between 1880 and 1930, racist intellectuals viewed the massive immigration of Europeans as further whitening the population (Latin America as a whole received about 12 million European immigrants between 1850 and 1930). At the end of the nineteenth century, Argentine elites could claim an already white nation with strong European roots and thus look down on their Brazilian neighbors.

Argentine racist thinkers—foremost among them José Ingenieros— were convinced of the merits of natural selection, claiming "the white race" would win out in an evolutionary struggle with "colored races," which were incompatible with "superior" white civilization. Argentine elites imagined theirs as a white country, and they pointed to the inevitable disappearance of Indians and blacks. With the rapid, huge influx of European immigrants, the Indian proportion of the population declined from 5 percent in 1869 to 0.7 percent of a total of nearly 4 million inhabitants in 1895 (Helg 1990:43). Blacks, who in the first third of the nineteenth century had made up 25 percent of the population of Buenos Aires, dropped to 2 percent by 1887.

What was not acknowledged were the terror and discrimination behind this supposedly natural process. Indians were the victims of continual military campaigns throughout the 1880s: They were killed, forcibly incorporated into the army, or forced to labor in agriculture or domestic service. Sporadic campaigns against them continued until the 1930s. Blacks were confined to a limited number of occupations and to poor living conditions.

The immigration wave of the period 1880–1930 was 43 percent Italian and 34 percent Spanish. Again, in breaking with mainstream racist thinking, Argentine elites chose not to make a distinction among those they considered white, believing the differences between Aryans and Latins were social and historical rather than biological.

Once the country was white, though, the elites' next task was to make it Argentinean. Many immigrants formed their own communities with separate institutions. Italians, Germans, Russian Jews, and others brought with them ideas of trade unionism, anarchism, and socialism that challenged the entrenched social order, and prosperous immigrants were excluded from the elites' inner circles. At the turn of the twentieth century, a revitalization of nationalism entailed glorification of the native Argentine (the *criollo*) and the definition of Argentine culture as characterized by the Spanish language and Hispanic culture, Catholicism, the family, paternalism, and order. This new nationalism had an anti-immigrant component. During the peak immigration years of the early 1900s, Jews represented between 2 and 6 percent of total immigration. In the context of anti-immigrant nationalism, they became visible and vulnerable targets, as anti-immigrant discourse and activity reached its depths with Catholic Church–inspired anti-Semitism and physical attacks on Jews.

Revolutionary Mexico provides an interesting contrast. In seeking to break with the widespread racist ideas and practices of the long dictatorship of Porfirio Díaz (1876–1911), the emergent thinkers, who gained prominence with the armed revolution beginning in 1910, constructed what became the official ideology of *indigenismo*. *Indigenismo*, or indigenism, as a doctrine had several components and relied on a number of cultural assumptions about "race." Fairly high consensus held that most Mexicans were *mestizos*. Such attributes as language, religion, dress, family form, and consciousness determined whether one were Indian or *mestizo*. And because these attributes were social in origin, they were amenable to change.

Indigenismo was not a movement initiated by the Indians; it was an elite ideology that advocated the gradual, nonviolent integration of the Indians into Mexican society, especially through education. It venerated Mexico's pre-Hispanic past and attempted to rescue the surviving Indian culture from oblivion. The *mestizo*, as the synthesis of the Indian and the European and, thus, neither one, was exalted as the true Mexican. Breaking with the scientific racism of the time, philosopher and politician José Vasconcelos referred to *mestizos* as the *raza cósmica* (cosmic race), "racial" hybrids who were to characterize Mexico and, eventually, the world at large. Those Indians who remained were to be absorbed into this "race."

As an explicitly antiracist ideology that reached its apogee in the 1930s and has essentially remained dominant since then, *indigenismo* represented a distinct departure from Westernism. Although disputing claims of Indian and *mestizo* inferiority, however, these thinkers believed in innate differences among the white, *mestizo*, and Indian "races." *Indigenismo* even led some to conclude that *mestizos* or Indians were actually "racially" and culturally superior to whites.

Given all its contradictions, then, official *indigenismo* meant Indians as such were marginalized because they were seen to be in the process of becoming what they needed to become to participate in national political life. Images of noble pre-Hispanic Indian culture with a glorious past were a cornerstone of *indigenismo*. But because it relied on notions of "race," it left the door open for contemporary Indians to receive separate and unequal treatment. *Indigenismo* could not legislate social change that would be accompanied by significant socioeconomic transformations. Notions that cultural and biological miscegenation could produce a new kind of human being are common in many Latin American countries, not only Brazil, Venezuela, and Mexico but also countries such as Ecuador, Colombia, and Peru. *Mestizaje* in its explicitly nationalist mode subordinates claims of ethnic distinctiveness to the ends of the nation. Therefore, those considering themselves indigenous have rejected at times the ideology of *mestizaje*. (*Mestizaje* has also been rejected by some Afro-Latins as well, as they look to associate with international signs of blackness.)

▨ Contemporary Patterns

The culture of ethnicity in Latin America and the Caribbean, however, has undergone significant modifications. Changes in language are principal indicators, to the extent that the *sociedad de castas* has been transformed, and at the same time the changes also testify that some of the colonial concepts have been reproduced. The language of "race" hides the arbitrary nature of words and terms believed to describe unchanging reality. Yet, studies of "racial" attitudes in Latin America reveal inconsistent attributions of "racial" terms.

For example, in studies by anthropologists Marvin Harris (1964b) and Harris and Conrad Kottak (1963), one hundred Brazilians in a Bahian fishing village were asked to identify the "race" of three full sisters depicted in photographs. Only six responses identified the three by the same "racial" terms. In fourteen responses, a separate term was used for each of the three sisters, most frequently *blanca* (white) for one and *mulata* or *morena* (brown) for one or both of the others. A particular Brazilian could be described by as many as thirteen terms by other members of the community. Another one hundred people were shown nine portrait drawings meant to depict nine different "racial" types. Around forty "racial" terms were discovered. The highest percentage that agreed on the "race" in any drawing was 70 percent; the lowest was 18 percent.

Mauricio Solaún, Eduardo Vélez, and Cynthia Smith (1987) conducted a study in the Caribbean port city of Cartagena, Colombia, that involved interviewing a sample of 120 adults from four social classes: upper, middle, working, and lower. These respondents were shown twenty-two photographs of individuals with varying ethnic identities and styles of dress and were asked to identify the "race" of each. For the twenty-two photographs, there were 128 different designations—an average of seventeen per photo. The authors show how much of the "racial" nomenclature of the *sociedad de castas* has remained, albeit with significant modification: The tendency now is to use descriptive terms. Individuals were perceived as *blanco aindiado* (white with Indian features) and *negro fileno* (black with a straight nose), for example. They were also *claro* (light), *trigueño* (wheat-colored), or *trigueño claro* or *blanco claro*. Many responses, then, included physical characteristics as well as "racial" ones: *rubio* (blond), *acanelado* (cinnamon-colored), *cobrizo* (copper-colored), *blanco no del todo* (white, but not completely so), or *blanco quemado* (burned white), for example.

Although the nomenclature in Cartagena includes terms and concepts that imply "racial" history, for example, *mulato*; "racially" neutral terms, for example, *claro*; and terms of physical description, for example, *negro por el pelo* (black because of hair texture), there is—as in the Brazilian studies—evidence that a wide variety of criteria are used to classify individuals. In the Cartagena study, the most frequent use of a term per photograph ranged from 24 to 71 percent, with no photo receiving more than 50 percent "racial" (as opposed to color or physically descriptive) terms; 60 percent of the responses were given only twice at the most.

In the Colombian study, when respondents were asked to describe themselves, only the upper class contained a majority of self-reported *blancos*, whereas no *blancos* were found in the lower class. Concomitantly, no *negros* were found in the upper class, where darker individuals referred to themselves as *moreno*. Virtually no respondents positively identified with blackness. Only a few called themselves *negro*, and terms denoting African ancestry were very rarely used. Only twelve respondents called themselves *mulato*. Collectively, these terms exhibit the effects of *blanqueamiento* and demonstrate the correlation between ethnicity and class, which, in turn, facilitates or impedes class mobility.

The Solaún, Vélez, and Smith research (1987) also showed the extent to which the stain of slavery still exists in Latin America. In perhaps every country in the region, with the exception of some in the non-Hispanic Caribbean, the use of the word *negro* is generally not polite or politically acceptable, as can be seen by the number of mostly pejorative modifiers that accompany its designation. Thomas M. Stephens (1989) listed fifty-nine separate entries of terms that entail *negro* and a modifier. *Negro humo* (smoke black) is a Colombian term that refers to physical description, whereas *negro catedrático* (a black "chaired professor") is a Cuban term used to refer to blacks thought to be feigning education and refinement by misappropriating "white" patterns of speech and upper-class modes of dress. Thus, use of this term is thought to be a way of keeping blacks "in their place."

Racial Democracy in the Caribbean: Cuba and Puerto Rico

The discourses of ethnicity and nationalism that crystallized in twentieth-century Cuba and Puerto Rico resembled Brazil's, explicitly comparing local ethnic relations favorably with those in the United States, promoting images of the nation in terms of "race" mixture, repressing black movements (in the case of Cuba), promoting an immigration policy designed to whiten the population (in the case of Cuba), and featuring white ideologues in politics, literature, and the social sciences who expounded on the racial democracy theme. Ethnic relations in present-day Cuba demonstrate that political and economic revolution does not necessarily entail fundamental social change. "Race" was a taboo subject in early revolutionary Cuba, as Fidel Castro tried to instill an official non-"racial" consciousness. The out-migration of an almost all-white Cuban oligarchy should have meant gains for blacks, even if by default. Indeed, evidence provided by Alejandro de la Fuente (1995, 2001) suggests that the revolution was successful in equalizing the educational and health status of whites, blacks, and *mulatos*, and there has been black and *mulato* mobility. But contradictions exist. Most of Cuba's top occupations and government positions are still in the hands of whites. Whites are even favored for service-sector jobs in the tourism industry, allowing for their access to foreign exchange and other perks. One still sees almost all menial occupations performed by blacks. And at the highest level, at times, a non-"racial" stance has even given way to official acknowledgments of blackness within Cuban culture and even, as in a historic address to the Communist Party Congress in 1986, recognition of racism in the party hierarchy by Castro himself.

In 1975, Castro declared Cuba a "Latin-African country." But many observers argue that rather than indicating a true show of solidarity with the African continent and culture, this declaration was for the consumption of the Cuban blacks who were called upon to fight in Cuba's military ventures in Africa. In 1983, for the first time in revolutionary Cuba, census statistics regarding "race" were published. These showed blacks representing 12 percent of the population, *mulatos* 21.9 percent, whites 66 percent, and Asians 0.1 percent (de la Fuente 1995:135, table 1). This seemed to many a vast overcounting of whites and, thus, an undercounting of blacks. As in other Latin American and Caribbean countries, blackness was being officially denied at the same time the nation was depicted as ethnically diverse. And as elsewhere, this was accomplished through the official promotion of culture, such as the ballet *folklórico*, which performs Afro-Cuban dances— some with religious significance.

As Michael Fleet shows in Chapter 12, many Cubans maintain a religious commitment to Santería, or Lukumí, as it is sometimes called. Similar in many ways to *vodou* in Haiti, this religion involves the blending of two religious traditions, in which Catholic saints are matched with Yoruba deities known as *orishas*. Santería worshippers are drawn from both the black and white populations. Even among Cubans who are not active worshippers, many believe in the efficacy of religious and spiritual forces and in the religion's spiritual leaders and practitioners.

In Puerto Rico, the discourse is one of the three *raices* (roots) of Puerto Ricanness: Spanish, African, and Amerindian (known as the Taínos). While Puerto Ricans are said to be the result of these three "races" mixing, the Spanish one tends to be valorized, that is, most highly valued. The *jíbaro*, imaged as a white peasant occupying the mountain ranges, is exalted as the authentic creole Puerto Rican. At the same time, blackness is relegated to folkloric status and Indianness to the past. Puerto Rican "cultural nationalism" is related to the island's status as a U.S. colony. As Arlene Dávila (1997) shows, transnational corporations, such as Winston cigarettes and Budweiser beer, help construct and trade in notions of Puerto Rican authenticity—to consume their products, they exhort, is to be a real Puerto Rican. Global capitalism and the commoditization of images has caused contradictory effects, meaning a more shared "global culture" and, as a reaction formation, a longing for particularism, the local, the exotic. This has meant that in Puerto Rico and elsewhere, there are groups who now claim Amerindian identity. However, it has also meant a resurgence of sex tourism in Cuba with the myth of the hypersexual *mulata* as an object of desire.

Comparative Social Status of Blacks and Indians

In Latin America, one occasionally hears *negrito* (little black one) as a term of endearment that might be used by an older family member when speaking to a child. But only certain kinds of family relationships permit this usage—a child would never address his or her parents in this way. The relationship construed even by the term *negrito* has parallels in a paternalism often exhibited by whites over nonwhites.

It is tempting to compare the place of *negros* with the position of Indians in Latin American nationalistic culture. In the five hundred years since the conquest, colonial and independent Latin American states' treatment of Indians has ranged from neglect to attempts at forced integration to genocide.[7] Nowhere in contemporary Latin America is the persecution of Indians as profound and cruel as in Guatemala. As David H. Bost and Margaret V. Ekstrom detail in Chapter 13, the irony was not lost on world observers when Rigoberta Menchú Tum was honored with the Nobel Peace Prize in 1992—the quincentennial of Columbus's first voyage.

As in many Latin American states in which Indians are numerous (they make up more than 60 percent of Guatemala's population, for example), the system of ethnic-class ranking holds that the elites are white, followed by *ladinos*—who are seen as *mestizos*—and then Indians. In many cases, the cultural and certainly the phenotypical differences between *ladinos* and Indians are not great. In class terms, however, the differences are stark: *ladinos* are found in a number of occupations and class levels, whereas most Indians continued to resist proletarianization through the late twentieth century.

Indians are a diverse group, and, as elsewhere through time, the construct "Indian" elides significant differences. Guatemalan Indians speak about twenty different Mayan languages. They are organized around the concept of community, and these communities differ from each other culturally in many ways. In the past, Indian identity has been rooted in the community rather than in some sense of pan-Indianness. Although they were not completely closed and isolated from the influences of the wider society throughout colonial conquest and independence, these communities are still able to act as corporate units in political and economic resistance against the state and entrenched economic interests.

In elite nationalism, the refrain was familiar. For non-Indians, a truly modern and prosperous nation not only required unity but also that Indians give up their separate identity and become integrated—on the oligarchy's terms—into national economic life. Indians wanted to retain what they see as their traditional ways and customs (whether these are actual continuities with the precontact past is beside the point), while participating as social and economic equals in a multicultural nation.

In Guatemala, integration and class exploitation have always been mediated by the state and its coercive capacities. The system of forced Indian plantation labor ended only in 1945 during the first elected government, which lasted from 1944 to 1954, when its land reform and social justice programs were seen as threatening U.S. interests. In the context of the Cold War, the U.S.-assisted military coup, backed by local and international capitalists, installed the military into a position of power it has not relinquished, though recently the military has relented and shares power with civil leaders.

In the 1960s, the beginnings of a guerrilla movement in the western highlands of Guatemala—where Indians predominate—gave the United States reason to assist the military further in setting up a counterinsurgency military program. Revolutionary groups tried to mobilize Indians who, in an effort to resist cultural and economic exploitation, sometimes joined. In response, beginning in 1975, the military began to use indiscriminate violence against "subversives," who were usually Indians who happened to reside in communities where any form of popular mobilization was taking place.

What has been called the "permanent counterinsurgency state" was now in place. The military, composed of *ladinos*, controlled civil society. Entire villages were massacred, rural leaders were tortured, and Indians' crops were destroyed. The military set up permanent bases in the highlands, conscripted around 20 percent of the male inhabitants into the army, and organized "civilian patrols" of Indians under direct military command. More than 120,000 people have been killed in the longer than thirty-year rebellion against repressive Guatemalan governments. Human rights agencies report that at least 50,000 Indians were killed during the 1980s, about 200,000 were forced into permanent exile, and at some point half of the 2 million highlands residents were displaced from their homes.

Notwithstanding these practices, Guatemala depicts itself with Indian symbols. The symbolic use of the *traje*, an indigenous dress, as the Guatemalan "national costume" appeals to international tourists and bolsters the local tourist industry. Profits rely on an image of the exotic, cultivated carefully and somewhat intentionally. But the concept of "Indianness as national essence" goes much deeper than any conscious manipulation of symbols for economic gain. Many *ladinos* assume some sense of identification with Indianness, taken in an almost spiritual way. This form of Guatemalan nationalism has clear parallels with other forms of nationalism in Latin

America, depicting the true soul of the nation as inhering in an Indian past.

Recent decades have seen Indians mobilize as indigenous people with common goals throughout Latin America. In many cases, it is to protect lands they consider theirs or to counter environmental threats. In the process, they develop a self-conscious discourse on what they define as distinctive indigenous culture, constructing identity in the process. A number of pan-Indian organizations have sprung up. And they speak in a language that power can understand. For example, some Amazonian Indian groups have utilized video and Internet technology to press their claims in the court of world opinion and to establish solidarity with indigenous groups elsewhere. Indigenous people in Ecuador have also been quite successful in their movement for equal treatment while retaining their distinctive cultures and languages.

Myths and Realities

The Latin American woman who represents perhaps the most strongly contrasting symbol to Rigoberta Menchú, who is a Quiché Indian, is the blond, blue-eyed, Brazilian, megamarketed superstar Xuxa (pronounced SHOO-sha). Xuxa is a former soft-porn movie actress and *Playboy* model, whose incredibly popular children's television show reaches millions in Brazil and elsewhere in Latin America; a U.S. version lasted only one season. (Brazil has more than 40 million television sets, placing it fourth in the world after the United States, Japan, and Great Britain; television reaches 99 percent of

Family Channel Photo

Brazilian performer Xuxa projects an image that has made her wealthy and famous.

the Brazilian population that watches an average of seven hours a day.) Xuxa is probably Brazil's best-known celebrity, a larger-than-life media creation who records best-selling records, stars in movies that attract huge audiences, has at least thirteen dolls bearing her likeness, and endorses a number of products, from surfboards to bicycles to soup to cookies. She has her own magazine with a circulation of 700,000. Her concerts are performed in sold-out stadiums, and her live performances garner her the highest pay of any Brazilian entertainer.

In 1991, Xuxa was ranked thirty-seventh on *Forbes* magazine's list of the forty highest-paid entertainers in the world—the first Latin American to make the list and one of only five women on the list. Although she has made millions of dollars, she claims, "I have no idea how much money I have; I don't even know where it is" (Simpson 1993:18).

In addition to crafting and marketing cultivated images of sexuality and consumerism that are intertwined, Xuxa also plays on—and trades in—whiteness, as Amelia Simpson (1993) showed in her fascinating study. Xuxa is simultaneously the blond ideal of beauty and the ideal of femininity—both of which become manifestly so because her image is ubiquitous in Brazil. Young girls dream of being Xuxa and go to great lengths to emulate her and the Paquitas, her blond clone teenage helpers on the children's show. Xuxa improbably incorporates (and herein lies her appeal) a number of contradictory images: she is at once a sexual, erotic figure and a domestic one, surrounded by masses of adoring children. She affirms the aesthetic superiority of whiteness while always assuring Brazilians of her Brazilianness. And to this end, her six-year public affair with soccer legend Pelé (Edson Arantes Do Nascimento), the most famous black man in Brazil, served as a legitimation of the veracity of the myth of *democracia racial*.

Xuxa's blond aesthetic is almost unquestioned in Brazil, yet her own words are revealing. Asked about the "race" issue and her show, Xuxa was quoted as saying, "Some people say that I shouldn't do a show because I am blond. . . . But Brazil is a country of mixed races. You can be blond, brunette, *mulato*; you can be anything." When asked why all of her cast members were white, she responded with racist assumptions: "Oh! I've already explained; the tests [auditions to be Paquitas] are very difficult." Continuing, she said, "I think blonds have more drive. Besides, we're all blond, but we're all Brazilian!" (Simpson 1993). And when her romance with Pelé ended in 1986, she told the press a story that clearly had insulting racial implications.

The rise of Xuxa—perhaps not coincidentally—comes with the relatively recent rise of a black consciousness movement in Brazil and the growth of a number of organizations whose aims are to empower blacks politically and economically and to promote a positive black self-image. Anthropologist John Burdick (1992b:40, 44) reported a conversation with a Brazilian man in a small bar in a working-class town on the outskirts of Rio de Janeiro: "There is no racism in Brazil! I have the blood of all races in me—white, black, Indian. How could we be racists?" But in a more reflective moment, he said, "There is a saying in Brazil: 'If you're not white you're black.' That's not really true, you know. Here, you can be other things, like me, I'm a *moreno*. But to a white man, I'm a *moreno* only if he likes me; if he doesn't like me, I'm a *mulato*, or I'm even a *preto* [black]. They play that game, you know? I guess the real saying should be, 'If you're not white, you lose.'" A principal aim of the black consciousness movement is to convince those Brazilians who identify themselves as *moreno* or *mulato* to identify themselves as *negro*.

"Race" as a category was left out of the 1970 census (which was taken during the period of military rule, 1964–1985). "Race" was included in the 1980 census; however, the results of that census were not released until two years later because the Census Bureau director apparently feared they would damage Brazil's image of harmonious ethnic relations. The results were damaging. They showed huge differences in income, with blacks earning 35 percent as much as whites and *pardos* earning 45 percent of what whites earned. This coincided with, and was part of, a general trend in which the rich got richer and the poor became poorer. The wealthiest 10 percent held 40 percent of the national income in 1960; by 1990, they held 53 percent of the national income. At the same time, the portion of the national income held by the poorest 50 percent of the population dropped from 17 percent in 1960 to 11 percent in 1990. More recent research and official statistics bear out this trend.[8]

Argentina provides an interesting contrast. By the late 1980s, Argentina had emerged from its most recent period of military rule (1976–1983). During this time, thousands of people were kidnapped, tortured, and murdered in the so-called Dirty War. The military leadership that instituted and reigned over the terrorist state, as it became known, justified these measures to "save Western Christian civilization." With the democratic election of Raúl Alfonsín, the self-termed Nationalists organized to oppose his regime, expressing continuity with the military government's ideological stance.[9] Their influence continued to threaten the elected regime of Carlos Menem and those of his successors.

The Nationalist strain is linked to far-right political groups and ideologies, and in practice its views are expressed by the *carapintadas* (painted faces), the dissident, antidemocratic military faction that sprang up in the late 1980s and protested the trials of those accused of atrocities in the Dirty War, along with Alerta Nacional (National Alert)—a terrorist group that had bombs, weapons, and links to the military and the police.

Nationalism as a Cultural Construct

Nationalist ideology is an almost textbook example of what historian Eric Hobsbawm (1983) called an "invented tradition," in which a mythical past is created and used to serve the needs of the present and the future. As David Rock (1993) has shown, the Nationalists called their movement an "authentically Argentine struggle for Catholic truth and Hispanic tradition," a "spiritual" as opposed to a "material" movement, whose aim was to prevent the "breakdown of the country's spiritual unity." They proclaimed that they were "heirs to a millenary civilization grounded on Christian teachings, Greek philosophy, and Roman order." They were on a "crusade" for "moral purification" and the "defense of the national soul." They supported authoritarian rule and were opposed to "liberal philosophy, formal democracy, and ideological colonization" (Rock 1993). Of course, not every Argentine is a Nationalist (with a capital N), but the influence of this movement in education, religion, and political and civil life cannot be overestimated.

It is rarely sufficient for the cultural constructions of a nation to proceed solely in a self-referential way. Usually, these constructions are brought about most effectively in contradistinction to some entity or group, which the nation is defined against negatively. That is, the nation is not what this group is, and this group is not of the nation. The Nationalists have no trouble finding scapegoats; they are constantly warning of the subversive influence of such foreign enemies as Marxism, communism, Freemasonry, and international Zionism.

Internally, anti-Semitism has continued to be integral to Argentine nationalism (at present more than 200,000 Jews live in Argentina). Similar to those who followed particular ideologies evident at the turn of the twentieth century, Catholic priests, bishops, and others in the 1980s criticized the Alfonsín government for the "many Jews" within it. Alfonsín's Radical Party government, which did include Jews, was termed *la sinagoga radical* (the radical synagogue) by right-wing critics. Some Spanish-language dictionaries define *sinagoga*, which is a Jewish house of worship, as "conspiracy." A 1988 survey of Buenos Aires by a University of Buenos Aires sociologist found that over 15 percent of those surveyed felt that they were manifestly anti-Jewish, and 13.5 percent admitted to anti-Jewish feelings (Elkin 1992:7). Perhaps the most famous Jewish victim of the Dirty War was journalist and publisher Jacobo Timerman, whose book *Prisoner Without a Name, Cell Without a Number* (1981) tells of his persecution and torture at the hands of the military government.

Nationalism often depends on depictions of people within the borders of the nation as not of the nation. The experience of numerically small ethnic groups in Latin America and the Caribbean varies from country to country. About half a million Jews live in Latin America. The Sephardic

Jewish community on the Caribbean island of Curaçao, founded in 1653, has the longest continuous history of all of the Jewish communities in the region. The group built up and maintained trading and merchant activities. Today, the three-hundred-member, economically powerful community is held together in its economic activities by kinship units known as *famiyas*, which serve to form business networks of capital and information. The experience of the Jews in Jamaica has been somewhat similar.

In addition to the arrival of relatively small groups of Europeans, such as the Germans in Brazil and Chile, and Middle Easterners, such as the Syrians and Lebanese found in the Caribbean and in Central and South America, there has also been significant immigration from Asia. About 200,000 Japanese immigrated to Brazil in the first half of the twentieth century, with another 30,000 landing in Peru. About 300,000 Chinese went, mainly as contract laborers, to Latin America and the Caribbean in the mid-nineteenth century. About 140,000 of the Chinese went to Cuba and 100,000 to Peru, where they were treated so poorly that a series of international incidents occurred, and Chinese officials launched investigations. A further 20,000 went to various Caribbean islands, and the rest went to Central America and elsewhere. In some places, they have maintained ethnically exclusive marriage and mating practices; in other places, they have been more apt to assimilate. Often visible and distinct as traders of dry goods and owners of grocery shops, they have occasionally been victimized in nationalist movements. Virtually the entire Chinese community of Sonora, Mexico, for example, was expelled in the 1930s in a particularly fierce moment of postrevolution nationalism.

The construction of a nation is not only the prerogative of antidemocratic regimes and movements, as seen in the Argentine example. The decolonization process in most of the English-speaking Caribbean, for example, legated functioning parliamentary democracy on a number of states that achieved independence from Britain in the 1960s. But colonialism also legated ethnic conflict between those who came to these plantation societies in differing circumstances and with differing legal and social statuses that corresponded to ethnicity.

In Trinidad and Tobago, universal adult suffrage in 1946 and independence in 1962 resulted in the displacement of whites in the political, but not the economic, sphere and in the institutionalization of ethnic voting between political parties organized by, and generally becoming identified with, the interests of blacks—the descendants of slaves—on the one hand and those identified with East Indians—the descendants of indentured workers brought from India between 1845 and 1917 to replace emancipated slaves on the sugar estates—on the other. At present, blacks and East Indians each make up a little more than 40 percent of the population. Very little intermarriage has occurred between these two groups. "Mixed" people, mainly of European and African ancestry, account for about 16 percent of the population. Whites represent less than 1 percent, as do Chinese, Syrian/Lebanese, and others. The "black" political party held power continuously from 1956 until 1986, doling out political patronage to its followers in the form of public-sector jobs. East Indians have benefited from educational improvements, but many continue to be economically marginalized. A number of visible East Indians have become wealthy capitalists, representing a counterweight to black political power and white economic power. Since 1986, there have been multiethnic political parties, and an East Indian prime minister has been elected, but this has not brought an end to ethnic politics.

Nationalism is related to ethnicity in countries such as Trinidad and Tobago, Guyana, and Jamaica in ways that significantly depart from the general Latin American pattern. Whereas Latin American nationalism is characterized by implicit or explicit references to and identification with the colonial past and the culture of the colonizers, in these countries nationalism is part of a two-pronged process.

First, multiculturalism is emphasized. Guyana is referred to as the "Land of Six Peoples." Jamaica's national motto is "Out of many, one people." Trinidad and Tobago's motto is "Together we aspire, together we achieve." The construction of ethnic and cultural difference proves and justifies contribution, authenticity, and citizenship.

Simultaneously, as Brackette F. Williams (1991) has argued, there is cultural contestation over which group historically has contributed the most to the nation, which, therefore, is constructed as "belonging" to that group. This construction is achieved through a conceptual move of inversion, in which the European-dominated, social-status hierarchy is turned on its head: The formerly subordinate, now politically ascendant, groups develop a view of the social-status hierarchy as composed of "givers" and "takers." Europeans become the takers who took more than they gave. Other groups, such as blacks and East Indians, wage a seemingly never-ending contest to prove they are the ultimate givers. It is only fair that the biggest givers, then, have the greatest say in the allocation of political and economic roles.

A homogenizing synthesis occurs when the conflation of nation/state/ethnicity exists to construct a nonethnicity, in which there are Trinidadians or Guyanese and there are "others"—that is, ethnics—who have retained their non-Trinidadian or non-Guyanese ways. In Trinidad and Tobago, elite blacks—perhaps unconsciously believing colonial stereotypes that blacks were stripped of their ancestral culture during the slavery experience and, in any case, that they did not have one worth saving—look to what they see as the real folk, creole culture as found in lower-class black creations, such as the steel band, calypso, and carnival, and term this national culture. Fortunately, this process has not led to the kinds of state terror that have occurred elsewhere in the region around these same issues.

▪ Conclusion

The complexities of ethnicity and class in an area as diverse as Latin America render most discussions incomplete and even, at times, contradictory. What is true in one context may be rather different in another. This chapter illustrates, however, how the phenomena of ethnicity and class and their manifestations in nationalism have evolved and will continue to be intimately interrelated in ways that are significant for the future of this region.

When North Americans encounter the ethnic, class, and national arrangements of Latin America and the Caribbean (through travel, residence, or study), they are surprised by the great gap between what is taken as "fact" and a very different Latin American reality. The cultural constructions of ethnicity and nationalism continue to structure reality for Latin Americans, as well as North Americans, in ways that are manifested in arrangements of power and influence in these societies. And this is so even in the modernizing movements brought about by Latin Americans' new and varied connections to international economic forces. Affected by an increasingly global popular culture that infiltrates the region through electronic transmissions and huge migratory flows that circulate from and back to the region, historically unique conceptions and configurations of ethnicity, class, and nationalism in Latin America are challenged. The present era is characterized by globalization entailing vast economic and cultural flows across borders, the so-called condition of postmodernity, where a more global capitalism is now engaged in regimes of "flexible accumulation" (Harvey 1989). In this process, the power of the state is challenged, and, indeed, under ruling policies and ideologies of so-called neoliberalism, the traditional role of the state is eroded, and the state's traditional responsibilities are put back onto the populace. New neoliberal discourses also encourage cultural rights—as long as these rights do not threaten the ruling groups still supported by the pared-down state. As a result, space is opened for ethnic and nationalist groups to operate in civil society, changing their public personae at the same time.

Protests against globalization are often staged in ethnic terms, but, as the result of the increased communication and travel that are concomitant with economic globalization, ethnic groups in Latin America and the Caribbean are often aware of the situations of those in North America and elsewhere and now make common cause with them. For instance, Latin

American Indian groups are not only forming coalitions across national borders, but they are more and more united with groups calling themselves indigenous around the world. And black groups in Brazil are now adopting more international symbols of blackness, such as Jamaican reggae music and U.S. African American ideologies of "race." It is not yet clear where these trends will lead, but both the historical structures and these newer processes of change require careful, empathetic analysis for a meaningful understanding of the contemporary scene.

▓ Notes

1. Strong condemnation of the apparently fraudulent 1994 election caused the Dominican Republic to disallow reelection of the president and to conduct the next presidential election after two, rather than the usual four, years. In 1996, Balaguer joined with longtime rival Juan Bosch to support Lionel Fernández in a successful run at the presidency, teaming up to prevent a Peña Gómez victory.

2. The question of how, if at all, the "racial"/ethnic/national systems of Latin America and the United States are converging is the subject of work by Skidmore (1993) and Winant (1999) considering a U.S.-Brazilian comparison.

3. By using the term "ethnicity" instead of "race," we convey that these are indeed cultural constructions. Therefore, in this chapter "race" appears in quotation marks to denote that it is a concept used in everyday life by Latin Americans but with no analytical or scientific value as so used. Similarly, ethnic terms such as white, black, *mulato*, Indian, and so on should be understood as referring not to some independent reality but to terms that are employed and have conventional meanings. As I have suggested, based on a related case study (Yelvington 1999), ethnicity is a flexible "umbrella" term, subsuming but not assuming "race," that facilitates cross-cultural comparison. It may be defined as an ideology, a definition of "peoplehood" that entails a theory of origins. Sometimes these links are constructed by the people in question as "racial," sometimes they are reckoned as "cultural," and sometimes they are deemed to be otherworldly, sacred, or spiritual in origins. At the same time, ethnicity is characterized by a theory of cause-effect relationships among these phenomena. Their specific combination varies from case to case. This is an empirical historical and cultural question rather than some either-or universal a priori proposition. However, it should be noted that this way of proceeding is not universally accepted. Established scholars of Latin America such as Wade (1997) have been critical of lumping "race" under ethnicity.

4. Culture is, for the most part, not discussed and implicit. It is, in the first instance, the result of human attempts to solve the problem of survival. Culture is not some entity that is enduring from time immemorial but is constantly made and remade under specific social conditions. Therefore, history and relations of power influence culture. At the same time, people often talk about their culture, about what they see as the culture that defines their group. This self-conscious discourse of culture, always political in nature, may or may not accurately reflect the present or past of a said group's cultural practices.

5. I want to make it clear here that in discussing *mestizaje* I am not talking about an objective process, independent from social and cultural processes. To do so would assume that "pure races" exist or existed and were therefore actually

"mixed" in this process. In other words, it would be to assign a false tangibility to *mestizaje*.

6. See Graham (1990).

7. See Olson (1991) for an ethnohistorical dictionary that serves as a reference guide, providing information about existing Amerindian groups of Central and South America. See also Coy (1985); Smith (1990); and Urban and Sherzer (1991).

8. For a more extended discussion of this theme in Brazil, see Andrews (1991, 1992); Crook and Johnson (1999); Fontaine (1985); Hanchard (1994, 1999); Lovell (1993, 1994); Mitchell and Wood (1998); Reichmann (1999a, 1999b); Silva and Hasenbalg (1992); Wood and Carvalho (1988); and Wood and Lovell (1992) for recent work.

9. David Rock's (1993) study examines in great detail the ideological bases for nationalism.

▓ Bibliography

Abraham–van der Mark, Eva. "Marriage and Concubinage Among the Sephardic Merchant Elite of Curaçao." In *Women and Change in the Caribbean*, edited by Janet H. Momsen. Bloomington: Indiana University Press, 1993, pp. 38–49.

Andrews, George Reid. *The Afro-Argentines of Buenos Aires, 1800–1900*. Madison: University of Wisconsin Press, 1980.

———. *Blacks and Whites in São Paulo, Brazil: 1888–1988*. Madison: University of Wisconsin Press, 1991.

———. "Racial Inequality in Brazil and the United States: A Statistical Comparison." *Journal of Social History* 26, no. 2 (1992):229–263.

Appelbaum, Nancy P., Anne S. Macpherson, and Karin Alejandra Rosemblatt (eds.). *Race and Nation in Modern Latin America*. Chapel Hill, N.C.: University of North Carolina Press, 2003.

Balaguer, Joaquín. *La isla al revés: Haití y el destino dominicano* (6th ed.). Santo Domingo: Editorial Corripio, 1990.

Baronov, David, and Kevin A. Yelvington. "Ethnicity, Race, Class, and Nationality in the Caribbean." In *Understanding the Contemporary Caribbean*, edited by Richard S. Hillman and Thomas J. D'Agostino. Boulder, Colo.: Lynne Rienner Publishers, 2003, pp. 209–238.

Brown, Diana De Groats. *Umbanda: Religion and Politics in Urban Brazil*. New York: Columbia University Press, 1994 [1986].

Burdick, John. "Brazil's Black Consciousness Movement." *Report on the Americas* 25, no. 4 (1992a):23–27.

———. "The Myth of Racial Democracy." *Report on the Americas* 25, no. 4 (1992b):40–44.

Carnegie, Charles V. *Postnationalism Prefigured: Caribbean Borderlands*. New Brunswick, N.J.: Rutgers University Press, 2002.

Carrión, Juan Manuel (ed.). *Ethnicity, Race and Nationality in the Caribbean*. San Juan: Institute of Caribbean Studies, University of Puerto Rico, 1997.

Conklin, Beth A., and Laura R. Graham. "The Shifting Middle Ground: Amazonian Indians and Eco-Politics." *American Anthropologist* 97, no. 4 (1995):695–710.

Coy, Peter. "Current Ethnic Profiles and Amerindian Survivals." In *The Cambridge Encyclopedia of Latin America and the Caribbean*, edited by Simon Collier,

Harold Blakemore, and Thomas E. Skidmore. Cambridge, UK: Cambridge University Press, 1985, pp. 155–160.

Crook, Larry, and Randal Johnson (eds.). *Black Brazil: Culture, Identity, and Social Mobilization*. Los Angeles: Latin American Center Publications, University of California at Los Angeles, 1999.

Cuba Commission Report. *The Cuba Commission Report: A Hidden History of the Chinese in Cuba*. With an Introduction by Denise Helly. Baltimore: Johns Hopkins University Press, 1993.

Daniel, Yvonne. *Rumba: Dance and Social Change in Contemporary Cuba*. Bloomington: Indiana University Press, 1995.

Dávila, Arlene M. *Sponsored Identities: Cultural Politics in Puerto Rico*. Philadelphia: Temple University Press, 1997.

Dávila, Jerry. *Diploma of Whiteness: Race and Social Policy in Brazil, 1917–1945*. Durham, N.C.: Duke University Press, 2003.

Dayan, Joan. "Codes of Law and Bodies of Color." *New Literary History* 26, no. 2 (1995):283–308.

de la Cadena, Marisol. *Indigenous Mestizos: The Politics of Race and Culture in Cuzco, 1919–1991*. Durham, N.C.: Duke University Press, 2000.

de la Fuente, Alejandro. "Race and Inequality in Cuba, 1899–1981." *Journal of Contemporary History* 30 (1995):131–168.

———. "Myths of Racial Democracy: Cuba, 1900–1912." *Latin American Research Review* 34, no. 3 (1999):39–73.

———. *A Nation for All: Race, Inequality, and Politics in Twentieth-Century Cuba*. Chapel Hill, N.C.: University of North Carolina Press, 2001.

Derby, Lauren. "Haitians, Magic, and Money: Raza and Society in the Haitian-Dominican Borderlands, 1900 to 1937." *Comparative Studies in Society and History* 36, no. 3 (1994):488–526.

Dosal, Paul J. *Doing Business with the Dictators: A Political History of United Fruit in Guatemala, 1899–1944*. Wilmington, Del.: Scholarly Resources, 1993.

Elkin, Judith Laikin. "Quincentenary: Colonial Legacy of Anti-Semitism." *Report on the Americas* 25, no. 4 (1992):4–7.

Feitlowitz, Marguerite. *A Lexicon of Terror: Argentina and the Legacies of Torture*. New York: Oxford University Press, 1998.

Fernández, Nadine. "Back to the Future? Women, Race, and Tourism in Cuba." In *Sun, Sex, and Gold: Tourism and Sex Work in the Caribbean*, edited by Kamala Kempadoo. Lanham, Md.: Rowman & Littlefield, 1999, pp. 81–89.

Ferrer, Ada. *Insurgent Cuba: Race, Nation, and Revolution, 1868–1898*. Chapel Hill: University of North Carolina Press, 1999.

Fiehrer, Thomas. "Political Violence in the Periphery: The Haitian Massacre of 1937." *Race and Class* 32, no. 2 (1990):1–20.

Fischer, Edward F. *Cultural Logics and Global Economics: Maya Identity in Thought and Practice*. Austin: University of Texas Press, 2001.

Fontaine, Pierre-Michel (ed.). *Race, Class, and Power in Brazil*. Los Angeles: Center for Afro-American Studies, University of California at Los Angeles, 1985.

Forte, Maximilian C. "Reviving Caribs: Recognition, Patronage, and Ceremonial Indigeneity in Trinidad and Tobago." *Cultural Survival Quarterly* 23, no. 4 (1999):35–41.

Fraginals, Manuel Moreno (ed.). *Africa in Latin America: Essays on History, Culture, and Socialization*. New York: Holmes and Meier, 1984 [1977].

Freyre, Gilberto. *The Masters and the Slaves: A Study in the Development of*

Brazilian Civilization. Berkeley: University of California Press, 1986a [1933].

―――. *The Mansions and the Shanties: The Making of Modern Brazil*. Berkeley: University of California Press, 1986b [1936].

Godreau, Isar P. "Missing the Mix: San Antón and the Racial Dynamics of 'Nationalism' in Puerto Rico." Ph.D. dissertation, University of California at Santa Cruz, 1999.

Gordon, Edmund T. *Disparate Diasporas: Identity Politics in an Afro-Nicaraguan Community*. Austin: University of Texas Press, 1998.

Gould, Jeffrey L. *To Die in This Way: Nicaraguan Indians and the Myth of Mestizaje, 1880–1965*. Durham, N.C.: Duke University Press, 1998.

Graham, Richard (ed.). *The Idea of Race in Latin America, 1870–1940*. Austin: University of Texas Press, 1990.

Guerra, Lillian. *Popular Expression and National Identity in Puerto Rico: The Struggle for Self, Community, and Nation*. Gainesville: University Press of Florida, 1998.

Hale, Charles R. "Travel Warning: Elite Appropriations of Hybridity, *Mestizaje*, Antiracism, Equality, and Other Progressive-Sounding Discourses in Highland Guatemala." *Journal of American Folklore* 112, no. 445 (1999):297–315.

―――. "Does Multiculturalism Menace?: Governance, Cultural Rights and the Politics of Identity in Guatemala." *Journal of Latin American Studies* 34, no. 3 (2002):485–524.

―――. *Más Que un Indio (More Than an Indian): Racial Ambivalence and the Paradox of Neoliberal Multiculturalism in Guatemala*. Santa Fe, N.M.: School of American Research Press, 2004.

Hanchard, Michael. *Orpheus and Power: The Movimento Negro of Rio de Janeiro and São Paulo, Brazil, 1945–1988*. Princeton, N.J.: Princeton University Press, 1994.

―――. (ed.). *Racial Politics in Contemporary Brazil*. Durham, N.C.: Duke University Press, 1999.

Harris, Marvin. *Patterns of Race in the Americas*. New York: Walker and Company, 1964a.

―――. "Racial Identity in Brazil." *Luso-Brazilian Review* 1, no. 6 (1964b):21–28.

Harris, Marvin, and Conrad Kottak. "The Structural Significance of Brazilian Racial Categories." *Sociologia* 25 (1963):203–209.

Harvey, David. *The Condition of Postmodernity: An Enquiry into the Origins of Cultural Change*. Oxford, UK: Blackwell, 1989.

Haslip-Viera, Gabriel (ed.). *Taíno Revival: Critical Perspectives on Puerto Rican Identity and Cultural Politics*. New York: Centro de Estudios Puertorriqueños, 1999.

Helg, Aline. "Race in Argentina and Cuba, 1880–1930: Theory, Policies, and Popular Reaction." In *The Idea of Race in Latin America, 1870–1940*, edited by Richard Graham. Austin: University of Texas Press, 1990, pp. 37–69.

―――. *Our Rightful Share: The Afro-Cuban Struggle for Equality, 1886–1912*. Chapel Hill: University of North Carolina Press, 1995.

Hendrickson, Carol. *Weaving Identities: Construction of Dress and Self in a Highland Guatemala Town*. Austin: University of Texas Press, 1995.

Hobsbawm, Eric. "Introduction: Inventing Traditions." In *The Invention of Tradition*, edited by Eric Hobsbawm and Terence Ranger. Cambridge, UK: Cambridge University Press, 1983, pp. 1–14.

Hoetink, H. "'Race' and Color in the Caribbean." In *Caribbean Contours*, edited by

Sidney W. Mintz and Sally Price. Baltimore: Johns Hopkins University Press, 1985, pp. 55–84.

Holzberg, Carol S. *Minorities and Power in a Black Society: The Jewish Community of Jamaica*. Lanham, Md.: North-South Publishing, 1987.

Hu-Dehart, Evelyne. "Immigrants to a Developing Society: The Chinese in Northern Mexico, 1875–1932." *Journal of Arizona History* 21 (1980):49–86.

Jackson, Jean. "Culture, Genuine and Spurious: The Politics of Indianness in the Vaupés, Colombia." *American Ethnologist* 22, no. 1 (1995):3–27.

Klich, Ignacio, and Jeffrey Lesser (eds.). *Arab and Jewish Immigrants in Latin America: Images and Realities*. London: Frank Cass, 1998.

Klor de Alva, J. Jorge. "Colonialism and Postcolonialism as (Latin) American Mirages." *Colonial Latin American Review* 1, nos. 1–2 (1992):3–23.

Knight, Alan. "Racism, Revolution, and Indigenismo: Mexico, 1910–1940." In *The Idea of Race in Latin America, 1870–1940*, edited by Richard Graham. Austin: University of Texas Press, 1990, pp. 71–113.

Kuznesof, Elizabeth Anne. "Ethnic and Gender Influences on 'Spanish' Creole Society in Colonial Spanish America." *Colonial Latin American Review* 4, no. 1 (1995):153–176.

Latortue, Paul R. "Neoslavery in the Cane Fields." *Caribbean Review* 14, no. 4 (1985):18–20.

Lesser, Jeffrey. *Negotiating National Identity: Immigrants, Minorities, and the Struggle for Ethnicity in Brazil*. Durham, N.C.: Duke University Press, 1999.

Levine, Robert M. *Race and Ethnic Relations in Latin America and the Caribbean: An Historical Dictionary and Bibliography*. Metuchen, N.J.: Scarecrow Press, 1980.

Lovell, Peggy A. "The Geography of Economic Development and Racial Discrimination in Brazil." *Development and Change* 21 (1993):83–101.

———. "Race, Gender, and Development in Brazil." *Latin American Research Review* 29, no. 3 (1994):7–35.

Maingot, Anthony P. "Race, Color, and Class in the Caribbean." In *The Americas: Interpretive Essays*, edited by Alfred Stepan. New York: Oxford University Press, 1992, pp. 220–247.

Márquez, Roberto. "An Anatomy of Racism." *Report on the Americas* 25, no. 4 (1992):32–33.

Martínez, Samuel. *Peripheral Migrants: Haitians and Dominican Republic Sugar Plantations*. Knoxville: University of Tennessee Press, 1995.

Martínez-Alier, Verena. *Marriage, Class and Colour in Nineteenth-Century Cuba: A Study of Racial Attitudes and Sexual Values in a Slave Society*. Ann Arbor: University of Michigan Press, 1989 [1974].

Mitchell, Michael J., and Charles H. Wood. "Ironies of Citizenship: Skin Color, Police Brutality, and the Challenge to Democracy in Brazil." *Social Forces* 77, no. 3 (1998):1001–1020.

Moberg, Mark. *Myths of Ethnicity and Nation: Immigration, Work, and Identity in the Belize Banana Industry*. Knoxville: University of Tennessee Press, 1997.

Moore, Carlos. *Cuba, the Blacks, and Africa*. Los Angeles: University of California at Los Angeles, Center for Afro-American Studies, 1990.

Mörner, Magnus. *Race Mixture in the History of Latin America*. Boston: Little, Brown and Company, 1967.

Olson, James S. *The Indians of Central and South America: An Ethnohistorical Dictionary*. Westport, Conn.: Greenwood Press, 1991.

270 Kevin A. Yelvington

Oostindie, Gert (ed.). *Ethnicity in the Caribbean: Essays in Honor of Harry Hoetink*. London: Macmillan, 1996.
Purcell, Trevor W. *Banana Fallout: Class, Color, and Culture Among West Indians in Costa Rica*. Los Angeles: Center for Afro-American Studies, University of California, Los Angeles, 1993.
Rahier, Jean Muteba. "Blackness, the Racial/Spatial Order, Migrations, and Miss Ecuador 1995–96." *American Anthropologist* 100, no. 2 (1998):421–430.
Ramos, Alcida Rita. *Indigenism: Ethnic Politics in Brazil*. Madison: University of Wisconsin Press, 1998.
Reichmann, Rebecca. *Brazil: Equality, Difference and Identity Politics*. Oxford, UK: Berg Publishers, 1999a.
———. (ed.). *Race in Contemporary Brazil: From Indifference to Inequality*. University Park: Pennsylvania State University Press, 1999b.
Rock, David. *Authoritarian Argentina: The Nationalist Movement, Its History and Its Impact*. Berkeley: University of California Press, 1993.
Sansone, Livio. *Blackness Without Ethnicity: Constructing Race in Brazil*. New York: Palgrave Macmillan, 2003.
Schwartz, Stuart B. *Slaves, Peasants, and Rebels: Reconsidering Brazilian Slavery*. Urbana: University of Illinois Press, 1992.
———. "Colonial Identities and the Sociedad de Castas." *Colonial Latin American Review* 4, no. 1 (1995):185–201.
Sheriff, Robin E. *Dreaming Equality: Color, Race, and Racism in Urban Brazil*. New Brunswick, N.J.: Rutgers University Press, 2001.
Silva, Nelso do Valle, and Carlos Hasenbalg. *Relações Raciais no Brasil Contemporâneo*. Rio de Janeiro: Rio Fundo, 1992.
Simpson, Amelia. *Xuxa: The Mega-Marketing of Gender, Race, and Modernity*. Philadelphia: Temple University Press, 1993.
Skidmore, Thomas E. *Black into White: Race and Nationality in Brazilian Thought*. Durham, N.C.: Duke University Press, 1993 [1974].
———. "Bi-racial U.S.A. vs. Multi-Racial Brazil: Is the Contrast Still Valid?" *Journal of Latin American Studies* 25. no. 2 (1993):373–386.
Smith, Carol A. (ed.). *Guatemalan Indians and the State: 1540–1988*. Austin: University of Texas Press, 1990.
Solaún, Mauricio, Eduardo Vélez, and Cynthia Smith. "*Claro, Trigueño, Moreno*: Testing for Race in Cartagena." *Caribbean Review* 15, no. 3 (1987):18–19.
Stavig, Ward. *The World of Tupac Amaru: Conflict, Community, and Identity in Colonial Peru*. Lincoln: University of Nebraska Press, 1999.
Stepan, Nancy Leys. *"The Hour of Eugenics": Race, Gender, and Nation in Latin America*. Ithaca, N.Y.: Cornell University Press, 1991.
Stephens, Thomas M. *Dictionary of Latin American Ethnic and Racial Terminology*. Gainesville: University of Florida Press, 1989.
Stutzman, Ronald. "*El Mestizaje*: An All-Inclusive Ideology of Exclusion." In *Cultural Transformations and Ethnicity in Modern Ecuador*, edited by Norman E. Whitten Jr. Urbana: University of Illinois Press, 1981, pp. 45–93.
Suárez Findlay, Eileen J. *Imposing Decency: The Politics of Sexuality and Race in Puerto Rico, 1870–1920*. Durham, N.C.: Duke University Press, 1999.
Thomas, Deborah A. *Modern Blackness: Nationalism, Globalization, and the Politics of Culture in Jamaica*. Durham, N.C.: Duke University Press, 2004.
Turits, Richard Lee. "A World Destroyed, A Nation Imposed: The 1937 Haitian Massacre in the Dominican Republic." *Hispanic American Historical Review* 82, no. 3 (2002):589–635.

Turner, Terrence. "Defiant Images: The Kayapó Appropriation of Video." *Anthropology Today* 8, no. 6 (1992):5–16.

Twine, France Winddance. *Racism in a Racial Democracy: The Maintenance of White Supremacy in Brazil.* New Brunswick, N.J.: Rutgers University Press, 1998.

UNESCO (United Nations Educational, Scientific, and Cultural Organization). *Race and Class in Post-Colonial Society: A Study of Ethnic Group Relations in the English-Speaking Caribbean, Bolivia, Chile and Mexico.* Paris: UNESCO, 1977.

Urban, Greg, and Joel Sherzer (eds.). *Nation-States and Indians in Latin America.* Austin: University of Texas Press, 1991.

Wade, Peter. *Blackness and Race Mixture: The Dynamics of Racial Identity in Colombia.* Baltimore: Johns Hopkins University Press, 1993.

———. *Race and Ethnicity in Latin America.* London: Pluto Press, 1997.

Warren, Kay B. *The Symbolism of Subordination: Indian Identity in a Guatemalan Town.* Austin: University of Texas Press, 1978.

———. *Indigenous Movements and Their Critics: Pan-Maya Activism in Guatemala.* Princeton, N.J.: Princeton University Press, 1998.

Warren, Kay B., and Jean E. Jackson (eds.). *Indigenous Movements, Self-Representation, and the State in Latin America.* Austin: University of Texas Press, 2002.

Whitten, Norman E., Jr., and Arlene Torres. "Blackness in the Americas." *Report on the Americas* 25, no. 4 (1992):16–22.

Whitten, Norman E., Jr., and Arlene Torres (eds.). *Blackness in Latin America and the Caribbean.* 2 vols. Bloomington: Indiana University Press, 1998.

Williams, Brackette F. *Stains on My Name, War in My Veins: Guyana and the Politics of Cultural Struggle.* Durham, N.C.: Duke University Press, 1991.

Winant, Howard. "Racial Democracy and Racial Identity: Comparing the United States and Brazil." In *Racial Politics in Contemporary Brazil,* edited by Michael Hanchard. Durham, N.C.: Duke University Press, 1999, pp. 98–115.

Wood, Charles H., and José Alberto Magno de Carvalho. *The Demography of Inequality in Brazil.* Cambridge, UK: Cambridge University Press, 1988.

Wood, Charles H., and Peggy A. Lovell. "Racial Inequality and Child Mortality in Brazil." *Social Forces* 70, no. 3 (1992):703–724.

Wright, Winthrop R. *Café con Leche: Race, Class, and National Image in Venezuela.* Austin: University of Texas Press, 1990.

Yelvington, Kevin A. "The War in Ethiopia and Trinidad, 1935–1936." In *The Colonial Caribbean in Transition: Essays on Postemancipation Social and Cultural History,* edited by Bridget Brereton and Kevin A. Yelvington. Gainesville, Fla.: University Press of Florida, 1999, pp. 189–225.

———. (ed.). *Trinidad Ethnicity.* Knoxville: University of Tennessee Press, 1993.

10

Women, Work, and Politics

Susan Tiano

Women were at the forefront of the dramatic changes that swept Latin America in the late twentieth and early twenty-first centuries, just as they have been in every previous historical epoch. What distinguishes the contemporary period is that women's achievements are more apt to be publicly acknowledged, acclaimed, and rewarded. In previous eras, Latin American women's multiform contributions to public life were obscured by images that defined women exclusively in terms of the private realm of family and the wife-mother role, thereby concealing their activities outside the domestic sphere. The long overdue attention to women's achievements has its intellectual roots in the burgeoning of feminist scholarship since the 1970s and its practical roots in the dramatic social changes that have transformed gender roles in recent decades. The global media have played a role in bringing information about women's public contributions to international and national awareness, often with far-reaching implications.

Argentina's political history, for example, was irrevocably altered by the globally disseminated media images of the Madres de la Plaza de Mayo, the women who helped topple Argentina's repressive military regime by staging weekly demonstrations in one of Buenos Aires' most public plazas. Their movement began informally, among housewives who had never been involved in politics, who had little in common except a tragic shared experience—a loved one, typically a son or a daughter, had "disappeared" at the hands of the military government.[1] As they made the rounds of government offices in a futile search for information about the missing person's whereabouts, they began encountering the same anxious faces in waiting lines and reception offices, and these women came to realize that many others shared their plight. Meeting in living rooms and other private spaces, they forged social networks enabling them to find other women in similar circumstances. In the face of continuing government unwillingness to respond to their requests for information, they settled upon a strategy for publicizing their concerns and protesting the government's lack of response to them. Tying white kerchiefs around their heads, they toted placards picturing their missing loved ones as they marched around the plaza in front of government headquarters. At a time when the regime's ban on political activity—often enforced through the same kind of "disappearances" that had separated the *madres* from their offspring—had completely curtailed men's public protest of the regime, the *madres'* weekly demonstrations were especially courageous. By centering their mobilization on their roles as mothers, the *madres* used a powerful symbolic identity to interpret their actions (to themselves, the press, and the government) in terms of their private roles in the household rather than the public world of politics, where women seldom ventured.

At first, the regime dismissed their activities as too insignificant to warrant repression. Instead, it impugned their legitimacy by calling them *las locas* (the crazy women) in the public press and by manipulating media accounts to distort their purpose and deny their concerns. As their protests continued, the regime tried other strategies, such as infiltrating their ranks and arranging for the "disappearance" of their founder, Azucena Villaflor. Nevertheless, the terms in which the *madres* framed their protests—as expressing their maternal responsibilities to their sons and daughters— insulated them from direct governmental repression. While the Argentine populace might tolerate and perhaps applaud the regime's wholesale repression of "terrorists" and "subversives," subjecting "mothers" to the same kind of treatment would threaten the regime's legitimacy. Thus, the *madres* were able to evade governmental repression until their activities had been too well publicized to be quelled without international protest and their cause had been adopted by international human rights organizations. The resulting political pressure was salient for Argentina's transition to democracy in 1983, showing the world an incontrovertible instance in which women's agency helped shape the course of a nation's history (Schirmer 1993; Bouvard 1994; Chant 2003:11).

The Argentine *madres'* experience is but one of many examples of Latin American women gaining long-neglected recognition for their contributions to public life. Another well-known, if less dramatic, example concerns the Mexican women working in multinational factories (*maquiladoras*, as the factories are called), who are stimulating industrial development along the U.S.-Mexican border by assembling products for export to global markets. Debates over the North American Free Trade Agreement (NAFTA) have generally portrayed *maquiladora* women to the U.S. public as docile, passive, and willing to work for a pittance—the antithesis of the unionized U.S. males whose employment base has eroded due to industrial downsizing and overseas investment. This image, which has been perpetuated in Mexico and elsewhere in Latin America to justify hiring women for *maquiladora* jobs, has been used in the United States to legitimate corporate internationalization and increasing investment in Mexico and elsewhere.[2] Such a narrow stereotype cannot possibly encompass the complex reality of diverse women's lives, but it is useful for shaping public perceptions, and its consistency with other stereotypes of Mexican women's roles gives it a certain credibility with both the Mexican and U.S. public (Sklair 1993; Tiano 1994).

Nevertheless, in at least two instances in recent years, women *maquiladora* workers have staged long-term, successful strikes for better wages and working conditions, and their collective action has begun to come to public awareness, both in Mexico and the United States. This is sparking cross-border organizing and support for Mexico's *maquiladora* workers from an increasingly broad sector of U.S. labor. As the fates of men and women workers on both sides of the border become increasingly intertwined with the spread of globalization, the scope of *maquiladora* women's contributions is too important to be ignored or occluded by misleading stereotypes (Bandy and Mendez 2003).

In short, Latin American women have always played key productive and political roles, but many have performed these activities in informal contexts hidden from the social consciousness or have had their roles obscured by ideologies that define them exclusively as wives and mothers. The increasing awareness of women's contributions to their communities reflects both a broadening of the scope of their activities and the growing commitment of researchers and the mass media to shed needed light on women's public roles.

Latin American women are a highly diverse group, reflecting the same regional heterogeneity that characterizes Latin America generally. As Kevin Yelvington illustrates in Chapter 9, women's lives are defined not only by their gender—the social and cultural meanings attributed to biological sex—but also by the complex ways gender interacts with class, race, and ethnicity to influence women's social roles and relationships. The world of a Mayan woman in highland Guatemala may seem light years away from that of an Afro-Latina in a Brazilian *favela* or a third-generation Italian woman in a cosmopolitan Argentine city. Yet, many features unite women across the region and permit generalizations about their history and contemporary circumstances. Like their male counterparts, women in most Latin American nations share an Iberian heritage that has molded their societies after the fashion of their Spanish and Portuguese colonizers. Women also share with men a history of external dependency that has shaped their nations' developmental trajectories and, as Richard Harper and Alfred Cuzán explain in Chapter 6, continues to dictate the terms under which their countries participate in the global economy. As this chapter reveals, the consequences of this heritage have posed challenges for women and men throughout Latin America, regardless of their specific circumstances. Nevertheless, Latin American women have other experiences in common by virtue of their gender that sharply divide them from the men in their societies. The next section describes concepts from feminist theory that illuminate women's gender-specific experiences.

■ Production, Reproduction, and the Gender Division of Labor

A useful starting point for exploring the changing roles of Latin American women is the conceptual distinction between production and reproduction and the gender-based division of labor that results from these interlinked activities. Production is the creation of socially useful goods and services. Its continuity requires reproduction—the replenishment of labor and other productive resources. Reproduction entails the day-to-day maintenance and emotional support of family members, some of whom provide the labor for the productive sphere. Reproduction also involves conceiving, bearing, and caring for children and preparing them for the roles they will occupy in adulthood. In precapitalist societies, both production and reproduction take place within the household and are oriented toward meeting the family's subsistence needs. Under capitalism, a separation exists between the private sphere of household and family, where reproduction occurs, and the public, formal sphere, which is the primary locus of production (Tiano 1984). At the interstice between the private and public spheres lies the informal sector of the economy. Informal activities, which often take place within the household, frequently involve such services as preparing and selling food, washing and ironing clothing, or tutoring children—all extensions of reproduction (Arizpe 1977). Yet, because informally generated products and services are typically sold on the market, they interpenetrate the public sphere.

Societies around the world have displayed considerable variety in the gender-specific tasks assigned to men and women. Yet, women consistently are responsible for reproduction, whereas men are allocated to productive roles in the public sphere. This gender-based division of labor between the private and public realms is supported by cultural ideologies that define women in terms of their wife-mother role, whatever their actual marital or childbearing status or their roles in public production (Beechey 1978:192). In Latin American societies, the dominant ideology of *marianismo*, the cult

Graffiti on a wall in Chiapas, Mexico, that
reads "Stop the repression of women."

of the Virgin Mary, glorifies motherhood and cultivates women to be self-sacrificing moral guardians of the family (Stevens 1973:94; Chant 2003:10). According to this belief system, the family is held together spiritually and emotionally through the mother's steadfast devotion. Women's dedication to their families is expected to extend beyond their selfless commitment to child rearing, domestic tasks, caring for the sick and elderly, and other reproductive roles; women must also maintain their purity by remaining within the safe haven of the household (Vaughan 1979:67). *Marianismo* supports the gender division of labor by deeming public participation to be inconsistent with women's inherent nature and familial responsibilities. Women are not only expected to refrain from undertaking waged employment but also are implored to avoid social or political activities that take them beyond the protective confines of the home. As the next section reveals, women's real-world circumstances have often dramatically contradicted this ideology; yet, it has persisted throughout Latin American history to circumscribe women's activities and define their self-concepts.

Women in Latin American History

At the time of first contact between the indigenous peoples of what would become Latin America and the Europeans, who would impose their way of life on groups throughout the continent, the status of indigenous women varied greatly. Most anthropologists posit an inverse relationship between women's status and the degree of class stratification in their societies (Gailey 1987:51–54). In relatively egalitarian hunting-and-gathering bands and in horticultural societies, where people gardened with handheld hoes and digging sticks, the complementary productive contributions of both genders offered women considerable economic parity with men (Etienne and Leacock 1980:6). Among the horticultural Bari of eastern Colombia, for example, women enjoyed a high degree of personal autonomy and social respect (Buenaventura-Posso and Brown 1980:119).

By contrast, in agricultural societies with elaborate cultivation systems, bureaucratic states, and hierarchically ranked social systems, women's status was below that of the men from their same class. Both the Aztecs, who built a sophisticated empire in what is now central Mexico, and the Incas, who controlled extensive territory in the Andean region, created societies in which women were deemed inferior to men and had more limited access to resources (Nash 1980:137; Silverblatt 1980:155).[3] Both empires had grown through a process of conquest in which the subjugated peoples were enslaved and forced to pay tribute to the empire. Similarly, the Carib-speaking people of the West Indies amassed considerable territory by subduing the more peaceful Arawaks, killing the Arawak men and retaining the women in a subordinate status for breeding and labor (Miller 1991:17). Such dynamics suggest that political conquest stimulated class and gender inequality among indigenous Latin Americans.

The imposition of colonial rule on the peoples of Latin America pro-

Brazilian woman preparing crushed manioc root, used in making *farofa* to be eaten with *feijoada* (black beans).

duced diverse outcomes, ranging from complete annihilation through disease and warfare to incorporation into radically new social relations intended to produce wealth for the colonial power. The indigenous populations that were forcefully assimilated into colonial societies were joined by the successive waves of African-born people who were imported to provide labor for the mines and plantations. Although each affected group experienced colonialism in its own way, certain commonalities cut across all colonized groups.

Regardless of women's circumstances prior to European contact, the imposition of colonial rule tended to diminish their status (Boserup 1970:53). Women in horticultural societies, whose productive contributions had given them relative parity with men, found themselves marginalized from socially valued roles and resources. Colonialism also weakened the position of women in stratified agrarian societies because even though precolonial systems had subordinated them to men, these arrangements were, nevertheless, more egalitarian than the social and legal systems imposed by the colonizers (Nash 1980).

As the colonial administrations implemented the mercantile capitalist economy that was emerging in Europe, indigenous people were immersed in new relations that often exploited their labor and divorced them from productive resources. The Spanish colonial regime instituted a system in which precious metals, agricultural products, and manufactured finery such as hand-woven textiles were used to enrich Spain's coffers and finance its military exploits. The British and Dutch developed more elaborate global trade networks in which agricultural products from their New World plantations were exchanged for commodities produced elsewhere (Chirot 1977:22). With the transition from subsistence to market-based production, land originally held in common and farmed cooperatively by both men and women became privately owned. The best land was claimed by the Europeans or awarded to indigenous elites as compensation for their loyalty. The reallocation of land disadvantaged most indigenous people, but it was especially harmful to women, whose ability to own and dispose of land was drastically limited under Spanish law. Women were denied official title to the land they worked, even after the death or desertion of the legally designated male head of household (Silverblatt 1980:167).

In some regions, both slave and free women labored along with men to produce agricultural goods for domestic or foreign markets. More typically, women were relegated to subsistence production, often on the most marginal land, producing the foodstuffs that sustained their households. Other women were confined to the domestic sphere, where they engaged in household labor and manufactured items, such as woven textiles, for family use or market exchange. Such manufacturing often occurred under highly exploitative conditions. In colonial Peru, for example, indigenous women were often sequestered in locked rooms and forced to weave cloth that colonial administrators appropriated for sale to European consumers. Yet, the exploitation of their labor was but one of the many indignities women suffered under colonial rule. Many women were raped or forced into concubinage by the Spanish and their indigenous allies (Navarro 1999:32). Women were often sexually victimized by priests, who forced them to prostitute themselves or serve as mistresses as a form of penance for presumed sins (Silverblatt 1980:169).

Women's responses to the colonial arrangements that limited their legal rights and exploited their labor and sexuality ranged from accommodation to resistance (Navarro 1999:24). A common accommodative pattern of women during the early colonial period was to become consorts or wives of the colonizers, thereby achieving relatively high status for themselves and their offspring. The Spanish initially encouraged these liaisons as a way of compensating for the scarcity of European women in the colonies but later saw them as a threat to the Spaniards' racial and cultural homogeneity (Nash 1980:141). By this time, however, the intermixing of indigenous, African, and European peoples had laid the basis for a complex class- and racially stratified society in which women at all levels derived their primary status from their roles as reproducers. Elite women were expected to bear children who would perpetuate upper-class privilege, whereas women of the popular classes were expected to breed children to replenish the rapidly dwindling labor force. The policies advanced by the Spanish crown to regulate marriage in the colonies blended with those of the Catholic Church, affecting the lifestyles and values of women across the class spectrum.

Even though colonialism reduced women's access to productive roles and resources, women in the preindependence and postindependence epochs were hardly idle. They performed many tasks that generated goods for household consumption and products for market exchange. Women's economic roles mirrored their positions in the race-class hierarchy. Upper-class women, whose work was typically confined to the private sphere, managed their households, oversaw the production and purchase of consumption goods, and regulated the care and training of their children. Women in the merchant and artisan classes often played entrepreneurial roles in family enterprises. Most lower-class urban women—both migrant and urban-born—worked as domestic servants or as laundresses, midwives, *curanderas* (healers), or food vendors. Rural women, in their capacity as subsistence agriculturalists, often not only provisioned their families but also produced a surplus to be traded or sold. In many rural regions, the lack of viable economic options led young women to leave for urban areas. Yet, the bulk of these women migrants, whose indigenous origins exposed them to frequent discrimination, found their employment options limited to domestic service and street vending.

An Indian woman of the
Salaseca tribe washing
wool in Ecuador.

UN Photo 155079/M. Grant

During the mid-nineteenth century, Argentina, Brazil, Chile, and Mexico introduced "normal" schools for teacher education and began admitting women to secondary schools and universities (Korrol 1999:73). These innovations enabled women whose families could afford their educational expenses to prepare for middle-class careers in health care, teaching, and other professions whose tasks and skill levels were presumed to parallel women's specialization in domestic tasks performed in the household. The proliferation of educational and occupational opportunities for women greatly expanded women's avenues for making important productive contributions to their communities. Yet, because most professional women were confined to jobs that were seen as mere extensions of their reproductive roles, their work was undervalued and badly compensated, and their achievements rarely won them much public recognition.

The twentieth century brought a division among Latin American nations, with some—such as Mexico, Argentina, and Brazil—developing labor-intensive manufacturing industries to produce basic consumption goods. Women formed the backbone of the labor force in the textile, tobacco, and food processing industries (Nash 1983:11; Towner 1979:49).[4] With the transition to capital-intensive industries during the 1930s and 1940s, however, the preference for male labor reduced women's share of the industrial workforce (Tiano 1994:42; Cravey 1998:28). In turn-of-the-century Mexico, when textile and tobacco production dominated manufacturing, about 76,000 women held factory jobs; after forty years of industrial diversification, only half as many women held jobs in manufacturing (Vaughan 1979:78). Similarly, in 1900, over 90 percent of Brazil's industrial labor force was female, but by 1940 women constituted only 25 percent of the manufacturing workforce (Schmink 1986:137).

Women's expulsion from industry sometimes occurred when male workers enlisted the state to penalize businesses for hiring women. In Puerto Rico, women had come to constitute such a large share of the manufacturing labor force by the 1930s that the male-dominated unions petitioned the government to help reverse the trend. When the state complied by granting subsidies to industries that hired men, there was a drastic reduction in women's industrial employment (Nash 1983:8). Similar trends have been documented for Mexico and Brazil (Vaughan 1979; Saffioti 1975). Despite equally discriminatory practices in many other employment sectors, women have continued to maintain a foothold in the formal economy. Yet, as discussed later, only in the 1970s did women begin to solidify their position in the labor force.

Women's contributions to the political life of their societies date from precolonial times, when many indigenous women were active in the movements that opposed European conquest (Navarro 1999:37–39). According to documents dating from the early conquest period, women's boldness on the battlefield terrified Spanish observers, who perceived them as incarnations of the Amazons (Miller 1991:16). Others resisted colonial incursion in less militaristic ways by fleeing to remote regions beyond Spanish domination. Thus, some women descendants of the Incas escaped Spanish rule by moving to isolated areas where they reinstated their native religious practices as a form of cultural resistance (Silverblatt 1980:179).

Women played active roles in the political mobilizations that culminated in the early-nineteenth-century independence struggles. Among those immortalized for their heroism in these wars of independence are Policarpa Salavarrieta, who was publicly executed by the Spanish for fomenting revolution in Colombia; María Quiteira de Jesús, who distinguished herself in battle in Brazil's independence movement; and Marie Jeanne a-la-Crete-a-Pierrot and Henriette St. Marc, who participated in Haiti's revolts against the French (Korrol 1999:61).

The surging political activity of the postindependence era was generally a masculine prerogative within the new postcolonial institutions, which, like their counterparts elsewhere in the Western world, denied women suffrage and other rights to participatory citizenship (Miller 1991). With formal political channels closed to women, those who wished to shape local or national politics did so informally, through their social networks within and outside their families. Their political activity was most apt to flourish in times of political upheaval, when grassroots resistance movements required their support. Just as women had figured centrally in the movements for independence from colonial rule, they also made key contributions to movements against what were perceived as unjust or dictatorial national regimes. During the Mexican Revolution, some women fought alongside men on the battlefields, and many others accompanied men to battle sites where they cooked, washed clothing, and tended the wounds of their embattled loved ones (Macias 1982:25). In Guatemala, women participated in the strike that helped to depose the autocratic regime of Jorge Ubico in 1944, inaugurating the first free elections in that country's history; in Bolivia, women staged street demonstrations and hunger strikes that helped to bring the Movimiento Nacionalista Revolucionaria to power in 1952. Cuban women were active in the revolutionary movement that unseated the Batista regime in 1959 and led to a socialist government that successfully promoted women's equality (Larguia and Dumoulin 1986).

Movements to transform political regimes were but one form of women's political participation during the pre- and postindependence periods. Much of their political energy was devoted to causes such as female suffrage, which directly affected women's well-being. By the late nineteenth century, women in Argentina, Uruguay, Chile, Brazil, Mexico, and Cuba had begun to develop movements that agitated for women's suffrage and other reforms to promote gender equality (Korrol 1999:84). The emergence of feminist political journals in this period gave women a forum for espousing their views on female equality; examples include the Brazilian journal, *O Sexo Feminino*, established in the 1870s, and *La Mujer*, which Chilean women published in the 1890s (Miller 1991:69).

Women also organized conferences such as the Congreso Feminino Internacional, which convened in Buenos Aires in 1910, and two feminist congresses held in 1916 in Mérida, Mexico (Korrol 1999:87). The Mérida conferences illustrated the deep divisions within the Mexican feminist movement: Whereas conservative Catholic women challenged proposals they viewed as threatening to women's traditional roles, the more progressive women advocated platforms deploring gender inequalities in education and employment and demanded legal reforms to ensure women's equal treatment before the law (Macias 1982:73–75). Regardless of their position, women at the Mérida and Buenos Aires conferences set the stage for the unique form of feminist consciousness that has characterized Latin American feminism in the twentieth and twenty-first centuries and has distinguished it from U.S. and European feminism. Rather than rejecting their feminine roles as wives and mothers, Latin American feminists have sought to eliminate conditions that interfere with women's ability both to successfully perform those roles and to use them as platforms for critiquing and transforming their societies (Miller 1991:74).

As the next sections reveal, contemporary Latin American women have acted in their capacities as mothers and wives to make lasting changes in the political tenor of their societies. At the same time, they have expanded their public participation in both the political and economic spheres. The discussion of women in contemporary Latin America begins by describing changes in women's employment patterns.

■ Women in the Formal Labor Force

As previously noted, Latin American women's employment patterns have traditionally been shaped by the ideology of *marianismo*, which deems formal labor force participation inappropriate for married women because it jeopardizes their ability to perform their domestic roles and, thus, threatens their families' well-being (Levenson-Estrada 1997:210). A woman is expected to work, if at all, only until she marries and has children, at which point she should leave the workforce to devote herself to full-time domesticity (Arizpe 1977:29; Fernandez-Kelly 1983). The assumption that her partner's wages will be adequate to support her and the household underlies this expectation. Partnered women who must generate income are expected to do so in the informal sector, where tasks and schedules are more compatible with reproductive duties than those of formal jobs (Beneria 1992:92). Even though they may need or want full-time jobs, the cultural injunction against married mothers working for wages leads to discriminatory hiring practices that restrict their employment opportunities. This ideology underlies protective legislation that circumscribes the range of jobs available to women, preferential hiring practices that favor men, gender-based wage discrimination, men's opposition to their wives' employment, and women's ambivalence about their wage-earning roles (Tiano 1987:227).

As a result of *marianismo* and the gender division of labor it supports, Latin American women's labor force participation has lagged behind that of women in most parts of the world. With the exception of northern Asia and the Middle East, where women have traditionally been rigidly secluded from public life, most African and Asian nations have had higher rates of female economic activity than have Latin American countries (Psacharopoulos and Tzannatos 1992:49–52). Latin American governments have encouraged this situation as a way of holding down unemployment levels in contexts where demographic growth has exceeded the economy's capacity to provide sufficient employment for the working-age population (Gregory 1986:21).

As the data in Table 10.1 demonstrate, until recently, traditional images of women's ideal roles shaped the Latin American workforce. These data describe trends in women's economic activity for three points in time—the 1960s, the 1980s, and the late 1990s. During the earliest period, women's labor force participation rarely rose above 25 percent and was less than 20 percent for the bulk of countries for which we have reliable data. Latin

Table 10.1 Labor Force Participation Rates for Working-Age Women and Men

Country	Year	Male Rate	Male Change	Female Rate	Female Change	Female/Male
Argentina	1960	92.8		24.4		26.3
	1980	90.8	−2.0	33.1	8.7	36.5
	1995	76.2	−14.6	41.3	8.2	54.2
Brazil	1960	95.0		18.2		19.1
	1980	92.4	−2.6	33.0	14.8	35.7
	1998	82.0	−10.4	52.8	19.8	64.4
Chile	1952	94.5		28.6		30.6
	1982	87.2	−7.3	28.9	0.3	33.8
	1999	74.4	−12.8	36.5	7.6	49.1
Colombia	1951	97.4		19.0		19.5
	1985	85.4	−12.0	39.4	20.4	46.1
	1999	79.8	−5.6	57.7	18.3	72.3
Costa Rica	1963	97.0		18.6		19.1
	1984	89.7	−7.3	26.4	7.8	29.4
	1999	81.5	−8.2	38.5	12.1	47.2
Ecuador	1962	97.8		17.7		18.0
	1982	87.7	−10.1	22.6	4.9	25.3
	1998	55.2	−32.5	36.8	14.2	66.7
Guatemala	1964	96.2		13.1		13.5
	1981	91.3	−4.9	14.7	1.6	16.5
	1999	87.9	−3.4	45.6	30.9	51.9
Honduras[a]	1961	52.7		7.7		14.7
	1974	48.8	−3.9	8.9	1.2	18.3
	1999	88.0	+39.2	45.8	36.9	52.0
Mexico	1960	96.5		19.1		19.8
	1980	92.4	−4.1	32.7	13.6	35.4
	1999	83.8	−8.6	38.5	5.8	45.9
Panama	1950	97.0		24.9		25.2
	1980	87.3	−9.7	35.7	10.8	40.9
	1999	79.7	−7.6	43.2	7.5	54.2
Peru	1961	96.8		22.7		23.3
	1981	91.3	−5.5	29.0	6.3	31.3
	1999	79.4	−11.9	58.1	29.1	73.2
Uruguay	1963	93.0		32.0		34.4
	1985	92.4	−0.6	46.0	14.0	49.8
	1998	55.8	−36.6	39.1	−6.9	70.1
Venezuela	1961	96.4		22.1		23.0
	1981	89.0	−7.4	35.0	12.9	39.3
	1997	53.2	−35.8	30.1	−4.9	56.6

Sources: George Psacharopoulos and Zafiris Tzannatos, *Case Studies on Women's Employment and Pay in Latin America: Overview and Methodology* (Washington, D.C.: World Bank, 1992); James Wilkie (ed.), *Statistical Abstract of Latin America*, Vol. 38 (Los Angeles: UCLA Latin American Center Publications, 2002).

Note: a. Honduran participation rates in 1961 and 1974 censuses were calculated differently from those of the other countries, whose rates are the ratio of the economically active population to the working-age (20- to 60-year-old) population. Early Honduran rates use the total population (all age categories) as the denominator for calculating male and female participation rates.

American nations showed considerable variation, with the more urbanized countries of Panama (25 percent) and the Southern Cone—Uruguay (32 percent), Chile (29 percent), and Argentina (24 percent)—showing higher female employment than the more rural Central American countries of Guatemala (13 percent) and Honduras (8 percent).[5] Yet, the common denominator among all Latin American nations during this period was a relatively low rate of female employment, particularly in contrast with male rates, which were uniformly above 92 percent during this period.[6]

The 1960s and 1970s witnessed considerable growth in the proportion of employed women. By the early 1980s, one-third of working-age women in Mexico, Brazil, Argentina, Venezuela, and Panama were in the labor force; almost 40 percent of Colombian women and almost half of Uruguayan women worked for wages. The most substantial rises in women's economic activity during the twenty-year period occurred in Colombia (20.4 percent), Brazil (14.8 percent), Uruguay (14 percent), and Mexico (13.6 percent), but most countries experienced gains of at least 8 percent. The exceptions to this trend include Chile (0.3 percent), where the seventeen-year Pinochet regime advocated policies designed to confine women to the home, and Guatemala, where political turmoil stunted the growth of both the male and female workforce.

Importantly, the general rise in women's economic activity was not accompanied by parallel growth in men's employment. During the 1950s and 1960s, upward of 93 percent of Latin American men were economically active, meaning that they either held jobs or were unemployed but actively seeking employment. These proportions encompassed most able-bodied men below retirement age who were not in school, producing a "ceiling effect," beyond which rates had little room to rise because the vast majority of men were already in the workforce. With men participating in the labor force in such large proportions, it would be reasonable to expect women's gains to occur at men's expense. This argument, which is often advanced as a rationale for maintaining traditional gender roles, envisages men and women as competitors for the same scarce employment opportunities. Feminist economists and sociologists, who see this "competitive" view as inconsistent with the way gender-segregated labor markets operate, have challenged it. Because labor markets channel the bulk of working women into a specific range of "female" occupations, such as teaching, nursing, and clerical work, rising female employment would not necessarily have to come at the expense of men's wage-earning opportunities.

The fact that men's economic activity decreased in all Latin American countries during the 1960s and 1970s, when women's employment was rising throughout the region, could be taken as evidence for the "competitive" scenario that women's increasing employment displaced men from the labor force. However, while this explanation may have some truth, it is clearly not the whole story. If women had expanded their employment primarily by taking jobs from men, the gains in women's rates would be roughly equivalent to the declines in men's. Yet, with the exception of Costa Rica, where the 7.8 percent increase in women's rates paralleled a 7.3 percent decrease in men's, the trends in women's and men's rates show little correspondence. In some countries, relatively large increases in women's employment went hand in hand with minimal declines in male activity. In both Brazil and Uruguay, for example, women's employment surged by 14 percent, while men's rates declined by only 3 percent in Brazil and a mere 0.6 percent in Uruguay. Even if the entire decline in male activity were due to women's movement into male jobs, this would only account for a tiny fraction of the rapid increase in women's employment rates, which would have been achieved at a proportionately small expense to male activity rates.

By contrast, in some countries, the decline in men's economic activity substantially exceeded the increase in women's. Thus in Ecuador, the 5 percent increase in women's participation could not compensate for the 10 percent decrease in men's labor force participation, nor could the 0.3 percent increase in Chilean women's activity make up for the 7 percent decline among Chilean men. In these cases, the drop in male activity was too large to be accounted for by women's increasing participation, even if it did occur at the expense of male employment, demonstrating that other factors played a role in the worsening employment scenario for men during the 1960s and 1970s.

The expansion of women's labor force participation continued, and in some countries accelerated, during the last two decades of the twentieth century. By the late 1990s, countries throughout Latin America reported female employment rates of 30 percent or higher.[7] Peru and Colombia, where 58 percent of women were economically active, topped the list, although Brazil was not far behind, with 53 percent female employment. With the exception of Venezuela (30 percent), all the remaining countries reported rates ranging between 37 percent (Chile and Ecuador) and 46 percent (Honduras and Guatemala). These two Central American nations showed the largest increase, with Guatemalan women's employment rising by 31 percent and Honduras showing a similar rise. In another group of countries (Peru, Brazil, Colombia, Ecuador, and Costa Rica), women's employment rose by 12 percent or more. With the exception of Colombia, which ranked above most countries in 1980, the nations showing the greatest gains during the period are the ones that had lagged behind in the earlier period and thus had the farthest to go. Similarly, of the countries that reported more modest increases or decreases, several, such as Uruguay, Argentina, and Panama, had such high rates during the 1980s that even with small increases they could rank in the middle of the continuum of countries by the late 1990s. By contrast, the slow expansion of women's employment in Mexico and Chile over the period pulled them into the bottom one-third of countries, while Venezuela's 5 percent decrease in women's economic activity caused it to plummet from the top one-third in 1980 to dead last in 1999.

During the 1980s and 1990s, men's economic activity declined, in some cases dramatically, throughout the region. By 1999, only a little more than half of working-age men in Uruguay, Venezuela, and Ecuador and three-fourths of men in Argentina and Chile were in the workforce. Men fared better in the rest of the region, with rates hovering around 80 percent in six countries (Mexico, Brazil, Costa Rica, Colombia, Panama, and Peru) and rising to 88 percent in Honduras and Guatemala. Unlike the previous period, in which there was no clear relationship between men's and women's changing labor force participation patterns, during the late twentieth century the trends in men's and women's rates across countries showed a closer correlation. Thus, in Guatemala and Honduras, in which women's economic activity reveals the largest increases during the period, men's labor force participation declined the least. Conversely, the only two countries in which female labor force participation actually decreased during the period, Venezuela and Uruguay, were also the ones in which male employment declined the most drastically. These patterns suggest that the same factors that contracted employment opportunities for women also restricted them for men, while those that greatly expanded women's employment options also mitigated the negative influences on male employment that were so pervasive in the rest of the region. We will return to this issue at a later point in this discussion.

The age-specific employment trends illustrated in Figure 10.1 provide insights into women's employment trends. The graphs in the figure illustrate how the employment pattern of a typical working woman changes over the course of her life cycle. By comparing the curves for the 1960s and 1980s, one can visualize how women's typical work histories changed during the period. In the early 1960s, women's economic activity tended to peak early in their life cycle—between the ages of 20 and 25—and to steadily decline with advancing age. This indicates that many women worked prior to marriage and childbearing and then left the workforce as they entered their late twenties and early thirties.

By the 1980s, a somewhat different pattern had emerged. In several countries (Chile, Costa Rica, Ecuador, Panama, Peru, Uruguay, and Venezuela), women's economic activity peaked at an older age in the 1980s than it had in the 1960s. Thus, whereas in the early 1960s economic activity was highest among 20- to 24-year-olds, in the 1980s it was most pronounced among women in their late twenties and early thirties. A related change concerns the age span during which women's employment remained at high levels and the point at which it began to decline steeply. During the 1960s, in every country except Mexico, women's participation dropped steadily after it peaked in their early twenties. By the 1980s, the age span of maximal economic activity had been extended, and women's employment generally did not drop substantially until a later point in their life cycle. These trends suggest that by the 1980s, growing numbers of women in their thirties and forties were remaining in the workforce. Thus, not only were more women joining the labor force, but more were remaining for a longer portion of their life cycles or were reentering after leaving to raise their children.

What might account for the rise in economic activity, particularly among women in their thirties and forties, who two or three decades earlier would likely have devoted themselves to full-time domestic roles? One way to illuminate this question is to use a conceptual distinction made by labor economists between "push" and "pull" factors. Push factors are forces such as economic need that impel women into the workforce to support their households. Pull factors are conditions that either attract women into the labor force or augment their employment opportunities. The availability of suitable jobs, the proliferation of schools and adult literacy programs, the weakening of norms that symbolically confine women to the household, and the attraction of noneconomic rewards, such as personal autonomy, may all operate as pull factors that draw women into the labor force. These two sets of factors need not be mutually exclusive. A woman may be compelled to enter the workforce because her household requires her income; at the same time, she may respond to the lure of financial independence, personal fulfillment, or other anticipated benefits of paid employment. Such considerations suggest that the growth in women's economic participation in the last half of the twentieth century reflected a complex mix of influences that both forced women to take jobs and augmented their incentives and opportunities for paid employment.

Considerable evidence suggests that many women joined the workforce out of economic need. Throughout the lost decade of the 1980s and continuing into the 1990s, Latin American nations were plagued by an economic crisis that dramatically eroded their living standards. As Richard Harper and Alfred Cuzán document in Chapter 6, the economic crisis ushered in several decades of rampant inflation, rising unemployment, and serial currency devaluations that jeopardized the well-being of all but the richest households (Cockroft 1983:260; Scott 1992:22). At the same time, the structural adjustment policies most Latin American governments adopted to stabilize their economies led to substantial cuts in state funding for health care, education, and other necessary social services and removed price supports for basic commodities (Chuchryk 1991:152; Lustig 1992:79). To make matters worse, governments often capped minimum

Figure 10.1 Female Labor Participation Rate by Age

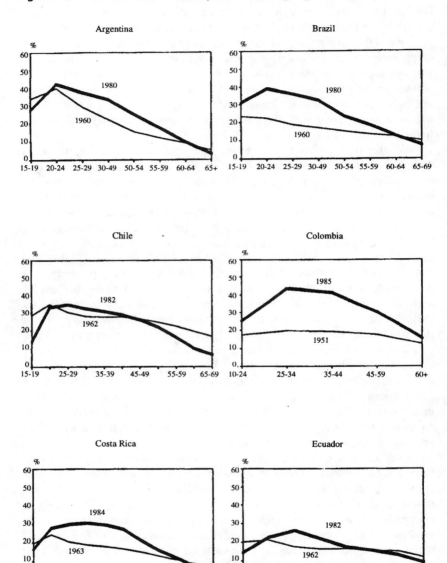

Figure 10.1 continued

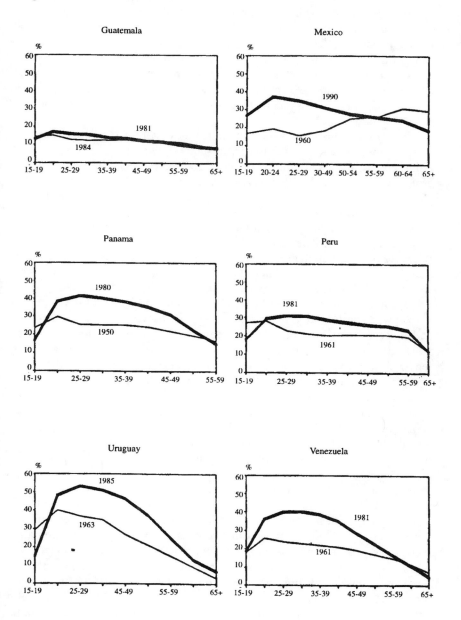

Source: International Labour Organization, *Yearbook of Labour Statistics: Retrospective Edition on Population Censuses, 1945–1998.* Geneva: ILO, 1990.

wage levels to counteract inflation, thereby limiting many workers' incomes. Rising levels of male unemployment and underemployment often prevented men from continuing in their traditional role of family breadwinner (Beneria 1992; Chant 1991). As the data in Table 10.1 demonstrate, the proportion of economically active men in all Latin American countries declined during the period as increasing numbers were marginalized from the formal labor force. Even those men who were able to hold down jobs often found their wages inadequate to support a household (Fernandez-Kelly 1983:56; Safa 1995:24).

These developments were particularly devastating for poorer households, whose already precarious circumstances were further eroded by the rising cost of food and other necessities and the elimination of vital government services (Safa 1995:33). Working- and middle-class households also experienced a drastic decline in their standards of living. Households formulated various strategies to cope with these deteriorating circumstances; most commonly, all working-age members, male and female, had to generate income (Beneria 1992:92). Daughters and sons were often forced to discontinue their schooling to enter the workforce or to postpone marriage to help support their parents' households. Many partnered women who had previously devoted themselves to domestic tasks or informal income-generating activities now had to take full-time jobs. Women's wages were particularly essential in households without adult members and those in which the men were unemployed or underemployed (Chant 1991:158). In some households, men's inability to support their families led to destructive behaviors, such as alcohol abuse, or caused them to desert their families (Beneria 1992:91). In others, the lack of employment options in the local community forced men to migrate elsewhere in search of stable wages (Safa 1995:32). Many women thereby became the primary economic providers for families without male household heads (Anderson and de la Rosa 1991:55). In short, economic necessity pushed many women into the workforce during the crisis-plagued years of the 1980s and early 1990s.

Yet, the upsurge in women's economic activity was not simply a result of economic need and rising male unemployment. Many other changes occurred during the mid- to late twentieth century to draw women out of the household, either by expanding their economy's demand for female labor or by increasing the supply of women willing and able to enter the workforce. One of the most important pull factors was the growth of women's employment opportunities. During the 1960s and 1970s, when many Latin American nations underwent rapid economic and political development, jobs proliferated for women in both the governmental and market sectors of their country's economies. The locus of women's employment opportunities shifted during the 1980s and 1990s, when the economic crisis brought a halt to the heady development of previous decades.

As the structural adjustment measures employed to restimulate economic growth have eroded barriers to foreign trade and investment, multinational corporations, with their well-known preference for female labor in many sectors of their workforce, have come to account for a growing proportion of jobs in Latin America. Jobs for women have proliferated in multinational agribusiness firms, which are flocking to Mexico, Chile, and elsewhere in Latin America to produce fruits and vegetables for export to global consumers (Barriento et al. 1999; Appendini 2002). The demand for women's labor has been particularly pronounced in the multinational manufacturing firms that have relocated their export-processing operations to Latin America (and elsewhere) in order to reduce production costs by employing low-wage workers to process products for export to global consumers (Fernandez-Kelly 1983; Korrol 1999:104). Beginning in the 1950s with Puerto Rico's Operation Bootstrap and the 1960s with Mexico's *maquiladora* program, export-led industrialization has become increasingly common throughout Latin America. Women are preferred for export-processing jobs because they tend to work for lower wages than men and are perceived as more docile, more manually dexterous, and better able to tolerate the monotony of repetitive assembly work (Fuentes and Ehrenreich 1983:12; Sklair 1993:171–172).

Maquiladora (textile factory) in Brazil.

The expansion of the Mexican *maquiladora* industry illustrates the impact of export-led industrialization on the female labor market. In 1967, two years after the *maquila* program was established, it encompassed seventy-two firms employing 4,000 workers, over 80 percent of whom were women. By 1990, the program had grown to include almost two thousand firms and over 460,000 workers (Sklair 1993:54, 68). The stimulus of NAFTA and the booming U.S. economy during the late 1990s greatly accelerated *maquila* investment, augmenting the workforce to 1.3 million people by the year 2000 (Tiano, 1999). In the program's early days, *maquilas* preferred to hire young, single, childless women who had completed secondary school. As the program grew, the *maquilas* relaxed their employment criteria and hired more older women, partnered women, and women with children, as well as more men (Tiano 1994:90). The *maquilas'* rapid proliferation and changing recruitment practices had a significant impact on Mexico's female labor market. By providing jobs for women, particularly those whose age and marital or motherhood status would otherwise have created employment barriers, *maquilas* dramatically increased their employment opportunities. Similar dynamics have been observed with export-processing industrialization programs in other Latin American countries (Safa 1995).

The increasing demand for female labor also stems from the rapid growth of the service sector, which encompasses many jobs that involve activities such as cleaning, cooking, serving food, and providing personal services, which are viewed as extensions of female roles. Even economic sectors that have traditionally employed men now include larger proportions of women. Thus, for example, women have begun to enter the mining and construction sectors, conventionally male preserves. In the 1960s, women constituted only 7 percent of workers in the Mexican mining industry; by 1980, the proportion had grown to 14 percent. During the same period, women's representation in the Peruvian mining industry grew from 2 percent to 6 percent, and Venezuelan women's share of the mining labor force increased from 5 percent to 10 percent. Similarly, during this period, women's share of the Mexican construction industry rose from 3 percent to 16 percent (ECLAC 1988:30). Thus, while some of the gains in women's employment occurred in sectors traditionally reserved for women, others reflected women's inroads into sectors that had once been male preserves.

Fortunately for women workers, the crisis-born conditions that forced many women to earn wages also stimulated the demand for female labor. The crisis and its aftermath compelled many businesses to minimize operating costs to weather the economic turbulence. Many accomplished this objective by turning to women as a low-cost labor source. Other employers began to recruit women because they viewed them as more reliable than men and less apt to organize potentially costly workers' unions. In countries such as Mexico with successful export-processing programs, firms' positive experiences with female labor induced other businesses to follow their example (Beneria and Roldan 1987:49).

The increased demand for women's labor and the growing acceptance of paid work for partnered women and mothers have augmented women's employment opportunities. But women need the necessary education to take advantage of these opportunities. Women's educational attainment reflects both objective conditions such as the availability of schools, and subjective factors such as parents' aspirations for their daughters. Since the 1960s, accelerated investment in public education by Latin American governments has led to a proliferation of rural and urban schools. Governments have encouraged parental support for their children's education through mass media campaigns urging parents to enroll and keep their sons and daughters in school (Rothstein 1982:118).

These efforts have led to substantial increases in school enrollments. By 1980, almost all Latin American children between ages 6 and 11 were enrolled in primary school (Stromquist 1992:1). The only countries in which boys outpaced girls in primary school attendance were Bolivia and Guatemala. Girls were less apt to attend secondary schools, whose female enrollment figures ranged from 65 percent in Panama to 17 percent in Guatemala, with only seven countries (Argentina, Chile, Costa Rica, Ecuador, Panama, Peru, and Uruguay) enrolling half or more of their adolescent girls in secondary school (Chant 2003:89). Boys shared with girls the difficulty in accessing secondary education; in only two countries (Bolivia and Peru) were girls less apt than boys to attend secondary school (ECLAC 1988:42). The subsequent decades witnessed continuing improvements in girls' secondary school enrollments; by 1993, rates approached 70 percent or above in Argentina, Chile, and Colombia, while Guatemala (at 23 percent) was the only country in the region where less than one-third of girls were enrolled in secondary school (Chant 2003:89). The progress of Latin American nations in providing postsecondary education was also considerable. In the mid-1980s, 17 percent of Latin Americans aged 20 to 25 were earning a university degree. Although men were somewhat more apt than women to pursue higher education, in several countries (Argentina, Cuba, Nicaragua, and Panama) women's participation exceeded that of men (Stromquist 1992:2).

The advances in public education have not spread evenly to all sectors of women. Older women, who were past school age when educational opportunities became widely available, often received few benefits from their government's investment in public schooling. By 1990, only 9 percent of women under age 25 were illiterate, but 23 percent of women above that age lacked basic literacy and numeracy skills (United Nations 1991:46). Similarly, rural women, particularly those in indigenous communities, often benefited only minimally from educational reforms. As recently as the 1990s in Guatemala, where indigenous groups constitute 60 percent of the population, 78 percent of rural women were illiterate; the disparity between comparable rates for rural men (60 percent) and those for urban women (36 percent) suggests that racism and sexism played a role in limiting indigenous women's access to educational resources. Indigenous women in Bolivia faced similar obstacles: whereas rural women's illiteracy rates reached 69 percent, only 37 percent of rural men and 23 percent of urban women were unable to read and write (Stromquist 1992:24). These disparities reflect not only the poorer quality of indigenous and rural schools but also the cultural and material hurdles indigenous women must overcome to attain an education.

In some contexts, the economic crisis and the structural adjustment policies implemented to eradicate it halted many of the educational gains of previous decades. For example, in Costa Rica, female secondary school enrollments dropped from 51 percent in 1980 to 49 percent in 1993, and in Nicaragua, from 45 percent to 44 percent (Chant 2003:89). Throughout Latin America, governments were forced to curtail spending on public education, while many young people had to discontinue their educations because their households could not bear the costs, and their economic contributions were needed for family survival. Many analysts worry that the crisis and the resulting structural adjustment policies have dealt a blow to public education—from which it will take Latin American nations decades to recover (Arizpe 1993:174). Nevertheless, although the crisis slowed the progress in educating women in Latin America, it was insufficient to undercut those gains entirely. Even after fifteen years of crisis, women in the 1990s were better prepared than their counterparts from the previous generation to compete for positions in the formal labor force. Thus, the region-wide gains in women's educational opportunities were another pull factor that augmented women's economic activity during the mid- to late twentieth century.

Women's rising labor force participation does not simply reflect the accelerating demand for women's labor, their growing educational preparation, and the increasing economic pressures on them to support their families. Regardless of how much her household may need additional income or how abundant her job opportunities might be, a woman cannot enter full-time employment if her reproductive responsibilities are too demanding. Most employed women, regardless of their marital status or household composition, receive little help with housework and childcare from male household members (Beneria and Roldan 1987:123). To avoid being crushed by their double burden, working women must find ways to balance the competing demands of their productive and reproductive roles. One solution is to have fewer children. Women with small families are better able than those with many offspring to make the necessary childcare arrangements to allow them to reenter the labor force, whether as soon after the birth as possible, or—if the woman can afford to stay home to raise her preschool children—when the children reach school age or beyond. The spread of family planning information and devices throughout much of Latin America during the late twentieth century made it easier for women who wanted smaller families to implement their choices. By the 1990s, the majority of Latin American women in their childbearing years (ages 15 to 49) used contraception, with rates ranging from a high of 84 percent in Uruguay to a low of 31 percent in Guatemala (Chant 2003).[8]

Women's growing ability to regulate their childbearing has led to a substantial decline in fertility throughout Latin America. Between 1960 and 1980, the average number of children per woman of childbearing age dropped from 6.0 to 4.6. In 1960, only three countries (Argentina, Cuba, and Uruguay) had fertility rates below 5.0, and thirteen countries had rates above 6.5. Two decades later, only five countries (Bolivia, Ecuador, El Salvador, Honduras, and Nicaragua) had fertility rates above 6.0, and seven countries averaged fewer than 4.5 children per woman. This trend continued throughout the 1980s and 1990s, such that by the year 2000, thirteen out of nineteen Latin American countries had fertility rates of 3.0 or less (Chant 2003:73). Women's declining fertility resulted from various factors, including increased public awareness of the links between overpopulation and economic and ecological difficulties, the growing commitment of Latin American governments to reduce population growth, and the spread of family planning technologies and information. The expansion of employment opportunities for women also contributed to their lowered fertility, both by augmenting women's economic incentives to have smaller families and by offering them an alternative to motherhood as a way of enhancing their social status (Blumberg 1991:110). Lowered fertility was thus both a cause and a result of women's rising labor force participation. The dramatic drop in fertility throughout Latin America was, therefore, another pull factor that increased women's employment.

An additional stimulus to women's economic activity reflects a change in the prevailing cultural ideology that defines appropriate roles for women. In a cultural context in which women are regarded exclusively as wives and mothers and work outside the home is considered detrimental to the performance of their domestic roles, women face extreme obstacles to formal employment. No matter how great her economic need, a woman will not be able to enter the workforce if no employer will hire her or if her partner will not allow her to leave the house. Similarly, if taking a job would lead to constant feelings of guilt over neglecting her children, emasculating her husband, or risking her feminine purity, a woman is unlikely to seek or long remain in paid employment.

Such considerations suggest that one of the most important incentives to women's rising economic activity was the relaxation of cultural norms against their paid employment, particularly for partnered women and mothers (Beneria and Roldan 1987:49). This normative change reflected a shift in the cultural ideology of *marianismo* and a reformulation of role expectations that consider men to be ineffectual or unmasculine if they cannot support their households without female assistance. As these rigid gender roles have begun to weaken, women's aspirations have changed accordingly, leading many to acquire the motivation and training to prepare for careers, to select partners who will not interfere with their occupational choices, and to plan their childbearing for increased compatibility with wage-earning activities. At the same time, the change in male role definitions has diminished men's resistance to their wives' and daughters' employment and has increased employers' willingness to hire partnered women without fear that spousal reprisals will hamper their successful job performance (Tiano 1994:93–96).

This gender role transformation is both a cause and a result of women's rising educational attainment. With advancing education, women tend to expand their occupational horizons and to question the validity of conventional gender roles for themselves and their daughters. Conversely, parents are more apt to make the necessary sacrifices to keep their daughters in school if they have abandoned conventional gender roles and believe educational attainment will foster their daughters' economic security in later life. In addition to promoting women's education, the erosion of traditional gender roles has expanded their opportunities in the workforce. Employers are more willing to hire women if they don't anticipate spousal resistance to their wives' employment and if they don't expect women to be so committed to their reproductive roles that they neglect their jobs. In turn, employers' increasing demand for female labor has helped to erode cultural norms proscribing women's employment. The desire to lower costs and achieve other benefits by hiring women has led many employers to reformulate their images of appropriate roles for women in order to justify their hiring practices. Similarly, governments hoping to attract corporate investment in *maquiladoras* and other industries that recruit female workers have ensured the availability of female labor through media campaigns and other strategies designed to weaken ideological constraints to female employment (Ruiz 1988).

Whereas this ideological shift may help to reconcile the cultural contradiction between *marianismo* and women's growing need for paid employment, it does not resolve the dilemmas the rapid flux in female roles is posing for Latin American women. Many women who find themselves forced to take jobs were raised to aspire to full-time motherhood and to view paid work and family duties as incompatible. Many resent their jobs for forcing them to neglect their families. Many others who are committed to their jobs feel guilty about deriving personal satisfaction from work that takes them away from their children (Tiano 1994:118; Tiano and Ladino 1999). And those who have resolved the conflicting emotions that surround their dual roles nevertheless struggle to balance the competing demands of their "double day" in contexts where governmental and private services for working mothers are sorely lacking (Safa 1990). Many women view this challenge as more than a personal struggle and are organizing to demand institutional changes, such as childcare and workplace reforms, to facilitate their abilities to perform their domestic and wage-earning roles simultaneously. Issues such as these are only a few of the many catalysts for the growing political mobilization of women.

▓ Women in Latin American Politics

Although women have always taken part in Latin American social and political movements, the past three decades have witnessed a dramatic upsurge in their participation (Jaquette 1991b:1). Women have mobilized in unprecedented numbers to support or protest political regimes, agitate for better working conditions, make demands on the state for improved services and affordable commodities, and transform legal and social barriers to gender equality. Much of their activity has avoided formal political channels—both because it often occurs within authoritarian climates, where political parties, trade unions, and mass demonstrations are illegal (Perelli 1991:101), and because women often consider institutionalized politics to be futile, corrupt, or inconsistent with their feminine roles (Pires de Rio Caldeira 1990:72). Instead, women have developed their own form of politics that stems from their reproductive roles and blurs the boundaries between the public world of politics and the private realm of the family (Safa 1990:355). The apolitical connotation of the wife-mother role has given women some immunity to protest despotic regimes that have brutally repressed political resistance (Perelli 1991:107).

The diversity of women's political objectives, agendas, and strategies precludes ready categorization. Most analysts distinguish between political activities, in which women join with men to pursue goals that transcend gender differences, and those that unite women around issues specific to them as women. The latter encompass both "feminist" movements, which explicitly aim to achieve gender equality, and nonfeminist "women's" movements, which are organized to satisfy needs or make demands that stem from women's reproductive roles and familial responsibilities (Chinchilla 1993).

Feminist Movements

During most of the twentieth century, feminist movements were confined to a small segment of middle-class women whose activities and goals were alien to most Latin American women (Miller 1991). Lower-class and indigenous women often saw feminist discourse as at best irrelevant and at worst threatening to their daily lives, in which survival depended upon their cooperation with men. Many middle-class women felt little resonance with feminist demands for employment parity, family planning programs, or divorce reform because they viewed these objectives as inconsistent with their roles as wives and mothers.

Not until the 1970s did the feminist movement gain more widespread appeal among Latin American women. Mexico City's selection to host the first United Nations International Women's Year Conference in 1975 increased the visibility of Latin American feminism within the region and internationally (Chinchilla 1993:46). The conference inaugurated a decade-long international effort to address women's needs and bring their issues to the forefront of public dialogue. The United Nations' Decade for Women stimulated conferences throughout the region that brought women together to define their needs and to formulate strategies for addressing them. The ensuing debates among the various branches of the feminist movement, each of which had its own agenda and objectives, and the often heated discourse between feminist and nonfeminist women helped to raise consciousness on all sides (Miller 1991:201).

In the wake of these debates, feminist movements have expanded their agendas to incorporate issues that reflect the race, class, and ethnic diversity of their membership and to increase their appeal to women who support conventional gender roles (Barrig 1991). Feminists have thereby continued the pattern set by their turn-of-the-century forebears, who embraced feminine roles as a source of personal power and as platforms from which to agitate for social change (Korrol 1999:84). Their theoretical contributions along these lines have given Latin American feminists an important voice within global feminist discourse that portends growing influence in the coming decades.

Mixed-Gender Movements

Latin American women have often joined men in political actions, ranging from short-lived spontaneous protests to long-term organized movements, that have operated both within and outside established political channels (Chinchilla 1993; Jaquette 1991a). Such activities have reflected the nature of the state and its responsiveness to popular demands; the availability of parties, unions, and other formal channels; and the social circumstances and class-based interests of the participants. As Thomas D'Agostino elucidates in Chapter 4, in many Latin American nations, elites have maintained class and racial hierarchies through authoritarian governments that have limited popular participation. Whereas upper-class women have sometimes mobilized to support these regimes, many nonelite women have participated in revolutionary struggles for democratization and social reform.

Early in the twentieth century, women typically supported revolutionary activities indirectly by preparing food, nursing the wounded, gathering intelligence, and providing other types of support for male combatants. The Cuban Revolution, in which women joined in the guerrilla activities, marked a turning point in women's revolutionary activity. The revolution's success in 1959 inspired growing numbers of women to participate, often as armed combatants, in the grassroots resistance movements that arose in Argentina, Brazil, El Salvador, Guatemala, Nicaragua, Peru, and Uruguay (Chinchilla 1993:41). Of those countries, in only one—Nicaragua—did the revolutionary forces succeed in changing the political system; in the others, their resistance movements provoked repressive government measures to regain "order," many of which led to authoritarian regimes that brutally repressed all forms of political opposition.

Whereas many women participated in regime-challenging movements on the political left, many others took part in right-wing movements that supported conservative measures aimed at maintaining the elite-dominated status quo. In Chile, for example, the "pots and pans" demonstrations of upper-middle- and upper-class women, who took to the streets to protest the rising cost of food, were instrumental in bringing down the socialist government of President Salvador Allende, which fell through a military coup that initiated the authoritarian government of General Augusto Pinochet (Miller 1991:182; Korrol 1999:99).

Many of the movements in which women have joined forces with men have not involved direct challenges to regimes. As women have entered the workforce in growing numbers, they have come to play more important roles in strikes, work stoppages, and other forms of resistance against poor working conditions (Chinchilla 1993:43; Levenson-Estrada 1997). Urban labor struggles have involved both working-class women, who have channeled their protests through unions, and middle-class women, who have expressed their grievances through professional organizations. Women have also participated in various student protest movements. In 1968, for example, when the Mexican government responded to a strident student demonstration by shooting at the unarmed protestors, many of the students who were killed were young women (Miller 1991:6).

Similarly, indigenous and peasant women have joined with men to demand land reform, improved working conditions on plantations and mines, and other remedies to perceived injustices. In Bolivia, indigenous Aymará and Quechua women have engaged in a century-long struggle to resist continual threats to their autonomy and the steady usurpation of their land (Cusicanqui 1990). Other examples of indigenous women's struggles include the activities of the Bolivian Housewives' Committee, who worked alongside men to protest labor conditions in the tin mines, and those of the Chiapan peasant women, who organized to protest the Mexican government's involvement in free-trade initiatives that threatened to impoverish the countryside (Barrios de Chungara 1978; Klubock 1997).

Yet, with the exception of the Central American revolutionary struggles of the 1970s and 1980s, these resistance movements have incorporated only a small proportion of Latin American women. Most women, including those who sympathized with the political activists' ideals, have remained aloof from politics (Pires de Rio Caldeira 1990:50). In a context in which women are defined exclusively as wives and mothers, women face a host of barriers to political activity, including opposition from male partners who demand their wives' constant presence in the household; male resistance to women's membership in their organizations; burdensome domestic and childcare responsibilities that limit their time, energy, and physical mobility; internalized images of politics as dangerous, useless, or simply inappropriate for women; and submissive self-conceptions that limit political agency. Indigenous women face additional obstacles that reflect their racial and cultural subordination. Given the pervasiveness of these obstacles to institutionalized political activity, it is not surprising that women's participation has more commonly taken alternative forms that are more consistent with their reproductive roles and their position within the gender division of labor (Jelin 1990:186).

Women's Movements

Recent decades have witnessed a burgeoning of grassroots movements in which women have been the primary or the sole participants. These movements react to conditions that hamper women's ability to perform their reproductive roles as wives and mothers or that threaten household survival. Their primary objective is to demand that the government rectify these conditions by providing needed services, transforming economic conditions, or abandoning oppressive political policies (Safa 1990:356).

Women's movements typically arise when institutionalized channels for participation are inoperative or are perceived as ineffective. Their creation signifies women's demands for incorporation into the political arena in a way that reaffirms their identity as women, particularly in their roles as custodians of family welfare (Schirmer 1993:32). In politicizing issues such as high food prices, unsafe drinking water, lack of sewerage and electricity, inadequate schools, and government cutbacks in health care services, these movements erode the traditional division between the private and public spheres (Jaquette 1991a:188). The boundary weakens when family concerns, traditionally viewed as beyond the scope of "normal" political debate, are defined as public issues and when women use their private roles as wives and mothers to legitimate their entry into the public world of politics (Chuchryk 1991:156).

Many women's movements emerge when women who share a common concern about a social issue in their community work through their social networks to publicize and gain support for their activities or to organize spontaneous demonstrations. Grounded in neighborhoods where women share common discourses and experiences that transcend ethnic, class, or religious differences, they typically involve issues such as cutbacks in basic government services that affect the entire community. This is one reason why poor women, whose economic disadvantage has traditionally muted their political voice, figure so prominently in many women's movements. Yet, the primary basis around which poor women organize women's movements is their gender rather than their class position: Although many are acutely conscious of the economic hardships that pervade their lives, they express their concerns as wives and mothers rather than as members of an impoverished class (Safa 1990:356).

Women's movements have taken various forms—depending on their objectives, their participants' circumstances, and the degree of involvement of sponsoring bodies, such as churches and international or local nongovernmental organizations (NGOs). Most fall within two broadly defined categories: neighborhood and community movements that focus on economic goals and human rights organizations that challenge repressive government policies. The former, which have cropped up throughout Latin America as a result of the economic crisis, address survival needs and demand essential government services. The latter, which have emerged in countries suffering under authoritarian regimes, address basic civic rights and demand political democratization. The crisis-born nature of both types of movements may explain their rapid explosion on the Latin American scene; it also helps to account for the widespread participation of women, particularly those from the lower classes, who ordinarily would not enter the political arena (Safa 1990:357).

Women's economic movements have stemmed from diverse sources. Some have their roots in the squatter movements of the 1960s, in which women were often leaders in organizing the overnight "invasions" of empty land by homeless urban dwellers whose makeshift settlements often evolved into stable urban communities (Jelin 1990:189). Others owe their existence to the liberation theology wing of the Catholic Church, which offered safe space for women to hold meetings and helped secure foodstuffs, clothing, and other items for collective distribution (Miller 1991:196). Some movements arose when spontaneous demonstrations protesting rising food costs, inadequate neighborhood infrastructure, or the elimination of state-sponsored community services forged networks of women who had similar concerns and a shared commitment to assuage those problems.

Regardless of their source, these movements have aimed to ameliorate material conditions that impair women's domestic role performance. Some movements' strategies have been geared toward helping members survive the economic crisis by offering them new ways to generate income or to reduce the rising costs of basic commodities. The communal kitchens organized in Peru, Uruguay, and other Latin American countries, through which households join together to purchase and prepare food, represent one collective strategy for reducing consumption costs (Chuchryk 1991:154). Another common approach has been to organize protest demonstrations and pressure groups to demand government services. In communities throughout Latin America, women's movements have demanded basic urban services, such as running water, sewerage, and electricity (Bennett 1995; Safa 1990:361). In nations such as Mexico and Argentina—where economic restructuring has reduced state spending on health care, education, and other community services—women's organizations have banded together to protest these cutbacks. Although these movements have met with varying degrees of success and have sometimes evoked heavy-handed treatment by governments aiming to silence women's protests, they have proved to be a valuable venue for translating women's "private" concerns into public discourse.

Women's human rights movements were galvanized by politically authoritarian regimes that sought to stamp out opposition by outlawing institutionalized political activities and brutally repressing any dissent against their policies. These regimes singled out trade union leaders, politicians, academicians, journalists, student activists, and anyone else considered subversive to the regime for imprisonment, torture, or murder. In Argentina, Chile, Guatemala, Uruguay, and elsewhere, many people were kidnapped by government agents who later denied any knowledge of their whereabouts. Public protest of these human rights violations was dangerous and often led to similar treatment for those brash enough to attempt it. Not surprisingly, those best able to form resistance organizations were those with the least political visibility; because women were viewed as apolitical guardians of family welfare, their activities were often immune to government scrutiny (Chuchryk 1993:87). Mothers' clubs and women's self-help organizations could operate in situations where men's organizations—even those with similar objectives—would be brutally repressed.

During the 1970s and 1980s, many women's organizations were formed to protest government abuses. In Chile, women's groups won international recognition for their plight by making *arpilleras*, or tapestries, that depicted the regime's violence and distributing them surreptitiously to global markets (Agosin 1993:20). In Guatemala, the Mutual Support Group for the Reappearance of Our Sons, Fathers, Husbands and Brothers has engaged in a decades-long struggle to account for the 38,000 people who have disappeared since the late 1970s (Schirmer 1993:40–44). In Argentina, the Madres de la Plaza de Mayo risked and sometimes lost their lives through their courageous efforts to expose their government's widespread human rights violations and efforts to demand punishment for the most egregious offenses, many of which have yet to be prosecuted (Bouvard 1994).

Women's economic and political movements have achieved varying degrees of success. In some cases, their issues and platforms have been adopted by governments or political parties that want women's support; in others, women's demands have been largely ignored or have been addressed symbolically by token gestures intended to mollify them without eliminating the root causes of their problems. Even when they have fallen short of their intended objectives, however, women's movements have profoundly affected their members' lives. In giving women a socially legitimate venue for entering the public arena, these movements have expanded women's horizons and provided them with a sense of personal agency (Chuchryk 1991:163). Women's participation has enabled them to acquire

Susana Ruíz Cerutti (center), former secretary of
state for foreign affairs for Argentina.

organizational skills and to forge social networks that decrease their isolation and augment their decisionmaking power within the household.
Although most women have retained their basic commitment to their roles
as wives and mothers, many have abandoned the submissive, self-sacrificing trappings of *marianismo* and now see themselves as empowered cham-
pions of family welfare. Such changes portend a transformation in gender
roles and relationships that will entail greater autonomy and growing political leadership for subsequent generations of Latin American women.

Conclusion

The last fifty years have brought dramatic changes for Latin American
women. Once symbolically confined to the household and the wife-mother
role, women are increasingly entering the public world of paid employment and political action. Their growing political and labor force participation has resulted from educational advances, declining fertility, and economic and political crises that have threatened the welfare of their
families. This participation also both reflects and further stimulates the
erosion of cultural ideologies that deem public participation to be inconsistent with women's reproductive roles. Women's public activities have
often been legitimated by cultural discourse and by women themselves as
necessary adjuncts to the successful performance of their domestic roles.
In defining wage work and political participation as effective means not
simply for self-fulfillment or needed social change, but also for caring for
their families more effectively, Latin American women are developing
their own unique role definitions that erode the rigid boundary between
private and public life. In forging these new bases for their identities,
Latin American women offer inspiring models for women around the
world.

Notes

1. As Thomas D'Agostino describes in Chapter 4, in 1976, a military junta
overturned a democratically elected government and seized power in Argentina.
During the seven-year dictatorship, the regime conducted a systematic campaign to
eliminate left-wing opposition. Often called the "Dirty War" because it involved
such widespread human rights violations, the campaign began as an effort to quell
the growing guerrilla violence in Argentina and was presented to the public as an
effort to stamp out "subversives" and "terrorists." Yet, while some of the people
who were detained and "disappeared" were political revolutionaries, the vast majority were ordinary Argentine workers, intellectuals, and students who had violated no
laws. Over 30,000 Argentines were imprisoned, tortured, and killed during this peri-

od. The "Dirty War" ended in 1983, when the regime, weakened by its humiliating defeat by the British in the Falklands War and unable to withstand the growing international pressure to eliminate human rights abuses, relinquished power.

2. According to this argument, for a corporation to stay in business in this globalizing era, with countries such as China emerging as industrial giants, nonunion, inexpensive labor power is essential to corporate competitiveness. Proponents of the *maquiladora* industry maintain that it is much better for the U.S. economy for U.S. companies to relocate their manufacturing operations to nearby Mexico, where they can more profitably maintain their links to other U.S. companies that supply manufacturing inputs, than to faraway Asian sites, where manufacturing inputs are apt to be purchased from Asian firms, thus accelerating deindustrialization in the United States (Sklair 1993).

3. Some recent writings suggest that gender roles among the Aztecs may have involved more complementarity and parallelism than previous interpretations would suggest. For a discussion of these alternative perspectives, see Navarro (1999:10).

4. For a firsthand account of the conditions of life and work in São Paulo's early-twentieth-century textile mills, see Veccia (1997:100–146).

5. Reported rates for Honduras in 1961 and 1974 were calculated differently from those reported by other Latin American countries, in a way that underestimates the actual rate of Honduran women's labor force participation. Rather than calculating the rate by comparing the number of wage-earning women to the number of women between the ages of 20 and 60, as did the other countries, the Honduran census compared employed women to the whole female population. This produces a misleading rate, because the relevant comparison should be confined to women of employment age and should not include children, adolescents, and the elderly, who are not normally members of the labor force. Had the Honduran census excluded the youth and the elderly, its rate would have risen by several percentage points, making it more similar to the rate of its neighbor, Guatemala. By 1999, the Honduran census had changed its procedure to make it conform to the rest of the Latin American countries, all of which calculated their rates by comparing employed women to the female population aged 15 and older.

6. Honduras once again provides an exception to this trend, in part because of the way employment rates were calculated, leading to underestimates of men's as well as women's employment.

7. Countries excluded from Table 10.1 because 1960 data were unavailable showed similarly high rates of women's labor force participation during the late 1990s. These include Bolivia (40.5 percent), Cuba (31.7 percent), Dominican Republic (28.3 percent), El Salvador (44.7 percent), and Paraguay (26.1 percent).

8. Latin American country censuses typically measure contraceptive usage only among married women (Chant 2003), although "marriage" is often defined in a way that includes women cohabiting with male partners, regardless of the official status of their union. If sexually active single women were included in these census surveys, the reported use of contraception would likely be much higher.

Bibliography

Agosin, Marjorie. "Introduction." In *Surviving Beyond Fear*, edited by Marjorie Agosin. New York: White Pine Press, 1993, pp. 15–28.
Anderson, Joan, and Martin de la Rosa. "Economic Survival Strategies of Poor

Families on the Mexican Border. " *Journal of Borderlands Studies* 6 (1991):51–68.

Appendini, Kirsten, "'From Where Have All the Flowers Come?' Women Workers in Mexico's Nontraditional Markets." In *Shifting Burdens: Gender and Agrarian Change Under Neoliberalism*, edited by Shahra Razavi. Bloomfield, Conn.: Kumarian Press, 2002, pp. 93–108.

Arizpe, Lourdes. "Women in the Informal Labor Sector." In *Women and National Development*, edited by Wellesley Editorial Committee. Chicago: University of Chicago Press, 1977, pp. 25–37.

———. "An Overview of Women's Education in Latin America and the Caribbean." In *The Politics of Women's Education*, edited by Jill Conway and Susan Bourgue. Ann Arbor: University of Michigan Press, 1993, pp. 171–182.

Bandy, Joe, and Bickham Mendez. "'A Place of Their Own': Women Organizers in the *Maquilas* of Nicaragua and Mexico."*Mobilization: An International Journal* 8, no. 2 (2003):173–188.

Barrientos, Stephanie, Anna Bee, Ann Matear, and Isabel Vogel. *Women and Agribusiness: Working Miracles in the Chilean Fruit Export Sector*. London: MacMillan Press, 1999.

Barrig, Maruja. "The Difficult Equilibrium Between Bread and Roses: Women's Organizations and the Transition from Dictatorship to Democracy in Peru." In *The Women's Movement in Latin America*, edited by Jane Jaquette. Boulder, Colo.: Westview Press, 1991, pp. 114–148.

Barrios de Chungara, Domitila, with Moema Viezzer. *Let Me Speak!* New York: Monthly Review Press, 1978.

Beechey, Veronica. "Women and Production: A Critical Analysis of Some Sociological Theories of Women's Work." In *Feminism and Materialism*, edited by Annette Kuhn and AnnMarie Wolpe. London: Routledge, 1978, pp. 155–197.

Beneria, Lourdes. "The Mexican Debt Crisis: Restructuring the Economy and the Household." In *Unequal Burden: Economic Crises, Persistent Poverty, and Women's Work*, edited by Lourdes Beneria and Shelly Feldman. Boulder, Colo.: Westview Press, 1992, pp. 83–104.

Beneria, Lourdes, and Martha Roldan. *The Crossroads of Class and Gender*. Chicago: University of Chicago Press, 1987.

Bennett, Vivienne. "Gender, Class and Water: Women and the Politics of Water Service in Monterrey, Mexico." *Latin American Perspectives* 22, no. 2 (1995):76–99.

Blumberg, Rae Lesser. "Income Under Female Versus Male Control." In *Gender, Family, and Economy: The Triple Overlap*, edited by Rae Lesser Blumberg. Newbury Park, Calif.: Sage, 1991, pp. 97–127.

Boserup, Ester. *Women's Role in Economic Development*. New York: St. Martin's Press, 1970.

Bouvard, Marguerite Guzman. *Revolutionizing Motherhood: The Mothers of the Plaza de Mayo*. Wilmington, Del.: Scholarly Resources, 1994.

Buenaventura-Posso, Elisa, and Susan E. Brown. "Forced Transition from Egalitarianism to Male Dominance: The Bari of Colombia." In *Women and Colonization: Anthropological Perspectives*, edited by Mona Etienne and Eleanor Leacock. New York: Praeger, 1980, pp. 109–133.

Chant, Sylvia. *Women and Survival in Mexican Cities: Perspectives on Gender, Labour Markets and Low Income Households*. Manchester, UK: Manchester University Press, 1991.

Chant, Sylvia, with Nikki Craske. *Gender in Latin America*. New Brunswick, N.J.: Rutgers University Press, 2003.

Chinchilla, Norma Stoltz. "Gender and National Politics: Issues and Trends in Women's Participation in Latin American Movements." In *Researching Women in Latin America and the Caribbean*, edited by Edna Acosta-Belen and Christine E. Bose. Boulder, Colo.: Westview Press, 1993, pp. 37–54.

Chirot, Daniel. *Social Change in the Twentieth Century*. New York: Harcourt Brace Jovanovich, 1977.

Chuchryk, Patricia. "Feminist Anti-Authoritarian Politics: The Role of Women's Organizations in the Chilean Transition to Democracy." In *The Women's Movement in Latin America*, edited by Jane Jaquette. Boulder, Colo.: Westview Press, 1991, pp. 149–184.

———. "Subversive Mothers: The Women's Opposition to the Military Regime in Chile." In *Surviving Beyond Fear*, edited by Marjorie Agosin. New York: White Pine Press, 1993, pp. 86–97.

Cockroft, James. *Mexico: Class Formation, Capital Accumulation, and the State*. New York: Monthly Review Press, 1983.

Cravey, Altha J. *Women and Work in Mexico's Maquiladoras*. Lanham, Md.: Rowman & Littlefield, 1998.

Cusicanqui, Silvia Rivera. "Indigenous Women and Community Resistance: History and Memory." In *Women and Change in Latin America*, edited by Elizabeth Jelin. London: Zed Books, 1990, pp. 151–183.

Economic Commission for Latin America and the Caribbean (ECLAC). *The Decade for Women in Latin America and the Caribbean: Background and Prospects*. Santiago: United Nations, 1988.

Etienne, Mona, and Eleanor Leacock. "Introduction." In *Women and Colonization: Anthropological Perspectives*, edited by Mona Etienne and Eleanor Leacock. New York: Praeger, 1980, pp. 1–24.

Fernandez-Kelly, Maria Patricia. *For We Are Sold: I and My People*. Albany: State University of New York Press, 1983.

Fuentes, Annette, and Barbara Ehrenreich. *Women in the Global Factory*. New York: South End Press, 1983.

Gailey, Christina Ward. "Evolutionary Perspectives on Gender Hierarchy." In *Analyzing Gender: A Handbook of Social Science Research*, edited by Beth Hess and Myra Marx Ferree. Newbury Park, Calif.: Sage, 1987, pp. 22–67.

Gregory, Peter. *The Myth of Market Failure*. Baltimore: Johns Hopkins University Press, 1986.

Jaquette, Jane. "Conclusion: Women and the New Democratic Politics." In *The Women's Movement in Latin America*, edited by Jane Jaquette. Boulder, Colo.: Westview Press, 1991a, pp. 185–208.

———. "Introduction." In *The Women's Movement in Latin America*, edited by Jane Jaquette. Boulder, Colo.: Westview Press, 1991b, pp. 1–17.

Jelin, Elizabeth. "Citizenship and Identity: Final Reflections." In *Women and Change in Latin America*, edited by Elizabeth Jelin. London: Zed Books, 1990, pp. 184–207.

Klubock, Thomas Miller. "Morality and Good Habits: The Construction of Gender and Class in the Chilean Copper Mines, 1904–1951." In *The Gendered Worlds of Latin American Women Workers*, edited by John D. French and Daniel James. Durham, N.C.: Duke University Press, 1997, pp. 232–263.

Korrol, Virginia Sánchez. "Women in Nineteenth- and Twentieth-Century Latin America and the Caribbean." In *Women in Latin America and the Caribbean:*

Restoring Women to History, edited by Marysa Navarro and Virginia Sánchez Korrol. Bloomington: Indiana University Press, 1999, pp. 59–106.

Larguia, Isabel, and John Dumoulin. "Women's Equality and the Cuban Revolution." In *Women and Change in Latin America*, edited by June Nash and Helen Safa. South Hadley, Mass.: Bergin and Garvey, 1986, pp. 344–368.

Levenson-Estrada, Deborah. "The Loneliness of Working-Class Feminism: Women in the 'Male World' of Labor Unions, Guatemala City, 1970s." In *The Gendered Worlds of Latin American Women Workers*, edited by John D. French and Daniel James. Durham, N.C.: Duke University Press, 1997, pp. 208–231.

Lustig, Nora. *Mexico: The Remaking of an Economy*. Washington, D.C.: Brookings Institution Press, 1992.

Macias, Anna. *Against All Odds: The Feminist Movement in Mexico to 1940*. Westport, Conn.: Greenwood Press, 1982.

Miller, Francesca. *Latin American Women and the Search for Social Justice*. Hanover, N.H.: University Press of New England, 1991.

Nash, June. "Aztec Women: The Transition from Status to Class in Empire and Colony." In *Women and Colonization: Anthropological Perspectives*, edited by Mona Etienne and Eleanor Leacock. New York: Praeger, 1980, pp. 134–148.

———. "The Impact of the Changing International Division of Labor on Different Sectors of the Labor Force." In *Women, Men and the International Division of Labor*, edited by June Nash and Maria Patricia Fernandez-Kelly. Albany: State University of New York Press, 1983, pp. 3–38.

Navarro, Marysa. "Women in Pre-Columbian and Colonial Latin America and the Caribbean." In *Women in Latin America and the Caribbean: Restoring Women to History*, edited by Marysa Navarro and Virginia Sánchez Korrol. Bloomington: Indiana University Press, 1999, pp. 5–57.

Perelli, Carina. "Putting Conservatism to Good Use: Women and Unorthodox Politics in Uruguay, from Breakdown to Transition." In *The Women's Movement in Latin America*, edited by Jane Jaquette. Boulder, Colo.: Westview Press, 1991, pp. 95–113.

Pires de Rio Caldeira, Teresa. "Women, Daily Life and Politics." In *Women and Change in Latin America*, edited by Elizabeth Jelin. London: Zed Books, 1990, pp. 47–78.

Psacharopoulos, George, and Zafiris Tzannatos. *Case Studies on Women's Employment and Pay in Latin America: Overview and Methodology*. Washington, D.C.: World Bank, 1992.

Rothstein, Frances. *Three Different Worlds: Women, Men, and Children in an Industrializing Community*. Westport, Conn.: Greenwood Press, 1982.

Ruiz, Vicki. "Mexican Women and the Multinationals: The Packaging of the Border Industrialization Program." Prepared for the Historical Perspectives on American Labor Conference, Ithaca, New York, 1988.

Safa, Helen. "Women's Social Movements in Latin America," *Gender and Society* 4, no. 3 (1990):354–369.

———. *The Myth of the Male Breadwinner: Women and Industrialization in the Caribbean*. Boulder, Colo.: Westview Press, 1995.

Saffioti, Heleieth. "Female Labor and Capitalism in the United States and Brazil." In *Women Cross-Culturally: Change and Challenge*, edited by Ruby Rohrlich-Leavitt. The Hague: Mouton, 1975, pp. 59–94.

Schirmer, Jennifer. "'Those Who Die for Life Cannot Be Called Dead': Women and Human Rights Protest in Latin America." In *Surviving Beyond Fear*, edited by Marjorie Agosin. New York: White Pine Press, 1993, pp. 31–57.

Schmink, Marianne. "Women and Urban Industrial Development in Brazil." In *Women and Change in Latin America*, edited by June Nash and Helen Safa. South Hadley, Mass.: Bergin and Garvey, 1986, pp. 136–164.

Scott, Katherine. "Women in the Labor Force in Bolivia: Participation and Earnings." In *Case Studies on Women's Employment and Pay in Latin America*, edited by George Psacharopoulos and Zafiris Tzannatos. Washington, D.C.: World Bank, 1992, pp. 21–38.

Silverblatt, Irene. "'The Universe Has Turned Inside Out . . . There Is No Justice for Us Here': Andean Women Under Spanish Rule." In *Women and Colonization: Anthropological Perspectives*, edited by Mona Etienne and Eleanor Leacock. New York: Praeger, 1980, pp. 149–185.

Sklair, Leslie. *Assembling for Development: The Maquila Industry in Mexico and the United States*. San Diego, Calif.: Center for U.S.-Mexican Studies, 1993.

Stevens, Evelyn. "Marianismo: The Other Face of Machismo in Latin America." In *Female and Male in Latin America*, edited by Ann Pescatello. Pittsburgh: University of Pittsburgh Press, 1973, pp. 89–102.

Stromquist, Nelly. *Women and Education in Latin America*. Boulder, Colo.: Lynne Rienner Publishers, 1992.

Tiano, Susan. "The Public-Private Dichotomy: Theoretical Perspectives on Women in Development." *Social Science Journal* 21 (1984):13–28.

———. "Gender, Work, and World Capitalism: Third World Women's Role in Development." In *Analyzing Gender: A Handbook of Social Science Research*, edited by Beth Hess and Myra Marx Ferree. Newbury Park, Calif.: Sage, 1987, pp. 216–243.

———. *Patriarchy on the Line: Labor, Gender, and Ideology in the Mexican Maquila Industry*. Philadelphia: Temple University Press, 1994.

———. "Feminization or Marginalization? The Changing Gender Composition of the *Maquila* Work Force Along the U.S.-Mexico Border." In *Border Women in Movement: Politics, Migration, and Identity at the U.S.-Mexico Border*, edited by Ellen Hansen and Doreen Mattingly. Tucson: University of Arizona Press, 1999.

Tiano, Susan, and Carolina Ladino. "Dating, Mating, and Motherhood: Identity Construction Among Mexican Maquila Workers." *Environment and Planning A* 31, no. 2 (1999):305–325.

Towner, Margaret. "Monopoly Capitalism and Women's Work During the Porfiriato." In *Women in Latin America*, edited by William Bollinger et al. Riverside, Calif.: Latin American Perspectives, 1979, pp. 47–62.

United Nations. *The World's Women 1970–1990: Trends and Statistics*. New York: United Nations, 1991.

Vaughan, Mary. "Women, Class, and Education in Mexico, 1880–1928." In *Women in Latin America*, edited by William Bollinger et al. Riverside, Calif.: Latin American Perspectives, 1979, pp. 63–80.

Veccia, Theresa R. "'My Duty as a Woman': Gender Ideology, Work, and Working-Class Women's Lives in São Paulo, Brazil, 1900–1950." In *The Gendered Worlds of Latin American Women Workers*, edited by John D. French and Daniel James. Durham, N.C.: Duke University Press, 1997.

Wilkie, James (ed.). *Statistical Abstract of Latin America*, Vol. 38. Los Angeles: UCLA Latin American Center Publications, 2002.

Education and Development

*Robert F. Arnove, Stephen Franz,
and Kimberly Morse Cordova*

The integral relationship between education and development has recently gained recognition.[1] Throughout the history of Latin America, education has functioned largely to maintain the status quo and to serve purposes determined by colonial powers or state authorities and elite groups. René de la Pedraja and Thomas D'Agostino point out in Chapters 3 and 4 that these purposes often ran counter to the interests of the majority.

During the colonial period, as Michael Fleet shows in Chapter 12, education served primarily to propagate the Catholic religion. Also, a small number of civil servants were trained to administer the Spanish and Portuguese empires. Following the various wars of independence (1810–1825) that liberated South and Central America from foreign rule, education was called upon to help create a sense of nationhood in newly emergent states. In countries such as Argentina, Chile, and Uruguay, which received large influxes of immigrants from Europe in the latter half of the nineteenth century, education—very much as in the United States—was used by state authorities to forge national unity. Kevin Yelvington discusses the influence of immigrants in Chapter 9.

Although education was viewed by many nineteenth-century policymakers and educators, such as Domingo Faustino Sarmiento of Argentina and Andres Bello of Venezuela, as a "civilizing" influence in the creation of citizens, the notion of mass-based public education systems available to all, from preprimary through higher education, remained an elusive goal up to the second half of the twentieth century. Formal education systems primarily served and benefited the children of the wealthy and powerful, particularly urban males. This largely but not totally changed in the period following World War II.

Beginning in the 1950s, social scientists and national governments began to view education in a different light. The principal shift in focus was from a concern with the political role of education in nation-state building to its economic role in contributing to the industrialization and technological development of a society. In the context of economic development, investigated in greater detail by Richard Harper and Alfred Cuzán in Chapter 6, schooling was viewed as a principal agency for teaching the knowledge, values, and attitudes that would modernize a society and undergird an industrial economy. Discussions of expenditures on public education as an investment in "human capital" or in the improvement of the skills of individuals that would contribute significantly to the economic growth of a country appeared in the work of economists, for example, Nobel laureate Theodore Schultz (1964). Previously, education had been viewed as a social service expenditure or as "consumption" that did not contribute to the total output of goods and services of a society as measured by the gross national product (GNP).

From the 1950s on, the notion of "development" emerged as a priority goal to be pursued by all governments in the so-called Third World, as did the idea that education was the key that could open the door to the modernization and development of societies (Coleman 1965). As this chapter points out, ideas of development have evolved, as have views concerning the role of education in sociopolitical change and economic growth.

Changing Notions of Development

In the post–World War II period, definitions of the term "development" passed through at least three stages (Fuenzalida 1985). During the first stage, development was defined primarily in terms of the expansion of an economy, of growth in the GNP of a country—which, in turn, was heavily dependent on acquiring the advanced scientific and technological knowledge of the industrialized countries of the North. By the end of the 1960s, a second stage emerged in which development was viewed not only in terms of the expansion of the productive capacity of a country but also with regard to (1) the more equitable distribution of the expanded output of goods and services and (2) the democratic participation of the majority of citizens in decisions concerning the direction and nature of change. During this stage, attention was also given to the notion of preserving national culture and safeguarding the political sovereignty of a country. As Susan Place and Jacqueline Chase show in Chapter 8, development was further defined in the 1970s (the third stage) to incorporate respect for the environment and the conservation of nonrenewable natural resources, as well as more equitable relations between the countries of the South and those of the North.

In the 1980s, further elaboration of the definition of development included the notion of sustainability, that institutional arrangements should be in place that guaranteed a country could continue to maintain progressive reforms to benefit a majority of its people. Closely coupled with an emphasis on sustainability was a concern with providing local communities and grassroots organizations with the skills and resources that would enable them to initiate and successfully implement efforts that would improve the health, education, and general well-being of the least privileged members of society.

As international definitions of development changed, so did conceptions of the role of education in society. The goals of education from 1950 to 1970 tended to emphasize the importance of technology and the sciences in national development. Attention was given more to the quality of education than to equality of educational opportunity, and higher education was emphasized. By 1970, it was evident that the goals of national development were better served by expanding access to schooling and democratizing opportunities for previously excluded populations to advance to the highest levels of education. In the 1970s and early 1980s, governments accorded priority to the provision of primary education and the first years of secondary education, as well as to literacy and adult basic education. The international debt crisis of the 1980s and 1990s, however, hampered many Latin American countries from achieving these goals. In recent years, the notion of efficiency has achieved preeminence, and policies have begun to emphasize the decentralization and privatization of education systems. Hence, higher education and adult education do not enjoy the priority they were given in previous decades.

Education and Technology

The transfer of technology, scientific institutions, and industry to underdeveloped countries requires the development of educational infrastructure capable of supporting the new technologies, sciences, and organizations. Secondary education, vocational education, and higher education are particularly important in this transformation.[2]

For his New Frontier policy, President John F. Kennedy adopted the growth theories of the 1950s, combined them with a new emphasis on sustained economic development in democratic societies, and empowered the United States Agency for International Development (USAID) to implement the plan—which has served as the principal model for development agencies worldwide. In Latin America, USAID sponsored community development programs that emphasized technical education in Brazil, Chile, the Dominican Republic, Ecuador, El Salvador, Honduras, Mexico, Panama, and Venezuela.

Latin America responded to the new emphasis on technical education with the Santiago Conference in 1962. Latin American education ministers, along with officials from the United Nations, attempted to respond to two fundamental questions: (1) How can economic development contribute to the improvement of educational systems, and (2) How can educational systems accelerate economic and social development in Latin America? The ministers believed the answers to these questions could be found in the development of secondary and higher education, technical and professional training, and improved teacher education.

During the 1960s, enrollments at the secondary and higher education levels increased significantly worldwide. Expansion of the Latin American secondary and higher education systems exceeded that of all other developing areas of the world. For example, between 1975 and 1985, enrollments at the secondary level in all developing areas increased from 31.4 percent to 37.6 percent, whereas in Latin America the secondary education sector expanded from 36.9 percent to 51.1 percent. Growth in enrollments in higher education during that period was even more significant. In all developing areas, higher education enrollments increased from 4.1 percent to 6.1 percent; in Latin America, enrollments increased from 11.8 percent to 15.6 percent. Between 1960 and 1970, enrollment in secondary education more than doubled, and enrollment in higher education almost tripled (see Table 11.1).

Enrollments in vocational education programs also increased in the 1960s. The cases of Brazil and Colombia are notable. In 1965 in Brazil, 380,459 students were enrolled in vocational programs; in 1971, that number rose to 797,487 students. Expansion of vocational education in

Students in a secondary school biology class in Kingston, Jamaica.

Table 11.1 Enrollment Numbers (in thousands) and Percentages (of total enrollment) by Level in Latin America, 1960 and 1970

Level	1960	1970
Primary		
Number	26,799	43,913
Percent	85.3	78.0
Secondary		
Number	4,053	10,800
Percent	12.9	19.2
Higher		
Number	570	1,615
Percent	1.8	2.9

Source: UN Educational, Scientific, and Cultural Organization, *Statistical Yearbook, 1974* (Paris: UNESCO, 1974), tables 2.1 and 2.2.

Table 11.2 Percentage of Total Public Education Expenditure by Level in Five Latin American Countries, 1965 and 1970

Country	Primary	Secondary	Higher
Argentina			
1965	55.0	26.4	18.6
1970	30.4	30.3	21.0
Ecuador			
1965	41.3	21.1	32.3
1970	45.9	41.1	9.9
Mexico			
1965	42.0	12.3	12.6
1970	50.0	27.2	10.4
Uruguay			
1965	44.9	39.8	15.3
1970	45.1	30.4	19.0
Venezuela			
1965	43.2	18.2	19.7
1970	38.3	20.6	25.5

Source: UN Educational, Scientific, and Cultural Organization, *Statistical Yearbook, 1974* (Paris: UNESCO, 1974), table 6.3.
Note: The figures do not add up to 100 percent because administrative expenses, adult education, and preprimary education costs are not included.

Colombia was also considerable, increasing from 96,834 students in 1965 to 173,737 in 1972.

Increases in educational expenditures paralleled the growth of school enrollments. These increases in expenditure, however, were not uniform at secondary and higher education levels. Some countries chose to invest heavily in secondary (including vocational) education, whereas others emphasized higher education (see Table 11.2).

As evidenced in Tables 11.1 and 11.2, enrollments and expenditures expanded at the secondary and higher education levels at the expense of the primary level. Between 1960 and 1970, total enrollments at the primary level, as a percentage of total enrollment, dropped from 85.3 percent to 78.0 percent. This means that a greater number of students were going on to higher levels, and not all students were concentrated at the primary level. Decreases were most apparent in Argentina, where total government expenditures for primary education dropped from 55.0 percent in 1965 to 30.4 percent in 1970.

Social scientists, however, also argued that the implementation of educational policies favoring technical, secondary, and higher education benefited only a small segment of the total population, thus widening the gap between the rich and the poor. They further argued that policies emphasizing technical, secondary, and higher education in the 1960s had limited participation by most of the population in the decisionmaking process, because decisions were made by government bureaucrats and outside technical advisers.

Finally, critics were concerned that material presented in vocational education programs was not relevant to local realities and that the equipment provided was outdated. Furthermore, curricula employed in rural areas had an urban bias. Generally, textbooks at all levels often presented images associated with a U.S. middle-class lifestyle that was unfamiliar to Latin American students.

By the early 1970s, Latin American education ministers began to discuss these and other issues related to the changing emphasis in the region's education. At the 1971 conference at Caraballeda, Venezuela, these ministers expressed concern with the growing economic disparities between socioeconomic classes. They recognized that those who benefited most were the children of middle-class families and not children whose parents were members of the working class.

Expanding Educational Opportunities

In light of these concerns, Latin American policy planners shifted emphasis away from technical education toward universal access to primary education and literacy. At a 1979 regional meeting of Latin American education ministers, participants developed the Principal Project for Latin America and the Caribbean. The objectives of the project redefined the goals of development and education: to extend compulsory basic education from eight to ten years, to eliminate illiteracy, and to improve the quality of basic education (Reimers 1991).

During the early 1980s, Latin American nations made some progress toward achieving these goals. Some nations extended basic compulsory education to nine or ten years, among them Costa Rica, El Salvador, Panama, and Venezuela. These efforts to expand access to education were closely related to increasing governmental expenditures. In 1980, a number of Latin American governments spent as much as 6 percent of their GNP on education (UNESCO 1993:table 4.1). By 1990, however, only eight of twenty Latin American nations had extended compulsory basic education to at least eight years, compared to six nations in 1985.

Among the most impressive achievements of the Principal Project were the gains made in the fight against illiteracy. During the 1980s, numerous Latin American countries sponsored literacy programs directed at illiterate adult populations, including Argentina, Chile, Colombia, Ecuador, Venezuela, El Salvador, Nicaragua, Panama, Cuba, Mexico, and the Dominican Republic. Most notable were the efforts of Cuba and Nicaragua, where accomplishments in extending literacy occurred in the midst of social and political revolutions.

In Cuba after 1959, a key element of Fidel Castro's revolution was the extension of social services to all sectors of the population. Education, including literacy, was seen as essential to the development of a socialist society in which every citizen had a moral responsibility to foster the country's development. By the end of the Cold War in 1989, the literacy rate in Cuba had reached 97 percent, one of the highest in the world.

Similarly, Nicaragua's Sandinista revolution in 1980 included a crusade against illiteracy as one of the key tenets of its social project. The crusade, undertaken during the social and economic turmoil of the initial months of the revolution, reduced the illiteracy rate from 50 percent to less than 25 percent in only nine months. The size of the campaign, the speed with which it was conducted, the difficult conditions under which it was pursued, and its impressive results mark the Nicaraguan literacy crusade as one of the most striking campaigns ever attempted.

By the late 1980s, despite international goals to improve the quality of basic education and despite increased spending by Latin American countries, it was evident that little had been accomplished in expanding access to educational opportunities. Unfortunately, the goals of the Principal Project (universal primary schooling, universal literacy, and improved educational quality) had not been tackled jointly. Critics began to realize that the three goals had to be pursued simultaneously to achieve significant results. Further, various literacy programs and campaigns had defined literacy differently. Some definitions were age based, others included math skills, others evaluated reading and writing ability, and others were based on the number of years in school. It became apparent that all programs had to function under the same definitions. Without a clear understanding of the scope of the problem in Latin America, it was difficult for planners to develop, implement, and evaluate programs designed to eradicate illiteracy (Torres 1990).

Throughout Latin America in 1960, less than 60 percent of primary school–age children were enrolled; in 1999, 92 percent were enrolled. Currently, approximately 82 percent of students throughout the region have completed six years of primary education. However, several Latin American countries lag behind. In Bolivia, Colombia, the Dominican Republic, El Salvador, and Nicaragua 40 percent or more of children failed to reach grade five. Repetition rates—direct indicators of educational quality—remained high despite educators' attempts to advance students to the next grade more consistently (see Table 11.3). Overall, the first-grade repetition rate for Latin America was 42 percent at the beginning of the 1990s. Currently, the repetition rate for Latin America for first through sixth grades is 16.4 percent (Wolff, Schiefelbein, and Schiefelbein 2002). The rate is as high as 42 percent for Brazil (Arnove et al. 2003). Repetition of students costs an estimated $4.6 billion per year (Wolff and de Moura Castro 2003).

Repetition rates were even higher among at-risk students living under difficult conditions, such as in urban slums and isolated rural areas. According to Laurance Wolff and colleagues (1994), students from the lowest socioeconomic stratum were more likely to repeat a grade than children in higher-income brackets. Those living in rural areas and members of indigenous populations were even more likely to repeat a grade than their urban counterparts. For example, in Chile, the highest repetition rates corresponded to the province with the largest indigenous population. Similarly, indigenous children in Bolivia were twice as likely to repeat as nonindigenous children. In many cases, indigenous children also have more difficulties because the language spoken at home may not be the same as the language of instruction. Rates of repetition for females tended to be lower than those for males. Data for the period 1990–1996 indicate that in not one single country did the repetition rates of girls exceed those of males (see Table 11.3).

Other factors contributing to the lack of progress in attempts to improve the quality of education were low teacher salaries, short school years, lack of textbooks, dilapidated schools, and high seasonal absenteeism associated with agricultural activity. These conditions were especially characteristic of students living in impoverished or marginalized circumstances.

Also contributing to low student retention and promotion rates are requirements in many Latin American countries that students pass standardized national examinations before proceeding to the next level of education.

Table 11.3   Latin American Repetition and Completion Rates in Primary Education and Male/Female Enrollment Ratios in Secondary Education, by Percentage

	First-Grade Repeaters, 1994–1996	Primary Entrants Reaching Grade 5, 1990–1995	Secondary Enrollment Ratio, 1990–1996	
			M	F
Argentina	9	—	73	81
Bolivia	3	60	40	34
Brazil	23	71	—	—
Chile	5	92	66	73
Colombia	12	58	62	72
Costa Rica	19	89	48	52
Cuba	0	94	78	82
Dominican Republic	—	58	34	47
Ecuador	6	77	50	50
El Salvador	12	58	30	34
Guatemala	27	—	25	23
Honduras	23	60	29	37
Mexico	11	84	58	59
Nicaragua	26	54	43	50
Panama	—	82	60	65
Paraguay	16	71	72	67
Peru	27	—	72	67
Uruguay	19	94	74	89
Venezuela	16	78	29	41
Latin America	15	74	51	55

Sources: UN Educational, Scientific, and Cultural Organization, *Statistical Yearbook, 1998* (Paris: UNESCO, 1998), table 3.6; UN Educational, Scientific, and Cultural Organization, *State of the World's Children, 1999* (Paris: UNESCO, 1999), pp. 106–109.

Because of the disparity in the quality of education between rural and urban areas, many rural students—as well as students who attend inferior urban schools—fail to pass these examinations and either drop out or repeat the same grade. This pattern is evident from the beginning of primary school. For example, in Brazil, El Salvador, Honduras, and Nicaragua, 71 percent or fewer students who enrolled in first grade completed fifth grade at the end of the 1990s (see Table 11.3). Data indicate that these dropouts are heavily concentrated in rural areas.

As stated previously, important urban/rural differences exist in equality of educational opportunities and outcomes. According to Muñiz (2000), 60 percent of 14-year-olds in rural Mexico are attending school, compared with 84 percent for the same age group attending schools in urban areas. These figures become more disparate for 15- and 16-year-olds. Attendance

Schoolgirls in a classroom in Lota, Chile.

figures for 15- and 16-year-olds in rural areas are 41 percent and 29 percent; in urban areas, these figures are 69 percent and 61 percent, respectively (Muñiz 2000).

Rural/urban completion rates are also disparate for Nicaragua and El Salvador. In 1999, 84 percent of urban Nicaraguan children completed primary education, whereas only 61 percent of rural children did so (PREAL 2001). In El Salvador, 92 percent of urban primary students completed the sixth grade, compared with 77 percent of rural children.

■ Education and the Debt Crisis

Latin America's inability to improve the quality of basic education in the 1980s was exacerbated by the region's debt crisis. As Richard Harper and Alfred Cuzán point out in Chapter 6, the 1980s have been termed the lost decade for development in Latin America. Economic expansion, experienced at high rates from the 1950s through the 1970s, slowed considerably in the 1980s and 1990s. In the 1960s, the average annual GNP growth rate for Latin American economies was 5.7 percent. In the 1970s, the average growth rate was 5.6 percent, despite difficulties caused by the oil crisis. By the 1980s, the average annual GNP growth rate for Latin American countries had dropped to 1.3 percent.[3] The falling GNP translated into decreasing per capita income for the majority of Latin Americans. On average, Latin American per capita incomes fell by 9 percent. In

Argentina, per capita income fell 22 percent, whereas in Brazil it fell only 5 percent.

In response to the ever-deepening economic crisis, during the 1990s most Latin American governments adopted the neoliberal fiscal stabilization and economic adjustment policies promoted by international donor agencies such as the International Monetary Fund (IMF) and the World Bank. These policies have led to a drastic reduction in the state's role in social spending, deregulation of the economy, and liberalization of import policies. The educational counterparts of these policies have included moves to decentralize and privatize public school systems.

Although neoliberal policies are designed to reduce a country's fiscal deficits and external debt while bringing inflation under control, they have also contributed to deepening poverty in the region. In many countries, the social safety net provided by government-subsidized services in health, education, and other basic areas has been removed. Consequently, social class differences have intensified. In the 1980s in metropolitan Buenos Aires, 25 percent of the poorest households lost 15 percent of their incomes, whereas 5 percent of the richest households increased their incomes by almost 20 percent. In the metropolitan areas of Rio de Janeiro and São Paulo, 25 percent of the poorest households lost almost 13 percent of their incomes, whereas 5 percent of the richest gained approximately 25 percent. Income losses were not only experienced by the poorest of the poor; 50 percent of the households located in the middle of the scale lost between 3 percent and 10 percent of their incomes.

As a result, in Latin America, class structures have become more polarized, with the rich and poor sectors separated by an increasingly wider gap. Between 1996 and 1998, the poorest 20 percent received less than 3 percent of incomes, while the top 20 percent received from 61 percent to 64 percent of total incomes (UNESCO 2001).

A salient illustration of this disparity is that, in 1994, forty-two of the world's 358 billionaires resided in Latin America and commanded total personal wealth of U.S.$73 billion. Mexico, with twenty-four billionaires, not only led all Latin American countries but was exceeded only by the United States, Japan, and Germany in total number of super-rich individuals (Button 1994). Although figures for 2002 are less dramatic, twelve of the 497 wealthiest individuals were Mexicans, one of whom was the richest man in Latin America and the seventeenth-richest individual worldwide (*Business Mexico* 2002).

Not only have the numbers of the poor increased and income disparities grown, but the structural adjustment policies have not lessened the debt of many countries in the region. For example, in 1995, Nicaragua's external debt was six times the size of its GNP with no prospect of being able to pay it off (UNICEF 1999). Many countries are spending more and more on debt reduction to the detriment of education.

With the economic downturn, all Latin American nations have experienced decreases in educational expenditures in terms of GNP and total governmental expenditure (TGE). For example, in Ecuador both the GNP and the TGE were cut drastically, with education's percentage of the GNP falling from 5.6 percent in 1980 to 3.5 percent in 1996. The percentage of TGE fell from 33.3 percent to 13.0 percent for the same time period (UNESCO 1998:table 4.1). In 1998, education percentages of the GDP and TGE for Guatemala, the Dominican Republic, and Uruguay, respectively, were 1.8 and 17.0, 2.2 and 13.8, and 2.5 and 12.2 (UNESCO 2001).

Under neoliberalism, significant improvements in education spending that took place during the 1960s and 1970s were effectively negated by drastic spending cuts in education. According to Fernando Reimers (1991:332), "On average, [unweighted] per capita expenditures in education in Latin America increased by 4.29 percent per year between 1975 and 1980, while they decreased by 6.14 percent between 1980 and 1985. The progress in educational finance made in the seventies was undone in the eighties."

For example, in Bolivia between 1975 and 1980, per capita expenditure on education increased at an annual rate of 3.62 percent. But between 1980 and 1985, that figure decreased at an annual rate of 42.03 percent (Reimers 1991:323).

The spending cuts in education in Latin America first affected recurrent expenditures, such as the purchase of teaching materials and the maintenance of school buildings. Because of the lack of funding, reforms designed in the 1970s and early 1980s were not implemented. Thus, in the late 1980s and early 1990s, teachers were working from curricula developed in the 1960s and with pedagogy designed to confront the challenges of the 1960s classroom.

Decreased expenditures, outdated pedagogies and curricula, and restricted access all contributed to the general decline in the quality of education. Low teachers' salaries were also a factor. The real value of teachers' salaries decreased steadily, as currencies were devalued and inflation increased during the economic turmoil of the 1980s and 1990s. In many Latin American nations, teachers are paid little more than domestic employees, and in Nicaragua, teachers receive even less.

Despite claims that teachers, given their long vacations and short work days, actually are paid relatively better than workers with similar qualifications, many are unable to support their families. In no country of Latin America do teachers' salaries exceed 60 percent of total family salary. The percentage ranges from a high of 56 percent in Costa Rica to a low of 20 percent in Paraguay. The percentage of teachers living in homes classified as "poor" or "vulnerable" by the Program for Educational Reform in Latin America (PREAL) generally was lower than that of comparable professional and technical workers in Bolivia, Brazil, Chile, Ecuador, and Paraguay (PREAL 2001). According to Organization for Economic Cooperation and Development (OECD) data, teachers in Argentina, Mexico, Brazil, and Uruguay receive salaries that are less than one-half of those earned by teachers in industrially developed countries (OECD 2000).

In recent years, many teachers have left the profession for higher-paying jobs. The exodus of teachers and the weeks and months of classroom time lost due to strikes have intensified already difficult circumstances in most Latin American classrooms. Overcrowded classrooms and the lack of up-to-date textbooks further added to the educational problems caused by the debt crisis.

By the late 1980s, it was evident to education ministers in Latin America that the deepening debt crisis would limit future funding. As a result, many ministries began to pursue other sources of revenue. One major source was to charge user fees to parents for their children's education. Another policy involved shifting a number of administrative responsibilities, including the financing of education, to departmental and municipal levels of education. These two policies (privatization and decentralization) are methods favored by the World Bank and the IMF for improving educational efficiency. Countries seeking access to international credit were obligated to implement such policies in education as they had in other social services. As Edward Berman (1992:69) has noted, "[Donor agencies] have advocated a decrease in the amount of government involvement in the education process, an increase in the private sector's role, and greater application of market principles to the organization of Third World educational systems."

Privatization and Decentralization

Privatization is the investment of private money into previously public institutions. It involves either charging user fees in public schools for services that were previously free of charge or converting some public institutions into private institutions. Privatization became more widespread in the educational sector because education budgets endured drastic cuts in the 1980s.

Carlos Torres and Adriana Puiggrós (1995) note that levying new fees for previously free services, such as textbooks, entrance examinations, and salaries for teachers in special subjects like computer applications, further restricts lower-class access to education. Students from marginalized sectors of society had previously benefited from services such as these that are not readily available outside the educational setting. Fees for educational services are a particular burden for poor families, because they have become even more impoverished as a consequence of recently initiated structural adjustment policies. In some cases, poverty-stricken families are unable to send their children to school because they cannot afford textbook rental fees, monthly tuition charges, or the purchase of a required uniform. In other instances, they may be induced to send their children to school for a free glass of milk or school lunch, which provides the only nutrition they are likely to receive.

In response to budget cuts, education ministries have also promoted the development and accreditation of private education institutions (primary, secondary, and higher education). Middle- and upper-class students have been particularly attracted to these institutions because they offer smaller classes, better facilities, and instruction in subject areas that address the market's demand for graduates in business administration and engineering.

Middle- and upper-class parents' ability to send their children to private schools has had adverse effects on public schools. Removing middle-class parents from the public school system eliminates the most vocal advocates for quality in the schools. The lower classes, although constituting the majority of the population, lack the economic clout necessary to promote quality in the public school system (Arnove, Franz, and Morse 1996). As a result, many public school systems have suffered from funding inadequacies.

In response to the debt crisis, the other primary reform pursued by Latin American education ministries has been administrative decentralization. In most Latin American countries, central education ministries have controlled all aspects of the educative process—for example, curriculum development, pedagogy, financing, and evaluation. Given this situation, decentralization is perceived as a positive governmental reform that grants more power to local authorities. Argentina (1976), Mexico (1978), Chile (1981), and Colombia (1986) have pursued decentralization programs, in which municipalities have been delegated the responsibility of administering school funding and curriculum development. For example, in Chile, which UNICEF (1999) considers to be a successful model of decentralization, municipalities are given a percentage of necessary funds and are responsible for paying the balance of educational costs.

A key element of decentralization theory is the belief that local decisionmaking will lead to superior schools. Proponents believe decentralization will result in curricula and pedagogies that are tailored to local needs and that streamlining a cumbersome bureaucracy will promote efficiency and cost-effectiveness. Attaching national subsidies to indicators of school efficiency, such as attendance rates, and school effectiveness, such as achievement scores, should contribute to improving the poor promotion and retention rates that have characterized Latin American education systems.

Market mechanisms are common components of decentralization policies. Competition for students, for instance, is seen as a means to improve the quality of educational offerings. The idea is that superior schools will attract more students and thereby increase funding capacity.

Competition in educational markets, however, has its downside. Although decentralization and market-driven policies are feasible in middle-class areas, they present serious problems for the residents of rural communities and marginalized urban areas. First, these areas are often unable to finance educational programs that are not funded by government subsidies. Second, residents in these areas often lack access to the information needed to make decisions regarding the market-driven elements of such educational reforms. Furthermore, standardized test scores in Spanish and mathematics do not indicate significant improvement in educational quality, especially for disadvantaged populations. On the contrary, in Chile after decentralization, results of Spanish and mathematics tests in 1982 and 1988 showed a 14 percent and a 6 percent decline, respectively. Moreover, the disparity between the highest test scores in private schools and the lowest test scores in high-risk municipal schools increased for this time period (Prawda 1993).

In 1993, Nicaragua implemented a decentralization program at the local school level that equates educational efficiency with high student-to-teacher ratios. As with Chile's program, the Nicaraguan Ministry of Education's plan allots extra funds to schools that increase their efficiency. Nicaragua's program emphasizes reduced dropout rates, thereby increasing the number of students in the classrooms. There is nothing particularly innovative about the program, however, in the areas of curriculum and pedagogy. In fact, any attempt to introduce more student-centered, inquiry-oriented pedagogy appears unlikely, if not impossible, considering the Ministry of Education's emphasis on a minimum of forty-five students per classroom as an indicator of efficiency (Arnove 1995).

Recent policies that diminish the role of the state in education and encourage users to pay the costs of their education have also affected higher education, as well as adult basic education programs, throughout Latin America. These policies in particular have generated tensions within higher education, which is considered the level of education most critically related to national development.

Higher Education

Despite their long-standing belief in the significance of higher education, in recent years international donor agencies such as the World Bank and the International Monetary Fund have accorded lower priority to public funding of higher educational systems than to primary education. The reason for this policy is that economic analyses suggest that the best investment for a country in terms of "rates of return" is primary education, followed by secondary education and finally higher education. Rates of return are calculated by comparing the present value of life-term earnings of people with different levels of education with the present costs, both public and personal, of schooling individuals to these levels (Psacharopoulos 1987).

Critics of such analyses point out that the benefits of higher education cannot be reduced to simply calculating wage differences. Benefits that are not immediately calculable include the fact that universities serve as the political conscience of many nations, often constituting the leading opponents of dictatorships, and that the research conducted by universities is indispensable to the general advancement of a society. In the absence of such research and ongoing intellectual activity, Latin American countries are condemned to dependence on the universities of the North for advanced scientific and technical knowledge. These critics warn of the dangers of emphasizing primary education, or *primarización,* to the detriment of higher education. They argue that Latin American countries need world-class universities that contribute to national development (Gorostiaga 1993). Indicative of this need is the fact that, according to Daniel Schugurensky (2003:299), Latin America represents less than 3 percent of the world's scientific production. In Mexico and Brazil, which lead Latin America in scientific production, there are, respectively, only 95 and 165 scientists and

Students at Madre y Maestra University
in Santiago, Dominican Republic.

engineers per million people, whereas in Sweden there are 3,714 and in Japan 5,677 scientists and engineers per million (Schugurensky 2003:299). Total public expenditures of all Latin American countries on research and development approximate those of several major multinational corporations (Schugurensky 2003). Moreover, with educational expansion, universities find it increasingly difficult to hire full-time faculty with the requisite educational qualifications—in part a reflection of the inadequate salaries and poor working conditions that they offer. As a case in point, the Latin American Studies Association Task Force on Higher Education noted that approximately 87 percent of university faculty in Brazil do not hold a doctorate or equivalent degree (LASA 1994:7).

In many Latin American countries, public universities charge no tuition, nor do they assess minimal fees. Recently, however, national governments have imposed tuition costs based on recommendations of the international donor agencies. Such initiatives have led to the paralysis of major universities, such as the National Autonomous University of Mexico (UNAM), where students effectively closed down the university by striking from April to October 1999. The minimal but symbolic tuition fee of $150, although well within the means of middle-class families, is often prohibitive for those from working-class backgrounds. This is especially the case in countries where as much as 70 percent or more of the population is living below the poverty level. Such policies threaten to erode the slow but steady gains made recently by the less privileged members of Latin American society to gain access to a higher education in recent years. According to Julia Preston (1999:A12), the Mexican strike "grew more intractable as it dragged on and turned into a battle for the soul of the university. The strikers want it to remain a place for the masses, where all kinds of young Mexicans get at least a little bit of college education."

While students and faculty have protested the imposition of tuition and fees at the undergraduate level in universities from Argentina to Nicaragua, this has not been the case with the introduction of quite substantial fees at the graduate level. With the need to upgrade faculty throughout the region, many instructors are now required to obtain advanced degrees. In many instances, a select few public universities and an increasing number of private institutions are offering master's and doctoral degrees.

One of the most remarkable trends in Latin American education over the past three decades has been the growth of private universities. In the 1970s, approximately 5 percent of higher education students were enrolled in private institutions; by 1994, over 30 percent attended private universities and colleges. Enrollment in private tertiary-level education is highest in El Salvador (75 percent), Chile (71 percent), and Brazil (61 percent). Countries with the largest public higher education enrollments are Cuba

(100 percent), Uruguay (84 percent), Bolivia (82 percent), Argentina (79 percent), and Mexico (79 percent) (UNESCO 2001).

There are many reasons for this growth in private higher education. Public universities in Latin America have a long history of political activism and radicalism. Private universities are generally less politically volatile, and the more privileged classes can send their children to them with the assurance that they will not be exposed to radical political ideas and movements that are likely to erupt into violence on campus. Also, believing graduates of private universities are better prepared academically and are less likely to harbor politically objectionable ideas, private-sector employers may be more likely to hire them. Furthermore, private universities in some countries, such as Brazil, may have less rigorous admissions standards because they depend on student tuition for their survival. Thus, they may recruit as many students as possible in low-cost fields, such as law, the social sciences, accounting, and administration.

Another significant trend is toward reliance on market forces and away from centralized efforts to plan higher education enrollment patterns in concert with national development goals. In the 1990s, enrollments in business administration and engineering programs grew disproportionately. This growth was matched by declining enrollments in the social sciences, education, and the humanities.

Although such shifts appear to reflect market realities, overall enrollment patterns by field of study manifest little relation to the so-called human resource needs of Latin American countries. Despite the agricultural basis of many of the region's economies, often fewer than 5 percent of students are enrolled in courses in agricultural sciences.

Cuba and Nicaragua in the late 1980s were possible exceptions because of university admissions quotas geared to national economic plans. Enrollments in agriculture, forestry, and fishery studies in Cuba constituted 10 percent of total enrollments (11,606 of 115,529 students). In Nicaragua, 15 percent of total enrollments (4,065 of 26,878 students) were enrolled in agriculture, forestry, and fishery studies (Schultz 1993:912). But that situation rapidly changed as a result of the 1990 national elections, which brought to power a government that greatly curtailed the authority of the higher education planning body, as well as scholarship funds for students in fields related to national development. By 1995, only 1,105 out of a total higher education enrollment of 50,769 were enrolled in agriculture-related studies (UNESCO 1998:table 3.11).

Throughout Latin America, one consequence of these enrollment patterns has been that graduates in overpopulated fields such as business administration have serious difficulty finding employment. Only graduates of the most prestigious institutions and fields—and, in many cases, those with the traditional advantage of family connections—can find employment that suits their expectations. One familiar outcome of frustrated expectations is the "brain drain" of high-level talent to the metropolitan centers of North America and Europe. In new fields of development (for example, petro-engineering), however, countries are forced to import experts from abroad (Arnove, Franz, and Morse 1996).

Literacy and Adult Education

Higher education is not the only level of education to be accorded low priority by international donor agencies and national governments. Although most Latin American countries paid lip service to the importance of literacy and adult education in preparation for the World Conference on Education for All in Jomtien, Thailand, in 1990, the fact is that literacy and adult education programs have been neglected in recent years.

Although Latin America has the lowest illiteracy rates of any of the developing regions, the region still had 43 million illiterate adults in 1999. The illiteracy rate in the region for 1999 was 14 percent overall: 15 percent for women and 12 percent for men (UNICEF 1999)—a decrease from 26 percent in 1950. Despite this gain, significant differences in literacy rates exist across and within countries. When the combined effects of social class, region, and gender are taken into account, the highest illiteracy rates, often over 60 percent, are found among poor women living in rural areas. Gender differences in literacy attainment become even sharper when ethnicity is considered, with indigenous groups registering the lowest levels of literacy (see Table 11.4).

The response of many governments to the problem of adult illiteracy has been to rely on nongovernmental organizations (NGOs) and the private sector to provide instruction. Although NGOs are particularly responsive to grassroots initiatives and local needs, their resources are often limited.

The case of Nicaragua is sadly typical of many countries. As a result of its impressive national literacy campaign in 1980, illiteracy was reduced from 50 percent to approximately 23 percent of the population over age 10. But by 1994, as a result of the war situation in the country during the 1980s, massive displacements of rural populations, economic setbacks, and declining resources for education, Nicaragua's illiteracy rate again reached 50 percent. In real numbers, the situation was even more discouraging. In 1980, there were approximately 723,000 illiterate Nicaraguans. In 1994, with over a decade of population growth, the number of illiterates exceeded 1 million. In 1992 and 1993, the government committed less than $25,000 to literacy and postliteracy programs. The Nicaraguan Ministry of Education, although providing literacy primers and some training for literacy workers, depended primarily on NGOs and volunteer teachers to carry the brunt of the adult education efforts. Such efforts reached less than one-

Table 11.4 Deficiencies in Educational Attainment in Urban and Rural Areas, by Percentage

				Interruption or Lag in:			
Country	Year	Geographic Area	Lag in Starting Primary Education	Repetition of First Two Grades of Primary School	Completion of First Four Grades of Primary School	Completion of Primary Education	Completion of Secondary Education
Argentina	1998	Urban	1	6	—	15	25
		Rural	—	—	—	—	—
Brazil	1997	Urban	3	24	29	43	71
		Rural	8	54	63	74	91
Chile	1998	Urban	1	8	5	9	31
		Rural	1	14	13	13	63
Colombia	1997	Urban	5	14	14	23	43
		Rural	9	41	46	59	82
Costa Rica	1998	Urban	1	16	14	13	53
		Rural	2	24	23	27	80
Ecuador	1998	Urban	3	9	8	9	46
		Rural	—	—	—	—	—
El Salvador	1998	Urban	6	14	15	22	55
		Rural	13	33	43	55	88
Honduras	1998	Urban	5	13	14	24	67
		Rural	10	22	31	40	91
Mexico	1998	Urban	2	—	—	8	34
		Rural	5	—	—	24	59
Nicaragua	1997	Urban	6	17	19	27	61
		Rural	—	—	—	—	—
Panama	1998	Urban	1	7	6	7	43
		Rural	3	12	16	18	68
Paraguay	1996	Urban	4	12	11	18	60
		Rural	—	—	—	—	—
Dominican Republic	1997	Urban	7	16	—	27	62
		Rural	7	36	—	51	79
Uruguay	1998	Urban	1	9	6	11	68
		Rural	—	—	—	—	—
Venezuela	1998	National Total	4	8	10	19	59

Sources: Comisión Económica para América Latina (CEPAL), *Panorama social de América Latina* (Santiago: CEPAL, 1999–2000), table V.8; Robert F. Arnove, Stephen Franz, Marcela Mollis, and Carlos Alberto Torres, "Education in Latin America: Dependency, Underdevelopment, and Inequality," in *Comparative Education: The Dialectic of the Global and the Local,* 2d ed., edited by Robert F. Arnove and Carlos Alberto Torres (Lanham, Md.: Rowman & Littlefield, 2003), p. 318.

tenth of those in need of literacy and follow-up adult basic education programs.

In contrast to state-sponsored adult education programs, a number of grassroots educational programs exist in Latin America that form part of a "popular education" movement. Although limited in resources and small in scope, these programs nonetheless are significant, in that they offer an alternative model of education that empowers individuals and communities to place demands on national governments for social services and resources that should be among the rights of all citizens of a country.

■ Popular Education and Other Educational Innovations

Since the 1960s, nonformal and popular education programs have been important alternatives to the formal education sector. Nonformal education implies an educative experience that occurs outside the standard education sphere. Popular education, a subset of nonformal education, is distinguished by its pedagogical and political characteristics (Fink and Arnove 1991).

Pedagogically, popular education programs emphasize nonhierarchical learning situations, in which teachers and students engage in dialogue, and learners' knowledge is incorporated into the content of instruction. According to Torres (1994:198–199), "Education appears as the act of knowing rather than a simple transmission of knowledge or the cultural baggage of society."

Politically, popular education programs tend to be directed toward meeting the special needs of marginalized sectors of society (women, the unemployed, peasants, and indigenous groups). These programs have offered marginalized sectors in Latin America opportunities for personal growth and socioeconomic and political participation. They have played a significant role in facilitating the development of collective survival strategies to confront the economic crisis of the 1980s and 1990s. Furthermore, the ultimate aim of many popular education programs is not just to facilitate adaptation or survival for hard-pressed populations but to bring about far-reaching social change that leads to more just societies (Torres and Puiggrós 1995:26).

In addition to the programs for women listed by Susan Tiano in Chapter 10, examples of popular education programs include Peru Mujer (Peru Woman) and REPEM (Popular Education Network of Women). Peru Mujer organizes and educates women in the fields of discriminatory labor codes and practices, inheritance and family law, and domestic violence issues. REPEM (based in Montevideo) links 140 organizations at the global, regional, and national levels. It serves as a focal point for research, information dissemination, and advocacy on behalf of low-income women with little formal education (REPEM 2003). A major goal of both Peru Mujer and REPEM is to meet women's demands for greater equality and opportunity and the chance to participate actively in the formulation of alternative social change strategies (Arnove et al. 2003:329).[4]

A number of popular education programs also address the special needs of indigenous populations. Multilingualism and multiculturalism are crucial elements of these programs in countries such as Guatemala, Mexico, and Bolivia. In addition, these programs build upon traditional knowledge in the agricultural and health fields and integrate various common forms of artistic expression into programs designed to foster self-pride and into civic and economic activities that contribute to viable communities.

Although popular education programs are generally effective on the community level, they often fail to bring about change at the level of governmental policy. One interesting case in which a leading proponent of popular education had an opportunity to effect large-scale educational change is that of Paulo Freire as secretary of education in the municipality of São Paulo, Brazil.

Paulo Freire and Educational Change

For more than thirty years, Paulo Freire, a theorist and innovator, redefined what educators all over the world think about the potential of education to contribute to social change. Freire's theories articulate the intimate relationship between education and development, particularly the connection between individual empowerment and democratic ideals. During his lifetime, Freire helped plan and implement literacy campaigns and popular education programs in countries worldwide. As municipal secretary of education between 1989 and 1991, Freire was involved in the development and implementation of numerous programs in São Paulo, which, with a population of over 14 million people, is South America's second largest city. The popular education programs put in place were designed to (1) increase access to schooling, (2) democratize school administrations, (3) improve instructional quality, (4) expand educational opportunities for working youths and adults, and (5) contribute to the formation of critical and responsible citizens (Lindquist Wong 1995:120).

Despite the egalitarian intent of Freire's program, Pia Lindquist Wong's analysis (1995) indicates that its implementation became mired in local politics and bureaucracies. This, unfortunately, is the case with many popular education programs. According to Rosa Torres (1990:464), the administration of adult and popular education programs is given to sectors of education ministries that "traditionally occupy a marginal place in the organizational structure and function of ministries of education, lack material and economic resources, and are staffed by bureaucrats showing little dedication."

Although such is the fate of many educational reforms, there are examples of less politically radical state-sponsored educational innovations that do benefit poorly served populations.

New Educational Approaches

An example of ambitious state-sponsored educational innovations that benefit traditionally underserved populations is Fe y Alegría (Faith and Happiness). This Venezuelan NGO began in 1955 by educating one hundred children in a single room. By 2001, the program had expanded to fourteen countries with more than 1 million students in formal and nonformal education programs in over five hundred centers, with over 33,000 teachers and staff. According to Reimers (1997:35), the mission of Fe y Alegría is to "provide quality education to the poor, as expressed in their motto 'Where the asphalt road ends, where there is no water, electricity or services, there begins Fe y Alegría.'" Although there is no "systematic evaluation" for Fe y Alegría, parents claim that these schools provide a better education than public schools. A Guatemalan case study, furthermore, indicates that 85 percent of students who entered Fe y Alegría at the preschool level completed primary education within seven years, as opposed to 34 percent in government schools. Reimers states that Latin American ministries of education usually do not embrace innovative programs such as Fe y Alegría until the programs have proved themselves. Fe y Alegría was initially privately funded but went on to secure substantial government funding in most cases. For example, the Venezuelan government funded over three-fourths of the program budget in the mid-1990s (Reimers 1997).

Another example of a state-sponsored innovation is La Escuela Nueva (the New School) in Colombia, which is designed to meet the special needs of rural schools and communities by creating a curriculum that emphasizes communal needs and values. The New School reform actively encourages a strong relation between schools and communities, and a flexible school calendar and promotion policy that is adapted to local agricultural production cycles. One of the goals of the New School is to teach civic values by encouraging both student and parent participation in important decisions concerning local educational policy. This emphasis on participation accords with the philosophical underpinnings of the reform movement, which are child centered and constructivist in nature. Between its initiation as a pilot project in 1979 and the mid-1990s, the program expanded to over 20,000 schools. The effectiveness of this education reform is one possible reason for the fact that Colombia is the only country in the 1997 UNESCO study of academic achievement in which rural third-grade primary school children outperformed their urban counterparts on standardized language and mathematics tests. New School students also demonstrate strong democratic values on various measures related to civic knowledge, skills, and attitudinal dispositions. Although widely admired and emulated, attempts to replicate the New School, without significant adaptation to local circumstances, have proved problematic, even within Colombia itself.[5] A key to the success of this reform, and any other, is the preparation of teachers and, as Henry Levin (1992) has pointed out, constant monitoring, problem solving, and adjustment.

In general, there are several types of state-initiated policies and practices that are likely to contribute to greater equality of educational opportunity for disadvantaged populations, including working-class and rural people, ethnic minorities, and women. Quality preschool and early childhood programs would improve with supplementary nutrition and health care services. Inadequate school infrastructures should be improved so that poor, rural, and indigenous children have the same amenities—such as school buildings, desks and chairs, electricity, running water, and toilets—enjoyed by their more advantaged peers in urban and private schools. Developing flexible academic calendars would be an appropriate response to the socioeconomic context of schools in different regions of a country. Sufficient supplies of textbooks, as well as culturally sensitive and socially relevant curricular materials in the appropriate languages, are also needed. There are significant instructional issues that ought to be addressed. This could be done through teaching guides adapted to transformed curricula and more student-centered, proactive pedagogies that involve collaborative work and personalized attention to each child. Teachers could benefit from significantly improved preservice and inservice teacher education and professional development programs and opportunities. Teachers working under difficult conditions would be well served by incentive pay, generally more adequate remuneration, and social recognition of the importance of teaching. Equally important would be an increase in participation of teachers, parents, and communities in the design of education programs to meet their self-defined needs, as exemplified by the Escuela Nueva.

Other state initiatives that are being employed to attract and maintain low-income children in schools involve subsidies for textbooks, uniforms, and transportation. Although the Inter-American Development Bank (IDB) (1998) reported mixed results for these policies, an even bolder initiative involving cash payments by governments to help poor children be pupils, not wage earners, shows promise of being effective. The largest program involving cash transfers to needy families is occurring in Brazil, where the government of President Luiz Inácio Lula da Silva has plans to reach 11.4 million families (more than 45 million people) by 2006 with incentive funds for their children to complete basic education (approximately six years). In Mexico, the program now reaches 20 million people. A rigorous evaluation of the Mexican program found that children in schools that receive transfer funds that include money for staples (such as rice, beans, eggs, and carrots) and school supplies were healthier and stayed in school longer than children in a control group (Duggan 2004:3). According to Laurance Wolff and Claudio de Moura Castro (2003:196), the Progresa Program in Mexico has increased entry rates into lower secondary schools in rural areas by almost 20 percent.

It is necessary to point out the important role that universities, through their research, development, and dissemination activities, can play in regard to the most disadvantaged members of their societies. In this role, universities can contribute to income and job generation to overcome the devastating effects of the debt crisis and the economic restructuring to control inflation and fiscal deficits. Higher education leaders, like the late Xabier Gorostiaga (former rector of the Central American University, UCA, of Nicaragua), have proposed a vision of a new role for "universities of the South." His vision calls for utilizing existing university departmental extension programs and research and development institutes affiliated with the UCA as nuclei for experimentation, training, and popular education. Building a university education around the knowledge generated by rural-based centers would contribute to the formation of professionals who, because they had a more realistic understanding of their society, would be better prepared to address its most pressing problems. Moreover, the work of such centers would contribute to empowering the "producing majority" to become major historical actors involved in the transformation of an unsatisfactory status quo that has marginalized and exploited them. According to Gorostiaga (1993:37), "All of these experimental nuclei offer an ideal place for our professors and students to bring their theoretical knowledge down to earth, to participate in research projects that directly benefit civil society" and to extend education to the majority of people excluded from secondary and higher education. Such efforts are critical to the development and dissemination of appropriate and self-sustainable technologies, and they offer prospects of collaboration between universities of the North and the South (Arnove 1996).

Mass Media and Education

Finally, in discussing education in Latin America, whether formal or non-formal and popular, it is necessary to mention briefly the role of the mass media as a parallel educational system. The mass media reaches more people on a more systematic basis and for longer periods of time than do formal education systems. Although the various forms of media are viewed, read, and consumed as entertainment, they nonetheless present an agenda of what merits society's attention. In addition to providing countless messages about products to consume, the mass media—particularly television soap operas (*telenovelas*) and popular comic books in picture form (*fotonovelas*)—reach vast numbers of people with a folk mythology about how society is constituted, which people and occupations are worthy of emulation, and how social change takes place.[6]

The mass media impacts Latin American youth and their classroom behavior. In fact, the pervasiveness of the information age, particularly the near-universal access to mass media, may have presented educators with a new crisis—one in which students are choosing some cultural legacies and rejecting others. While students reject the authoritarianism of past generations, "at the same time, students are increasingly ignorant of both their own national past and world history . . . they are indifferent to collective values or notions of solidarity . . . and are apolitical in their attitudes" (Torres and Puiggrós 1995:20).

Although there are always differences between generations, the gap that exists between teachers and their students appears to be greater than ever. These cultural differences between adults and youth are only part of a larger set of issues concerning whether Latin American education systems can continue to play their historical role of transmitting common values, preparing citizens for a unified nation-state, and equipping citizens to be participating members of democratic polities.

Education and Democracy in Latin America

The prospect of Latin American countries establishing democratic polities is greater now than at any time in the history of the region. The emergence of democratically elected regimes in the Southern Cone countries (Argentina, Chile, and Uruguay) and Brazil after two or more decades of military dictatorships is particularly encouraging, as is the termination of civil wars in Central America (El Salvador and Nicaragua), and installation of democratically elected governments in Honduras and Guatemala (countries with a tradition of military rule). But as Thomas D'Agostino makes clear in Chapter 4, democratic institutions throughout Latin America are very fragile.

The enormous debt burden of the region, the increasing impoverishment of the less privileged social classes in these societies, and the willingness of individuals and groups to resort to violence to press their demands on national governments do not bode well for either social stability or political democracy. To counter these negative trends, educational systems in a number of countries have been called upon to teach civic values. Particularly important is the need to teach toleration of differences by promoting a willingness to engage in dialogue with those with whom one disagrees.

Although there are examples of countries, such as the Dominican Republic and Ecuador, that reached a national consensus in the early 1990s around their educational systems and the role of education in development, in many other countries, as Robert Arnove (1995) has noted, education is "contested terrain." Different governments and groups have attempted to use education to indoctrinate students into accepting certain political dogmas and religious doctrines. Schools have become battlegrounds in which ideologically and politically opposed groups fight not only over curriculum, textbooks, and who is qualified to teach but also over the governance, organization, and financing of education. Moreover, rather than building on the best of previous governments' education programs, newly elected governments have often dismantled them, wasting years of effort in rebuilding what had already been achieved. If consensus, harmony, and respect for differences—values critical to democracy—cannot be achieved in an education system, what hope is there for the larger society?

▪ Conclusion

Despite the apparently bleak future of education in Latin America, both past and present reforms, such as popular education, grassroots projects, and community self-help programs, all point to a persistent ability of people to turn discouraging situations into positive developments. Furthermore, the evolving definitions of development and education indicate a constant move away from theories that reinforce the status quo toward ideals that promote individual empowerment and faith in egalitarian principles.

Another encouraging sign is the general realization on the part of education and political decisionmakers that if education is to contribute to national development, the issues of improvements in access and quality must be tackled simultaneously. In addition, there is an increasing effort to use educational resources more efficiently and effectively to reach the most disadvantaged populations. Many policymakers also realize that all levels of an education system, from preprimary through university and adult education, are important and that continuity and articulation must exist among all levels of the system so that conditions are created for ongoing and lifelong education.

Finally, there is a growing awareness that all of the major stakeholders—international donor agencies, national governments, intergovernmental agencies, private bodies, nongovernmental organizations, local governments, communities, and individuals—need to join forces. If consensus can be reached around these goals and processes, it may be possible to provide meaningful education to all sectors of society. If this is accomplished, the prospects will be bright indeed for education systems to contribute both to the development and the democratization of Latin American countries.

▓ Notes

1. This chapter represents an updated and revised version of the earlier chapter by Robert F. Arnove, Stephen Franz, and Kimberly Morse Cordova, "Education and Development in Latin America," in *Understanding Contemporary Latin America*, edited by Richard S. Hillman. Boulder, Colo.: Lynne Rienner Publishers, 2001, pp. 297–322.
2. Data in this section are drawn from UNESCO reports.
3. Data in this section are drawn from CEPAL and the World Bank.
4. Information was provided by Vicky Semler, executive director of the International Women's Tribune Centre, New York City, in a telephone conversation of January 7, 2003.
5. Conversation with Vicky Colbert, president of the Fundación Volvamos a la Gente and cofounder of la Escuela Nueva, August 19, 2002, Bogotá, Colombia.
6. The authors are indebted to the late Rose Goldson of the Sociology Department at Cornell University for these insights.

▓ Bibliography

Arnove, Robert F. "Education as Contested Terrain in Nicaragua." *Comparative Education Review* 39, no. 1 (1995):28–53.
———. "Partnerships and Emancipatory Movements: Issues and Prospects." *Alberta Journal of Educational Research* 42, no. 2 (1996):170–177.
Arnove, Robert F., Stephen Franz, Marcela Mollis, and Carlos Alberto Torres. "Education in Latin America: Dependency, Underdevelopment and Inequality." In *Comparative Education: The Dialectic of the Global and the Local* (2d ed.), edited by Robert F. Arnove and Carlos Alberto Torres. Lanham, Md.: Rowman & Littlefield, 2003, pp. 313–337.
Arnove, Robert F., Stephen Franz, and Kimberly Morse. "Latin American Education." In *Latin America: Perspectives on a Region,* edited by Jack W. Hopkins. New York: Holmes and Meier, 1996, pp. 123–137.
Berman, Edward. "Donor Agencies and Third World Educational Development, 1945–1985." In *Emergent Issues in Education: Comparative Perspectives,* edited by Robert Arnove, Philip Altbach, and Gail Kelly. Albany: State University of New York Press, 1992, pp. 57–74.
Business Mexico. "Mexicans in *Forbes*," 2002. Available online at www.amcham.com.mx/hotissues/abril02/hotissues0401-1.html (accessed June 17, 2004).
Button, Graham (ed.). "The Billionaires: *Forbes'* Eighth Annual Survey of the

World's Wealthiest People," *Forbes,* July 18, 1994 (section on Latin America), pp. 186–198.

CEPAL (Comisión Económica para América Latina). *Transformación productiva con equidad.* Santiago: CEPAL, 1990.

———. *Panorama social de América Latina.* Santiago: CEPAL, 1991.

———. *Panorama social de América Latina.* Santiago: CEPAL, 2001.

Coleman, James S. (ed.). *Education and Political Development.* Princeton, N.J.: Princeton University Press, 1965.

Duggan, Celia W. "To Help Poor Be Pupils, Not Wage Earners, Brazil Pays Parents." *New York Times,* January 3, 2004, pp. A1, 3, 6.

Fink, Marcy, and Robert Arnove. "Issues and Tensions in Popular Education in Latin America." *International Journal of Educational Development* 11, no. 3 (1991):221–230.

Freire, Paulo. *The Politics of Education: Culture, Power, and Liberation.* Critical Studies in Education. Westport, Conn.: Greenwood Press, 1984.

Fuenzalida, Edmundo. "Development and Education." In *The International Encyclopedia of Education,* Vol. 3, edited by Torsten Husén and T. Neville Postlethwaite. New York: Pergamon, 1985, pp. 1374–1379.

Gorostiaga, Xabier. "New Times, New Role for Universities of the South." *Envío* 12, no. 144 (1993):24–40.

IDB (Inter-American Development Bank). "Education: The Gordian Knot: Shortfalls in Schooling Are at the Root of Inequality," 1998. Available online at http:///www.iadb.org/idbamerica/Archive/stories/1998/eng/e1198e4.htm (accessed January 28, 2004).

LASA (Latin American Studies Association). *Latin American Task Force Report on Higher Education,* 1994, p. 7.

Levin, Henry. "Effective Schools and Comparative Focus." In *Emergent Issues in Education: Comparative Perspectives,* edited by Robert F. Arnove, Philip G. Altbach, and Gail P. Kelly. Albany: State University of New York Press, 1992, pp. 229–245.

Levy, Daniel C. *Higher Education and the State in Latin America: Private Challenges to Public Dominance.* Chicago: University of Chicago Press, 1986.

Lindquist Wong, Pia. "Constructing a Public Popular Education in São Paulo, Brazil." *Comparative Education Review* 39, no. 1 (1995):120–141.

Muñiz, Patricia. "The Schooling Situation of Children in Highly Underprivileged Rural Localities in Mexico." In *Unequal Schools, Unequal Chances: The Challenges to Equal Opportunity in the Americas,* edited by Fernando Reimers. Cambridge, Mass.: Harvard University Press, 2000, pp. 290–314.

OECD (Organization for Economic Cooperation and Devlopment). *Education at a Glance: OECD Indicators, 2000.* OECD, August 2000.

Plank, David N., José Amaral Sobrinho, and Antonio Carlos de Ressurreição Xavier. "Obstacles to Educational Reform in Brazil." *La Educación* 117, no. 1 (1994).

Prawda, Juan. "Educational Decentralization in Latin America: Lessons Learned." *International Journal of Educational Development* 13, no. 3 (1993):253–264.

PREAL (Programa de Promoción de la Reforma Educativa en América Latina y el Caribe). "Quedándonos atrás: Un informe del progreso educativo en América Latina." December 2001, pp. 7–8. Available online at www.preal.org.

Preston, Julia. "University Officials Yield to Student Strike in Mexico." *New York*

Times, June 8, 1999, p. A12.

Psacharopoulos, George. "Economic Aspects of Educational Planning." In *Economics of Education: Research and Studies,* edited by George Psacharopoulos. New York: Pergamon Press, 1987, pp. 311–314.

REPEM (Popular Education Network of Women). wwwpersonal.umich.edu/~fiatlux/td/eccher/ctc.html, 2003.

Reimers, Fernando. "The Impact of Economic Stabilization and Adjustment on Education in Latin America." *Comparative Education Review* 35, no. 2 (1991):319–362.

———. "Role of NGOs in Promoting Educational Innovation: A Case Study in Latin America." In *Education and Development: Tradition and Innovation,* Vol. 4, *Non-formal and Non-governmental Approaches,* edited by James Lynch, Celia Modgil, and Sohan Modgil. London: Cassell, 1997.

Schugurensky, Daniel. "Higher Education Restructuring in the Era of Globalization: Toward a Heteronomous Model?" In *Comparative Education: The Dialectic of the Global and the Local* (2d ed.), edited by Robert F. Arnove and Carlos Alberto Torres. Lanham, Md.: Rowman & Littlefield, 2003, pp. 292–312.

Schultz, Theodore William. *Transforming Traditional Agriculture.* New Haven, Conn.: Yale University Press, 1964.

———. "Investment in Human Capital: The Role of Education and of Research." *New Statistical Abstract of Latin America 1993.* Los Angeles: University of California at Los Angeles, 1993.

Torres, Carlos Alberto. "Paulo Freire as Secretary of Education in the Municipality of São Paulo." *Comparative Education Review* 38, no. 2 (1994):198–199.

Torres, Carlos Alberto, and Adriana Puiggrós. "The State and Public Education in Latin America." *Comparative Education Review* 39, no. 1 (1995):1–27.

Torres, Rosa María. "Illiteracy and Literacy Training in Latin America and the Caribbean: Between Inertia and a Break with the Past." *Prospects* 20 (1990):461–468.

UNESCO (United Nations Educational, Scientific, and Cultural Organization). *UNESCO Statistical Yearbook, 1974.* Paris: UNESCO, 1974.

———. *Boletín de educación: Publicación semestral de la oficina regional de educación* 19 (January–June 1976):1–75.

———. *UNESCO Statistical Yearbook, 1993.* Paris: UNESCO, 1993.

———. *UNESCO Statistical Yearbook, 1998.* Paris: UNESCO, 1998.

———. "Latin America and the Caribbean: Regional Report." 2001. Available online at www.unesco.org.

UNICEF (United Nations Children's Fund). *State of the World's Children, 1999.* New York: UNICEF, 1999.

Wolff, Laurence, and Claudio de Moura Castro. "Education and Training: The Task Ahead." Institute for International Economics, 2003. Available online at www.iie.com.

Wolff, Laurence, Ernesto Schiefelbein, and Paulina Schiefelbein. *La educación primaria en América Latina: La agenda inconclusa,* 2002. PREAL, available at www.preal.org.

Wolff, Laurence, Ernesto Schiefelbein, and Jorge Valenzuela. *Improving the Quality of Primary Education in Latin America and the Caribbean.* Washington, D.C.: World Bank, 1994.

World Bank. *Brazil: Public Spending on Social Programs, Issues and Options.* World Bank Report 7086-BR. Washington, D.C.: World Bank, 1988.

12

Religion
in Latin America

Michael Fleet

The most striking aspect of religious life in Latin America today is its diversity. Over 70 percent of the region's residents still say they belong to the Catholic Church, but the number of Protestants has risen dramatically in nearly all countries in the last thirty years. In fact, some observers have argued that Protestants make up close to 30 percent of the population of Guatemala and close to 20 percent in Chile and Brazil.[1]

Within each of these broader communions, however, divergent factions, tendencies, and denominations can be found. Many self-proclaimed Catholics, for example, practice popular or folk versions of Catholicism that combine Catholic and non-Christian (such as spiritist) beliefs. Others cling to the socially and theologically conservative beliefs associated with the church in the years prior to the Second Vatican Council (1962–1965). In recent years, under Pope John Paul II, there was a resurgence of conservatism, and those who adhere to these beliefs appear to be growing in numbers. In the past forty years, influential social Christian and liberation tendencies have arisen, and while they were minority currents in most countries, they have given the Catholic Church a more progressive image than it had in the past.

Among Protestants, mainline churches continue to exist but have been overwhelmed by numbers and visibility in a myriad of small and not so small Evangelical and Pentecostal churches, whose theologies, interest in social questions, and positions on leading moral and cultural issues differ considerably.[2]

Some observers have viewed the reforms undertaken by the Catholic Church during the 1960s, 1970s, and 1980s as part of a strategy to compete with the Evangelical Protestant movement.[3] The Catholic Church's initia-

343

tives may well have revitalized substantial numbers of working- and middle-class members. However, the reforms also appeared to alienate more conservative Catholics of both upper- and lower-class backgrounds, and the church's innovations did not seem to diminish the growing appeal or success of Evangelical Protestantism, which continued to expand into the 1990s.[4]

In addition to the many tendencies and orientations within the Catholic and Protestant churches, a variety of spiritist cults and movements continue to flourish in the region. They are most numerous and visible in Brazil and the Caribbean, where large numbers of African slaves were brought beginning in the seventeenth century. They can also be found in other locales, interwoven with both Catholic and Protestant faiths. To Christians and non-Christians alike, spiritist movements, such as *umbanda, candomblé, santería, obeah,* María Lionsa, and *vodou,* offer additional means of mitigating or averting personal misfortune and disasters. In Chapter 9, Kevin Yelvington shows how most syncretic religions have served as sources of popular identity and of resistance to social and political authorities. However, for the most part, adherents of these religions or movements direct their energies at placating, or escaping the reach of, more powerful forces; are less interested in acquiring or extending power of their own; and, thus, tend to support the social and political status quo.

Religious beliefs are both formative elements and faithful reflections of Latin America's popular cultures. They directly affect the region's prospects for economic growth and social modernization and, in turn, will be affected by any growth and modernization that take place. Historically, religion and politics have always been very closely intertwined in Latin America. As René de la Pedraja illustrates in Chapter 3, the Spanish and Portuguese adventurers who colonized the Western Hemisphere in the fifteenth and sixteenth centuries and came ashore with crosses and swords, found religion and politics similarly intertwined in the Aztec, Mayan, Incan, and Araucanian civilizations. Since then, as Thomas D'Agostino shows in Chapter 4, church and state authorities have worked both with and against one another in attempting to inform and control their common subjects.

The affinity between religion and politics is compelling. Religions are organized communities of faith, worship, and witness whose members define and attempt to maintain proper relationships with transcendent powers. Religious leaders define what is most important in life and what people need to do to live properly—for example, proclaim beliefs, observe rituals and practices, and order their social lives and relationships accordingly. More than a few religious leaders have looked to the power and sanctions of secular authorities for help in performing these vital functions. Just as frequently, civil authorities have sought the blessing of religious institu-

UN Photo 129/94/J. Frank

Worshippers outside
the Villa de Guadalupe
shrine in Mexico City.

tions as a means of strengthening or extending their claims to temporal power.

Historically, movements calling for the separation of religion and politics have arisen when more than one religion existed in a country, when the official religion developed more liberal tendencies, or when state authorities wanted to be free of the power of conservative religious authorities. The goal of Western European liberal movements in the seventeenth century, for example, was to enable people to remain religiously faithful and yet live in harmony. With the establishment of religious toleration and the separation of civil and religious authority, each side was denied use of the other's sanctions and rewards.

Because Roman Catholicism was unchallenged in the religious sphere and conservative forces continued to dominate the social and political arenas, Latin Americans felt little need to separate church and state until the early twentieth century. At that point, Protestant missionaries began arriving, but because their numbers were relatively small they played only a minor role in the movement to separate church and state. This achievement was more the result of pressure from secular elites and anticlerical middle- and working-class activists, who were beginning to emerge as a force within the political arena in many countries. These groups were critical of the Catholic Church's close ties to dominant economic and political elites. In countries where these reforms were carried out, religious institutions and elites retained their political influence but were less able to dictate their people's thoughts and actions.

Today, despite decades of Protestant growth, Roman Catholicism remains the region's dominant religion. During the papacy of John Paul II, newly appointed bishops and those transferred to more influential sees generally reflected the Vatican's insistence on unwavering support of hierarchical authority and traditionally conservative teachings with respect to divorce, contraception, abortion, homosexuality, and other issues. But the church remains more diverse than ever at the level of grassroots believers, and it must now compete for hearts, minds, and sociopolitical influence with Protestants, spiritists, and an increasingly secularized mass culture.

The remainder of this chapter describes the religious beliefs of Catholic, Protestant, and spiritist groups and analyzes their respective social and political influence at institutional and grassroots levels.

■ Catholicism

From its earliest days, the Roman Catholic Church has claimed to be the authoritative embodiment of a single, united Christian people, valid for men and women of all times and circumstances and led by authorities claiming to be the direct successors of the original apostles. Roman Catholics believe that Christ's sacrifice redeemed human beings from their sinful natures but that their pursuit of salvation should be a communal, not an individual, undertaking. They need one another's support, the guidance of bishops and priests possessing special knowledge, and the spiritual nourishment afforded by grace-giving sacraments.

The Catholic Church has been the world's largest Christian denomination for nearly two thousand years. It has weathered the assaults of numerous religious and secular challengers, due to its efficient organizational structures, astute leadership at crucial junctures, and the ability to identify itself with the national cultures of the different countries in which it functions.

In such worldwide contexts, the church's following consists largely of so-called cultural Catholics, that is, popular-sector Catholics who are neither sacramentally nor organizationally active in the church but who retain, to varying degrees, the sentiments and practices of Catholic culture. These include processions, festivals, and other devotional practices involving Catholic images and saints, to whom promises and commitments are made in exchange for intercession and assistance. Concern for formal doctrines and teachings is limited and is often colored by indigenous and non-Christian notions and practices. In fact, it is from these cultural Catholics that Evangelical and Pentecostal Protestants have recruited most successfully in recent years. The cultural environments in which most Latin Americans live and work are noticeably less Catholic than in the past, while people who have long thought of themselves as Catholics are now more open to the appeals of other churches and movements.

The Catholic bishops of Latin America are social and cultural elites with ready access in most instances to state, party, and military elites. The bishops' views and concerns are taken seriously because of (1) their religious stature; (2) the influence they are believed to exert over their countries' citizens; and (3) the value of the health care, educational, and cultural institutions and programs they oversee. In special circumstances, individual bishops, national episcopal conferences, and even local-level priests and nuns play active roles in the political process and can affect its course when certain issues are involved. Since the 1930s, Catholic lay men and women, acting at both local and national levels, have come to speak for the church as well. Accordingly, this chapter's discussion focuses both on the institutional church and on Catholics acting on their own at both local and national levels.

The Institutional Church

From the early fourth through the late nineteenth centuries, the Catholic Church relied on the patronage of socioeconomic and political elites to help it fulfill its religious mission.[5] It endorsed governments and dominant elites who were willing to proclaim Catholic values and protect the church's interests. The arrangement worked reasonably well until the late 1800s, when commercial elites, secular liberals, and middle-class businesspeople and professionals began to challenge the conservative patrons.

In Latin America, liberals and conservatives fought for control of national governments and their policies during much of the 1800s and early 1900s. Catholic authorities generally took the conservative side in this struggle. They paid a heavy price by allowing outsiders to dictate episcopal appointments, failing to undertake internal reforms, and further alienating those who believed the church cared little for them.

Evidence of the Catholic Church's disarray was increasingly apparent as the twentieth century began. It could be seen in declining rates of religious practice, in the inroads Protestant missionaries were making among lower- and middle-class nominal Catholics, in the anticlericalism of both middle- and working-class forces, and in the development of Marxist and socialist movements. Aware that their church was in trouble, Catholic authorities began to devise new strategies and forms of organization. Their embrace of modern, liberal values was aided by a renewed emphasis on the utopian side of the Christian vision and the rediscovery of alternative conceptions of church and mission.

From its inception, the Catholic Church has been of two minds regarding secular history and authority. It has viewed human history as a vale of tears to be endured with an eye to the better world beyond and as an evil to be resisted and made to conform to gospel values (peace, justice, community, self-sacrifice, and so on). For most of its history, the church has acted in line with the first of these views. As long as their relationship with socioe- conomic and political elites was "working"—that is, safeguarding their institutional interests, as these were understood—church authorities were reluctant to abandon their allies. But when they began losing ground to emerging class and political adversaries, church leaders examined them and their policies more critically.

As Catholic leaders studied the opposition's views, they started to rethink the church's mission and its relation to society and history. They were aided by their rediscovery of the early Christian Church—a church rather different from the centralized, hierarchical, and almost exclusively sacramental church most of them assumed had always existed. In effect, biblical scholars introduced these leaders to a church that was more com- munitarian, more service oriented, and more committed to preaching the gospel. These features of the early Christian Church became models or precedents for the development of new pastoral strategies.

Without repudiating the institutional conception of the church (one that emphasized hierarchy, outward conformity, and legal status), Catholic lead- ers began to restore the communitarian, servant, herald, and sacramental dimensions of church life within it. In doing so, wittingly or not, they vali- dated many of the concerns of Protestant reformers centuries earlier. Church leaders in some countries began earlier and carried their reforms further than those in others, but by the late 1970s, virtually all had embraced several principles.

First, they endorsed the principle of religious freedom and agreed to a substantial separation of church and state; nevertheless, the church still enjoys a relatively privileged legal status among religions, Catholic schools continue to receive government subsidies, and the Catholic catechism is taught in public schools in most Latin American countries. Initially, some bishops viewed these moves as unfortunate but necessary concessions. In the end, however, even ecclesiastical and theological conservatives embraced them as measures effectively freeing the church from harmful external constraints.

Second, the leaders assigned lay Catholics to evangelical (gospel preaching) work traditionally reserved for clerics. They trained lay men and women in the church's moral and social teachings and then gave them both educational and organizational responsibilities. This helped to compensate for the shortage of clerics, and it strengthened the religious understanding and commitments of many middle- and working-class Catholics. It also developed a Catholic presence among social forces, both professionals and workers, who had drifted away from the church over the years.

Third, Catholic leaders embraced the idea of pastoral ministry in social justice. They came to see the achievement of social justice within history and society as part of the salvation process; at the same time, they recognized that the gospel's values must be brought to people's attention in concrete and socially relevant terms if they were to appreciate and respond to them and to the church positively.

Fourth, the leaders came to view the defense of other universal values—including freedom, equality, and the rights of women—as part of Christian witness and ministry. Their partial realization on earth was part of God's plan, requiring a strong defense from the church—particularly if other forces were unable to provide these basic rights and conditions.

The church's appreciation of such modern, liberal-democratic ideals was strengthened by the Second Vatican Council's reintroduction of the notion of church as sacrament. In the Catholic tradition, a sacrament is a ritual that mediates God's grace. It is a symbol (an "outward sign") that points to a spiritual reality beyond itself even as it embodies that reality. Jesus was the perfect sacrament, since he pointed to his Father's power as the source of his works and yet possessed and embodied that power as well. By analogy, substances used in Jesus's name (such as water in baptism; bread and wine in the Eucharist; and oil in confirmation, ordination, and last rites) brought his life into the person receiving them. But from a biblical perspective, humanity itself was sacramental as well; it pointed to God and was an image of God in human flesh. In this light, everything that was humanly good could be viewed as sacramental and as having religious value. The church was a more perfect sacrament because it mediated God's grace and truth as fully revealed in Jesus. But other religions or "noble" causes were also, albeit less perfect, expressions of truth that should be celebrated as sacraments as well.

In fact, according to the Second Vatican's conciliar documents, the bishops proclaimed that God's presence in the world was to be found, above all, in the human conscience, a person's "most sacred core and sanctuary," and in the "authentic freedom . . . an exceptional sign of the divine image" that is also present in all people. The church would defend these values by passing "moral judgments, even on matters touching the political order, whenever personal rights . . . make such judgments necessary, and would denounce any kind of government that blocks civil or religious liberty" or "multiplies victims of political crimes." People should be able, they said, "to defend their own rights . . . against any abuse of . . . authority" and "to choose their governments and the methods used for selecting their leaders" (Abbott 1966:213–214, 289, 284, 283).

These perspectives have helped the church to play a progressive role in support of social change, human rights, and democracy in Latin America since the early 1960s. At this point, the bishops of many countries endorsed agrarian and tax reforms, promoted expanded suffrage, and urged greater government spending on health and education. With financial help from European and U.S. churches, they initiated literacy programs, production and marketing cooperatives, credit unions, and health and nutrition projects. In these ways, they sought to promote peaceful change and to head off violent revolution. In the process, they gave additional impetus to modernization and reformist forces within the church itself.

Simultaneously, the Latin American church took up the prophetic function of defending universal moral values. From the late 1960s through the 1980s, military governments and establishments assaulted the civil, political, social, and economic rights of their citizens. With the help of the larger church's organizational and financial resources, many local parishes and communities became havens that offered human warmth, material and legal assistance, and logistical support for those who were repressed. Some served as staging grounds for nonviolent resistance, and Catholic activists were soon prominent in movements calling for the restoration of civilian rule. When the poor protested the lack of jobs and the unjust distribution of resources under these regimes, church authorities began to link violations of personal and civil liberties to structural and ideological causes. These included maldistribution of land and wealth, the lack of participation by the poor in the institutions that affected their lives, and a conception of national security that subjugated individual rights to state and ruling elite interests.

With financial assistance from Europe and North America, Catholic bishops mounted or expanded national human rights programs. Agencies that monitored violations and provided lawyers for those accused of political "crimes" were established in Chile, Brazil, Paraguay, Bolivia, Argentina, El Salvador, Guatemala, and Nicaragua. Other programs distributed food and clothing to families of the imprisoned and of those who had disappeared, treated people who had been abused while imprisoned, set up employment projects, and even generated research on social movements, alternate economic and political models, and transitions to democratic rule.

Frequently, these programs offered refuge and support to activists and intellectuals who came to work in them, first as volunteers and later as paid staff members. Many were disaffected Catholics or Marxists who were skeptical of religion. Some began to attend mass again or joined their fellow workers in reflection, communal prayer, or Bible study groups. Others gained new respect for the church as a moral and institutional force.

By the early and mid-1980s, episcopal conferences in Argentina, Brazil, Chile, and Uruguay were advocating a return to democracy as the only lasting guarantee for preserving human rights and resolving social and economic problems. In some instances (Bolivia, Chile, and Paraguay), bishops sought to help contending factions work out the conditions for the restoration of constitutional government. In others (El Salvador and Nicaragua), they mediated between governments and their guerrilla opponents. In fragile democracies (Peru, Haiti, and Guatemala), they urged respect for democratic procedures and policies aimed at solving chronic economic and social problems.

A priest celebrates mass with residents of Cinquera,
who are returning to the town after abandoning it
during El Salvador's twelve-year civil war.

The church's new pastoral emphases have helped it to counter challenges to its survival and relevance. Although accepting church-state separation and partisan neutrality, it has developed new ways of evangelizing
middle- and working-class Catholics and has retained—probably even
enhanced—its national presence and influence. The decentralization of its
structures, greater use of the Bible, modification of forms of prayer and
worship, and greater lay involvement in its ministries have helped the
Catholic Church to offset staffing problems resulting from the decline of
priestly vocations in recent years and may have helped to limit its loss of
followers to the Protestant churches. Finally, its defense of the rights and
interests of ordinary people has helped the church to win back estranged
followers and gain the respect of others, including leftist activists.

Lay and Grassroots Involvement

The emergence of a more engaged and committed laity has greatly
enhanced the Catholic Church's vitality and social influence in the past
fifty years. Often in close cooperation with the bishops but at times fairly
independent of them, Catholic citizens have come to represent the church's
values and beliefs in a variety of social and political contexts.

Beginning in the early 1920s, lay people were schooled in Catholic doctrine and spiritual practices. The idea was to prepare middle- and working-class Catholics to evangelize on the job, in their schools and neighborhoods. These efforts culminated in the Catholic Action Movement, which emerged in Europe following World War I and was brought to Latin America in the 1930s by charismatic priests returning from studies in France and Belgium. They gathered students (including young women) and middle-class professionals around them, introduced them to Catholic social teaching, and sent them into secular contexts to defend Catholic values and interests.

Latin America proved fertile ground for these activities. During the 1930s and 1940s, Argentina, Brazil, Chile, Colombia, Mexico, and Peru were industrializing while their educated middle and working classes were growing. So, too, were the numbers of university students and labor leaders, whom the church hoped to protect from the perils of modernity (urbanization, secularization, and Marxism). Although they represented only a small percentage of the total Catholic population (less than 2 percent in both Chile and Peru, for example), those involved in these efforts had important formative experiences. Many went on to become priests, bishops, and national business and political leaders, giving the church a new, more socially progressive presence in many countries for years to come.

Lay activists tended to disperse themselves politically. Many were skeptical of existing parties and movements, preferring to spend their time and energies in social movements and church-related activities. If they were politically affiliated, it was generally with the progressive, social-Christian wing of a pro-Catholic conservative party (Mexico, Nicaragua, and Colombia), an emerging social-Christian or Christian Democratic party (Chile, Venezuela, Peru, Uruguay, and El Salvador), or—where these did not exist—a populist-reformist party (Argentina and Brazil) that was not excessively anticlerical.

A second wave of lay evangelization came in the 1960s, as men and women were encouraged to take more active roles in religious ministries and in church-sponsored charitable and social programs. Married men were admitted to the deaconate and given sacramental and other responsibilities, including preaching. The bishops created pastoral councils composed of priests, women, and religious and lay people to advise them. With the establishment of national and regional episcopal conferences, bishops began to act in a more collegial manner and to draw more fully on the expertise of lay advisers and administrators.

The church also sought to deal directly with its chronic shortage of priests. During the 1950s and 1960s, extensive financial and human resources were channeled to the Latin American churches from both Europe and North America. Missionary priests and nuns from these areas were assigned to staff high schools and service parishes in rural and urban slum areas where local clerics rarely ventured. Most brought resources with them and sent for more when they were settled. They helped to set up and sustain the clinics, cooperatives, credit funds, and training programs that were encouraged by reform-minded bishops. International church aid agencies, which had shifted from relief to development activities following World War II, were an additional and increasingly important source of financial aid.

But even with the arrival of additional priests and nuns (more than three thousand priests and six thousand nuns by the early 1960s), the church was still unable to reach all of its "faithful" through traditional pastoral structures. At their conference in Medellín, Colombia, in 1968, the Latin American bishops endorsed decentralized neighborhood groupings called *comunidades eclesiales de base* (CEBs; ecclesial base communities), most of which were located in the countryside or in poorer areas (slums and densely populated neighborhoods) of large cities. They were small and socially homogeneous enough to allow for personal fraternal contact among members. They combined prayer, Bible study, preparation for the reception of sacraments, and service to their areas or neighborhoods.

CEBs reached only a fraction of the general Catholic population. In Brazil, an estimated 100,000 such groups, many with twenty or thirty members, had arisen by the mid-1980s but accounted for only 2.5 percent of the country's baptized Catholics. Nonetheless, they gave the church a presence in working- and popular-class neighborhoods, where few priests had penetrated previously. Given the scarcity of priests and the low levels of church affiliation among working-class men, the leaders of many of these CEBs were nuns and married women. In some communities, they preached, taught the Bible, baptized, distributed Holy Communion, and officiated at weddings and funerals—helping to chip away at the tradition of male clerical domination in the church.

Lay Catholics, however, remained politically dispersed. Many soured on both Christian Democratic and populist reformism, frustrated by the limited extent and pace of reforms, the meager economic growth, and the resulting social conflict. Some were driven in opposing directions, some back to the moderate right and others leftward to socialist revolution. Most of the latter were younger-generation Catholic activists who had come into contact with Marxist sociology in their university studies and were disillusioned with both church authorities and their own political elders.

Ironically, many of them abandoned the church and the faith just as liberation theology was beginning to emerge. Theologians and priests who had gone to live in popular neighborhoods to understand and serve the poor more fully developed this new, radical Christian response to the problems of poverty, exploitation, and underdevelopment. Their ideas were the outgrowth of pastoral practice, biblical reflection, and consideration of the findings of the contemporary social sciences. They stressed the primacy of the poor in the prophets and the teachings of Jesus and how in the Jewish Scriptures knowledge and experience of God were at their peak whenever the poor were attempting to free themselves from injustice—for example, during the exodus of the Jewish people from slavery in Egypt. From such a perspective, religious salvation was neither an otherworldly phenomenon nor something to be mediated exclusively through prayer, sacramental practice, or personal acts of faith. It involved the liberation of the full human person, body and spirit. Conversely, as sin was both individual and collective, to liberate the poor was to reject sin and begin a process of personal and collective salvation.

For most liberationists, effective gospel witness required active involvement with the poor in their struggle for liberation. For some, this meant joining political parties or movements that sought to replace capitalism with some type of participatory socialism. For others, it meant helping to build strong organizations to defend popular interests but leaving issues of economic and political systems to lay people and political parties.

In Argentina, Chile, Colombia, and Peru, organizations of radical priests emerged, attacking capitalism and capitalist development policies and calling for a united popular movement in which Christians would join with Marxists and other progressives to build a socialist society and thereby liberate the poor and oppressed. Their public statements and their willingness to challenge their bishops on both political and ecclesial matters gained them considerable notoriety. However, none of these organizations ever developed an appreciable lay following. Most Catholic lay people, peasants and workers in particular, remained loyal to moderate Christian Democratic or populist parties and were unwilling to collaborate with Marxists.

These radical priests and nuns did accomplish a number of things, however. With the help of outside money, they set up and equipped parish centers, outreach programs, and social and religious networks—greatly enhancing the church's organizational capacity in local communities and in popular and slum neighborhoods. These structures were pressed into service in the late 1960s and early 1970s, when repressive military governments took power in many Latin American countries. Parish centers and small Christian communities became free spaces in which people could meet, reflect, and organize. Not all of these groups developed radical social or political perspectives, but many took in people, Christian or not, who were being sought or persecuted by authorities, and most spoke out against these abusive practices.

With parties and political institutions suspended, leftists and reformists under fire, many people out of work, and much practical "survival" work to do (for example, in food kitchens, milk programs, job-training projects, and sewing and knitting cooperatives), Catholics and leftists found it easier to work together, and the ideas of liberation priests had much greater appeal. Their religious character gave these organizations relative—although by no means total—immunity to repression and reprisal. Many functioned as cells of resistance and opposition to military regimes and appeared, both to these regimes and to conservative church leaders, more radical than they actually were. In fact, their less-than-radical character became clear when the region's military regimes were replaced by elected civilian successors. When this happened, most Catholics reverted to the apoliticism and dispersion of the premilitary years. Many supported right-wing parties like ARENA (Republican National Alliance) in El Salvador and the UNO (National Opposition Union) coalition in Nicaragua. Even those calling themselves leftists (for example, Catholics who belonged to Peru's United Left or to the Socialist Party of Chile) held moderate "reformist" views.

Tensions and Attempts at Restoration

The Catholic Church thus has exerted a generally progressive political influence over the past thirty years through its institutional and grassroots expressions. Its active defense of human rights and of social and liberal causes, however, has produced tensions, divisions, and fragmentation within its own ranks. Some Catholics have been won back to the fold, while others have been alienated. The new collegiality among bishops, greater independence and organizational development among priests and nuns, and the expanded dignity and role of lay men and women have generated greater vitality and commitment at all levels of the church. However, this has occurred at the expense of institutional authority and coherence. Increasing numbers of Catholics are making moral decisions based on the dictates of their own consciences rather than on the instructions of church authorities.

Alarmed by these developments, conservative Catholics have sought to rein in progressive elements—that is, to pull them back from political involvement—and to restore hierarchical prerogatives and practices that had been abandoned. Pope John Paul II, elected in 1978, headed this movement. Under him, retiring or deceased bishops (many of them progressives, who were named by Popes John XXIII and Paul VI) were replaced by conservative successors. In this manner and in the twenty-six years during which John Paul II was pope, the character and orientation of the Latin American church's leadership was changed fundamentally. In fact, more than 90 percent of the prelates serving as residential bishops or archbishops in the countries of Latin America were appointed, that is, consecrated as bishops and placed in charge of a diocese, or transferred or promoted from one diocese or archdiocese to another—by Pope John Paul II.[6]

These new leaders are not uniformly conservative. Some hold conservative positions on all questions—be they ideological, moral, theological, ecclesial (church functions and structures), or pastoral (how best to serve and lead their fellow Catholics). Many others, while conservative on moral, theological, and ecclesial matters, are—as was Pope John Paul II himself—ideologically or politically more progressive and favor democracy (except with respect to moral issues), greater social equality, and leniency for debtor countries.

In addition, theologically liberal seminaries have been closed, and the faculties and curricula of others—together with lay leader training programs—have been restructured to emphasize prayer, biblical scholarship, church history, canon law, and individually oriented pastoral counseling. Finally, loyalty to official church teachings is being stressed, and pastoral agents are urged to compete with Protestants to prevent nominal Catholics from being drawn away into Evangelical or Pentecostal churches.

Part of the Vatican's concern with strengthening hierarchical authority and reaffirming strict Catholic teaching on moral issues reflects the evidence that a majority of Catholics reject and/or ignore official church positions on birth control, divorce, and, in some cases, abortion in most Latin American countries.[7]

These changes have affected the church's relations with social and political processes in many countries. Its political visibility and influence have declined from their peak (in most countries) during the 1970s and early 1980s. With a drop in the incidence of human rights violations and with secular parties and movements resuming their normal activities, the church's role would have diminished in any event. But the directions taken by its new leaders further strengthened that tendency. In some instances, for example, Chile, the church's efforts to reduce its political profile actually helped it to play a more positive and influential role in the transition to democracy. Elsewhere, as in Peru, these efforts tended to produce and sustain a vacuum into which nondemocratic forces were able to insert themselves.[8]

The Catholic bishops have not entirely abandoned social issues. In their individual dioceses, and at regional conferences, such as Puebla in 1979, Santo Domingo in 1992, and the Synod for America in 1997, they have continued to speak out forcefully on issues of poverty and inequality, and they have argued that the neoliberal economic policies currently being pursued by most Latin American governments are making things worse for most people. But when they do speak out, they seem to be going through the motions—that is, reminding civil authorities of the need to do more but stopping short of insisting that they change course or redefine their objectives.[9] The lack of any follow-up, as well as the general aversion and suspicion with which the church's new leaders view politics, simply reinforce this impression. Unfortunately, their moderation is no longer palatable to upper-class Catholics, who do not think the bishops should be speaking on such matters at all, nor does it appear to console the working- or popular-class citizens whom the bishops claim to defend.

With their emphasis on traditional moral and ecclesiastical (church-oriented) issues, the bishops appear to have lost at least some of the esteem in which both working-class Catholics and secular liberals or leftists held them during the years of military rule. Secular liberals are unhappy with the church's conservative positions on moral issues and its unwillingness to let people themselves decide what to think or do. They have been quick to point out the contradiction between the church's earlier insistence (in urging a return to democracy) on greater respect for the rights and opinions of one's fellow citizens and its refusal to show such respect itself in these matters.

Somewhat surprisingly, upper-class Catholics are not favorably disposed toward the bishops' positions on sexual matters. Working-class and popular-sector Catholics are more likely to agree on some of these issues (sex before marriage and abortion, for example), but they are also jealous of the autonomy they have come to enjoy in the church in recent years and are not about to surrender it. Some conservative bishops have brushed such resistance aside, but other Catholic authorities have been more indulgent. They are aware of the inroads made by Protestant churches, of the continuing scarcity of priests, and of the consequences of dismissing or defrocking the "independents" or dissidents among either group.

Church leaders will no doubt continue to press political authorities directly in connection with moral issues, and the social and political forces with which they worked so effectively on behalf of human rights and democracy just a few years ago are again among their leading critics. But how the positions of church leaders will affect the social and political engagement of individual Catholics remains to be seen. Church leaders have been heartened, in recent years, no doubt, by the growth of well-financed lay-Catholic movements, such as Opus Dei, the Legionaires of Christ, and others, and by their emergence as a potent political force in a number of countries, most notably Chile, in connection with divorce legislation and other moral issues.

Even here, however, the church's influence may be limited to matters that significant segments of a country's population already identify with, because its ability to bring people around or back to its way of thinking will be more limited than in previous eras. As to the progressive movements and communities that represented the Latin American church in the public's mind—if not in actual numbers—during the years of military rule, some observers believe that they will survive the hierarchy's attempt at restoration and will continue to play an active and critical role in politics. But others question whether these groups can continue to function on their own without the resources, the moral authority, and the politically good offices of the institutional church.

Renewed Vitality

In the face of ongoing globalization and modernization, the Latin American Catholic Church has shown remarkable vitality and renewed staying power in recent years. In this regard, it resembles more the U.S. than the European pattern of responding to secularizing forces. For one, Latin Americans unhappy with Catholicism are more likely to have migrated to an Evangelical Protestant church than to have abandoned religion altogether, as their European counterparts have tended to do. For another, the church itself has exhibited renewed vitality in responding to both secularizing forces and the Protestant challenge.

Those who follow the Latin American church note, for example, that the number of priests and of men and women embracing the religious life actually has been increasing since the early 1990s in Latin America and not declining, as in the United States and Europe. They also point out that the portion of the population saying it belongs to the Catholic church has either stabilized or actually increased in many countries, that the percentage of the Catholic population reporting that it attends mass (services) at least once a week has increased in many countries as well, and independently organized lay Catholics are an increasingly visible and effective political force in a number of countries. Developments such as these have led some to conclude that, as in the United States, religion in Latin America is successfully resisting the demise to which modernizing and secularizing forces were inexorably supposed to lead it. A closer look at the evidence of renewed church vitality paints a more mixed picture, however.

It is true that the number of diocesan and religious priests increased by 8.7 percent between 1995 and 2001 and that the number of nuns also increased, though only by 1 percent.[10] Most of these gains have been confined, however, to the secular or diocesan clergy, such as deacons, whose ranks have increased by 15 percent in Mexico alone, and by 20 percent for South America as a whole. Among ordained priests, however, numbers are generally down (by 1 percent) despite gains in Mexico, Central America, and the Caribbean, and those for religious women are only up even marginally because gains of 10.2 percent in Mexico and Central America have compensated for a decline of 2.5 percent in South America.[11] Because the Catholic population itself has continued to grow, the overall increase in pastoral agents has not been able to prevent the ratio of numbers of Catholic faithful to priests from continuing to rise or to arrest the decline in the number of Catholics being baptized, marrying in the church, being confirmed, or receiving First Communion.[12]

With respect to affiliation and levels of practice, the data is also less clear than commonly reported. Church vitality is less evident in the region's more developed and, arguably, more modern secular societies. World Value Survey data are available for Argentina, Brazil, Chile, Colombia, Mexico, Peru, and Venezuela for much of the period since the early 1980s. Table 12.1 summarizes levels of affiliation ("belonging" to the Roman Catholic Church) and the extent of practice or observance (the percentage of those indicating that they attend services at least once a week).

Two distinct patterns emerge from these data. Four of the region's most advanced and culturally cosmopolitan countries, Argentina, Brazil, Chile, and Venezuela, exhibit still relatively high but steadily declining attachments to Catholicism, coupled with much lower but apparently stable levels of practice. This suggests that while the church has lost its hold on many in these increasingly secular countries, it retains the loyalty of a solid core of highly devout followers and may also have attracted newer adherents among the young and those who had fallen away from the church. This pattern, that is, a general trend of declining religiosity combined with renewed

Table 12.1   Levels of Affiliation and Practice Reported in World Values Surveys, 1981–2002

	Percentage Belonging to Roman Catholic Church	Percentage Attending Weekly
Argentina, 1984	80.7	30.7
Argentina, 1991	75.9	31.8
Argentina, 1995	77.4	25.4
Argentina, 1999	78.3	24.5
Brazil, 1992	69.9	33.6
Brazil, 1997	69.9	36.3
Chile, 1990	67.7	27.7
Chile, 1996	71.2	25.0
Chile, 2000	53.7	31.3
Colombia, 1997–1998	83.9	45.8
Mexico, 1981	87.3	54.1
Mexico, 1990	78.8	43.4
Mexico, 1995–1996	63.5	46.4
Mexico, 2000	72.3	54.8
Peru, 1996	82.5	42.9
Peru, 2001	82.3	47.1
Venezuela, 1995	82.5	30.9
Venezuela, 2000	65.6	30.5

Source: World Values Survey, 1981–1984, 1990–1993, 1995–1997, 1999–2002, available online at www.worldvaluessurvey.org.

fervor and vitality among those remaining "faithful" can be found in the European and U.S. experiences as well.

Constituting a second, contrasting pattern are two of the region's less modern and less developed societies, Colombia and Peru. Colombians and Peruvians display high levels of loyalty both to the church and to the practice of their religious faith. Mexico, however, while clearly modernizing rapidly, was closer to the first group of countries through the mid-1990s before undergoing a substantial shift in both allegiance and levels of practice and, thereby, joining Colombia and Peru.

A revitalization of Latin American Catholicism thus appears to be taking place, but it is not uniform in either level or locale. With the exception of recent trends in Mexico, a renewal of church attendance seems to be strongest in countries where less development and modernization have taken place and weakest, as in the United States and Europe, where they have been most pronounced. Those Latin Americans who have remained Catholic or who recently have returned to the church are more devout and regular in their practice than the Catholics of previous periods. Many of these appear to have drifted away, if not into atheism then into "noninstitutional religiosity," thereby validating, at least partially, the secularization thesis. But their places have been taken up by younger or returning Catholics who are part of a Catholic renewal that is a response and a potentially countervailing force to that very same secularization.

Protestantism

Latin America's Protestant churches have grown dramatically since the 1960s. According to some studies, between 10 and 15 percent of the roughly 540 million people living in Latin America today identify with one or another of the more than three hundred distinct Protestant denominations operating in the region. Almost half have been baptized or converted since 1980. Growth has been most notable in Guatemala, where Protestants are said to constitute more than 25 percent of the population; in Honduras and El Salvador, where between 17 and 16 percent of the people, respectively, are affiliated with one or another Protestant denomination; and in Brazil and Chile, where the figure is 15 percent.[13] These data are drawn from national censuses, CID-Gallup polls, and other "country" studies; unfortunately, the labels and criteria used are not uniform, and some believers may well have been counted as belonging to more than one church. Data from World Value Surveys presented below suggest that these figures may be inflated in the cases of Brazil, Chile, and Argentina, and understated in those of Mexico, Colombia, and Venezuela. In fact, it appears that Latin American Protestantism is no longer growing as rapidly as was once thought and that many of the men and women who no longer find Catholic beliefs and practices responsive to their needs are abandoning organized religion, as such, instead of turning to an "alternative" church.

Protestantism first came to Latin America through the so-called mainline (and relatively liberal) Anglican, Lutheran, and Presbyterian churches that came to minister to European and North American immigrants who had settled in the region in the late nineteenth and early twentieth centuries. Since then, however, Protestant expansion has been dominated by more conservative Evangelical and Pentecostal Christian groups, which now make up over 80 percent of the total Protestant population. Mainline groups comprise 12.5 percent and are strongest in countries such as Barbados, the Bahamas, Jamaica, Guyana, Suriname, and Belize, which were settled originally by non-Catholic Europeans. Marginal or eschatological groups (like Mormons, Jehovah's Witnesses, and Seventh Day Adventists who believe the world is coming to an end) make up the remaining 7.5 percent.

Although they quickly became independent, most of Latin America's Evangelical and Pentecostal communities were spawned by Evangelical Protestant churches in the United States. The twelve largest denominations or churches account for more than 90 percent of all Protestants. The Assemblies of God, with more than 10 million members, is the largest single denomination. But given the autonomy both Evangelical and Pentecostal churches extend to local chapels and communities, it is difficult to speak of cohesive churches or a dominant theological perspective.

Protestant Beliefs

The Protestant reformers arose in the sixteenth century in opposition to the way in which Catholic authorities had structured and guided the church. They believed God watches over his people and speaks through all believers, not just through a church's central authorities or ordained ministers. In addition, most reformers favored the translation of the Bible into vernacular languages and encouraged believers to read and reflect on it regularly. Most also were critical of "selling" indulgences and other religious favors for exorbitant fees and questioned the propriety and efficacy of sacraments such as Penance (could a cleric forgive one's sins?); the Eucharist (was Christ truly present in the bread and wine?); and Extreme Unction (could it bring physical as well as spiritual healing?).

None of the early reformers (Martin Luther, Ulrich Zwingli, Henry VIII, and John Calvin) advocated either religious freedom or separation of church from state, however. In fact, their churches were quickly enveloped in the same collusion with political interests and powers they had objected to so strongly in the Catholic Church. They were also unwilling to grant the freedoms of conscience and belief to their dissenters that they had demanded from Rome. And even the groups—Puritans, Pietists, Baptists, and Methodists—that later broke with the original reform churches were as intolerant of their nonconformists as Luther, Calvin, and the Anglicans had been of them. Only the Quakers, who fled to Pennsylvania to escape persecution in England, preached and practiced tolerance.

The Quakers' insistence on the integrity of the individual conscience, their belief that the Holy Spirit was potentially present in all believers, and the autonomy they granted to their local churches might have led other Protestants to embrace toleration and separation on their own. But they had to be forced to do so by the secular reformers who helped to write the U.S. Constitution. The Protestants who came to the United States in search of tolerance initially condemned these notions when Thomas Jefferson and others proposed them. Over time, however, they came to embrace them. Apparently, they were able to see that no religion could be free unless each shared its freedom with others, and the notion of an established church was thus abandoned.

Some Protestants who came to the United States retained their affiliation with a historical or mainline church, for example, Presbyterian, Baptist, Reformed, and Congregational. Many others, such as Methodists, Puritans, and Nonconformist Anglicans, came to escape the mainline churches' jurisdiction or to consolidate themselves as newly independent churches. The latter groups came to be known as Evangelical Christians. They disagreed on the degree of autonomy to be given to local churches, the degree of hierarchy or equality within any church, and the way to read the Bible, but they shared three basic tenets: (1) the reliability and final authority of the Bible, (2) the need to be saved through a personal relationship with Jesus Christ, and (3) the importance of spreading the message of salvation to every nation and person. Most Evangelical Christians felt the mainline churches lacked proper missionary fervor; they were more interested in defining the word of God for their existing communities than in bringing it to new ones. But even the Evangelicals had difficulty agreeing on how to preserve "fundamental" beliefs and still enlarge or expand the faith community. Those who give priority to the preservation of beliefs are generally referred to as fundamentalists; those who favor the growth of the community are called neo-Evangelicals.

Mainline and Evangelical Protestant churches developed simultaneously in the United States during the nineteenth century. The mainline denominations flourished in the larger cities of the eastern seaboard; the Evangelical communities tended to settle or emerge in smaller towns, rural districts, and frontier areas, where they enjoyed greater freedom to maneuver. Both groups developed an interest in Latin America, although for different reasons. Beginning in the 1850s, the mainline churches sent pastors to minister to European and North American immigrant communities in

Latin America. The Evangelicals, more missionary in orientation, were determined to save Latin American souls from disbelief or from, in their view, the clutches of corrupt Catholic priests.

The Evangelical churches led most of the Protestant missionary efforts in the twentieth century. In recent years, the Pentecostal denominations and communities have been particularly active. Although most Evangelical Christians believe in the presence of the Holy Spirit at all levels of the church, their meetings and prayer services tend to be orderly and reserved.

From the earliest days of evangelism in England, however, exceptionally "enthusiastic" pastors and communities could be found within the movement and in Methodism in particular. These people claimed to have received God's Spirit in the form of special gifts of prophecy, faith healing, and the ability to speak in languages or "tongues," in which they had never been trained. They were generally at odds with more reserved church officials, but they survived and occasionally developed large followings—particularly among lower-income and less-educated sectors.

These enthusiastic elements emerged full blown among poor blacks and whites in the United States in the early twentieth century, forming a series of Pentecostal churches and sects. They took their name from the occasion on which the Holy Spirit descended upon the apostles in tongues of fire, bringing them the ability to speak in unknown languages. Claiming and displaying the gifts of prophecy, tongues, and healing, they quoted readily and literally from the Bible and called for people to repent of their sins, accept Jesus as their personal savior, and be born again to Christian life through a second baptism. They swept the country—performing to packed houses, often accepting generous donations, and leaving behind small Pentecostal communities.

The largest single Pentecostal church in the United States, the Assemblies of God, is also the largest single Protestant denomination in Latin America with more than 10 million affiliated members. Other Pentecostal churches—including the Word Church of Guatemala, the Pentecostal Methodist Church of Chile, Brazil for Christ, and the small Pentecostal communities of indigenous peoples in southern Mexico—are among the largest and most influential Protestant churches in their respective countries.

The bulk of Protestant growth in Latin America in the past thirty years has been among the Pentecostal churches. The keys to their spectacular growth have been their appeal to Latin American religious sensibilities and an ability to attract or recruit pastors from local communities. Apparently, the emotion of their liturgies and the emphasis on faith healing have been responsive to the needs, anxieties, and feelings of many minimally educated and lower-income Latin Americans.

Pentecostals and Evangelicals also differ on the issue of social involve-

ment and in the way they approach the Bible. Evangelicals are generally
more open to the idea of materially assisting their own people and the poor
and underprivileged. Most Pentecostals view the world and society with
fear and distrust and see social causes as distracting to religious life. But
some groups do recognize a responsibility to improve the quality of life of
their own immediate community and of society as a whole. With respect to
the Bible, Evangelicals are divided between neo-Evangelicals, who reject
literal renderings or interpretations altogether, and moderate fundamentalists, who believe that the Bible is generally reliable and that its apparent
discrepancies are the result of "dispensations" or changes in the divine
plan. Most Pentecostals tend to deny the existence of discrepancies and to
insist on unerring and literal interpretation by all sincere believers.

In practice, however, most Evangelical and Pentecostal Protestants
occupy similar, middle-ground positions with respect to these issues. Only
very liberal Evangelicals and radical Pentecostals hold truly incompatible
positions. Moreover, the attitudes of particular communities appear to have
as much to do with the character of their leaders, the social conditions in
which they live, and the political options or threats they face as they do
with the positions of the church, whether Evangelical or Pentecostal, with
which they are affiliated.

How Strong Is Latin American Protestantism?

Counting Protestants in Latin America has never been easy or free of controversy. Labels and criteria differ markedly from study to study. Some of
the data is taken from the churches themselves and may well reflect both
the hopes and subjective impressions of pastors and staff people, whose
registration procedures are not always either elaborate or uniform. These
uncertainties have been underscored by the data by the World Values
Surveys for seven of the region's larger and more prominent countries.
Levels of Affiliation and Practice reported in World Values Surveys
1981–2002 are given in Table 12.2.

These data are striking in their implications, which suggest that in
these seven countries, among Latin America's largest and most cosmopolitan, Protestantism, even of the Evangelical variety, is much less widespread
than the churches themselves have claimed and than those who study them
have believed to this point. They further suggest that Catholicism's loss of
adherents in recent decades has swelled the ranks of those professing no
religion to a greater extent than it has those of Protestant churches. To be
sure, there could be serious problems with some of the data. The percentages of Protestants in Brazil seem implausibly low, just as those for ortho-
dox Christians in Chile, and the jump in the percentage of Chileans claiming no religion in 2000 seem implausibly high. While the Chilean survey

Table 12.2   Religious Affiliation for Selected Countries, by Year of Survey

	Percentage Belonging to Roman Catholic Church	Percentage Belonging to a Protestant Denomination	Percentage Belonging to None
Argentina, 1984	80.7	.1	12.8
Argentina, 1991	75.9	1.8	15.6
Argentina, 1995	77.4	1.9	13.7
Argentina, 1999	78.3	4.9	13.0
Brazil, 1992	69.9	3.5 (+8.5)[a]	11.7
Brazil, 1997	69.9	3.5 (+14.4)	11.9
Chile, 1991	67.7	9.3 (orthodox)[b]	18.5
Chile, 1996	71.2	9.3 (orthodox)	12.2
Chile, 2000	53.7	7.6 (Evangelical)	33.8
Colombia, 1997–1998	83.9	9.4	4.7
Mexico, 1981	87.3	7.7	3.9
Mexico, 1990	78.8	5.2	15.2
Mexico, 1995–1996	63.5	8.4	22.5
Mexico, 2000	72.3	4.6	20.5
Peru, 1996	82.5	6.2	7.0
Peru, 2000	82.3	9.5	4.7
Venezuela, 1996	82.5	6.3	7.5
Venezuela, 2000	65.6	6.7	27.0

Source: World Values Survey, 1981, 1990–1993, 1995–1997, 1999–2002, available online at www.worldvaluessurvey.org.

Notes: a. The figures in parentheses following the percentages of Protestants in Brazil indicate percentages of those responding "other," who may include both spiritists and Evangelical Protestants.

b. The terms included in parentheses following the percentages for Chile indicate the label under which Protestants were counted.

was directed by the very people who have studied religion extensively,[14] that may not be the case for all countries. But despite possible glitches here and there, the thrust of these data is clear. Secularization is a fact and a force of life in Latin America, and the success of religious institutions in resisting and responding to it should be placed in that larger context.

The Protestant Impact on Politics

Although it was generally progressive when the Catholic Church was aligned with the state and the dominant classes, Protestantism's political impact grew more conservative in the mid- and late twentieth century. This assessment requires qualification. With respect to short-term effects, there are enough exceptions to the general rule to preclude categorical generalization. In the long run, even conservative Pentecostal churches and communities may actually contribute to the further liberalization of Latin American societies, much as they have done in North America.

At the source of the political conservatism of many Evangelical and Pentecostal churches are the strongly anticommunist, antiliberal convictions of their U.S. pastors, sponsors, and benefactors—most of whom come from southern or western frontier states. Another factor in this direction has been the support of the U.S. government and military officials, for whom these groups were useful foils against secular leftists or progressive Catholic groups in Guatemala, Nicaragua, Costa Rica, and elsewhere.

Most Protestant pastors are Latin Americans, and their churches and communities (for example, the Pentecostal Methodist Church of Chile) are pointedly independent of their U.S.-based parent organizations. Most of these groups accept a conservative interpretation of authority that—even in morally questionable regimes—comes from God and warrants full obedience and respect. Moreover, they want no part of earthly power or politics, as only violence and evil can come of them. Indeed, they come to their religious communities seeking refuge from such sordid business and are highly critical of others, primarily Catholics and liberal Protestants, who advocate social and political involvement. Social and political abstentionism need not have inherently conservative consequences. In Latin America, however, where religion and politics have long been intertwined, religious affiliation does tend to legitimate and further strengthen those in power in most cases.

Additionally, some pastors (including those who inveigh against involvement in worldly affairs) will negotiate with regimes that offer something of value in return. In Chile, where the Catholic Church was very critical of the military regime's policies and practices, the regime courted Evangelical and Pentecostal pastors, offering them facilities, subsidies, and authorizations in exchange for implicit or explicit expressions of support. These churches were not always comfortable with their new allies or sponsors, but they apparently preferred to align themselves with forces (right-wing) that claimed to be Christian than with those (secular left-wing) that readily acknowledged they were not.

In a number of countries (such as Mexico, El Salvador, Chile under Allende, and Brazil), however, Pentecostal groups have adopted progressive positions. Under certain circumstances, Evangelical and Pentecostal doctrines can be taken in politically moderate and progressive directions. Much depends, it seems, on the views of a group's leader, the socioeconomic conditions in which particular communities live, and the concrete political alternatives the members confront.

In the long run, however, even conservative Protestant groups are likely to have a liberalizing effect on Latin American society and politics. First, their continued existence and expansion will further erode the link between Catholicism and national identity and with it the vestiges of established status that remain in some countries. Second, the corresponding development of religious pluralism will make it difficult for any religion or group of religions, whatever the extent of their followings, to dictate government policies on moral issues (such as divorce, birth control, and abortion) on which diverse opinions exist. Finally, even when a faith's content and immediate political implications are conservative, the fact that it constitutes a free social space where people can meet, speak, choose, and act as they see fit strengthens their sense of identity and civil rights vis-à-vis state officials and, to that extent, enhances the tendency toward further delimitation of political authority.

Spiritism

The third significant religious tradition in Latin America today is the family of movements and cults broadly referred to as spiritism. Spiritists can be found in virtually all Latin American countries but are particularly prominent in areas such as Brazil and the Caribbean, where West Africans were brought as slaves from the seventeenth through the nineteenth centuries. In addition, the beliefs of the Aztec, Incan, and Mayan traditions contain spiritist elements that survive to this day in eclectic or syncretic combination with the Catholic and Protestant creeds to which their followers were "converted" centuries earlier.

Spiritists believe the dead continue to "live" as spiritual bodies with whom communication through special mediating agents is possible. They believe in the gradual purification of souls across various incarnations and believe benign and not-so-benign spirits exert significant influence (for better and for worse) on the world of the living. The identity of the principal spirits, the methods employed by mediating agents, the extent to and means by which evil spirits can be countered, and the degree to which spiritist beliefs blend or conflict with Christian notions (for example, the overlapping of spirits and patron saints) vary from movement to movement, as do the socioeconomic and cultural characteristics and concerns of their members. Here, I discuss briefly Kardecian spiritism, *umbanda, candomblé,* and *vodou* (or voodoo). Others, such as *obeah, santería,* Pocomania, Zion Revival, and the cult of María Lionsa, display similar characteristics.

Spiritist Beliefs

There are three major spiritist movements in Brazil alone: spiritism proper, *umbanda,* and *candomblé.* The first of these is associated with the nineteenth-century French psychologist Allan Kardec. Appealing primarily to middle- and upper-class Brazilians of European descent, Kardecian spiritism is more a philosophy than a religion. The spirits on which it calls are the "great voices of history"—that is, Asian sages and Western intellectuals.

Umbanda is a more religious version of spiritism that appeals to blacks, whites, and *mulatos* of popular- and middle-class backgrounds. Its spirits are both Brazilian (indigenous Brazilians known as *caboclos*) and African (*pretos velhos* or old blacks), who are paired or "identified" with Christian saints that have similar characteristics or functions. They advise people about health- and work-related problems and about personal relationships, using sensitive mediums who receive them and transmit their prescriptions through trance speaking or "automatic" writing. Some mediums develop large personal followings, attracting people from far and wide and acquiring near saint or cult status. The advice many give is in part recognizably Christian, stressing free will, charity, reincarnation, and the new millennium. Most *umbanda* centers hold daily sessions and offer a full range of cultural activities and medical, physical, and social services. Whereas the Kardecian spiritist movement has developed its greatest following in the São Paulo area, the *umbanda* movement's principal base of operation is Rio de Janeiro.

The third major tendency in Brazilian spiritism is *candomblé* (also known as *macumba* or *xangô*), a descendant of the Yoruba religion West African slaves brought with them in the eighteenth century. Its spirits, known collectively as *orixas*, are closer to the Greek and Roman gods—with strong but clearly imperfect characters—than to the Kardecian or *umbanda* spirits. They, too, are linked to the Christian saints; for example, the wise spirit Oxala is identified with Jesus, the lively Xango with Saint Jerome, gentle Oxun with the Virgin Mary, and the vigorous Ogun with Saint George. Such connections, however sincere, help *candomblé* followers assuage the fears of both the religious and secular authorities who are concerned with their country's Christian character.

Candomblé differs from *umbanda* in terms of its constituency—which is poorer, less educated, and racially "blacker"—and its more consciously religious character. Whereas *umbanda* rituals focus on practical advice—healing bodies and purging evil energies and spirits—those of *camdomblé* are more celebratory. They pay homage to the gods, the *orishas*, with whom believers mingle and enjoy the dancing, eating, processions, and pageantry that have long been a part of their religious tradition.

A more aggressive and violent form of spiritism is *vodou,* a generic term referring to the various spiritist cults that grew up among Haiti's slave population. *Vodou* was instrumental in the country's independence and abolition movements in the late 1700s and has continued to exert religious and political influence in the two centuries since. Its origins are also West African, although they are more varied than those of *candomblé*. *Vodou* has adapted to or more fully assimilated the conditions and forces slaves confronted in the various regions of Haiti. *Vodou* also differs from other Latin American spiritist movements in the thorough politicization to which it was subjected during the Duvalier dictatorships (1957–1986).

Vodou spirits are called *loas*. Their personalities and functions vary from temple to temple. Some are clearly mixtures or amalgams of African, native indigenous, and Catholic figures. Contact is normally "arranged" by priests called *houngans*, whose authority rests on their charisma, their knowledge of herbal healing, and their ties to certain spirits and to local political or military authorities. Spirits sometimes make themselves available in sacred places, such as trees or posts, or appear as they take possession of someone during community dances or festivals. Their help is usually sought in connection with curing ailments or heading off anticipated or forewarned disasters. Individual temples or networks of temples tend to identify with different spirits and frequently become embroiled in conflicts of both a personal and political nature, in which context spirits can be invoked to attack or neutralize one another.

For most of the 150 years following independence, *vodou* communities operated on an essentially clandestine basis. They were outlawed and persecuted episodically by most Haitian governments, usually at the urging of the country's French (and thus white) Catholic bishops. Throughout this period, however, *vodou* groups provided cultural enclaves in which Haitian blacks developed and maintained their own identity. As the various temples and communities were set up along territorial lines, they developed into organizational networks, in which smaller temples identified with a larger or more established mother temple, and priests or temple heads functioned as local power brokers. These features made them useful cells for the black power movement launched by François Duvalier in the mid-1950s. Duvalier legitimated *vodou* and used its organizations, in particular its imposing militias (known as Tonton Macoutes), to win the 1957 presidential elections and to repress, intimidate, and control enemies and potential adversaries for the next thirty years.

Santería, the form Yoruba spiritism has taken in Cuba, was brought by African slaves beginning in the late eighteenth century. Its spirits offered help with personal and health problems. For the most part, it helped the slaves to make the best of their generally miserable lot. In the nineteenth century, however, the sense of ethnic identity and community that *santería* helped them to nurture served as the basis for slave uprisings that ultimately led to abolition.

Santería's deities are similar to those of *candomblé*. In time, they came to be identified with Christian personalities or saints. Jesus, Mary, and

Catholic saints were accepted as extensions or equivalents of Yoruba deities, and *santería* believers adapted their festivals to the Catholic calendar. This syncretism (the reconciliation of conflicting beliefs) was both honest and calculating. As one *santería* sage put it, "They [white people's saints] must be very powerful since they have made them [the whites] masters and us [blacks] slaves" (Efunde 1983:15). But having experienced periodic suppression at the urging of Catholic authorities, believers also hoped to protect themselves by moving closer to the church.

With Cuba's emancipation in 1888, the movement developed a new, more sinister strain. Younger men, unable to find work as freemen, saw criminal potential in their reputed ability to negotiate with the spirit world. Borrowing from Haitian *houngans* and *bocors* (medicine men), they used black magic and sorcery for criminal purposes—kidnapping and sacrificing small children, casting spells on people for money, and helping people arrange accidents or misfortune for their enemies. With the emergence of this darker side of *santería*, the movement lost much of its respectability, and its more peaceable priests (*jawalowos*) were often blamed for the violent and sordid practices of others.

The Spiritist Impact on Politics

The impact of these spiritist movements on the politics of their countries has been mixed. Insofar as they encourage spiritual explanations and solutions of secular problems, their impact has been conservative. But at specific junctures in the histories of several countries, they have helped to forge and sustain identities and to strengthen progressive abolition, independence, and cultural autonomy movements.

Clearly, much depends on the socioeconomic conditions and political alternatives of individual countries. It can be argued that the *umbanda* and *candomblé* movements in Brazil have provided a basis for popular class identity and consciousness that is independent of the country's elite-dominated, mainstream institutions (including the Catholic Church). But the *vodou* experience in Haiti offers a forceful reminder of the potential that spiritist structures and practices hold for manipulation by repressive, sectarian regimes that seek to rally people against foreign enemies and then control and exploit them.

The fact that a majority of the country's population believed in and practiced this "illegal" cult, as well as the lack of any alternative organizational structures at the grassroots level made *vodou* particularly susceptible to such politicization. In turn, however, the reputation for power enjoyed by certain priests, many of them members of the Tonton Macoutes, contributed to an equally pervasive "vodouization" of Haitian politics. In other words, the systematic recourse to *vodou* methods and practices by some of the country's leading military and political figures served to legitimize their domination and abuse of citizens.

■ Conclusion

The role of religious beliefs in Latin American social and political life has been profound. With respect to Catholicism, its authority and influence have been substantial at key moments during the past thirty years but now appear to be in decline. Once solidly Catholic constituencies are increasingly pluralistic, more open to secularizing influences and more assertive of their own autonomy and responsibility, particularly with respect to sexual norms and conduct.

Although constantly calling attention to the moral and religious dimensions of public issues, the Catholic Church has assumed a more visible and leading political role when secular political forces are either deadlocked or prevented from functioning normally. In these cases, it has been easier for the church to achieve consensus in its own ranks and to rally practicing and cultural Catholics and secular forces in defense of social justice, human rights, and an end to dictatorial rule. With the return to civilian rule, however, secular forces resume their normal functions, and the policy issues become more complex and debatable. Under these circumstances, the

UN Photo 159535/J. Bleibreu

A wedding party walks to church in El Salvador.

church has shifted its focus to more traditional and personal moral concerns on which, amid growing secularization and pluralism, its authority and influence are weaker and in connection with which its authorities are probably unwilling to push more forcefully for fear of further alienating dissident clergy and laity.

The Protestant churches are likely to retain their appeal with the popular-sector groups on which the Catholic Church has focused much of its attention in recent years. Although the days of the Protestant churches' dramatic growth may have come to an end, the link that once existed between Catholicism and national culture and identity has been broken. A person's national identity no longer points him or her in a particular religious direction.

Although Catholic parishes have introduced charismatic prayer services, in which lay members play a leading role, they do not appear to draw as well as their Pentecostal rivals. As far as the small Christian communities (the CEBs) are concerned, the return to civilian rule in most countries has caused them to diminish in number and vitality, although they continue to maintain a presence in the lives of many popular neighborhoods. It may be, as some observers have suggested, that the CEBs continue to appeal to believers who are comfortable studying (as opposed to just quoting) the Bible, dealing with complex ideas, and making and following through on social and political commitments but that they have lost appeal among the majority of Latin American Christians and cultural Catholics, who appear to prefer more emotion and less intellectualism.[15]

As pointed out by Susan Tiano in Chapter 10, both lay and religious women have played more central, leading roles, at least in local communities. Catholicism, however, continues to project the image of a large, male-dominated institution in which women occupy subordinate positions and exercise only limited responsibilities. Conversely, the more decentralized structure of Protestant churches makes the prominent role women play in local churches and communities appear to be more significant and is, therefore, probably more attractive to many women.

Politically, mainline, Evangelical, and Pentecostal Protestants are divided into liberal and conservative camps over the issues of divorce, birth control, abortion, and religious education. Moreover, although many continue to eschew the affairs of the world, others are taking up issues of poverty, social justice, and growth with equity—particularly where the lot of the poor is deteriorating. Finally, whereas some Protestants actually sit in national legislatures in countries such as Guatemala and Peru, others continue to view politics as inherently violent and corrupting.

Given the diversity of opinions within Roman Catholicism on both moral and social issues, greater public policy consensus may exist across denominational lines than within any particular church. Conservative

Catholics, backed by conservative Evangelicals and the resources of wealthy and well-organized Catholic movements, are an increasingly formidable political force in connection with moral issues and could conceivably extend their agenda. More liberal Christians, Catholics and Protestants alike, however, are not as numerous, cohesive, resourceful, or well organized, but they may be able to counter the efforts of more conservative elements in some instances. Trends are not yet clear and predictions remain hazardous. But such developments could lead to the further secularization of political power and to a shift in the debate on moral and ethical matters from the political to cultural arenas, such as the role of the news media, and, as we saw in Chapter 11, the universities of Latin American countries.

Notes

1. As will be seen below, survey data for Chile and Brazil raise serious questions about these claims.

2. Most are against abortion and homosexuality, although they are divided on whether to permit divorce and on how actively to support or oppose political initiatives dealing with these issues.

3. The most prominent of these is Gill 2000.

4. Survey data available for many of the larger Latin American countries from 1990 suggest that the extent of Protestant expansion may have been inflated and that these churches are no longer growing at all, much less at the rates attributed to them earlier.

5. This discussion draws on chapter 1 of Fleet and Smith (1997).

6. By 2000, 545 of the 608 serving bishops had been either initially designated or subsequently promoted or transferred by John Paul II, and the trend continued in the next four years. Data on these matters are readily available from national episcopal conferences and can be found online at www.alapadre.net or www.riial.org and in the yearly editions of the *Annuario Pontificio*, which contains biographical information on church officials throughout the world.

7. World Values Survey data since the early 1980s indicate that fewer than 30 percent of Latin American Catholics agree with its opposition to divorce, although a majority apparently continue to oppose abortion unless the life of the mother is in danger.

8. See Fleet and Smith (1997:chapters 5 and 7).

9. In response to their critics, a number of bishops have protested that they are "pastors," not economists.

10. I have arrived at these figures using data from yearly editions of the *Annuarium Estatisticum Ecclesiae* (AEE), a Vatican publication providing detailed statistical information on the church worldwide.

11 The number of ordained priests also fell by 2.5 percent in South America as a whole, with only Colombia, Paraguay, and Peru escaping the trend. These indications that the church's revitalization is most modest in the region's largest, socioeconomically most advanced, and culturally most cosmopolitan countries (i.e., Argentina, Brazil, Chile, and Venezuela) suggest it may be premature to dismiss the secularization thesis entirely. Further evidence in this same vein is presented below.

12. Table 6 of the AEE for 2000 and 2001 shows the Catholics per priest ratio to have fallen only in Mexico and Central America (7,671 in 1995 to 6,854 in 2001) and to have risen from 7,760 to 8,316 and from 7,013 to 7,176 in the Caribbean and South America respectively. Data regarding reception of sacraments is provided in tables 30 and 31 of the AEE.

13. For data see the website of the Latin American Studies Center of Providence College (www.providence.edu/las), table 7.

14. The survey was conducted by Latinobarómetro and headed up by the veteran and widely respected pollster and sociologist Marta Lagos.

15. One such observer is Phillip Berryman, who offers a thoughtful discussion of the competing visions and appeals of radical Christian communities and Evangelical Protestant groups in chapter 7 of *Stubborn Hope* (Berryman 1994).

▓ Bibliography

Abbott, Walter J. (ed.). *The Documents of Vatican II*. New York: Guild Press, 1966.

Annuario Pontificio, per l'Anno 1999. Vatican City: Libreria Editrice Vaticana, 1999.

Berryman, Phillip. *Stubborn Hope: Religion, Politics and Revolution in Central America*. Maryknoll, N.Y.: Orbis Books, 1994.

Efunde, Agun. *Los Secretos de la Santería*. Miami: Ediciones Cubamérica, 1983.

Fleet, Michael, and Brian Smith. *The Catholic Church and Democracy in Chile and Peru*. Notre Dame, Ind.: University of Notre Dame Press, 1997.

Gill, Robin (ed.). *The Cambridge Companion to Christian Ethics*. Cambridge: Cambridge University Press, 2000.

Hess, David. *Samba in the Night: Spiritism in Brazil*. New York: Columbia University Press, 1994.

Laguerre, Michel S. *Voodoo and Politics in Haiti*. New York: St. Martin's Press, 1989.

Levine, Daniel. *Popular Voices in Latin American Catholicism*. Princeton, N.J.: Princeton University Press, 1992.

Martin, David. *Tongues of Fire: The Explosion of Protestantism in Latin America*. London: Basil Blackwell, 1990.

Marzal, Manuel M. *Los Caminos Religiosos de los Inmigrantes en la Gran Lima*. Lima: Pontificia Universidad Católica del Perú Fondo Editorial, 1989.

Smith, Brian H. *Religious Politics in Latin America: Pentecostal vs. Catholic*. Notre Dame, Ind.: University of Notre Dame Press, 1998.

Stoll, David. *Is Latin America Turning Protestant?* Berkeley and Los Angeles: University of California Press, 1990.

13

Latin American Literature

David H. Bost and Margaret V. Ekstrom

L iterature reveals much about how people interpret their physical and
social environments and their place in the world. Their values, beliefs,
and aspirations are reflected in tales about past and daily experiences.
Hence, literary expression is an important consideration for students of
contemporary Latin America.

Previous chapters have explored specific aspects of Latin America,
past and present. In this chapter we look at the perceptions of interpreters
and writers who have contributed an artistic and intellectual account that
illuminates our understanding of the culture in which they lived.

■ The Colonial Heritage

Native American Literature

As René de la Pedraja reports in Chapter 3, the Spanish explorers and *conquistadors* of the early 1500s were astonished to find that the New World
had civilizations that in some ways rivaled those in Europe. The Mayas,
Aztecs, and Incas were accomplished architects, artists, musicians, sculp-
tors, and dancers. Most pre-Columbian literature was oral and was quickly
forgotten after the conquest. A few Native American texts, however, were
transcribed in the sixteenth century by Spanish clerics and educated
Indians. These texts exist today as evidence of a rich literary tradition that
flourished in the centuries before the discovery of America.

The Mayas were the only Native American civilization that had written
texts, in hieroglyphic form, almost all of which perished in the chaotic
years after the conquest. A few of these books survive as Spanish transla-

tions, however. For example, *Popul-Vuh* (the Mayan Bible) is a collection of myths, history, philosophy, and legends. *Chilam Balam* is a compilation of history, religion, astronomy, and medicine. It was written in Mayan a few years after the conquest by an anonymous author who used the Spanish alphabet. Some fragments of Mayan codices and stone inscriptions do remain.

The Incas and Aztecs had no actual written language but had an active oral literary culture. The Aztecs used some pictorial representations, whereas the Incas kept accounts on colored, knotted strings called *quipus*. Many performances—often a combination of theater, song, and dance—were ceremonial and ritualistic in nature. The Incan *taqui*, for example, was a ritual dance that represented the Incan calendar and principal mythological characters. The Aztecs had highly developed theater that was performed in the large open spaces of Tenochtitlán (most of which now lies under the foundations of Mexico City). Drama in the Aztec and Incan empires often constituted an official ceremony performed at the royal court and events reenacted from their historical or mythological past. The Aztecs and the Incas also composed lyric and epic poetry that was performed at public ceremonies.

Spanish missionaries who lived among the Indians and learned their languages also wrote extensively about the Native American tribes of Mexico and Peru and produced some of the earliest accounts of Indian culture. Diego de Landa, for example, translated Mayan hieroglyphs into the Roman alphabet.

Native American culture survived long after the conquest of the New World. The most important native-born chronicler of Incan society was Garcilaso de la Vega. Son of a Spanish captain and an Incan princess, Garcilaso spent his childhood in Peru and his adult years in Spain serving as an officer in the military. Garcilaso was truly bicultural; he spoke fluent Quechua as well as Spanish and spent his later years writing his monumental *Comentarios reales del Perú* (*Royal Commentaries of Peru*, 1609), a history and analysis of Incan culture and the Spanish conquest of Peru. The commentaries repeat many of the stories and legends Garcilaso heard as a child growing up among his Incan family. He wanted to correct the misconceptions of Spanish historians who, in his opinion, had misrepresented the history and culture of his maternal ancestors. Today, his work is one of the most important historical, anthropological, and literary sources for scholars studying ancient Peruvian culture. Garcilaso is perhaps better known in the United States for his detailed history of the ill-fated 1539 De Soto expedition, *La Florida* (1605).

A contemporary of Garcilaso's was Guamán Poma de Ayala. His *El primer nueva crónica y buen gobierno* (*First New Chronicle and Good Government*, 1615) is an illustrated history of Peru that challenged the legitimacy of the Spanish conquest of the New World and called for an end to Spain's colonial domination.

Chronicles of the Conquest and Colonization

With the exception of the novel, virtually every literary form was cultivated during the early colonial period. Much of the historical writing was testimonial; soldiers, explorers, and missionaries felt compelled to give their version of events in which they had taken part. Columbus's diary of his first voyage (1492) is considered by many literary historians to be the earliest text in Latin American literature. As a writer, Columbus faced a monumental challenge: to communicate an image of the New World in ways that were understandable and compelling to his European audience. Hence, Columbus justified further exploration and ultimate conquest by tempting his readers with exaggerated reports of gold and tales of a generous and trusting people who lived in an idyllic paradise.

The conquests of Mexico and Peru were recorded by active members of the expeditionary forces that defeated native rulers Montezuma and Atahuallpa. Hernán Cortés, the Spanish captain who led the overthrow of the Aztec Empire, kept Emperor Charles I abreast of events as the Spaniards marched on Tenochtitlán. His letters to the monarch are one of the most valuable sources of information on one of history's most remarkable military victories. These records were written in part as an attempt to seek monetary or political reward for service to the crown. Cortés wanted to be named ruler of the lands he conquered, a wish the emperor ultimately fulfilled.

Bernal Díaz del Castillo wrote a remarkable account of the fall of Mexico, narrated from the point of view of an ordinary soldier. His book, *Historia verdadera de la conquista de la Nueva España* (*True History of the Conquest of Mexico*, 1557), is based primarily on his own observations and recollections. Bernal Díaz had an incredible eye for detail: he remembered such things as the number of steps on different Aztec sacrificial temples, the names of horses, and the identity of common soldiers other historians had ignored or forgotten. His work is one of the best colonial Latin American examples of a literary treatment of a historical event. Bernal Díaz, who lacked the formal academic training of a professional historian, relied on novelistic language and devices to tell his story more eloquently. Hence, many portions of his text sound like a popular tale from a novel of chivalry.

Most historical accounts of the colonial period, professional or otherwise, were strongly influenced by literary language and models. Popular historians, such as Bernal Díaz del Castillo, incorporated many elements from popular literature. Learned historians, those commissioned by the crown to write the official story of the conquest and colonization, were well versed in classical historiography and often used ancient Latin masters as their ideals. Gonzalo Fernández de Oviedo wrote his *Historia general y natural de las Indias* (*General and Natural History of the Indies*, 1557) using such classical historians as Pliny as his model. Oviedo, nurtured on classical literature through his immersion in Italian Renaissance culture, wrote in extraordinary detail about virtually everything he witnessed during his long residence in the New World.

Perhaps the most important characteristic of Oviedo's work and that of other official chroniclers is their passionate defense of Spain's conquest of America. Oviedo and many others felt it was Spain's imperial destiny to dominate and Christianize the New World, even if this meant the virtual annihilation of Indian culture. There were a few worthy opponents to this position, however. Dominican priest Bartolomé de las Casas was the most articulate defender of the Indians in history; in his many historical works, it is difficult to avoid his strongly favorable characterizations of Indians. In contrast, Oviedo and many others depicted the Indians in an extraordinarily negative fashion.

Oviedo was succeeded by generations of official chroniclers who were charged not only with writing general histories of the colonies, but also with censoring other histories in an effort to protect Spain's image in the international community. Spain suffered for many years from the Black Legend, the belief in many European countries that Spain had committed numerous atrocities in the New World in the name of religious conversion. The debate over the Indian—helpless victim or godless savage—is one of the most pervasive themes in the colonial as well as contemporary eras. Indianist novels of the nineteenth and twentieth centuries examined the prejudices toward the Indian that still exist hundreds of years after the conquest. Contemporary writers Mario Vargas Llosa, Carlos Fuentes, Octavio Paz, and Rigoberta Menchú Tum—among many others—continue to explore the presence of Indian culture in contemporary Latin American life.

Not every official in the Spanish army was contemptuous of Indians. In 1542, Alvar Núñez Cabeza de Vaca wrote an extraordinary account of his eight-year journey through the North American Southwest, living among the Indians first as a captive and later as their leader. His book of these experiences has recently been translated as *Castaways* (*Naufragios*, 1993). Cabeza de Vaca, one of the few who survived a shipwreck off the Texas coast, felt great sympathy for the Indians he had befriended during his long trek toward Mexico City. His account of his travels is a veritable treasure of ethnographic and historical information on tribes that have long since vanished. *Castaways* is fairly typical of many Latin American historical works of the colonial period in its reliance upon literary themes and motifs: There are prophecies told and revealed; suspense; betrayals; the supernatural; and a fascination with an immense, exotic, and virtually unknown world ready for exploration, conquest, and eventual settlement.

Captivity among the Indians was a popular topic for colonial historians. In several cases, prisoners returned to their former countries with fascinating stories. The captives were sought out by Spanish authorities because of their valuable information regarding the Indians. Yet, the returning captives were not always entirely sympathetic to the conquest and its methods of subjugating the Native Americans.

One of the most remarkable characteristics of certain captive narratives is that the authors reported their assimilation into the foreign culture. Francisco Núñez de Pineda y Bascuñán wrote *Cautiverio feliz* (*The Happy Captive*, 1673) as a record of his seven-month captivity among the Araucanian Indians in southern Chile. His story is one of adventure, action, and intrigue. A young captain stationed on the frontier, Bascuñán was captured by the fierce Araucanians during a raid on the outpost. His extended residence among the tribe gave him considerable insights into a group of people generally regarded as savages. His story does something that was remarkable for the time: He individualized his descriptions of the Indians and avoided the generalizations that were common with earlier historians. Bascuñán did not deny that his captors could behave in a savage fashion, but he also revealed that these people were capable of extraordinary generosity and benevolence.

Spanish captivity and residence among the Indians have also fascinated contemporary novelists. Argentinean writer Abel Posse, for example, has published a novel based on Cabeza de Vaca's experiences entitled *El largo atardecer del caminante* (*The Long Afternoon of the Walker*, 1992). And Mexican novelist Eugenio Aguirre (1980) has written about Gonzalo Guerrero, the first Spaniard ever captured by Native Americans, who apparently led his Mayan captors in a revolt against the Spanish invaders.

The Imaginative Construction of History

By the mid-seventeenth century, many of the testimonial accounts of the colonization of the New World gave way to histories that were more literary in nature. One of the most imaginative accounts of Colombian history is Juan Rodríguez Freyle's *El carnero y Conquista y descubrimiento de Nuevo Reino de Granada* (*The Conquest of New Granada,* 1636). Rodríguez Freyle wrote a traditional history of the founding and settlement of his native Santa Fe de Bogotá, but his work also contains tales of sorcery, stories of adultery, lurid accounts of criminal activity in the colony, and myths and legends about the Native Americans. Rodríguez Freyle was one of the most innovative and expressive writers during the colonial period; his text reveals a dimension of life in the colony that other historians had either ignored or understated.

At first glance, it may seem unusual for a historical account like *The Conquest of New Granada* to have so many imaginative stories. It was fairly common, however, for historical writers during the Latin American colonial era to rely on literary models to invest their stories with a more expressive language. In the sixteenth and seventeenth centuries, often no clear distinction could be discerned between historical and fictional writing with regard to truth or reliability. It was not uncommon, for example, for historians such as Rodríguez Freyle, Garcilaso de la Vega, or Oviedo to depict individuals, situations, or events with little or no textual evidence. Historians often speculated fairly freely about events and their significance. Some of Rodríguez Freyle's stories were justified as examples of what the author viewed as moral decay within the colony.

One of the best examples of a literary treatment of history in the later colonial period is *Infortunios de Alonso Ramírez* (*The Misadventures of Alonso Ramírez*, 1690) by Mexican intellectual Carlos de Sigüenza y Góngora. Much like a novel, the work is an account of Ramírez's extraordinary journey around the world. Alonso Ramírez was a sailor who, through a series of mishaps, shipwrecks, and captivity, circumnavigated the planet—a remarkable feat for his day. He told his story to Sigüenza y Góngora who, in turn, constructed an entertaining tale of Alonso's life.

Sigüenza y Góngora's book is very similar to a picaresque novel. Alonso left his native Puerto Rico for Mexico City, where he held a succession of jobs with a number of masters. He went to the Spanish Philippines, where he briefly had a prosperous career as a sailor, traveling and trading widely throughout the Asian Pacific. His most dramatic misfortune occurred, however, when he was captured by English pirates who abused and humiliated their prisoners and treated them as slaves. Alonso's crew quickly perished under captivity. Of the original twenty-five who were captured, only eight survived. The pirates finally gave Alonso and his crew the opportunity for freedom: They placed them in a small boat with minimal provisions and arms.

Sailing west from Madagascar, Alonso and his crew's boat wrecked on the Yucatán shore, and the men eventually wandered back to civilization. Once back in Mexico City, Alonso reported his story to Sigüenza y Góngora. In spite of the historical foundations of this story, many novelistic elements are at work that give Sigüenza's narrative its strong literary quality: its sense of adventure, humor and irony, political intrigue, first-person narration, and episodic structure.

Sigüenza y Góngora was intensely interested in the American experience and wrote many other works of scientific, anthropological, and historical value. In many of his works, it is possible to detect a nascent American consciousness. Sigüenza bristled with anger, for example, whenever Europeans made disparaging references to the so-called inferiority of the Creoles who populated the New World.

Poetry and Drama

Although poets and dramatists in colonial Latin America generally attempted to copy the literary conventions and styles of their Spanish and European counterparts, many tried to depict the American reality in their literature. Epic poets were among the first to compose literary homages to the individuals who had orchestrated the principal events of the discovery and conquest of the New World.

The greatest epic poem written in colonial Latin America is Alonso de Ercilla's "La Araucana" ("The Araucanian," 1569–1589), depicting the prolonged wars with the fierce Araucanian Indians of Chile. Ercilla's poem is both testimonial—based on his experiences in fighting the tribe—and epic. Perhaps the most unique quality of the poem is that Ercilla did not shy away from showing profound admiration for the honor and valor of these warriors who, year after year, effectively thwarted the best efforts of the Spanish army to defeat them. Ercilla depicted the Araucanians as a highly organized, well-disciplined army. In many regards, the poem is more the story of Caupolicán, the head of the Araucanian forces, than of Pedro de Valdivia, the Spanish leader. "The Araucanian" was extraordinarily popular during its day and for many years afterward, spawning numerous imitations.

The epic tradition was continued into the seventeenth century by Mexican poet Bernardo de Balbuena, whose poem "Grandeza Mexicana" ("Mexican Greatness," 1604) is an exuberant tribute to Mexico. Balbuena's careful examination of the Mexican reality is a precursor to the nineteenth-century literary movement of *costumbrismo*, in which writers recorded in minute detail virtually all aspects of daily life. Because of his passionate interest in describing Mexico in all of its complexity, Balbuena has been regarded by some literary historians as the first genuinely American poet.

Not all poetry written during the colonial era was an epic tribute to the great events that had given shape to Spain's American empire. Satirists, such as Juan del Valle y Caviedes (c. 1645–1697), were bitter critics of many members of colonial society, particularly those who sought to better themselves at the expense of others. Few escaped Caviedes's wrath: Aristocrats, religious officials, women, and doctors were among those who were ridiculed in his poetic compositions. His disregard for doctors was legendary. One of his most widely read poems is "Coloquio que tuvo con la muerte un médico moribundo" ("Conversation That a Dying Doctor Had with Death," c. 1680), a savage attack on the practice of medicine in colonial Peru.

Like most satirists, Caviedes hated hypocrisy and deceit. In the sonnet, "Para hallar en palacio estimaciones" ("How to Succeed at Court," c. 1690), Caviedes depicts the "perfect" courtier, one who is certain to get the attention of the viceroy: He will be a liar, a clown, a deceiver, a gossip, and, above all, a yes-man. Honesty and integrity have no place in the colonial court. Like Juan Rodríguez Freyle, Caviedes was interested in exploring the dark underside of colonial life in an effort to portray an increasingly complex society many years past the conquest.

Caviedes was one of many in the late seventeenth century who openly admired the Mexican nun, Sor Juana Inés de la Cruz, generally regarded as colonial Latin America's greatest writer. Poet, dramatist, essayist, and scholar, Sor Juana's intellectual reputation was rather unusual, of course, for women in the seventeenth century. Unable to attend the university, Sor Juana was almost entirely self-taught. Before entering the convent she was a well-known figure at the viceregal court, where she often dazzled onlookers with her amazing intelligence and learning.

Sor Juana often found it necessary to defend her life of learning and erudition. One such instance is seen in her famous correspondence with the bishop of Puebla, who had criticized her for spending too much time in her intellectual pursuits to the detriment of her religious duties. Sor Juana's response to these accusations is the *Respuesta de la poetisa a la muy ilustre Sor Filotea de la Cruz* (*Reply to Sor Filotea de la Cruz*, 1691), an autobiographical statement that, among other things, defends her right to a life of study and reflection—an inclination that, she argued, God had given her. Sor Juana finally succumbed to the ecclesiastical authorities in 1694, when she sold her impressive library for charity and dedicated herself fully to her religious calling.

Sor Juana was a gifted and prolific poet. Her many poems dealt with religion, morality, love, jealousy, death, and other literary topics that were common during the baroque period. Feminist literary critics have recently read with great interest her compositions that criticize men for their unbridled arrogance toward women. One of Sor Juana's best-known poems is "Hombres necios" ("Foolish Men," c. 1690), a work that asks sarcastically why men expect women to be good when it is men who so often lead women astray. Her love poetry, known for its passionate language, is unusual considering the restrictions of her religious order. Her most ambitious poetic attempt is "Primero sueño" ("First Dream," 1692), a long, complex poem that is a philosophical meditation on her search for knowledge and the elusive nature of reality.

Sor Juana was also an accomplished dramatist. Writing during the last years of the golden age of Spanish theater, Sor Juana was heavily influenced by Calderón de la Barca, generally regarded as Spain's premier play-wright. Sor Juana wrote both secular and religious drama and utilized all of the major styles of her era.

Much of the dramatic literature that preceded Sor Juana was religious in nature. Many of the plays in the sixteenth and seventeenth centuries were written by missionaries interested in using drama as a means of converting the Indians to Christianity. Missionaries often mixed Spanish with native languages and incorporated elements of Indian theater into their religious plays. Following some of the practices of Aztec and Incan theater, mission-aries staged many of their plays in outside settings, frequently utilizing cos-tumes and scenery of the indigenous tribes. The best-known playwright of the sixteenth century was Gonzalo de Eslava, a Mexican priest who wrote primarily religious plays. Eslava, not unlike Bernardo de Balbuena, infused his literature with many references to Mexico.

Seventeenth-century playwrights include two Peruvians, Juan del Valle y Caviedes, who wrote satirical plays on the folly of love, as well as satiri-cal poetry mentioned earlier, and Juan de Espinosa Medrano, whose princi-pal work was based on the Bible. The greatest name associated with theater in the Latin American colonial period is Mexican-born Juan Ruiz de Alarcón, a writer who emigrated to Spain at an early age. Alarcón, more properly affiliated with Spanish golden age theater, was an extremely popu-lar and respected writer of comedies of manners and honor.

■ The Nineteenth and Twentieth Centuries

The First Novel and Short Story
Nineteenth-century Latin American literature marked the beginning of a new age brought about by independence and a growing sense of national identities. Many literary achievements occurred during this period: the pub-lication of the first novel and short story; the attempt to produce literature that was unique to the many new countries; and the creation of modernism, the first literary movement Spanish America gave to Spain.

Critics generally agree that the first novel published in Spanish America was José Joaquín Fernández de Lizardi's *El periquillo sarniento* (*The Itching Parrot*, 1816). In some ways, Lizardi's novel owes more to the eighteenth-century Age of Reason than to the Age of Revolution: It is didactic in tone, containing long, moralizing passages on education and the proper upbringing of young people. The story is about an orphan named Pedro who, like a typical character from Spanish picaresque literature, serves a series of masters while observing and remarking ironically on vir-tually every aspect of Mexican society. Much like his literary predecessor, Alonso Ramírez, Pedro also sails for the Philippines, is shipwrecked on a desert island, and eventually returns to Mexico, where his life is finally put into some moral order. Lizardi was a well-known social critic in prerevolutionary Mexico, often writing newspaper articles under the pen name "the Thinker." Once imprisoned for speaking out against the colonial viceroy, Lizardi used *The Itching Parrot* as a vehicle for satirical commentary on the need for radical social reform.

Political and social commentary are also the thematic bases for Latin America's first short story, Esteban Echeverría's "El matadero" ("The Slaughterhouse," 1838), published in Argentina. Set during the tyrannical reign of the infamous despot Juan Manuel Rosas, the story tells in graphic detail how a young man from the opposition Unitarian Party is captured by a mob and brutalized. Echeverría's political and social messages were clear: If Argentina was going to prosper in the era of independence and self-rule, it would need a centralized, representative government with an educated populace acting responsibly.

One of the lasting legacies of such foundational works as *The Itching Parrot* and "The Slaughterhouse" is the use of literature to bring about social and political change. A great deal of nineteenth- and twentieth-century literature—novels, short stories, poetry, and drama—protests some situation or condition brought about by the abuse of power and privilege.

Toward an American Identity

Much of the literature written during the decades following independence was a celebration of the diversity of the new nations that emerged from the years of colonialism and conflict. Following the European literary models of romanticism and realism, Latin American authors invested their literature with references to the uniqueness of their newly formed republics. Poets were especially effusive in their depiction of the shifting American reality. Ecuadorian poet José Joaquín Olmedo is credited with being the first Spanish American poet to commemorate in verse America's independence from Spanish rule. His ode, "La victoria de Junín" ("The Victory of Junín," 1826), is, among other things, an elegy to Simón Bolívar and his leadership during the revolutionary period. Similarly, Venezuelan Andrés Bello, one of Bolívar's former teachers, urged his fellow writers to search for inspiration in authentic American topics rather than copying European models.

The poetic elaboration of the American experience perhaps reached its peak in nineteenth-century literature with the publication of José Hernández's narrative poem, "Martín Fierro" (1872), a work that laments the gradual disappearance of the *gaucho*, long a symbol of the Argentine pampas. The poem is the story of a *gaucho* (cowboy) who, against his wishes, is forced to serve in the military, where he is mercilessly abused and exploited. Fierro eventually deserts the army and joins with the Indians, embittered over the loss of his freedom and autonomy. "Martín Fierro" is the literary predecessor of *Don Segundo Sombra* (1926), Ricardo Güiraldes's famous novelistic rendition of the *gaucho* and his importance to Argentine cultural identity.

The description of the Argentine consciousness was a central concern of Domingo Faustino Sarmiento, one of the nineteenth century's greatest essayists and intellectuals. Sarmiento wrote a classic essay delineating Argentina into two opposing camps, the urban and the rural. Unlike Hernández, Sarmiento perceived the urban mentality as offering his country education, enlightenment, progress, democracy, and industrial development. Sarmiento was an unabashed admirer of Europe. He felt the ignorance, superstition, tyranny, and isolation of rural Argentina—characterized by the pampas and the ever-present *gaucho*—symbolized all that kept his country from emerging from its barbaric past.

Sarmiento's essay, "Civilización y barbarie o vida de Juan Facundo Quiroga" ("Facundo," or "Civilization and Barbarism," 1845), is ostensibly a psychological study of Juan Facundo Quiroga, a prototypical rural tyrant who was a supporter of the *caudillo* Juan Manuel Rosas. In this work, Sarmiento examined what he felt was the root cause of many of Argentina's political problems during the early years of the republic. Surrounded by and containing vast pampas, Argentina suffered from extreme isolation, which made effective governance virtually impossible. Sarmiento argued that Argentina's future salvation would occur through dramatic improvement of the educational system and effective centralized government.

The political and social realities of Argentina and the other Latin American countries were fully represented in the nineteenth-century novel. Novelists were deeply concerned about the failure of liberal democracy to flourish in the new age of independence. Political oppression, economic hardship, and social injustices were common maladies throughout Latin America during much of the nineteenth century, and novelists felt compelled to call attention to the problems affecting their countries.

One of the most prominent political novelists of the period was José Mármol, whose *Amalia* (1855) depicts Argentina suffering under the regime of Juan Manuel Rosas, thematically similar to Echeverría's "El matadero." *Amalia,* typical of literature from the romantic school, includes conspiracies, political intrigues, hidden identities, and the tragic death of two lovers, the main characters, shortly after their wedding. As with many novelists who are committed primarily to writing about social and political circumstances, Mármol's work contains much commentary on contemporary issues of national concern. Critics have argued that such political literature—which was even more commonplace during the twentieth century—is too severely compromised to constitute an effective work of literary art.

Yet, virtually all of Latin America's major contemporary writers, including its Nobel laureates, have at some time written literature that carries an obvious political or social message.

In addition, the theme of the struggle with nature was developed by several authors, including Jorge Isaacs of Colombia in his romantic novel *María* (1867), and more recent writers, such as José Eustacio Rivera, who described the Colombian jungle in *La vorágine* (*The Whirlpool*, 1924); Martín Luis Guzmán, with his portrayal of the Mexican Revolution in *El águila y la serpiente* (*The Eagle and the Serpent*, 1928); and Rómulo Gallegos of Venezuela in *Doña Bárbara* (1929), a work contrasting civilization and barbarism.

The novel was an effective vehicle during the nineteenth century for examining and presenting qualities that reflected a nation's particular identity. Ignacio Manuel Altamirano used the nineteenth-century Mexican novel in the same way Bernardo de Balbuena had used epic poetry centuries earlier to defend all that was uniquely Mexican. Altamirano joined Andrés Bello in his fervent desire to incorporate American themes into what was envisioned as a national literature. *Clemencia* (1869), for example, was written against the historical backdrop of the French intervention in Mexico in 1863. In *La Navidad en las montañas* (*Christmas in the Mountains*, 1871), Altamirano romanticized life in rural, mountainous Mexico, using the novel to expose the beauty and serenity of life far away from the capital city.

Although Altamirano had a somewhat romantic, perhaps even idyllic view of rural life, he was also an astute observer of the customs and traditions of regional Mexico. One of his purposes was to incorporate into his novels as many traits of Mexican life as possible, in an effort to show that Latin Americans had ample subject matter for their literature in their own history and traditions. By the late nineteenth and early twentieth centuries, it had become commonplace for authors to write in great detail about subjects that seemed particularly appropriate for their specific countries. Peruvians and Ecuadorians wrote about the plight of the Indian and of Andean culture in general. Chilean novelists, heavily influenced by European naturalism, began to examine the economic and social effects of copper mining on daily life. Argentineans followed the course set by José Hernández and continued to explore the life of the *gaucho* in a rapidly changing world.

The best example of a nineteenth-century writer who found inspiration in his country's mythological and historical records was Peruvian Ricardo Palma. Palma wrote short sketches, anecdotes, and characterizations based on people and incidents from old Peru. His short folkloric compositions, *Tradiciones peruanas* (*Peruvian Traditions*, 1872–1883), are humorous, ironic, satiric narratives that deeply mine Peru's rich colonial and indigenous heritage, ingeniously mixing fact with fiction. As director of the

National Library, he had easy access to a wealth of original documents that provided source material for his creations. Many of his stories fairly accurately reproduce speech patterns, customs, popular sayings, and common beliefs of the time. Scholars have noted that Palma is one of the most important precursors of the contemporary Spanish American short story.

Modernism

The first major literary movement that took root in Spanish America and was passed to Spain, modernism was heavily influenced by French symbolist poets and philosophical currents of the late nineteenth century. Modernists—attempting to renovate literary language, style, themes, and techniques—significantly departed from the subject matters that were characteristic of realism and naturalism. Rather than giving detailed descriptions of regions and local traditions, they opted to write about exotic lands that captivated the poetic sensibilities of this new generation of writers. Captivated by ideas of beauty, elegance, sensuality, and refinement, modernists infused their literary language with references to ancient Greece, the Far East, and the medieval world.

Whereas their realist counterparts were interested in portraying an accurate image of the world around them, a world that was often squalid and dangerous, modernist writers depicted realms that were creations of fantasy—places inhabited by princesses and knights, swans and nightingales. "Art for art's sake" was the battle cry of the modernists, who at times sought to divorce literature from the sordid economic and social realities that characterized their world. Above all, modernism was a movement that attempted to create a new Hispanic literary language, one that was essentially poetic in nature and reflected the new aesthetics of cosmopolitan refinement and literary renovation.

Many names are associated with modernism: Cuba's José Martí, Manuel Gutiérrez Nájera of Mexico, Colombia's José Asunción Silva, Cuba's Julián del Casal, and Argentina's Leopoldo Lugones. Yet no one embodies the spirit of modernist thought and practice better than Rubén Darío, a Nicaraguan poet whose work spans the entire movement and defines its basic tenets. Critics often mark the beginning and end, respectively, of modernism with the publication of Darío's *Azul* (*Blue*, 1888) and his death in 1916. Darío was unquestionably the best-known and most widely imitated Hispanic poet of his generation. His poetry exemplified grace, cultural refinement, extraordinary literary depth, and stylistic elegance. Elevating Hispanic poetry to unprecedented heights in his efforts to revolutionize concepts about literature, Darío showed that it was possible to break from the realist and romantic schools of thought. He wrote about Wagnerian swans, ancient Persian cities, medieval Spanish poets, classical deities, and mythological characters. Yet Darío's greatest contribution to Latin American literature may have been his extraordinary renewal of poetic language.

Of the dozens of Darío's poems that embody the modernist spirit of innovation and originality, "Sonatina" (1893) perhaps best captures the mood of exoticism and elegance. The poem describes a beautiful young princess whose melancholy mood contrasts sharply with her opulent home. She lives a life of unparalleled luxury, yet she is limited by her excessive wealth. Her fairy godmother reassures her that she will soon be rescued from her "prison" by a knight "who [will] arrive from afar, conqueror of Death." The poem is filled with arcane references to figures from classical mythology, exotic locations, and unusual plants and wildlife.

It is a common misconception to regard modernism as a literary movement that completely broke from many Latin American writers' concern with social and political issues. Modernists were concerned primarily with the renovation of literary language, yet they never abandoned some of the issues that had preoccupied earlier generations of writers, such as how Latin America differed fundamentally from North America. For example, a number of Darío's poems—including "A Roosevelt" ("To Roosevelt," 1905), which takes issue with Theodore Roosevelt's militant nature—openly accuse the United States of being overly aggressive toward its Latin American neighbors, suggesting that North American foreign policy was imperialistic.

Criticism of the United States was common among writers of Darío's era. Uruguayan José Enrique Rodó, the greatest essayist of the modernist generation, published *Ariel* (1900), a philosophical treatise on the essential distinctions between Latin America and the United States. Although openly admiring U.S. economic and political power, Rodó was deeply opposed to what he viewed as a U.S. obsession with materialism. Rodó considered Latin Americans to be far more spiritually inclined than North Americans and urged his readers to weigh the benefits of material progress against the advantages of spiritual and cultural achievements.

Darío and Rodó initiated a trend among Latin American writers in the twentieth century to use the United States as a point of reference in their analyses of their own culture and society. Octavio Paz, Mexico's contemporary Nobel laureate, for example, wrote *El laberinto de la soledad* (*The Labyrinth of Solitude*, 1950), a book that incisively compares popular Mexican culture with that in the United States, searching the history of each nation for root causes of the vast distinctions between them. Similarly, Carlos Fuentes's *El espejo enterrado* (*The Buried Mirror*, 1992) is a modern critique of Latin American cultural history.

The impact of modernism on Latin American literature was profound and enduring. The modernist renewal and invigoration of literary language occurred in both prose fiction and poetry. Writers nurtured on realist modes of exposition discovered that their stories could be far more expressive and effective if they focused on the eloquent possibilities of language. The long, cumbersome, detailed passages that were common in documentary realism gave way to shorter, more poetic narratives that were highly metaphorical in construction.

Darío was a masterful prose writer as well as poet, and his work provided models and inspiration for countless others—even writers whose subject matter was largely social and political. Mariano Azuela, whose *Los de abajo* (*The Underdogs*, 1915) is considered the classic novel of the Mexican Revolution, incorporated modernist literary techniques in his vivid descriptions of the Mexican countryside. Regionalist and Indianist novelists—who continued the centuries-long struggle for justice on behalf of the Indian well into the twentieth century—were strongly influenced by modernist innovations in language and literature. Modernism, for example, helped to teach regionalist writer Horacio Quiroga how to condense his stories—generally set in the Latin American wilderness—into brief exposés on the tragic nature of human existence.

Literature of the Vanguard

Modernism was succeeded by a period that invited an enormous variety of literary styles, techniques, and concerns. The documentary tendency of realist fiction continued to flourish, and most poetry became a more intimate, personal expression. Women writers had far greater visibility, most notably, poets Delmira Agustini, Alfonsina Storni, Juana de Ibarbourou, and Gabriela Mistral—Latin America's first Nobel laureate in literature. The most dramatic development of the postmodernist era was unquestionably the eruption of the literature of the vanguard.

The vanguard was to literature what cubism was to painting: a complete upheaval of traditional expectations regarding the fundamental premises of artistic expression. By the 1920s, art had witnessed a revolutionary plunge away from realism and into abstraction, and literature soon followed suit. Literature of the vanguard attempted to push verbal expression away from the rational into the irrational, away from conventional forms of literature in favor of newly created forms, away from old themes toward a new registry of poetic topics that reflected the sensibilities of a new age of technology. The modernists had their swans; the vanguard had airplanes, trains, factories, and cities. Spanish philosopher José Ortega y Gasset wrote at the time about the "dehumanization" of art that occurred during the period following World War I, a reference to what he felt was an absence in art of elements that reflected the human experience.

The poetic manifestations of vanguard literature include a total disregard for formal grammatical and stylistic conventions; punctuation, for example, is often random and arbitrary. Poets would often avoid a logical exposition of themes and subjects; their poems at first glance often appear to be chaotic jumbles of images and incoherent metaphors.

Perhaps the most vivid example of a Latin American poet of the vanguard is Chilean Vicente Huidobro, whose long, rambling poetic meditation, "Altazor" (1919), was an invitation to literary anarchy: The only rule was that there were no longer any rules. Huidobro was especially fond of creating words simply for the sound they represented or the rhyme scheme they momentarily fulfilled. "Altazor" has segments that are merely a collection of invented words that seem to exist for no purpose beyond the sound they create within the poem. Huidobro called his poetic efforts "creationism." His thesis, typical of the vanguard generation, was that the poet alone was exclusively responsible for the burden of inspiration and creativity.

As with all literary movements, the period of the vanguard had its day, yet its legacy was enduring. Literature was imbued with an experimental verve that has lasted from the vanguard until the present. Novels and short stories of the famous "boom" of the 1960s, for example, are indebted to the vanguard for opening the door to literary experimentation, which characterized Latin American literature for most of the twentieth century.

▓ Magical Realism and the Boom

It was Cuban author Alejo Carpentier who first made extensive use of the term magical realism (*lo real maravilloso, la maravillosa realidad,* or *el realismo mágico*), after a 1943 trip to Haiti during which he was greatly impressed by the influence of African culture on Haiti. These influences included myth and music; language and perception; and unexpected alternations of reality, metamorphosis, and magic. They involved a cultural ability or tendency to perceive or emphasize mysterious and magical elements that could be found in everyday reality, in common activities, thus mixing reality and fantasy. Numerous examples of this literary technique are found in Carpentier's novel, *El reino de este mundo* (*The Kingdom of This World,* 1949).

Characteristics of magical realism, however, can be traced back to the earliest cultural encounters between Europeans and the indigenous peoples of the Americas. Columbus, Cortés, and the other early explorers of the 1500s were not prepared for the New World they encountered. There was initial confusion about whether they had arrived in some part of Asia (China or India). Their languages lacked words for many of the new things they found; they had to borrow from the indigenous languages. They were often amazed by the peoples, plants, animals, locales, and customs in the new lands. Their reactions thus combined their own wonder with the obvious reality of their surroundings. In some cases, they embellished their "discoveries" to impress their rulers or supporters back in the old country.

As the explorers began to learn about indigenous myths and religious practices, the blending of magic and reality continued, albeit on a predominantly subconscious level. As they attempted to impose many of their own beliefs on the indigenous peoples, an almost inevitable syncretic evolution of hybrid cultural forms occurred. The introduction of African cultural elements, predominantly in the Caribbean, added substantially to the mix. Thomas D'Agostino in Chapter 4, Kevin Yelvington in Chapter 9, and Michael Fleet in Chapter 12 show how this process of amalgamation occurred in politics, ethnic relations, and religious practices, respectively.

Although the participants may not have had a specific name for this process, it continued nevertheless. Known as "El Inca," Garcilaso de la Vega of Peru tried to present the indigenous perspective and reaction to the encounter by explaining some of the myths and practices of his people. Mexican author Fernández de Lizardi later combined some elements of indigenous language and belief in his nineteenth-century descriptions of colonial life. As mentioned previously, the most profound and effective blending of these early tendencies to combine history and fiction (reality and myth) occurred in the works of Ricardo Palma. His *Tradiciones peruanas* (*Peruvian Traditions*, 1872–1883) combined researched historical fact with local legends and personal commentary, often in an ironic or satirical tone. Jorge Luis Borges, the famed twentieth-century Argentine author, also used this technique with success, giving a veneer of historical reality to his creative fantasies in works such as *Ficciones* (*Fictions*, 1944) and *El aleph* (*Aleph*, 1949). Borges is universally renowned for his use of the basic elements of magical realism, including time shifts, dream sequences, and multicultural references.

Authors of the modern Latin American literary "boom" (c. 1960–c. 1970) raised magical realism to the exalted level of a renowned, worldwide literary movement—gaining international stature, recognition, and respect for the previously all-too-often neglected realm of Latin American literature. This boom was exemplified by the unprecedented explosion of Latin American writing on the international literary scene. Many of the works achieved universal appeal, critical acclaim, and financial success.

Interests and characteristics of the boom authors include magical realism, native cultures, myths, combinations of history and fiction, circular time, dreams, the other or the double, creative language, multiple viewpoints, and experimentation. The reader becomes an active participant rather than a passive observer in the work, because the reader has to untangle the varied literary threads. An excellent example is seen in Julio

Cortázar's novel *Rayuela* (*Hopscotch*, 1963), in which the reader can select chapters in a varied order, thus altering the plot development. Several of the boom authors were also fond of intellectual games and occasionally referred to other authors, works, or characters in their writings.

In addition, the ideals of the boom include some allegiance to certain tenets of the Cuban Revolution—such as greater rights for the poor, individual liberty with group social consciousness, a fairer distribution of wealth, and an improvement in general living standards. The institution Casa de las Américas, which was renamed the Organization of American States (OAS), fostered the new interest in Latin American literature with wider publication of both classic and recent texts.

Many authors can be included in the boom; among the most notable are Cuba's Alejo Carpentier; Mexico's Carlos Fuentes (*La muerte de Artemio Cruz* [*The Death of Artemio Cruz*, 1962]); Peru's Mario Vargas Llosa (*La ciudad y los perros* [*The City and the Dogs*, 1962]); Argentina's Julio Cortázar; Colombia's Gabriel García Márquez (*Cien años de soledad* [*One Hundred Years of Solitude*, 1967]); Guatemala's Miguel Ángel Asturias (*El Señor Presidente* [*Mr. President*, 1946]); and Mexico's Juan Rulfo (*Pedro Páramo*, 1955).

By 1970, several disagreements had developed among the various authors of the boom. There were political and ideological differences, especially when the Cuban Revolution failed to live up to its original promise. There were also social and creative differences, with a desire by some for greater liberty in literary subject matter and style. Although the boom declined, many of its members continued to write and evolve within this genre, even as new authors appeared on the scene.

The techniques of magical realism had become well established and were continued in later works by several authors. It is interesting to note that of the five Latin Americans who have won the Nobel Prize for literature, at least three were from the boom. The Nobel laureates include Gabriela Mistral of Chile (1945, poetry); Miguel Ángel Asturias of Guatemala (1967, novels/stories); Pablo Neruda of Chile (1971, poetry); Gabriel García Márquez of Colombia (1982, novels/stories); and Octavio Paz of Mexico (1990, poetry and essays).

Beyond the Boom

Although interest in magical realism continued after the boom, some writers reacted unfavorably to certain techniques employed during that movement. Some opposed the intellectual games played out in a few texts. Differences occurred on many levels—political, social, stylistic, ideological, and creative. Although many of the boom authors have continued to work and are still popular, they have evolved with changing times.

Contemporary literature has made room for many more varied voices, including more women authors. Some who have achieved wide recognition are Rosario Castellanos of Mexico (*Balún Canán*, 1957); Elena Poniatowska of Mexico (*La noche de Tlatelolco* [*The Night at Tlatelolco*, 1971]); Luisa Valenzuela of Argentina (*El gato eficaz* [*The Clever Cat*, 1972]); and Isabel Allende of Chile (*La casa de los espíritus* [*The House of the Spirits*, 1982]). Gioconda Belli of Nicaragua, Edwidge Danticat of Haiti, and Anacristina Rossi of Costa Rica have achieved literary recognition in recent years, as well, with works often critical of political developments in their countries. It is also worth noting that several authors of Latino/Hispanic descent are writing in the United States in both English and Spanish, including Luis Rafael Sánchez, Miguel Méndez, Oscar Hijuelos, Rudolfo Anaya, Julia Alvarez, Sandra Cisneros, and Rolando Hinojosa-Smith.

Interest has also continued in the multicultural nature of Latin American society. Peruvian José María Arguedas has written of the indigenous influences in *Los ríos profundos* (*Deep Rivers*, 1958). The African cultural heritage has been vividly described in the poetry of Nicolás Guillén of Cuba and Luis Palés Matos of Puerto Rico. Peruvian poets have defended the poor (César Vallejo) and the Jewish heritage (Isaac Goldemberg). Both Ariel Dorfman and Antonio Skármeta of Chile have written powerfully on the theme of exile.

One of the most popular forms of literature in Latin America in the years following the boom of the 1960s has been the historical novel. The contemporary history novel has inherited many of the literary techniques and thematic concerns of magical realism, such as multiple narrators, fluid depiction of time and space, Native American mythology and culture, and fantasy. The colonial era has a powerful fascination for contemporary novelists because it provides a basis for understanding many of the historical issues of concern today throughout Latin America: the discovery and its political, social, and economic consequences; the plight of the Indian during the conquest; the inception of a nationalistic consciousness; and the movement toward independence.

In what is sometimes an obvious parody of the great figures of early Latin American history—Columbus, Cortés, and the *conquistadors*—a number of writers have presented highly imaginative visions of the past that challenge, distort, and contradict standard accounts of history. In Alejandro Paternain's *Crónica del descubrimiento* (*Chronicle of the Discovery*, 1980), for example, a tribe of Indians crosses the Atlantic and "discovers" Europe, a land the Native Americans consider to be highly uncivilized. Cuban writer Alejo Carpentier, in many ways the father of magical realism, wrote several novels in which conventional distinctions of time are completely disregarded. His *Concierto barroco* (*Baroque*

Concerto, 1974), for example, juxtaposes elements from modern music—jazz, electric guitars, and Louis Armstrong—with the musical culture of eighteenth-century Venice.

Carpentier is one of many writers who incorporate primary historical documents in their literary treatments of the colonial period, making virtually no distinction in their novels between historical and fictional language. Antonio Benítez Rojo's *El mar de las lentejas* (*Sea of Lentils*, 1979), a book about Latin America's first one hundred years, uses historical accounts from the era to underpin his fictional story about Columbus's second voyage to America. Virtually all of Latin America's most noted novelists have contributed to this literary genre, including Gabriel García Márquez (*El general en su laberinto* [*The General in His Labyrinth*, 1989]); Carlos Fuentes (*La campaña* [*The Campaign*, 1990]); and Mario Vargas Llosa (*La guerra del fin del mundo* [*The War of the End of the World*, 1981]).

As Kevin Yelvington observes in Chapter 9, the world learned about Indian rights activist Rigoberta Menchú with the publication of her 1983 autobiography, *I, Rigoberta Menchú: An Indian Woman in Guatemala*, which eventually appeared in eleven languages. Her accounts of Quiché Mayan life and culture in the northwest highlands, hardships growing up helping her parents tend their tiny plot and traveling with them to work on coffee and sugar plantations, and state terror directed against her people earned her the Nobel Peace Prize in 1992. In her autobiography, Menchú vividly recounts the torture and death of her parents and brother at the hands of the Guatemalan military. Rather than happily mark the five hundredth anniversary of Columbus in the New World in October 1992, she was quoted as defiantly insisting that "the celebration of Columbus is for us an insult." Some critics, such as anthropologist David Stoll, have questioned the accuracy of certain historical and interpretive aspects of Menchú's text. She has defended her work and produced a new volume, *Crossing Borders* (1998).

■ Brazil and the Circum-Caribbean

Brazil followed a pattern similar to that of the other Latin American nations though with Portuguese language and culture. Some of the best-known Brazilian writers lived during the nineteenth century: Machado de Assis, Joaquim Nabuco, José de Alencar, Gonçalves Dias, and Castro Alves. The twentieth century also produced important authors in Brazil, including Mário de Andrade, Oswald de Andrade, Carlos Drummond de Andrade, Cecília Meireles, Raquel de Queirós, Jackson de Figueiredo, Graça Aranha, Coelho Neto, and Jorge de Lima.

João Guimarães Rosa published one of his major works, *Grande sertão, veredas* (*Big Country, Footpaths*), in 1956. Jorge Amado treated social themes in such works as *Mar morto* (*Dead Sea*, 1936) and *Capitães de Areia* (*Captains of Sand*, 1937). Other notable writers from the Brazilian republic include regionalists and social realists such as Gilberto Freyre and José Lins do Rêgo; stylist Graciliano Ramos; experimental novelists with innovative narrative techniques such as Erico Veríssimo; and writers who employ powerful, poetic, and magical language such as Clarice Lispector and Nélida Piñón.

Other non-Spanish-speaking nations of the Circum-Caribbean have produced several writers of considerable stature whose works should be included in the discussion of Latin American literature. For example, Orlando Patterson of Jamaica wrote *The Children of Sisyphus* in 1964, which reveals the struggle for survival in Kingston's shantytown society. Jamaican novelist John Hearne wrote *Faces of Love* (1957) and *Autumn Equinox* (1959), which study the nation's complex social and psychological relationships. From Dominica in the West Indies, Jean Rhys published her novel, *Wide Sargasso Sea*, in 1966, which deals with the representation of the Creole Caribbean woman. From French-speaking Guadeloupe, Simone Schwarz-Bart wrote two novels, *Pluie et vent sur Télumée miracle* (*The Bridge of Beyond*, 1972) and *Ti Jean L'Horizon* (*Between Two Worlds*,

Nobel Prize winner Rigoberta Menchú (center) makes her way through a gauntlet of reporters on her way to a press conference in Guatemala City.

1979), which depict the cultural interconnections of the region. These and works by Trinidadian writer V. S. Naipaul (*Guerrillas*, 1975); Antiguan author Jamaica Kincaid (*At the Bottom of the River*, 1983); and St. Lucian epic poet Derek Walcott (*Omeros*, 1990) provide additional perspectives on the Circum-Caribbean.

■ Popular Culture

The literature and society of Latin American nations have been strongly influenced by popular culture. Numerous street theaters throughout the region have served as models of social reform, political protest, and artistic creativity. Such artists as Diego Rivera and Frida Kahlo participated in international politics. As Susan Tiano discusses in Chapter 10, the protest movement of the mothers of the Plaza de Mayo in the 1970s helped bring about the downfall of the Argentine dictatorship that was responsible for the disappearances of many citizens. Nonfiction writing in essays and newspapers also has played an important role in the development of Latin American society.

Film became a powerful cultural medium in the twentieth century. Argentina's Manuel Puig wrote *La traición de Rita Hayworth* (*Betrayed by Rita Hayworth*, 1968); his *El beso de la mujer araña* (1976) became the important film, *Kiss of the Spider Woman*, which condemned dictatorial excess and prison cruelty. *The Official Story* (1985), directed by Luis Puenzo, is another award-winning film that grew out of the protests against the Argentine military dictatorship.

As cinema developed as a dominant artistic form, attempts were gradually made to transfer literary magical realism to film, which presented interesting challenges. The technique of flashback can be used with considerable success to convey the interplay of past, present, and future that is so important to magical realism's sense of the circularity of time. The use of ancestral or legendary spirits (even ghosts) that appear in works of magical realism can be portrayed through various split-screen and related cinematic techniques. Magical realism should not be confused with horror films or science fiction; it has a lighter, subtler touch than those popular genres. A cinematic version of Carlos Fuentes's *Aura* (1962) might run the risk of such confusion, for example, because of its depiction of otherworldly beings who even seem to return from the dead.

Perhaps the best-known work of magical realism is García Márquez's *Cien años de soledad* (*One Hundred Years of Solitude*, 1967). One episode from the novel was developed into another story by the author, which became the film *Innocent Erendira* (1982). Several of García Márquez's stories were developed for the film series, *Love in the Time of Cholera* (named after his novel with this title published in 1988). García Márquez has now written part of his life story (*Vivir para contarla*; translated into English as *Living to Tell the Tale*, 2003), which reveals some of the fantastic elements of his long creative career.

Indeed, memoirs have become increasingly popular with Latin American authors in recent years. Marjorie Agosín described her childhood as a Jewish girl growing up in Chile in *A Cross and a Star* (1997). Another Chilean writer, Isabel Allende, told the very personal tale of the fatal illness of her daughter in *Paula* (1994). Gioconda Belli wrote vividly about her life in Nicaragua in *El país bajo mi piel* (2001, translated into English as *The Country Under My Skin* in 2002). Cuban author Reinaldo Arenas offered his life story in *Antes que anochezca* (published posthumously in 1992), which has been translated into English and produced on film as *Before Night Falls*.

Chilean author Isabel Allende's novel, *La casa de los espíritus* (*The House of the Spirits*, 1982), was also later brought to the screen in an English-language version. Mexican author Juan Rulfo's novel, *Pedro Páramo* (1955), appeared on screen in a Mexican film version in the 1970s. Rulfo's story of the life of a local *patrón* involved magical realism to a considerable degree through flashbacks to different time periods in his life and references to characters, living and dead, who appeared in the work.

The independent film *El norte* (*The North*) was a joint U.S.–Latin American production that came out in 1983, directed by Gregory Nava. Although not directly based on a novel, it beautifully evoked on film the spirit of magical realism. It follows the lives of two young refugees from the violence in Guatemala—a brother and sister who escape north through Mexico and finally into the United States. One of the most popular recent attempts to bring magical realism to film was the successful screen adaptation of Mexican scriptwriter Laura Esquivel's imaginative novel, *Como agua para chocolate* (*Like Water for Chocolate*, 1992). The author deftly combined the popular themes of food preparation and romance in a work that portrayed some of the most memorable scenes in the novel. This and other recent films have emphasized the importance of family in Hispanic life as well.

Magical realism has been used or adapted in films from non–Latin American countries, but it seems most suited to its place of origin. Carpentier's *El reino de este mundo* (*The Kingdom of This World*, 1949) contains scenes that seem perfectly adaptable to the screen—such as one character's juxtaposition of the wax heads in a wig shop display, the animal heads in a butcher shop, the royal heads on stamps in a philately store, and the author's imaginative vision of the beheading of guillotined French overlords during the French Revolution, as he ponders the possibility of rebellion in Haiti to overthrow French domination. There is also a scene involving an African Haitian cultural hero, the leader of a revolt, who appears to escape execution at the hands of the French; the two cultures view the same scene in a different way. Some of the scenes at the end of the novel, when the main character rules his gentle imaginary kingdom and eventually disappears in a storm, seem to cry out for film adaptation.

Like *One Hundred Years of Solitude*, however, *The Kingdom of This World* has not had a successful cinematic interpretation. Several auspicious forces must be brought into play with skilled treatment if literary magical realism is to be successfully transferred to film within the sphere of popular culture. Perhaps the reader of a literary work has developed imaginary mental pictures of the elements of magical realism in the piece. He or she expects those images to be reinforced through the film adaptation. Creating a successful cinematic rendition from such disparate images is a daunting challenge, especially if cross-cultural boundaries are to be bridged as well. Miguel Ángel Asturias wrote a lovely collection of *Leyendas de Guatemala* (*Legends from Guatemala*, 1930) that evokes the powerful beauty of indigenous myths, yet it might be difficult to produce a screen version of the work. As the popular success of *Like Water for Chocolate* has shown, however, the goal of bringing literary magical realism to the screen can be achieved. The PBS television series, "American Family," directed by Gregory Nava of *El norte* fame, depicts some aspects of Latin American history and culture through several generations of a Mexican American family. As the new millennium continues to unfold, this medium of popular culture in Latin America can be more fully explored.

*   *   *

In sum, literature and artistic expression contribute to the cultural richness of Latin America. These genres and others that are beyond the scope of this chapter, such as the graphic arts and music, help us to understand Latin American perceptions of reality.

▪ Bibliography

Alonso, Carlos J. *The Spanish American Regional Novel*. New York: Cambridge University Press, 1990.

Baddeley, Oriana, and Valerie Fraser. *Drawing the Line: Art and Cultural Identity in Latin America*. New York: Routledge, Chapman and Hall, 1989.

Beezley, William, and Judith Ewell. *The Human Tradition in Latin America: Twentieth Century*. Wilmington, Del.: Scholarly Resources, 1987.

Beverley, John, and Marc Zimmerman. *Literature and Politics in the Central American Revolutions*. Austin: University of Texas Press, 1990.

Burton, Julianne (ed.). *Cinema and Social Change in Latin America*. Austin:

University of Texas Press, 1986.

Chanaday, Amaryll (ed.). *Latin American Identity and Constructions of Difference.* Minneapolis: University of Minnesota Press, 1994.

de los Santos, Nancy. *The Bronze Screen: One Hundred Years of the Latino Image in Hollywood.* Questar video, 2002.

Dorfman, Ariel. *Some Write to the Future: Essays on Contemporary Latin American Fiction.* Durham, N.C.: Duke University Press, 1991.

García-Pinto, Magdalena, and Trudy Balch. *Women Writers of Latin America: Intimate Histories.* Austin: University of Texas Press, 1991.

Gautier, Mari-Lise Gazarian. *Interviews with Latin American Writers.* Elmwood Park, Ill.: Dalkey Archive Press, 1989.

González-Echevarría, Roberto, and Enrique Pupo-Walker (eds.). *Cambridge History of Latin American Literature* (3 vols.). New York: Cambridge University Press, 1996.

Goodrich, Diana Sorensen. *The Reader and the Text: Interpretive Strategies for Latin American Literatures.* Purdue University Monographs in Romance Languages 18. Erdenheim, Pa.: John Benjamins Publishing, 1986.

Gracia, Jorge J. E., and Mireya Camurati. *Philosophy and Literature in Latin America: A Critical Assessment of the Current Situation.* Albany: State University of New York Press, 1989.

Hart, Stephen. *Companion to Spanish American Literature.* London: Tamesis, 2001.

Hart, Stephen, and Richard Young (eds.) *Contemporary Latin American Cultural Studies.* London: Arnold, 2003.

Hillman, Richard S., and Margaret V. Ekstrom. "Political Cynicism in Contemporary Caribbean Fiction," *Secolas Annals* 21 (March 1990):71–78.

Kaminsky, Amy K. *Reading the Body Politic: A Feminist Criticism of Latin America.* Minneapolis: University of Minnesota Press, 1993.

Keen, Benjamin. *Latin American Civilization and History.* Boulder, Colo.: Westview Press, 1986.

Kerr, Lucille. *Reclaiming the Author: Figures and Fictions from Spanish America.* Durham, N.C.: Duke University Press, 1992.

King, John. *Magical Reels: A History of Cinema in Latin America.* London and New York: Routledge, Chapman and Hall (Verso), 1990.

Lindstrom, Naomi. *Twentieth Century Spanish American Fiction.* Austin: University of Texas Press, 1994.

León-Portilla, Miguel. *Pre-Columbian Literatures of Mexico.* Norman: University of Oklahoma Press, 1986.

Mac Adam, Alfred J. *Textual Confrontations: Comparative Readings in Latin American Literature.* Chicago: University of Chicago Press, 1987.

Martin, Gerald. *Journeys Through the Labyrinth: Latin American Fiction of the Twentieth Century.* New York and London: Routledge, Chapman and Hall (Verso), 1989.

Menton, Seymour. *Latin America's New Historical Novel.* Austin: University of Texas Press, 1993.

Ortega, Julio. *Poetics of Change: The New Spanish-American Narrative.* Austin: University of Texas Press, 1984.

Pagden, Anthony. *European Encounters with the New World.* New Haven, Conn.: Yale University Press, 1993.

Payne, Judith, and Earl Fitz. *Ambiguity and Gender in the New Novel of Spanish America.* Iowa City: University of Iowa Press, 1993.

Pérez-Firmat, Gustavo (ed.). *Do the Americas Have a Common Literature?* Durham, N.C.: Duke University Press, 1990.

Schroeder, Shannin. *Rediscovering Magical Realism in the Americas.* Westport, Conn.: Praeger, 2004.

Shaw, Donald L. *The Post-Boom in Spanish American Fiction.* Albany: State University of New York Press, 1998.

Smith, Paul Julian. *Representing the Other: "Race," Text and Gender in Spanish and Spanish American Narrative.* New York: Oxford University Press, 1992.

Solé, Carlos A. (ed.). *Latin American Writers* (3 vols.). New York: Macmillan Publishers, 1989.

Stevens, Donald F. (ed.). *Based on a True Story: Latin American History at the Movies.* Wilmington, Del.: Scholarly Resources, 1997.

Swanson, Philip. *Landmarks in Modern Latin American Fiction.* New York: Routledge, Chapman and Hall, 1990.

———. *The New Novel in Latin America.* Manchester: Manchester University Press, 1995.

———. (ed.). *The Companion to Latin American Studies.* London: Arnold, 2003.

Taylor, Diana. *Theatre of Crisis: Drama and Politics in Latin America.* Lexington: University Press of Kentucky, 1991.

Weiss, Rachel (ed.). *Being America: Essays on Art, Literature of Latin America.* Fredonia, N.Y.: Inbook (White Pine Press), 1991.

Williams, Raymond L. *The Postmodern Novel in Latin America.* New York: St. Martin's Press, 1995.

Zamora, Lois Parkinson. *Writing the Apocalypse: Historical Vision in U.S. and Latin American Fiction.* New York: Cambridge University Press, 1989.

14

Trends and Prospects

Richard S. Hillman

An interesting contribution to the study of the future holds that "just as it is possible for the professional historian to infer from incomplete records why people acted the way they did in the past . . . it is possible to infer how they will act in the future, as long as we are clear about the ideas that give rise to such action" (Goodman 1993:3). With respect to the need for clarity, in this volume, we have tried to bring about an interdisciplinary understanding of Latin America—to overcome myths, stereotypes, and prejudices that are often derived from a myopic view or insufficient knowledge. Each chapter provides information, analysis, and a variety of viewpoints that we hope will contribute to a clear, broadened, and empathetic vision of an extremely complex, increasingly important, yet widely misunderstood region. Moreover, throughout our survey of important aspects of Latin America's background, society and culture, and geopolitical and socioeconomic settings, we have included informed speculation about what might lie ahead. It is, therefore, appropriate in our final chapter to summarize likely short- and long-term projections that could influence the region, the Western Hemisphere, and the world.

Forecasting Latin America's future, especially in times of great upheaval, is challenging and requires not only a realistic and empathetic understanding but also critical analysis and imagination. We should recognize, therefore, that although inferences about Latin American socioeconomic and political realities can help us predict the future, this exercise necessarily yields many more open questions than definitive answers. In light of these considerations, several trends and prospects that appear to suggest future directions for Latin America can be extrapolated from our broadened vision.

We have learned that contemporary Latin America is a diverse region with similar underlying patterns and experiences. Not only has the region been shaped by its past, but it also has been transformed by the pressures of modernization and the requirements of a new world order. Traditional institutions and values that have been derived from a long colonial experience have endured and blended with emergent patterns of leadership, political dynamics, economic strategies, ethnic relations, and gender roles. Even deep-seated religious beliefs have undergone significant changes. All of these uniquely Latin American transformations are given expression in a rich literature and popular culture, as well as in the ways countries of the region interact with each other and with the rest of the world.

As a dynamic interplay between integrative and disintegrative political and socioeconomic forces has begun to define the twenty-first century, it is precisely in the realization of unity amid diversity that we find promise for the future. A Latin American synthesis, based on patterns of fusion and amalgamation, could contribute to a model worthy of global application. Although the region continues to struggle with resilient legacies of its past and difficult current challenges, the future lies within the context of this transitional process.

Traditional patterns have been resilient, adaptable, and persistent, as urbanization, industrialization, and technological advances have made Latin America even more complex and diversified—with more literate, politically conscious, and politically active populations. Thus, political leaders have had to recognize the need to be responsive to both tradition and change, as well as to challenges and obstacles ranging from extensive poverty, profound inequality, dependent economies, and rapid transition. However, in the short term, populations with rising expectations have been disillusioned by their governments' inability to provide adequate services; at the same time, governments' capacities are overwhelmed by citizens' limitless needs that often cannot be fulfilled. Hence, Latin American politics are more belligerent and explosive due to the emergence of new political actors in this competitive, pluralistic environment. On the one hand, governments have not been able to satisfy all groups struggling for control over limited national resources, which has made the people in these groups feel cynical, frustrated, and left with a heightened sense of relative deprivation. On the other hand, democratization and the promise of economic growth has given citizens hope that, in the future, their countries and Latin America as a whole will attain satisfactory levels of development and stability. A variety of factors are involved in the quest to resolve this dilemma.

One crucial factor in how the future will be shaped is the military, which for centuries supported traditional authoritarianism but is now changing as a result of a new regional and global context. The national security state of the 1960s through the 1980s lacked legitimacy. Moreover,

the experience of repression, the apparent failure of state socialism globally, and the problems of state-led development in Latin America made the
region more susceptible and receptive to international influence. In
response to these changes, the military had to modernize, professionalize,
and restructure itself.

Economic difficulties, however, have limited the availability of funds
for military modernization, and the potential for social turmoil continues to
provide a pretext for the military to intervene in domestic politics. In fact,
the armed forces in some countries have split within their ranks over their
theoretical subordination to civilian political authority. Although the armed
forces in Latin America essentially appear to be participating in one way or
another in the process of democratic consolidation, their precise role in the
future continues to be unclear.

Despite periods of prosperity under liberal regimes, economic benefits
have never been evenly distributed in the region. Experiments with economic nationalism and *dirigismo* failed to correct this problem; thus, most
states have been adopting neoliberal policies. Latin America's enormous
external debt, low investor confidence, capital flight, hyperinflation, and
devastating rate of unemployment, however, continue to pose serious challenges to countries attempting to improve their economic performance.
This raises troubling questions about the relationship in the region between
economics and politics. What is the significance of past correlations
between economic development and authoritarianism on the one hand and
between economic stagnation and democracy on the other?

Knowledge of Latin American history and society suggests a cautious
response. While the region is well endowed with natural resources and a
good supply of labor, it has a shortage of managers, persistent dominance
by the elites, and high levels of corruption. Nevertheless, if present trends
continue toward freer markets, export-oriented growth, more secure and
widely distributed property rights, a better climate for foreign investment,
and fiscal and economic restraint, then Latin America may begin to develop
its great potential in an era of democratization.

Unfortunately, Latin American countries have suffered from rapid
development, which has led to environmental pollution, ineffective use of
resources, and underdevelopment—which, in turn, have yielded poverty
and socioeconomic inequality. Ironically, the region's economic dynamism
has often existed at the expense of social justice. Therefore, environmental,
demographic, and urbanization challenges require that Latin America confront the social and political issues associated with ecological balance and
environmental conservation. It is important to recognize that the experiences of hunger, illiteracy, premature death, substandard housing, and
underemployment are profound despite the region's marginal contribution
to global ecological disorder. In fact, the region could contribute to a new,

sustainable level of development if its long-term potential can be tapped in a productive and harmonious way that overcomes short-term disruption.

Intimately interrelated with these questions and issues in ways that are significant for the future of this region are the uniquely Latin American functions of race, ethnicity, gender, class, and nationalism. These roles continue to influence arrangements of power and, thus, require careful, empathetic analysis for a meaningful understanding of the contemporary scene. For example, women and their organizations have begun to contribute to change in Latin America. Despite their participation in revolutions, grassroots movements, and international political meetings, however, inhibiting traditional gender roles continue, tying most women to the home and family in subservient positions. Thus, their participation in formal political institutions and organizations has been limited. Significantly, the contemporary women's movement in Latin America, despite its limitations, has emphasized democratic practices. Activists desire an end to authoritarianism and seek the extension of basic human rights, such as the right to clean water, sanitary housing, medical care, and education. Similarly, notwithstanding deep-seated ethnic and class divisions, ongoing Eurocentrism, and socioeconomic obstacles to racial democracy, emergent conceptions of the unique Latin American fusion of peoples and cultures may contain the seeds for a potentially harmonious future.

Of crucial importance to the evolution of societies that are based on ethnic and racial tolerance and equality of opportunity is *education*. Despite the considerable problems of education in Latin America, reforms have occurred, including the institution of popular education, grassroots projects, and community self-help programs. Moreover, the evolving definitions of development and education indicate a continuing move away from theories that reinforce the status quo toward ideals reinforced by policies that promote individual empowerment and faith in democratic principles. There is also a growing international awareness that effective educational systems can contribute both to the development and democratization of Latin American countries.

The role of religious beliefs in Latin American social and political life has been profound. Traditionally, the Catholic Church has been a leading political actor, especially when secular political forces were ineffective. The region, however, has become increasingly pluralistic and more open to secularizing influences. As Protestant churches have grown, the strong link between Catholicism and national identity and culture has eroded. In the future, liberals and conservatives may cross denominational lines to pressure public officials on socioeconomic matters. Such developments could lead to the further secularization of political power and a shift in the debate on moral and ethical matters from religious to political and cultural arenas.

Each of these factors is influenced not only by internal dynamics but also by changes in the international environment. As in the past, the United States—the dominant military and economic power in the Americas—continues to be far more important to Latin America than the region has been to the United States. Hence, as the perception of communist influence in the region virtually disappeared with the end of the Cold War, the U.S. and international community's support for continuing the processes of democratization and liberalization in Latin America became overshadowed by more immediate and problematic issues in other areas of the world. For example, the suicide attacks on the twin towers of the World Trade Center in New York and the Pentagon in Washington, D.C., on September 11, 2001, shifted interest to international terrorism.

But even with global attention diverted from Latin America, the illicit narcotics trade, immigration problems, excessive international debt, and prospects of hemispheric trade to offset European and Pacific Rim competition have required reassessment of relations with the region. Venezuela, the world's fifth largest petroleum exporter, continues to supply 14 percent of U.S. oil imports. However, the emergence of a "social revolution" in Venezuela has prompted reevaluation of the traditional relationship between the two countries (Cardozo and Hillman 2003). Similarly, although Colombian drug cartels constitute a hemispheric threat, little consensus exists about what approach to take to reduce or eliminate their influence. The same is true with regard to Mexican, Central American, and Caribbean immigration controversies. Would improved socioeconomic conditions in Latin America reduce the number of undocumented aliens seeking upward mobility in the United States? If so, what are the most effective methods for fostering development of these improved conditions within the region? Should the U.S. embargo against Cuba be lifted in order to allow for normalized trade and interaction? Would involvement in Cuba enhance U.S. influence? Can Latin America evolve to the level of stability required for equal partnership in an integrated hemisphere?

Clearly, accelerating interdependence and economic issues will remain high on the regional agenda. Progress has been made in renegotiating the terms of debt agreements and also toward greater interregional and intraregional trade. In fact, regional integration appears to be encouraging greater economic efficiency and expanded cooperation in politics and defense. Therefore, we should see enhanced common strategies for fostering increased economic cooperation through existing common markets, customs unions, and regional institutions. Undoubtedly, one of the most important trends in contemporary Latin America is the movement toward free-trade zones that provide an emerging infrastructure for facilitating hemispheric integration.

The move toward a Free Trade Area of the Americas (FTAA) is an excellent example of an integrative trend. At the December 1994 Summit of the Americas, leaders of thirty-four nations in the Western Hemisphere committed their countries to participate in forming a hemispheric free-trade area by the year 2005. Although this has yet to be accomplished and has received a lower priority by the Bush administration than the "war on terrorism," the goal continues to inform policies articulated throughout the hemisphere. In their "Declaration of Principles," these elected heads of state reiterated a firm adherence to the principles of international law and the purposes of the United Nations to preserve and strengthen the community of democracies in the Americas, promote prosperity through economic integration and free trade, eradicate poverty and discrimination, and guarantee sustainable development and environmental conservation.

Although these are lofty ideals, they nevertheless address—at least rhetorically—the major challenges confronting contemporary Latin America. For example, the discussion of the consolidation of democracy reveals an acutely realistic recognition of the need to attack pervasive corruption, empower independent judiciaries, and battle against narcotrafficking and terrorism on multiple levels. There is also clear recognition of the ways in which "democracy and development reinforce one another" ("Summit of the Americas: Declaration of Principles" 1994:2). The objectives are to create employment opportunities; improve access to education and health care; end discrimination based on race, gender, national origin, or religious affiliation; and thereby attain greater social justice for all sectors of society to improve the general quality of life. Such investments in the future can only have salutary effects. What remains to be seen is the extent to which these principles can be translated into operational reality through the implementation of concrete policies and programs.

Unfortunately, ongoing and increased challenges unresolved by the worthy intentions expressed at the Summit of the Americas characterize the early stages of the twenty-first century. Although Chile has begun integration into an incipient hemispheric free-trade zone and established a bilateral Free Trade Agreement (FTA) with the United States in June 2003, other Latin American nations have faced difficulties in achieving their objectives in ongoing negotiations. In fact, Richard Bernal, the Jamaican representative and spokesperson for developing areas, walked out of a World Trade Organization (WTO) conference held in Cancún, Mexico, in 2003, in order to protest what he claimed was the unwillingness on the part of the United States to negotiate in good faith. Bernal proclaimed, "There is nothing for us small countries in this proposal. We don't want any of this."[1] Consequently, Brazil's President Luiz Inácio Lula da Silva began to push for a separate South American trade pact. In March 2005, Brazil and Venezuela entered into an enhanced trade pact.

Moreover, many countries in the region are experiencing the debilitating effects of declining living standards, increased crime and violence, corrupt political institutions that fail to deliver on their promises, and the concomitant discrediting and even delegitimization of democracy (Blake 2005). The election of several populist and authoritarian leaders, whose platforms and policies reflect legacies of the past, could constrain progress toward democratization and raise new concerns about Latin America's future.

Recent elections and actions within the armed forces in several countries raise further questions about the fragility of democratic institutions and stability within the region. Alberto Fujimori, for example, gained an uncontested third term as president of Peru when Alejandro Toledo along with international observers withdrew in protest against a fraudulent electoral process in May 2000. Later, Fujimori fled the country when his complicity in corruption schemes with Vladimiro Montesinos, his principal adviser, came into question. Toledo was elected president in July 2001. Yet, he has also faced much criticism by Peruvians seeking socioeconomic and political development.

After Paraguay's Vice President Luis Argana was assassinated in 1999, President Raúl Cubas was impeached and resigned, accused of complicity in the assassination. Paraguay continued under a state of siege after an attempted coup in May 2000, and a similar outcome occurred in Bolivia in April 2000. Ecuador's President Jamil Mahuad was ousted after attempting a "dollarization" policy, and Vice President Gustavo Noboa was installed by the military. Ecuador's election of Lucio Gutiérrez in January 2003 and the October 2004 election of Tabare Vázquez in Uruguay, along with Chile's Ricardo Lagos in March 2000, Argentina's Nestor Kirchner in May 2003, Brazil's Lula da Silva in January 2003, and Venezuela's Hugo Chávez in February 1999 suggest a recent trend toward the left and moderate left in Latin America. Sandinista victories in Nicaragua's local elections in November 2004 also appear to reflect the leftward drift.

Venezuelan "megaelections," in which the presidency and over 6,000 offices were to be filled in compliance with the newly rewritten constitution, were postponed when the National Electoral Commission resigned in disgrace in May 2000. When elections were held in July 2000, former coup leader Hugo Chávez and his Fifth Republic Movement (MVR) won handily. However, Venezuela has become so politically polarized that, despite President Chávez's surviving a series of strikes against the government and a recall election in 2004, his opposition has refused to recognize the legitimacy of his regime (Ellner and Hellinger 2003).[2]

Charges of corruption were rampant in Mexico as the PRI attempted to maintain its long-standing control. Finally, PAN candidate Vicente Fox emerged victorious in December 2000. Will a two-party or multiparty system continue to develop with transparent elections? The July 2006 election could prove to be decisive in Mexico's democratization process.

The civil war between guerrillas and the government persists in Colombia with no end in sight. Haitian elections were marred by violence, gang warfare, and the forced exile of President Jean-Bertrand Aristide in 2004. In Guatemala, President Alfonso Portillo allied himself with former military leader Efraín Rios Montt, who became president of the Congress. Chile's President Ricardo Lagos remains at odds with the country's military leadership over the human rights case against Augusto Pinochet. The debate continues; the former dictator's house arrest was suspended, and charges were brought against him by Judge Juan Guzmán. Pinochet remains under house arrest and unable to go to trial due to illness. But the Chilean courts ruled that he was mentally competent to stand trial.

Poverty, occasioned by the maldistribution of wealth, as in much of Latin America, continues to rise in most of the insular Caribbean. The all-time-high crime rate in Jamaica is a direct consequence of widespread poverty and alienation. Although there are fewer Haitian "boat people," *balseros* (Cuban exile rafters) continue to attempt entry into the United States as much for economic as political reasons.

A general societal malaise throughout Latin America resulted at the commencement of the twenty-first century as a consequence of challenges and obstacles that appeared to be insuperable—in the absence of real economic development, which did not materialize via political institutions in which the people placed their confidence and trust. Programs of economic structural adjustment have been very unpopular except among the wealthy elites; thus, political parties, legislatures, and judiciaries have been deeply discredited. Such political delegitimization left a vacuum into which charismatic populists have entered. These strong presidents have rewritten national constitutions, attempted to lead "social revolutions," and ruled through "plebiscitory democracy" or "democracy by referendum." *Democradura*, a governing style exhibiting "characteristics that are neither strictly authoritarian nor truly democratic" (Hillman and D'Agostino 1992), appears to have emerged within the context and continuity of Latin American political culture as a response to the societal malaise. As one analyst suggests, "Many citizens appear willing to give up some measure of democracy and accept authoritarian governments that they believe can solve their problems" (Hakim 1999–2000:107).

Do these challenges and obstacles mean that Latin America is condemned by its past and, therefore, destined to fail in the quest to promote political and socioeconomic development? None of the authors included in this text believe that the future of Latin American nations is determined exclusively by past political and social patterns. The impact of historical legacies, however, must be understood in order to deal effectively with the present.

Perhaps *democraduras*, strong presidencies, plebiscitory democracies, and democracies by referendum are a phase within the transitional process?

There is little doubt, for example, that in Venezuela the consociational dominant party system unraveled prior to the definitive election of Hugo Chávez (McCoy and Myers 2004). Chávez's popularity represents not only a rejection of past failures, but also hope that his "social revolution" can deliver palpable results to masses of Venezuelans whose quality of life had diminished during elitist regimes. Despite Fujimori's *autogolpe* and resignation under a cloud of corruption charges, many Peruvians perceive a more stable country with diminished threats from the Sendero Luminoso and some renewed prospects for economic development. Elections in the Dominican Republic were conducted without incident, and a peaceful transfer of power resulted in the defeat of Joaquín Balaguer after decades of manipulation. The PRI, which chose its candidate not by *dedazo* (president's pointing of his finger to designate a successor) but by an open primary, was defeated in Mexico. Chile freely elected a socialist president. Brazil's economy shows signs of potential growth. Mercosur (the Southern Common Market) has been reinforced. These trends may be part of a transition toward a uniquely Latin American solution to political and socioeconomic challenges.

Although the raised expectations engendered by the end of the Cold War and the first years of the new millennium have given way to disappointments, and legacies of the past continue to constrain the realization of much of Latin America's promise, some countervailing trends indicate healthy prospects for the future of a region that continues to define and redefine itself in terms of its unique qualities. Significantly, no country in the region faces a real possibility of violent revolution. Nor are the new leaders likely to create true military dictatorships. Almost all of the Latin American regimes are attempting to improve their economies by linking them more effectively to global markets. Moreover, each nation is operating within some conception of democratic politics. In sum, "[n]owhere in Latin America today is democratic rule threatened by military takeover" (Hakim 1999–2000:113).

The opportunities for the region continue to be great. Vast natural and human resources, an evolving culture of unity within diversity, recognition of the need for political and social democratization, expanded economic productivity and markets, as well as great potential in all of these areas make Latin America a vital part of an increasingly interrelated world. Achievement of an integral and positive role in the contemporary global era will largely be a consequence of overcoming stereotypical myths through the promotion of enhanced mutual understanding. There are many signs that this process has already begun, and every citizen has a responsibility to ensure that it continues.

Human rights and economic considerations regarding the Chiapas conflict in Mexico and the Colombian civil war have expanded attention well beyond their local origins. In March 2001, for example, international as well as domestic pressures prompted Mexico's President Fox and Colombia's President Pastrana to meet with leaders of the Zapatistas (EZLN) and the Revolutionary Armed Forces of Colombia (FARC), respectively. Subcomandante Marcos, with international support, arrived in the Mexican capital on March 11, 2001, as a champion of indigenous rights, while FARC leaders continued to negotiate with the Colombian government over socioeconomic and political issues that have gained an international audience. Unfortunately, neither of these conflicts has been resolved, and negotiations between the rebels and their respective governments were sporadic in 2004.

Although the United States has rhetorically supported the peace negotiations in Mexico—primarily to promote the North American Free Trade Agreement (NAFTA)—the U.S. antinarcotics policy has prohibited U.S. representation in discussions with the FARC. In fact, in March 2001, the U.S. Congress proposed that the "war on drugs" (detailed in Plan Colombia) be expanded to Bolivia and Peru. Such U.S. military intervention has met with almost as much resentment as U.S. "certification" of Latin American countries' success in combating human rights abuses and drug trafficking. Thus, there has been tension between Latin American initiatives and U.S. policy regarding the resolution of conflicts engendered by socioeconomic and political conditions in these countries. Despite the global focus on international terrorism, the internationalization of these and other essentially local conflicts and problems underscores the ongoing importance of Latin America in contemporary world affairs.

Notes

1. This was reported by Elizabeth Becker in "Poorer Countries Pull Out of Talks on World Trade," *New York Times*, September 14, 2003, p. 14.
2. I have observed that polarization regarding the Chávez regime is profound enough to divide families and friends. Venezuelan politics is rapidly becoming a zero-sum game. In February and March 2005, Chávez accused the United States, and specifically President Bush, of planning to attack Venezuela and assassinate Chávez. He has reiterated these charges and threatened that if he is harmed, Venezuela would cease to export petroleum to the United States (14 percent of U.S. oil imports). The Bush administration has responded by adopting a policy of "containment" against Chávez's alleged "drive to subvert Latin America's least stable states" (*Finanical Times,* London, March 13, 2005, p. 21).

Bibliography

Blake, Charles H. *Politics in Latin America*. Boston: Houghton Mifflin, 2005.
Cardozo, Elsa, and Richard S. Hillman. "Venezuela: Petroleum, Democratization,

and International Affairs." In *Latin American and Caribbean Foreign Policy*, edited by Frank O. Mora and Jeanne A. K. Hey. New York: Rowman & Littlefield, 2003, pp. 145–165.

Carothers, Thomas. *Aiding Democracy Abroad: The Learning Curve.* Washington, D.C.: Carnegie Endowment for International Peace, 1999.

Diamond, Larry, Jonathan Hartlyn, Juan Linz, and Seymour Martin Lipset (eds.). *Democracy in Developing Countries: Latin America* (2d ed.). Boulder, Colo.: Lynne Rienner Publishers, 1999.

Diamond, Larry, Juan Linz, and Seymour Martin Lipset (eds.). *Politics in Developing Countries: Comparing Experiences with Democracy* (2d ed.). Boulder, Colo.: Lynne Rienner Publishers, 1995.

Dietz, James L. (ed.). *Latin America's Economic Development: Confronting Crisis* (2d ed.). Boulder, Colo.: Lynne Rienner Publishers, 1995.

Ellner, Steve, and Daniel Hellinger (eds.). *Venezuelan Politics in the Chávez Era: Class, Polarization, and Conflict.* Boulder, Colo.: Lynne Rienner Publishers, 2003.

Everingham, Mark. "Latin America and the International Development Community: Revisiting or Redefining the Relationship?" *North-South Issues* 4, no. 2 (1995).

Goodman, Allan E. *A Brief History of the Future: The United States in a Changing World Order.* Boulder, Colo.: Westview Press, 1993.

Hakim, Peter. "Is Latin America Doomed to Failure?" *Foreign Policy* (Winter 1999–2000):104–119.

Hillman, Richard S., and Thomas J. D'Agostino. *Distant Neighbors in the Caribbean: The Dominican Republic and Jamaica in Comparative Perspective.* New York: Praeger, 1992.

McCoy, Jennifer L., and David J. Myers. *The Unraveling of Representative Democracy in Venezuela.* Baltimore and London: Johns Hopkins University Press, 2004.

"Summit of the Americas: Declaration of Principles." Florida International University. Available online at www.summit-americas.org/eng/miamisummit.htm.

Vanden, Harry E., and Gary Prevost. *Politics of Latin America: The Power Game.* New York: Oxford University Press, 2002.

Acronyms

AD	Democratic Action (Venezuela)
APEC	Asia-Pacific Economic Cooperation
APRA	American Popular Revolutionary Alliance (Peru)
ARENA	Republican National Alliance (El Salvador)
CACM	Central American Common Market
CARICOM	Caribbean Common Market
CARIFTA	Caribbean Free Trade Association
CDRs	Committees for the Defense of the Revolution (Cuba)
CEBs	*comunidades eclesiales de base* (ecclesial base communities)
CFC	chlorofluorocarbon
CIA	Central Intelligence Agency (United States)
DBCP	dibromochloropropane
DINA	National Intelligence Directorate (Chile)
EC	European Community
ECLA	Economic Commission for Latin America, known as CEPAL in Spanish
ECLAC	UN Economic Commission for Latin America and the Caribbean
ELN	National Liberation Army (Colombia)
EU	European Union
EZLN	Zapatista National Liberation Army
FARC	Revolutionary Armed Forces of Colombia
FMLN	Farabundo Martí National Liberation Front
FSLN	Sandinista National Liberation Front (Nicaragua)
FTA	Free Trade Agreement
FTAA	Free Trade Area of the Americas
GATT	General Agreement on Tariffs and Trade
GDFI	gross direct foreign investment

GDP	gross domestic product
GMOs	genetically modified organisms
GNI	gross national income
GNP	gross national product
IAEA	UN International Atomic Energy Agency
ICA	International Coffee Agreement
IDB	Inter-American Development Bank
IEF	index of economic freedom
IMF	International Monetary Fund
ISI	import substitution industrialization
LAFTA	Latin American Free Trade Area
LAIA	Latin American Integration Association, known as ALADI in Spanish
Mercosur/ Mercosul	Mercado Común del Sur/Mercado Comum do Cone Sul (Southern Common Market)
MNC	multinational corporation
MNR	National Revolutionary Movement (Bolivia)
MRTA	Tupac Amaru Revolutionary Movement
MVR	Fifth Republic Movement (Venezuela)
NAFTA	North American Free Trade Agreement
NGO	nongovernmental organization
NIEO	new international economic order
NPT	Nuclear Non-Proliferation Treaty
OAS	Organization of American States
OECD	Organization for Economic Cooperation and Development
OPEC	Organization of Petroleum Exporting Countries
PAN	National Action Party (Mexico)
PNR	National Revolutionary Party (Mexico)
PRD	Dominican Revolutionary Party (Dominican Republic)
PRI	Institutional Revolutionary Party (Mexico)
SAP	structural adjustment program
TOI	trade openness index
TGE	total governmental expenditure
TNC	transnational corporation
UFCO	United Fruit Company (United States)
UNESCO	United Nations Educational, Scientific, and Cultural Organization
UNO	National Opposition Union (Nicaragua)
UNMOVIC	UN Monitoring, Verification and Inspection Commission
URNG	Guatemalan National Revolutionary Union
USAID	United States Agency for International Development
WTO	World Trade Organization

Appendix 1:
Basic Political Data

This Basic Political Data Appendix was compiled by Amin Alexander Choukairi. Data for capital city, independence date, population, current leadership, and elections categories were obtained from *The CIA World Fact Book* (available at http://www.cia.gov/cia/publications/factbook/index.html), which was current as of mid-2004. Types of government were compiled by Thomas J. D'Agostino. The human development index (HDI) cited below was drawn from the *Human Development Report 2004: Cultural Liberty in Today's Diverse World*, published for the United Nations Development Programme (UNDP). The HDI ratings range from 0.0 (lowest) to 1.0 (highest) as a representation of the general state of affairs for each nation's citizenry. More specifically, the HDI reflects a combination of average literacy, life expectancy, and per capita income levels. As useful points of reference, consider the following HDI averages: Average World HDI: 0.729; Average Latin American and Caribbean HDI: 0.777; a typically high HDI: 0.915; a typically medium HDI: 0.695; and a typically low HDI: 0.438. Parliamentary elections may be held at any time but must be scheduled by the dates listed.

Antigua and Barbuda
Capital City Saint John's
Date of Independence from Great Britain November 1, 1986
Population 68,320
HDI Score 0.800
Current Leader Prime Minister Baldwin Spencer (since March 2004)
Type of Government Parliamentary democracy
Elections Last held in March 2004. Next elections by 2009.

Argentina
Capital City Buenos Aires
Date of Independence from Spain July 9, 1816
Population 39,144,753
HDI Score 0.853
Current Leader President Nestor Kirchner (since May 2003)
Type of Government Republic
Elections Last held in May 2003. Next elections in May 2007.

Bahamas, The
Capital City Nassau
Independence from Great Britain July 10, 1973
Population 299,697
HDI Score 0.815
Current Leader Prime Minister Perry Christie (since May 2002)
Type of Government Parliamentary democracy
Elections Last held in May 2002. Next elections by May 2007.

Barbados
Capital City Bridgetown
Date of Independence from Great Britain November 30, 1966
Population 278,289
HDI Score 0.888
Current Leader Prime Minister Owen Seymour Arthur (since September 1994)
Type of Government Parliamentary democracy
Elections Last held in May 2003. Next elections by May 2008.

Belize
Capital City Belmopan
Date of Independence from Great Britain September 21, 1981
Population 272,945
HDI Score 0.737
Current Leader Prime Minister Said Musa (since August 1998)
Type of Government Parliamentary democracy
Elections Last held in March 2003. Next elections by March 2005.

Bolivia
Capital City La Paz
Date of Independence from Spain August 6, 1825
Population 8,724,156
HDI Score 0.681
Current Leader President Carlos Diego Mesa (since October 2003, when his predecessor, Gonzalo Sánchez de Losada, resigned)

Type of Government Republic
Elections Last held in June 2002. Next elections in June 2007.

Brazil
Capital City Brasília
Date of Independence from Portugal September 7, 1822
Population 184,101,109
HDI Score 0.775
Current Leader President Luiz Inácio Lula da Silva (since January 2003)
Type of Government Federal republic
Elections Last held in October 2002. Next elections in October 2006.

Chile
Capital City Santiago
Date of Independence from Spain September 18, 1810
Population 5,823,957
HDI Score 0.839
Current Leader President Ricardo Lagos Escobar (since March 2000)
Type of Government Republic
Elections Last held in December 1999. Next elections in December 2005.

Colombia
Capital City Bogotá
Date of Independence from Spain July 20, 1810
Population 42,310,775
HDI Score 0.7730
Current Leader President Álvaro Uribe Vélez (since August 2002)
Type of Government Republic
Elections Last held in May 2002. Next elections in May 2006.

Costa Rica
Capital City San José
Date of Independence from Spain September 15, 1821
Population 3,956,507
HDI Score 0.834
Current Leader President Abel Pacheco (since May 2002)
Type of Government Republic
Elections Last held in April 2002. Next elections in February 2006.

Cuba
Capital City Havana
Date of Independence from Spain December 10, 1898
Date of Independence from United States May 20, 1902
Population 11,308,764

HDI Score 0.809
Current Leader President Fidel Castro Ruz (since February 1959)
Type of Government Communist state
Elections Last held in March 2003. Next elections in March 2008.

Dominica
Capital City Roseau
Date of Independence from Great Britain November 3, 1978
Population 69,278
HDI Score 0.743
Current Leader Prime Minister Roosevelt Skerrit (since January 2004)
Type of Government Parliamentary democracy
Elections Last held in October 2003. Next elections by October 2008.

Dominican Republic
Capital City Santo Domingo
Date of Independence from Haiti February 27, 1844
Population 8,833,634
HDI Score 0.738
Current Leader President Leonel Fernández Reyna (since August
    2004)
Type of Government Republic
Elections Last held in May 2004. Next elections in May 2008.

Ecuador
Capital City Quito
Date of Independence from Spain May 24, 1822
Population 13,212,742
HDI Score 0.735
Current Leader President Alfredo Palacio (since April 2005 after the aust-
    ing of Lucio Gutiérrez)
Type of Government Republic
Elections Last held in October 2002. Next elections in October 2006.
    (One-term limit.)

El Salvador
Capital City San Salvador
Date of Independence from Spain September 15, 1821
Population 6,587,541
HDI Score 0.720
Current Leader President Antonio Elías Saca (since June 2004)
Type of Government Republic
Elections Last held in March 2004. Next elections in March 2009.

Grenada
Capital City Saint George's
Date of Independence from Great Britain February 7, 1974
Population 89,357
HDI Score 0.745
Current Leader Prime Minister Keith Mitchell (since 1995)
Type of Government Parliamentary democracy
Elections Last held in November 2003. Next elections by November 2008.

Guatemala
Capital City Ciudad de Guatemala
Date of Independence from Spain September 15, 1821
Population 14,280,596
HDI Score 0.649
Current Leader President Óscar José Rafael Berger Perdomo (since
    January 2004)
Type of Government Republic
Elections Last held in November 2003. Next elections in November 2007.

Guyana
Capital City Georgetown
Date of Independence from Great Britain May 26, 1966
Population 705,803
HDI Score 0.719
Current Leader President Bharrat Jagdeo (since August 1999)
Type of Government Republic
Elections Last held in March 2001. Next elections in March 2006.

Haiti
Capital City Port-au-Prince
Date of Independence from France January 1, 1804
Population 7,656,166
HDI Score 0.463
Current Leader Interim President Boniface Alexander (since February
    2004 after the resignation of Jean-Bertrand Aristide)
Type of Government Republic
Elections Last held in November 2000.

Honduras
Capital City Tegucigalpa
Date of Independence from Spain September 15, 1821
Population 6,823,568

HDI Score 0.672
Current Leader President Ricardo Maduro (since January 2002)
Type of Government Republic
Elections Last held in November 2001. Next elections in November 2005.

Jamaica
Capital City Kingston
Date of Independence from Great Britain August 6, 1962
Population 2,713,130
HDI Score 0.764
Current Leader Prime Minister Percival James Patterson (since March 1992)
Type of Government Parliamentary democracy
Elections Last held in October 2002. Next elections by October 2007.

Mexico
Capital City Mexico City (Federal District)
Date of Independence from Spain September 16, 1810
Population 104,959,594
HDI Score 0.802
Current Leader President Vicente Fox Quesada (since December 2000)
Type of Government Federal republic
Elections Last held in July 2000. Next elections in July 2006.

Nicaragua
Capital City Managua
Date of Independence from Spain September 15, 1821
Population 5,359,759
HDI Score 0.667
Current Leader President Enrique Bolaños Geyer (since January 2002)
Type of Government Republic
Elections Last held in November 2001. Next elections in November 2006.

Panama
Capital City Ciudad de Panamá
Date of Independence from Spain November 28, 1821
Date of Independence from Colombia November 3, 1903
Population 3,000,463
HDI Score 0.791
Current Leader President Martín Torrijos Espino (since September 2004)
Type of Government Republic
Elections Last held in May 2004. Next elections in May 2009.

Paraguay
Capital City Asunción
Date of Independence from Spain May 14, 1811
Population 6,191,368
HDI Score 0.751
Current Leader President Óscar Nicanor Duarte Frutos (since August 2003)
Type of Government Republic
Elections Last held in April 2003. Next elections in April 2008.

Peru
Capital City Lima
Date of Independence from Spain July 28, 1821
Population 27,544,305
HDI Score 0.752
Current Leader President Alejandro Toledo Manrique (since July 2001)
Type of Government Republic
Elections Last held in April 2001. Next elections in April 2006.

Saint Kitts and Nevis
Capital City Basseterre
Date of Independence from Great Britain September 19, 1983
Population 38,836
HDI Score 0.844
Current Leader Prime Minister Denzil Douglas (since July 1995)
Type of Government Parliamentary democracy
Elections Last held in March 2000. Next elections by July 2005.

Saint Lucia
Capital City Castries
Date of Independence from Great Britain February 22, 1979
Population 164,213
HDI Score 0.777
Current Leader Prime Minister Kenneth Davis Anthony (since May 1997)
Type of Government Parliamentary democracy
Elections Last held in December 2001. Next elections by December 2006.

Saint Vincent and the Grenadines
Capital City Kingstown
Date of Independence from Great Britain October 27, 1979
Population 117,193
HDI Score 0.751

Current Leader Prime Minister Ralph E. Gonsalves (since March 2001)
Type of Government Parliamentary democracy
Elections Last held in March 2001. Next elections by July 2006.

Suriname
Capital City Paramaribo
Date of Independence from the Netherlands November 25, 1975
Population 436,935
HDI Score 0.780
Current Leader President Runaldo Ronald Venetiaan (since August 2000)
Type of Government Republic
Elections Last held in May 2000. Next elections in May 2005.

Trinidad and Tobago
Capital City Port-of-Spain
Date of Independence from Great Britain August 31, 1962
Population 1,096,585
HDI Score 0.801
Current Leader Prime Minister Patrick Manning (since March 2002)
Type of Government Parliamentary democracy
Elections Last held in February 2003. Next elections by February 2008.

Uruguay
Capital City Montevideo
Date of Independence from Brazil August 25, 1825
Population 3,399,237
HDI Score 0.833
Current Leader President Tabare Vázquez (since March 2005)
Type of Government Republic
Elections Last held in October 2004. Next elections in October 2009.

Venezuela
Capital City Caracas
Date of Independence from Spain July 5, 1811
Population 25,017,387
HDI Score 0.778
Current Leader President Hugo Chávez Frias (since February 1999; remained in office after a failed recall referendum in August 2004)
Type of Government Federal republic
Elections Last held in July 2000. Next elections in 2006.

Appendix 2: Nonindependent Territories

The list of nonindependent territories, is based, with minor adjustments, on the Nonindependent Territories list published in *Understanding the Contemporary Caribbean* (Lynne Rienner Publishers, 2003). Although the Falkland (Malvinas) Islands, as well as the South Georgia and South Sandwich Islands under British control, are technically in the South Atlantic Ocean, they were included for geopolitical reasons. First, they are located on the eastern edge of the Scotia Sea, which is a maritime extension of the South American continent. Second, these territories' political past and present are very much a part of colonial history in South America—with particular reference to the Falkland Islands War between Great Britain and Argentina.

South America
French Guiana Overseas Department of France (1946).
Falkland Islands Under British administration since 1908. Briefly occupied by Argentina in 1982. Currently listed as being administered by Great Britain while claimed by Argentina.
South Georgia and the South Sandwich Islands Under British administration since 1908. Briefly occupied by Argentina in 1982. Currently listed as being administered by Great Britain while claimed by Argentina.

Central America and the Caribbean
Anguilla Under the British Commonwealth since 1982.
Aruba Domestically autonomous member of the Netherlands Antilles since 1986.
Bonaire Domestically autonomous member of the Netherlands Antilles since 1954.
British Virgin Islands British Crown Colony since 1967.
Cayman Islands British Crown Colony since 1972.

Curaçao Domestically autonomous member of the Netherlands Antilles since 1954.

Guadeloupe Overseas Department of France since 1946.

Martinique Overseas Department of France since 1946.

Montserrat British Crown Colony since 1966.

Puerto Rico Commonwealth associated with the United States since 1952. Labeled a "Free Associated State."

Saba Domestically autonomous member of the Netherlands Antilles since 1954.

St. Barthélemy Administrative district of Guadeloupe since 1946.

St. Eustatius Domestically autonomous member of the Netherlands Antilles since 1954.

St. Maarten Domestically autonomous member of the Netherlands Antilles since 1954.

St. Martin Administrative district of Guadeloupe since 1946.

Turks and Caicos British Crown Colony since 1976.

U.S. Virgin Islands Self-governed territory of the United States since 1968.

The Contributors

Robert F. Arnove is professor emeritus of international and comparative education at Indiana University, Bloomington.

David H. Bost is professor of modern languages at Furman University, Greenville, South Carolina.

Jacqueline Chase is assistant professor of geography and planning at California State University, Chico.

Alfred G. Cuzán is professor and chair of political science at the University of West Florida, Pensacola.

Thomas J. D'Agostino is executive director of international programs and adjunct professor of political science at Hobart and William Smith Colleges, Geneva, New York.

Margaret V. Ekstrom is professor of modern languages at St. John Fisher College, Rochester, New York.

Michael Fleet is professor of political science at Marquette University, Milwaukee, Wisconsin.

Stephen Franz is a doctoral student in education policy at Indiana University, Bloomington.

Cleveland Fraser is professor of political science at Furman University, Greenville, South Carolina.

Richard K. Harper is associate professor of economics at the University of West Florida, Pensacola.

Richard S. Hillman is distinguished professor emeritus of political science at St. John Fisher College, Rochester, New York, and director of the consulting firm Hemisphere Research in Hudson, Florida.

Kimberly Morse Cordova is a graduate student in history at the University of Texas, Austin.

René de la Pedraja is professor of history at Canisius College, Buffalo, New York.

Susan E. Place is dean of graduate, international, and interdisciplinary studies and professor of geography and planning at California State University, Chico.

Marie Price is associate professor of geography and international affairs and director of Latin American Studies at George Washington University, Washington, D.C.

Susan Tiano is professor of sociology at the University of New Mexico, Albuquerque, New Mexico.

Kevin A. Yelvington is associate professor of anthropology at the University of South Florida, Tampa.

Paul W. Zagorski is professor of political science at Pittsburg State University, Pittsburg, Kansas.

Index

438   *Index*

Indigenous peoples, 1; Christianization of, 42; civilizations of, 43; confrontation/accomodation among, 6; conversion to Catholicism, 48; crops grown by, 16; decimation of, 146; decline in population of, 29–30, 44; discrimination against, 247; displacement of, 214; economic exploitation of, 146; enslavement of, 42; European alliances with, 42; immigration and, 250–252; labor of, 147; languages, 35; marginalization of, 252; migration routes, 31*map*; mortality rates, 213; in peonage, 148; population decline, 147; resettlement of, 213; resilience of, 29; resistance from, 42, 44; seminomadic, 214; settlement zones, 16; social status of, 256–258; socioeconomic status of, 147; subjugation of, 41

Industrialization, 75, 152; acceleration of, 187; capital-intensive, 281; domestic, 151; export-led, 293; import substitution, 75; large-scale, 92; promotion of, 151, 152; rapid, 78; state-managed, 154; urban working class and, 76; women and, 281

Industrial Revolution, 70

Inflation, 7, 92, 93, 98, 100, 105, 155, 158, 180

Infrastructure: border, 228; development, 81, 92; economic, 70; educational, 315; expansion of, 70; financial, 149; funding, 168; government, 226; housing, 223; human, 127; improvements in, 79; physical, 127, 149; urban, 228

Ingenieros, José, 250–252

Inquisition, 48, 49

Institutional Revolutionary Party (Mexico), 77, 103, 104

Institutions: colonial, 46, 69; democratic, 69, 101, 102, 103; development of, 79, 108, 109; duplication in New World, 44; electoral, 104; European, 44; formation of, 70; international, 10*n1*; military, 107; modern, 77; political, 6, 7, 119, 209; regional, 187; republican, 119; social, 6, 119;

traditional, 77; transplantation of, 44, 63, 67; viable, 78

Intelligence: domestic, 137–139; military role in, 137–139

Inter-American Conference (1889), 186–187

Inter-American Conference (1948), 189

Inter-American Development Bank, 216, 336

Inter-American Treaty of Reciprocal Assistance, 189

Interdependence in international relations, 183–184

Interest rates, 92, 98, 99, 154, 155

International Monetary Fund, 99, 159, 180, 193, 216, 323

International relations, 110, 177–207; dependency and, 182–183; historical legacies in, 184–188; interdependence and, 183–184; politico-military affairs in, 181; popular opinion in, 181; realism and, 181–182; regional framework for, 187; subsystems, 180–181; terrorism and, 8

Investment, 92, 98, 155; capital, 150; decline in, 158; domestic, 185; foreign, 9, 70, 71, 87, 91, 100, 148, 160*tab*, 161, 171, 185, 215, 216; indigenous, 185; influx of, 70; international, 168–170; spending, 168–170

Iraq, 201; weapons of mass destruction and, 201, 202

Irygoyen, Hipólito, 125

Isaacs, Jorge, 386

Italy: immigration to Latin America from, 15

Iturbide, Agustín de, 61

Jamaat-Al-Muslimeen, 90

Jamaica, 22, 49; education in, 316; IMF riots, 100; labor disturbances in, 77; labor movements in, 109; multiculturalism in, 263; narcotrafficking and, 96, 196; nationalism in, 263; political violence in, 90; Protestantism in, 361; racial issues in, 263; sugar production in, 51; U.S. intervention in, 89

Japan: economic performance in, 163,

About the Book

Thoroughly updated to reflect recent events and trends, this new edition of *Understanding Contemporary Latin America* treats the range of issues facing the region in the first decade of the twenty-first century.

The authors provide current, thorough analyses not only of history, politics, and economics, but also of environmental concerns, class and ethnicity, the role of women, religious beliefs, education, and cultural expression. Each topic is covered in an accessible style, while incorporating the latest available scholarship. Maps, photographs, and a table of basic political data enhance the text, which has made its place as the best available introduction to Latin America.

Richard S. Hillman is distinguished professor emeritus of political science at St. John Fisher College. He is author of *Democracy for the Privileged: Crisis and Transition in Venezuela,* coeditor (with Thomas J. D'Agostino) of *Understanding the Contemporary Caribbean,* and coeditor (with John Peeler and Elsa Cardozo) of *Democracy and Human Rights in Latin America.*